D0891583

Culture and the Development of Children's Action

A Theory of Human Development

Second Edition

JAAN VALSINER

John Wiley & Sons, Inc.

New York • Chichester • Weinheim • Brisbane • Singapore • Toronto

Library of Congress Cataloging-in-Publication Data:

Valsiner, Jaan.
    Culture and the development of children's action: a theory of
human development/Jaan Valsiner.—2nd ed.
        p.   cm.
    Includes bibliographical references and index.
    ISBN 0-471-13590-9 (cloth: alk. paper)
    1. Child psychology—Philosophy. 2. Children—Nutrition—
Psychological aspects. 3. Children—Nutrition—Social aspects.
4. Environmental psychology. I. Title.
BF722.V34   1997
155.4—dc21   96-46293

Printed in the United States of America

10 9 8 7 6 5 4 3 2 1

Foreword

Science touches the lives of us all, and in advanced industrial societies it is a familiar and powerful feature of our world. And yet it is not easy to define or even to capture its essence. For many, science seems to be about facts, hard facts, facts that are in some way better than those of history, literature, or philosophy. Science is associated confidently with knowledge and progress, but as Lewis Thomas has so elegantly pointed out in his *Late Night Thoughts on Listening to Mahler's Ninth Symphony:* "Science, especially twentieth-century science, has provided us with a glimpse of something we never really knew before, the revelation of human ignorance."

In reality, scientific conclusions are much more tentative than most nonscientists and many scientists think. Even a brief examination of 20th-century science will show that dogmas come and go with astonishing rapidity even in those areas designated the exact sciences. Scientific progress is commonly talked about, and institutions and societies of various sorts exist throughout the world to further it. But what is scientific progress and how do we measure it? The usual indicators are in terms of money attracted and expended, number of papers published, or citations scored, and so on, but the validity of these is so obviously questionable as not to require further comment.

The task of science is to provide us with a better, fuller, and clearer comprehension of the natural world in which we live. To do science, particularly good and original science, requires a mix of some seemingly conflicting qualities. It requires, at one and the same time, confidence and iconoclasm. It demands a mind that automatically doubts and questions but at the same time has the confidence needed to pursue, develop, and press home ideas. The practice of science needs a mixture of rigor and imagination. It requires that ideas be put to the toughest tests that can be devised, and, at the same time, it demands vision and the courage to cut loose from the constraints of currently accepted dogmas.

Most of contemporary scientific activity in psychology consists of carrying out empirical investigations whose purpose is to add to our store of "facts." But facts exist only within a theoretical context, and there is consequently a danger that the activity of science, the conduct of investigations, becomes an end in itself. The activity takes on a life of its own, and the primary purpose of furthering our understanding of the natural world is subordinated to organizational

iii

needs. In this important book, Dr. Valsiner argues that many developmental psychologists have lost their way, and he illustrates this by his quote from Wittgenstein, the essence of which is that one cannot sort out conceptual confusions by experimental methods.

Science, like any other human activity, is influenced by the culture in which it is embedded. In Western industrialized societies, the predominant and most influential branch of science, the one that forms the "scientific culture" in which other branches are embedded, is classical physics, which stresses *things*. But is the world of things, the Democritean world, a satisfactory model for psychology—and developmental psychology in particular? Valsiner thinks not, and he argues persuasively that if we are to understand development, then a better—indeed, a necessary—starting point is a Heraclitean view of the world as composed of processes. Envy of physics and mathematics, which have been held up as the goal to which other sciences should aspire, has often misled and ill served the social and biological sciences.

Three features make this book unusual. First, it is unashamedly and primarily concerned with theory. As Valsiner sees it, epistemological progress is the key to evaluating scientific progress, to deciding whether we have gained a clearer comprehension of nature. From an examination of basic assumptions underlying psychological research, Valsiner proceeds to a consideration of several theories of development and on to the presentation of his own theory about the development of children's actions and thinking. The second major feature of the book is that it deals with behavioral change taking place in the natural, normal, socially rich, and varied contexts of children's everyday lives. The way in which culture shapes the behavior of infants in some quite specific settings, such as that of a meal, is thus explored and described. The joint action of adult and child in the setting of a meal is brought out vividly in three longitudinal cases that are analyzed. The third feature that distinguishes this work from the bulk of what is published in developmental psychology is the range of the author's scholarship. He draws on sources in ancient and modern philosophy, on several branches of psychology, on neurobiology, genetics, mathematics, anthropology, political theory, history, sociology, philosophy of science, education, artificial intelligence, and theoretical physics. He integrates work from European, American, and Soviet traditions, and, through his meticulous scholarship, he shows us that many of the central questions and approaches are not new; we had simply forgotten earlier work. Drawing attention to important and, still today, highly significant work done 50 or more years ago is a valuable corrective in an age obsessed with what might appear in next week's *Nature* or *Science*.

The preceding paragraphs are derived from my comments after having read the typescript of the first edition of this book. Later, after the book had been published, I read the comments again. I had not been guilty of hyperbole; this is a fascinating and important work that challenges much of contemporary developmental psychology. The second edition has changed in a number of respects and much new material has been added, but, at root, Valsiner grapples with the question: How shall we understand development? He continues to struggle also with what he describes, rather vividly, as the "epistemological windmills of psychology." His challenge can be summed up succinctly in two lines from a poem by T.S. Eliot:

> Where is the wisdom we have lost in knowledge?
>
> Where is the knowledge we have lost in information?

Those who read the first edition of this book will want to read the second, and those who did not certainly should.

KEVIN CONNOLLY

March 1997

Preface to the Second Edition

It has been an interesting experience to reread and reconstruct the text of the first edition. One discovers easily that the rough and rambling expressions of ideas that were abundant in the earlier edition have become slowly transformed into different indications of the author's intellectual development over the past decade. This streamlining may reflect gained wisdom, or the loss of youthful readiness to tilt at the rigid epistemological windmills of psychology.

However the author's development from the first to the second edition might be interpreted, this book continues the same intellectual journey—one hopes, in a constructive way. Developmental psychology in general has not solved most of the problems to which the author's young finger was pointed earlier. Tendencies toward looking for solutions have emerged, yet they largely remain in a state of blind search. The focus of psychology at large remains overwhelmingly empiricist. What have not flourished in contemporary developmental psychology are the persistent asking of basic questions about the organization of development, and an appropriate methodology that could unite the theoretical and empirical sides of the knowledge-construction process. Empirical investigation without theoretical relevance is empty restatement of the obvious (or conglomeration of uninterpretable and nonobvious) knowledge. On the other side, pure theorizing for its own sake is an idle exercise of the human mind. Therefore, the focus in this book continues to push our thinking toward integration of the general and the specific.

The second edition continues the direction of the first edition, in the sense of being unclassifiable into usually accepted categories of "research." It would not fit into the category of observational research, even though the description of children's mealtime actions might lead toward such a category. It remains theoretical in its focus, yet it cannot be categorized as purely theoretical in the usual sense of "theories and systems," which has become accepted in much of psychology. It continues to borrow from the historical roots of developmental psychology (rather than from their contemporary elaborations), yet it is not a book on the history of psychology. It may touch on very general philosophical issues, such as the problem of determinacy and indeterminacy, yet it lacks the sophistication of a "real" philosophy book. Finally, the author makes numerous methodological claims (and even provides some concrete elaborations), yet this is not a book on methodology.

viii   *Preface to the Second Edition*

The key to understanding this edition lies in departing from the usual classi-fications that psychologists of our postmodern era so easily accept. Efforts to classify this book are the best starting point for failing to understand where its complex deconstructive and reconstructive actions on psychology from a strictly developmental perspective are leading. At the least, the book is not meant for intellectually lazy readers; rather, it addresses active thinkers who are ready to get rid of much of the social conventionalism that governs both the "traditional" and "social constructionist" versions of psychology, and who are trying to construct a new understanding of theory in close proximity to actual psychological phenomena. Thus, the book will not "contribute to the literature" (as a conglomerate of accumulated texts), but might trigger some efforts to modify theoretical perspectives.

In comparison with the first edition, the general methodological focus has been upgraded here. A focus on constraining in the intrapsychological sphere—by semiotic mediation—has been added. There is a further extension of the issue of relations of psychology with societies in which it is embedded (the so-ciology of psychology). These are directions in which the author has developed his thinking over the past decade. The empirical parts of the book (Chapters 6 and 7) have remained basically as they were in the first edition.

In the past ten years, I have benefited from a number of collaborative ties with colleagues all over the world. Joint work with Jeanette A. Lawrence, of the University of Melbourne, and with Ingrid E. Josephs, at the Otto von Guericke University of Magdeburg, has been crucial for my slowly developing under-standing of the processes of internalization and externalization. Continuing joint work and close friendship with René van der Veer have led us to develop the notion of intellectual interdependency on the material of the history of ideas in developmental psychology. Historical reconstruction of the thinking of Lev Vygotsky, Pierre Janet, George Mead, James Mark Baldwin, and other socio-genetic thinkers has led to a new way of seeing how history is relevant in the process of theory construction in the present. This has fortified the tendency—evident in the first edition—to look into the past for innovative, yet abandoned or forgotten, solutions to complex problems. Collaboration with Angela U. Branco, of Universidade de Brasilia, and Terry Winegar, from Randolph-Macon College, has advanced the methodological domain of my work. I have been glad to know Dietmar Görlitz of the Technische Universität Berlin and to learn from him much about the history and forgotten domains of German psychology. The richness of much of the intellectual heritage of that psychology seems to be at risk for vanishing; psychology in Europe has become increasingly "American-ized," rendering the meaning of that term fuzzy indeed.

Many others have challenged my intellectual efforts in various scientific and nonscientific ways. I remain grateful to all for the experience. Different institu-tions' support of my work over recent years needs to be acknowledged. Thanks to the 1995 *Alexander von Humboldt Forschungspreis für Geisteswissenschaften,* and the year in Berlin that it made possible, many of the ideas included in this edition could be advanced into their current form. The actual preparation of the manuscript was done in Brasilia, thanks to a generous Serial Lecturing and Research Award from the William J. Fulbright Foundation. The environment of the Colina turned out to be exactly the context needed for the work on the book to proceed very quickly, largely under the influence of *forró*. For the smooth and thoughtful organization of my working conditions in Brazil, I am particularly indebted to the Comissão Fulbright of Brazil (Director: Prof. Marco Antonio da Rocha), and to the Instituto de Psicologia of Universidade de Brasilia.

I am glad this book has warranted a new edition, and I hope that it will be of use to an interested readership. Its author continues his wandering in the field of human development and the curious science of psychology.

JAAN VALSINER

March 1997

Preface to the First Edition

This book is a result of an intellectual journey—its author's experience with different traditions of psychologists' thinking in different countries. That experience had its beginning in Estonia, a country that due to historical coincidences has been a part of the Soviet Union over the last four decades. The intellectually stimulating and nonconformist atmosphere that characterized the Psychology Department of Tartu University in the 1970s, where I received my higher education and subsequently became involved in research, served as the background for my later endeavors. I am indebted to a number of the "angry young men" of Estonian psychology of the 1970s with whom I shared ideas, collaborated in joint research projects, and wrote papers. Among them, Jüri Allik constantly challenged my thinking, so that I began to try to transcend ideas that at any time happen to be popular in psychology literature originating in any particular country, and Peeter Tulviste introduced me to the cultural–historical thinking in psychology which is one of the foundations of the theoretical perspective outlined in this book. Mati Heidmets and I undertook a number of efforts to understand how the society and personality are interdependent within environmental contexts. My original interest in the organization of human social interaction and its development was greatly facilitated by joint work with Henn Mikkin. He, together with Peeter Tulviste, also provided me with my first exposure to the relevance of the history of psychology for better understanding and improvement of its contemporary state. I may have, somewhat stubbornly, refused to understand that "modernizing function" of history at that time. However, it will be evident from this book that the historical roots of the suggested theoretical framework are of primary importance in my contemporary thinking.

After my luck in gaining an opportunity to leave the Soviet Union for good in 1980, my experiences in Western Europe and North America have had a profound impact on the development of the theoretical structure that is described in this book. My six-month stay at the Justus-Liebig-Universität in Giessen, arranged by Klaus R. Scherer and Paul Ekman, provided an opportunity for an insider's look into the theoretical inclinations of the contemporary Continental-European psychologies. My subsequent work in the United States, first at the Institute of Child Psychology of the University of Minnesota, and then at the University of North Carolina at Chapel Hill, has provided me with ample opportunities to contemplate the relationships of psychological theories (and empirical research traditions) with the cultural–historical contexts of the researchers. Interaction with many friends and colleagues on both sides of the Atlantic Ocean has been very important for the development of ideas that are in the core of this book. Frequent meetings with Robert B. Cairns, devoted to discussion of basic developmental ideas, have been particularly rewarding and pleasant. The multiple opportunities for working in the Istituto di Psicologia of Consiglio Nazionale delle Ricerche in Rome during a number of summers, and continuing collaboration and friendship with Laura Benigni, have significantly contributed to the formation of ideas presented in this book.

The function of this book is to present to the readers a systematic and thorough overview of the present author's theoretical system, its methodological consequences, and the empirical data that follow from those. I have deliberately covered all the levels of analysis, from the most abstract (philosophical) to the most concrete (empirical phenomenology of children's development in their everyday life contexts). The focus of the coverage is on the interdependence of the levels of the system. Therefore, this is primarily a theoretical book, furnished with empirical illustrations of some of the aspects of the theory. In this emphasis, it is deliberately out of place among the majority of contemporary publications in developmental psychology which suffer from the ethos of empiricism, and that often reduce theoretical discourse about "the data" to some relatively simple set of ideas, derived from the socialized intuitions of members of the given culture at the given time. As I argue in the book, the epistemological status of "empirical data" as the foundation for an "objective developmental psychology" is no simple matter, and depends on the theoretical system within which the data are constructed from observable phenomena. The conceptual difficulties with the idea of development that child psychologists have persistently encountered make it imperative to address difficult issues first theoretically (although in close connection with the observable phenomena), and then proceed to construct scientific methodologies that fit the developmental nature of the phenomena that are studied. My motivation to undertake the difficult task of working toward a better theoretical and empirical understanding of developmental processes stems from the growing dissatisfaction with the oftentimes dogmatic ways in which the most interesting phenomena are turned into highly uninteresting and inconclusive "data" by conventional application of strategies of "data analysis" that are meant for the use of stable (not developing) phenomena.

A number of people deserve my great gratitude in conjunction with writing this book. Kevin Connolly provided very helpful feedback on the first draft of the manuscript, and has encouraged my work in many ways from its beginning. The empirical research reported in the book was performed thanks to a grant from the Foundation for Child Development (located in New York). The help of Debra Skinner and Kathryn Luchok in the work with participating families, as well as the readiness of parents to participate in the study, is acknowledged with gratitude. Albrecht and Elzbieta Lempp helped me out by doing the photographic work. The Editorial Staff of John Wiley & Sons Ltd., and especially Michael Coombs, were helpful in many ways in scheduling the writing of the manuscript, and in bringing it to its final state. The book itself, of course, constitutes a milestone on the author's way toward better understanding of development. It is not meant to be a final or "absolutely true" system which is published with the aim of converting readers into a new faith. Instead, it will hopefully raise more questions than it provides answers for. In this case, the whole writing of the book will be considered by its author not to have been in vain.

JAAN VALSINER

July 1986

Acknowledgments

The author wishes to acknowledge the use of copyrighted material from the following sources:

M. Rutter, *Scientific Foundations of Developmental Psychiatry,* 1980. Reproduced by permission of William Heinemann Medical Books Ltd.

J. Shotter, "'Duality of structure' and 'intentionality' in an ecological psychology." *Journal for the Theory of Social Behaviour, 13,* 19–43, 1983. Reproduced by permission of Basil Blackwell Limited.

Excerpts reprinted from *The Concept of Activity in Soviet Psychology,* edited by James V. Wertsch, by permission of M. E. Sharpe, Inc., Armonk, NY 10504.

T. R. Williams, *Socialization and Communication in Primary Groups,* 1975. Reproduced by permission of Mouton De Gruyter, The Hague.

Excerpt from pp. 145–146 from *The Sociology of Child Development,* Fourth Edition, by James H. S. Bossard and Eleanor Stoker Boll. Copyright 1948, 1954 by Harper & Row, Publishers, Inc. Copyright © 1960, 1966 by Eleanor Stoker Boll. Reprinted by permission of Harper & Row, Publishers, Inc.

A. Freud, The concept of developmental lines, *The Psychoanalytic Study of the Child, 18,* 251 and 252, 1963. Reproduced by permission of International Universities Press, Inc.

M. M. Gergen & K. J. Gergen, "The social construction of narrative accounts." In K. J. Gergen & M. M. Gergen (Eds.), *Historical Social Psychology.* Copyright © 1984 by Lawrence Erlbaum Associates. Figures 9.1–9.5 reproduced by permission of Lawrence Erlbaum Associates.

Contents

1

Developmental and Nondevelopmental Orientations in Psychology, and Their Contexts

The confusion and barrenness of psychology is not to be explained by calling it a "young science": its state is not comparable with that of physics, for instance, in its beginnings. (Rather with certain branches of mathematics. Set theory.) For in psychology there are experimental methods and *conceptual confusion*. (As in the other case conceptual confusion and methods of proof.) The existence of the experimental method makes us think we have the means of solving the problems which trouble us; though problem and method pass one another by.

Ludwig Wittgenstein (1958, p. 232)

Comparison of a state of affairs in one science with that in another is a problematic enterprise, that is, nevertheless, of heuristic value. Wittgenstein's description of the conceptual confusion in psychology becomes particularly relevant when one tries to sort out the basic differences between developmental and nondevelopmental perspectives within psychology. Even in that part of the discipline that is labeled *developmental psychology,* conceptual confusion prevails. Often, basic assumptions of the developmental view are not made explicit, and empirical research methods, together with their backgrounds, are imported wholesale from nondevelopmental psychology. Simultaneously, one can observe efforts by developmental psychologists to provide solutions to problems that are perceived to be of social relevance. One is tempted to risk another, quite unfavorable comparison: Psychology in our time may be approximately where chemistry was at the end of its prescientific (i.e., alchemical)

1

era. Similar to alchemists, psychologists all too eagerly undertake applied efforts that cannot succeed in principle, and they perform empirical research that merely pretends to prove empirically what is known to them by way of their everyday-language backgrounds. The latter kind of research is *pseudoempirical* (Smedslund, 1994, 1995). The former applied efforts may be compared to alchemists' attempts to turn mundane objects into shining and valuable substances.

No science progresses in a linear fashion. It moves interdependently with the society in which it is embedded, making use of narrative forms in describing itself to its insiders and outsiders. The rhetoric of scientists about their science is therefore necessarily inconsistent (Valsiner, 1994a). Sciences are both social institutions within a society, and social organizations that attempt to build universal knowledge. For psychology to be simultaneously knowledge-constructing and self-reflexive is a complicated task. Nevertheless, self-reflexivity guides the actual construction of knowledge.

This book has three objectives. First, it analyzes the epistemological state of affairs in the discipline of psychology as a whole. It offers elaborate analyses of the embeddedness of the discipline in its social context, together with a general analysis of psychology's methodology. Both analyses are given through the contrast of developmental and nondevelopmental perspectives within psychology. Elaboration of the latter distinction is the second objective of the book. Within the same social-institutional framework of psychology, two diametrically opposite perspectives have found their home. Issues of psychological development are closer to the perspectives of developmental biology than to those of nondevelopmental psychology. Hence, the recent tendencies toward discussion of developmental science (Cairns, Elder, & Costello, 1996) as well as reanalyses of different theoretical perspectives that are considered developmental (Shanahan, Valsiner, & Gottlieb, 1997) help to clarify this distinction.

Finally, the book provides a positive scenario for theory development in the area of human cultural-historical ontogeny. It sets forth a theoretical system, built deductively on the notion of *limits on variability,* and then links these theoretical elaborations with empirical phenomena. These phenomena are shown to be culturally organized, and the actions involved in guiding the processes of human development are shown to be sign-mediated (semiotic) in their nature.

The crucial aspect of the presented theory is the multilevel, hierarchical nature of the constraining systems that includes actions, semiotically mediated reflections on actions, metasemiotic reflexivity on reflection on action, and so on. The human psychological system is hierarchically integrated in such a way that adjacent levels of the hierarchy constrain themselves and one another. The theoretical issue of human psychological development is the regulation of the interdependent levels. Construction of a theoretical language that captures this multilevel constraining process and development of a methodology that fits this systemic complexity constitute a way out of the conceptual confusion that caught Wittgenstein's eye.

1.1   THE ROOT DISTINCTION: DEVELOPMENTAL AND NONDEVELOPMENTAL APPROACHES IN PSYCHOLOGY

In the most general sense, development entails *change in the organizational state of a system in time,* which is *maintained* (rather than lost) *once the conditions of its emergence disappear.* When seen in these terms, development refers to *reorganization of the structure* of a system, as a result of the system's constant relating with its surrounding conditions. Development is therefore possible only in open systems (Bertalanffy, 1950)—systems that exist in constant exchange relations with their environments.

In other words, the developmental perspective concentrates the researchers' attention on the time-dependent *phenomena of becoming,* or emergence of a new structural order of the phenomena from their previous state. That process of becoming can be studied at different levels of magnitude of the phenomena:

In the course of a here-and-now situation (which amounts to the *microgenetic* view; Draguns, 1984);

In the course of an organism's life span (the *ontogenetic* view);

During the time of existence of the given species (the *phylogenetic* view);

During the period of existence of semiotically constructed, specifically human forms of organization of mental, emotional, and social lives (the *cultural-historical* view).

All these levels of focus form a hierarchy based on the time scale used to describe them. Thus, the widest time-scaled view—that of phylogenesis—includes the cultural-historical view (as a phenomenon of one species—*homo sapiens*—and established within phylogeny). Phylogeny and cultural history include ontogenesis as well as microgenesis.

In contrast, the nondevelopmental (or ontological) perspective leads researchers to look at constant and stable aspects of the phenomena, and to pay no special attention to the irreversible nature of time. The contrast with the developmental approach is further elaborated in Table 1.1.

The ontological approach eliminates from investigation the possible transformation of the phenomena it studies. Any transformation is considered error or noise, because the underlying axiom of the ontological view is to consider the phenomena in a form that is basically stable. If there are demonstrable fluctuations in the phenomena over time, they are assumed to be occasional perturbations around the stable *true nature* of being. Hence, it is not surprising that the ontologial perspective, within which the focus on the fluctuations around a mean (or prototype) is considered irrelevant, proliferates—in the form of the *law of large numbers.* Because the time dimension is viewed merely as a locus within which independent specimens of the phenomena occur (rather than transform from one state to another), it is possible to emphasize the notion that

TABLE 1.1. Comparison of Nondevelopmental and Developmental Approaches in Psychology

Topic	Nondevelopmental	Developmental
1. Object of investigation.	The "being," i.e. the constant and stable aspect of psychological phenomena.	The dynamic, "becoming" aspect of psychological phenomena.
2. Source of "noise" in research.	The dynamic, unstable aspects of phenomena. These are often dealt with as "error" and eliminated from the study.	The static, stable aspects of phenomena, since these do not pertain to the issues of "becoming" and can obscure the dynamic processes hidden beneath the static appearance.
3. Source of concepts for theories.	Platonic philosophical concepts that emphasize the stability aspect in phenomena and eliminate the time dimension (and time-related change) from scientific discourse.	Different philosophical backgrounds, all of which emphasize the variable aspect of phenomena (Heraclitus, Goethe's romanticism, Hegel, marxist theoreticians of different kinds).
4. Dominant research design.	Cross-sectional accumulation of data, excluding any information on time-related change in the phenomena.	Longitudinal—awareness of the danger of eliminating information about development through aggregation of data over time and subjects.
5. Emphasis in theoretical discourse.	Theoretical discourse often operates with concepts that capture some outcomes (products) of psychological processes. Processes are expected to be revealed through investigations of their outcomes.	Theoretical discourse concentrates on the analysis of the processes (that produce outcomes), attempting to study these processes directly, rather than through their outcomes.

accumulation of the phenomena over time reveals to us the true nature of the given issue.

None of these axioms can fit the developmental approach. It concentrates on the phenomena of becoming—and therefore the dimension of time is not a mere locational dimension in which the phenomena occur, but an inherent organizer of the life-sequence of the developmental transformation. Implications of this axiom for methodology are profound (see Chapter 3). The developmental approach takes a systemic perspective, based on the traditions in philosophy that have emphasized the dynamic nature of the world (Heraclitus), or romantic or fluid transformations (Goethe's natural philosophy and Hegel's dialectics). The prevailing methodological orientation focuses on the processes of transformation, and the outcomes of such processes are assumed to be mute as to an explanation of these processes.

The developmental approach does not deny the moments of stability that can be observed in phenomena. However, instead of considering those stability states as the core of the phenomena, it views them as temporary steady states that, under some conditions, will transform into other states. So, both the ontological and the developmental perspectives can agree that a given system is currently in a stable state and can be described as such; yet the former considers that state its normal ("true") state, whereas the latter views it as an "anchor state" for further transformation.

1.1.1 Human Psychological Development: Attempts at Definition

Surprisingly few efforts have been made to define *development* in developmental psychology. This omission may be partly attributable to psychology's preoccupation, in recent decades, with fragmented research questions of an empirical kind. Construction of general-level theoretical models has been rare. Yet it is exactly for the value of empirical research efforts that such general definitional efforts are necessary—again, to overcome the conceptual confusion in the discipline.

The following definition, offered by Richard Lerner and Donald Ford, is perhaps the most comprehensive one that can be found in contemporary developmental psychology:

> Individual human development involves *incremental and transformational processes* that, through a *flow of* interactions among current characteristics of the person and his or her current contexts, produces *a succession of* relatively enduring changes that *elaborate or increase* the diversity of the person's structural and functional characteristics and the patterns of their environmental interactions *while maintaining* coherent organization and structural-functional unity of the person as a whole. (Ford & Lerner, 1992, p. 49, emphasis added)

The emphasis added to this quotation indicates the complexity of the phenomenon of development, which any definition must capture. Development entails recognizable continuity of the system as such; at the same time, the focus of a developmentalist is on the phenomena that transform the system into a novel state. The question of emergence of novelty on the basis of previous states is the central issue in the developmental perspective. It touches on two issues: (a) the distinction of (and relation among) processes and their outcomes, and (b) the relationship between the developing system in its present form and its potential future states.

1.1.2   Processes, Outcomes, and the Focus of the Developmental Approach

A systemic view of organisms considers developmental phenomena to be based on *processes*—the particular functioning of a developing system in its relations with its internal parts and its external environments. Biological organisms exist only because of such functioning processes, obvious examples being blood circulation, breathing, assimilation/dissimilation, protein synthesis, and so on. Each of these processes leads to some outcome, such as a state of readiness to act, or body buildup of a specific kind.

It is not difficult to see that outcomes of processes are artificially constructed static "slices" of the processes themselves. A particular outcome of a process may be an external result (from the impact of the process), or a "fixed" temporary state of the process itself. Thus, in a process described by a sequence of transformations A $\rightarrow$ B $\rightarrow$ C $\rightarrow$ A (i.e., a cyclical process), any part (A, B, or C) of the cycle can be conventionally considered a temporary outcome of the process cycle as a whole. Yet each of these outcomes emerges because the whole cycle operates in continuous time. Elimination of that time, and consideration of any outcome (A, B, or C) as representing the process that generates it (cycle A $\rightarrow$ B $\rightarrow$ C $\rightarrow$ A), is therefore an inadequate construction of entities where processes rule.

In a similar vein, psychological processes that take place in irreversible time (i.e., they proceed as the time flows) can be viewed as bases for different psychological phenomena that occur as their outcomes. Thus, processes of feeling, thinking, expecting, or worrying can be viewed as leading to the appearance of specifiable outcomes: feelings, thoughts, expectations, or worries. Such outcomes are transitory; they feed further into the process from which they have emerged. Thus, a particular thought (an outcome, and a relatively static state of mind) can enter into the process of thinking at the next time moment, thus reorganizing the dynamic side of that process.

Nevertheless, the process–outcome distinction can serve as a useful starting point in this demonstration of the distinction between developmental and ontological approaches in psychology. The two approaches treat the process and the outcome quite differently. Table 1.2 gives an overview of the contrast between the two approaches.

Consider the first cell (1.1) in the table. A particular psychological process is viewed as being stable and unmodifiable, and is assumed to generate stable

TABLE 1.2.   Developmental and Nondevelopmental Aspects of the Study of Psychological Processes and Outcomes

	Outcomes	
Processes	*Static*	*Dynamic*
Static	1.1 Nondevelopmental	1.2 Nondevelopmental
Dynamic	2.1 Developmental	2.2 Developmental

outcomes. An example of this kind of process might be a computer program that works exactly the same way at each run, producing the same result (e.g., a program in which the addition of numbers always leads to the same outcome, if the input numbers are the same; so $2 + 3$ will always equal 5, or there is an error in the program). In the realm of human psychological functions, any formal-logical operation—like syllogistic reasoning of the first form (i.e., major premise = all X are Y; minor premise = A is Y; conclusion = A is X)—is an example of this static process–static outcome combination (cell 1.1). The thinking person using the syllogistic process always reruns it according to its logical correctness, which leads to a similar kind of fixed outcome. This form of process–outcome interrelation is a good example of the nondevelopmental approach.

The statically organized process can also produce dynamically variable outcomes (as depicted in cell 1.2 of Table 1.2). A particular nonlinear algorithm that remains the same in different modeling efforts would generate qualitatively variable outcomes. Examples have been demonstrated by Paul van Geert's computer models (van Geert, 1991, 1993, 1994a, 1994b). The nonlinear algorithm remains the same in each run of the computer program, but the input material it uses may lead to a wide variety of growth curves, which, if viewed only as outcomes, suggest that completely different underlying mechanisms exist for each curve. Yet the same algorithm generates all the curves, and the *algorithm itself is not changed* in the process of generating that variety of outcomes. Hence, cell 1.2 also belongs to the nondevelopmental versions of process–outcome relations.

Cells 2.1 and 2.2 of Table 1.2 represent the developmental versions of process–outcome relations. For both cells, *transformation of the process* that is generating the outcome is assumed to be possible. Hence, as they feed into the process that has generated them, the outcomes change the process. In the static (stable) outcome (cell 2.1), we can consider a state where repeatedly steady-state outcomes are at first generated by process mechanism X and are then transformed to be generated by process mechanism Y, without corresponding alteration in the outcome. Many control systems, where the goal is to maintain the outcome within certain stable conditions, can be used as examples. If a shop assistant needs to add numbers 2 and 3 to arrive at the sum 5, this can be done in his or her mind, on paper, with an abacus, by counting fingers, or with a calculator. The specific media that guarantee arrival at the same result are qualitatively very different and provide examples of the cultural-historical transformation of the process of calculation (from counting body parts to using abacus, paper, and calculator). Hence, cell 2.1 of Table 1.2 reflects the development of underlying processes that cannot be observed from looking at the outcome. The emergence of new forms of the process—new technological devices—has been promoted by a need either to reach a wider range of outcomes, or to achieve the outcomes more quickly, yet the actual outcomes remain invariant under changed processes.

Cell 2.1 reflects a condition in which multiple processes become available for the generation of the same outcome. This condition of *equifinality* is characteristic of open systems. It also illustrates how stable outcomes may be latently developing, even when that development does not become visible in the outcome. For nondevelopmental psychology, such latent transformation of the process mechanisms is of no interest; it is assumed that a description of the outcomes can explain the process that underlies it. From the developmental point of view, this assumption cannot be accepted; in fact, if a researcher starts from observing some outcomes of hidden processes (e.g., number of words recalled in a memory task), there is no direct way to recover the memorizing–retrieving process from the outcome depiction. One process of that kind may be involved, but there can also be more than one—perhaps complementary, mutually linked, or mutually substituting processes. Hence, from a developmental viewpoint, analyzing the processes can explain the outcomes, but analyzing the outcomes cannot explain the processes.

Cell 2.2 of Table 1.2 indicates a transformation of the processes underlying the conditions of generated outcomes, where further variability is produced in these outcomes. Finding examples of this transformation in the realm of physical objects is complicated, because physical objects do not undergo development. Phenomena of human development, however, provide a multitude of examples. When a child learns to speak, this accomplishment involves the acquisition of the acoustic form and semantic function of the first words. Once these signs have become part of the child's lexicon, the child's action is qualitatively transformed by the use of the signs. Previously an outcome of the child's learning process, the use of signs now becomes a means that is part of the new form of mental self-regulation processes (Luria, 1979). What had been an outcome of a process has now fed into that process and changed it qualitatively, leading to the generation of new outcomes.

Similar examples of process ⟷ outcome relations, where one leads to a qualitative leap in the other, can be found in human cultural history. Consider the invention—or introduction—of literacy in an illiterate society. This innovation makes it possible to guarantee the fulfillment of some important task—for instance, memorializing the society's corpus of myths—in a novel way. Instead of being preserved by oral retelling of the texts, these texts now become captured in writing. As a consequence, the demands on the memory skills of individual persons within the given society may be reduced and changed into a novel task context. The possibility that texts will be preserved accurately is enhanced by literacy; however, the high-level memory skills of the preliterate people may be gradually replaced by limited memory skills of people living in the environments of external memory devices (computers of gigabyte memory capacities, etc.). Transformation of processes as a result of changed outcomes includes both emergence of new processes and disappearance of old ones.

1.1.3 An Example: Where Is Piaget's Developmental Theory?

The claim that developmental and nondevelopmental perspectives are rarely clearly distinguished in contemporary psychology—including developmental psychology—can be illustrated by referring to different readings from the contributions of Jean Piaget to psychology. Piaget's theoretical constructions are analyzed later (see Chapter 4); here, it is sufficient to capture two alternative readings of Piaget's work—one from the ontological and the other from the developmental perspective.

In contemporary discourse in child psychology, Piaget's description of stages in children's cognitive development is usually given high priority, and this stage description is often labeled "Piaget's developmental theory." However, the description of stages entails merely an account of ontogenetic intermediary outcomes of development. Piaget's stage description is only a *classification* of emerging cognitive functions into *similarity classes* (of sensorimotor, preoperational, concrete-operational, and formal-operational kinds). Surely there exists a sequence of transitions (with age) from one similarity class to the next (i.e., the classification has sequential order based on the course of childhood development); yet the description of these intermediate outcomes does not explain the transition from one stage to the next. Thus, to claim that a child becomes *concrete-operational* because he or she was *preoperational* before would amount to the use of one intermediate, externally detected outcome, in place of a causal agent, to explain the emergence of another intermediate outcome. Piaget's description of ontogeny of cognitive stages is not his theory of development but merely a description of outcomes that occur in the course of ontogeny.

Piaget, of course, has a theory of development—that of equilibration of cognitive structures (see Chapter 4). The processes of equilibration and disequilibration lead both to maintenance of the present cognitive state of the developing child and to qualitative transformation of the outcomes and the processes themselves into a new form.

1.2 PRESENT AND FUTURE: THE LEADING EDGE OF DEVELOPMENTAL PERSPECTIVE

The developmental approach entails a look at the transformation of organizational forms of systems, in their relations with their environments. The actual occurrence of a transformation is detectable *after* it has taken place, yet the interest of researchers in development is fueled by the desire to learn, *before* a transformation takes place, what it might be like, and often to try to modify it in some desirable direction by way of intervention. The developmental perspective has to deal with the uncertainties of transition between the present and the immediate future; in fact, the focus on emergence is a focus on the *making of the new present* out of possibilities projected into the future.

1.2.1 Irreversibility of Time: Inevitable Complication for the Study of Development

Once the developmental perspective is located in the realm of transformation of the organizational form of phenomena from their present state to that of the immediate future, the major philosophical complication of such research becomes obvious. Any research account of development abstracts from its own time-locked encounter with the developmental phenomena, whereas the latter are bound to their specific time loci. In other words, accounts of development cannot belong to the realm of developmental phenomena, by being a process-oriented constant explanation of otherwise unique, transitory phenomena of development.

From the nondevelopmental perspective, the inevitable irreversibility of developmental phenomena guarantees that the developmental perspective cannot be scientific—from an ontological viewpoint. If the phenomena targeted by the developmental perspective are unique (never recurring) and transient, basic canons of the scientific approach, viewed ontologically—such as replicability of empirical studies (see Van der Veer, Van IJzendoorn, & Valsiner, 1994), or comparisons of experimental and control cases, as well as accumulation of data in general—cannot be put into practice. Yet a similar challenge to ontological scientific norms currently exists in the area of thermodynamics (Prigogine, 1973, 1976a, 1976b; see also Chapter 3). The irreversibility of time is not an obstacle but merely a challenge on the way to constructing basic knowledge about regular, yet indeterministic, processes, the uniqueness of which reflects some general principles. Probably the social distinction between *idiographic* and *nomothetic* perspectives in sciences has slowed down the search for universality in uniqueness.

In an ironic historical twist, the basic developmental thought of the 1890s has reentered psychology 100 years later, brought back from Prigogine's now celebrated thought system of emergence of structural novelties at far-from-equilibrium states, and via chaos theory in its many popularized forms. Prigogine's thermodynamics is built on the time-philosophical roots of the thinking of Henri Bergson (1907/1945), who, in his turn, synthesized ideas of different developmental biologists and psychologists of the turn of the century (e.g., James Mark Baldwin; see Chapter 4).

1.2.2 Henri Bergson's *Durée*

Bergson's critique of the notion of time used in the physical sciences was centered on the translation of time into a parameter similar to that of space.

Although this approach could be appropriate for the physical sciences, which study objects, Bergson denied this translation in the life sciences. Instead, he introduced the concept of duration *(durée)* that unified the introspectively lived-through experiences with the irreversibility of time:

> Pure duration is the form which the succession of our conscious states assumes when our ego lets itself *live,* when it refrains from separating its present state from its former states. For this purpose it need not be entirely absorbed in the passing sensation or idea; for then, on the contrary, it would no longer *endure.* (Bergson, 1911, p. 100)

This emphasis on the psychological "flow" was similar to William James's "stream of consciousness" (Chapter 9 in James, 1890). However, there is a strong constructivist emphasis in the notion of duration. For Bergson, duration is not merely one lived-through instant replacing another, but "continuous progress of the past which gnaws into the future and which swells as it advances" (Bergson, 1911, p. 7; original: *"La durée est le progrès continu du passé qui ronge l'avenir et qui gonfle en avancant"; Bergson, 1907/1945, p. 22).* The concept of duration (durée) is intricately linked with the *process of enduring,* which entails the creation of novelty as its main feature:

> The more we study the nature of time, the more we shall comprehend that duration means invention, the creation of forms, the continual elaboration of the absolutely new. . . . It is true that in the universe itself two opposite movements are to be distinguished . . . "descent" *["descente"]* and "ascent" *["montée"].* The first only unwinds a roll ready prepared. In principle, it might be accomplished almost instantaneously, like releasing of a spring. But the ascending movement, which corresponds to an inner work of ripening or creating [un travail intérieur de maturation ou de création], endures essentially *[dure essentiellement],* and imposes its rhythm on the first, which is inseparable from it. (Bergson, 1911, p. 14; French formulations added via Bergson, 1907/1945, p. 28)

Bergson's conceptualization of enduring included the unity of two processes: construction and deconstruction, or evolution and involution. Undoubtedly, the process of construction dominates over its counterpart. What is being constructed in the process of biological evolution is complexity, which culminates in the advent of consciousness.

1.2.3   Irreversibility, Duration, and Adaptation

A central concept of Bergson's developmental thought was the notion of adaptation. That concept—popular as it was (and is)—can carry different meanings. First, it has been seen as a direct reaction to the conditions that are causing change—either positive (by giving rise to new variations) or negative (by eliminating emerged variations that are misfits). Bergson disagreed with both these meanings on the basis of their mechanistic elaboration (see

Bergson, 1911, p. 63); rather, he saw adaptation in the process by which novel mechanisms emerged in ways *coordinated with* context demands but not molded or shaped by those demands. Thus, in psychological development, the psychological functions develop new organizational forms that allow them to encounter new possible conditions in the future (as opposed to the idea of fitting in with the environmental demands of the present). The adaptations are organic (systemic) growths, oriented toward a set of future possibilities, which, because they do not exist in the present, cannot be precisely defined. Nevertheless, these new forms canalize the further encounters of the organism and the environment (see Bergson's 1911 discussion of canalizing involved in vision [pp. 105–108] and the role of concepts in canalizing conscious processes [pp. 305–308]). In the case of creative adaptation, the organizational forms that emerge in adaptation go beyond fitting with the present state of the survival conditions; they set the basis for facing the challenges of possible future demands.

Bergson was preceded by a rich philosophical tradition of the Occident, in which issues of stability and transformation were episodically queried.

1.3   FROM HERACLITUS AND ARISTOTLE TO CONTEMPORARY DEVELOPMENTAL SCIENCES

The emergence of developmental ideas in occidental philosophy can be traced to ancient Greece, and to the philosophical system of Heraclitus of Ephesus (c. 500 B.C.). Heraclitus's thinking emphasized the permanence of change in nature: Things were considered never to remain the same over time. An emphasis on change of things across time is an essential prerequisite for any developmental perspective on the nature of things.

Within ancient Greek philosophy, the developmental and nondevelopmental ideas existed concurrently. The nondevelopmental thought frameworks were prominently represented by Parmenides's (c. 470 B.C.) theory of being, and Plato's (427–347 B.C.) theory of forms. In general, the conceptual problem of how to deal with the issue of change occupied the minds of many philosophers, who often attempted to find *the real,* which constitutes the permanent something that underlies change. In other words, the causal mechanism that produces change was assumed itself to be unchangeable (similar to the condition in cell 1.2 in Table 1.2).

1.3.1   A Glimpse into Aristotle's Thinking: Stable Quality, Variable Quantity

An example of the unchangeable mover of change may be found in Aristotle's thinking. He made use of a conceptual trick that has remained prominent in contemporary psychology: By separating the qualitative and quantitative aspects of a phenomenon, it is possible to account for change (quantitative variation) without giving up the notion of sameness of the core of the phenomenon (stable quality). Thus, Aristotle claimed:

[T]hat which is losing a quality has something of that which is being lost, and of that which is coming to be, something must already be. And in general if a thing is perishing, there will be present something that exists; and if a thing is coming to be, there must be something from which it comes to be and something by which it is generated, and this process cannot be *ad infinitum*. But leaving these arguments, let us insist on this, that it is not the same thing to change in quantity and in quality. Grant that in quantity a thing is not constant; still it is in respect of its form that we know each thing. (*Metaphysica*, Book 4, 1010, quoted in Smith & Ross, 1908)

This suggested separation of quality (the permanent essence) and quantity (the extent of appearance of that essence) served as a conceptual means for fitting together both the constant and the changeable aspects of the world. The primary relevance of the former was emphasized by Aristotle in his insistence on the permanence of the *first mover:*

Evidently again those who say that all things are at rest are not right, nor are those who say all things are in movement. For if all things are at rest, the same statements will always be true and the same always false—but they obviously are not; for he who makes a statement himself at one time was not and again will not be. And if all things are in motion, nothing will be true; everything therefore will be false. But it has been shown that this is impossible. Again, it must be that which is that changes; for change is from something to something. But it is not the case that all things are at rest or in motion *sometimes,* and nothing *forever,* for there is something which always moves the things that are in motion, and the first mover must itself be unmoved. (*Metaphysica*, Book 4, 1012, quoted in Smith & Ross, 1908)

Aristotle was less than enthused by the possibility of qualitative change. Yet he had to accept the reality of change, treating it as a transfer from one to another essence, *expressed* in variable ways. The dual structure of stable essence (being) that may express itself in quantity (including disappearance), and giving way to a takeover by some other essence (also expressing itself quantitatively) creates a system of explanation in which any change can be explained by activation or deactivation of a large but finite number of previously unexpressed essences.

1.3.2 Wandering from Aristotle to the World of Toddlers

Child psychology is filled with explanatory constructions that follow Aristotle's conceptual trick of strict separation of quality and quantity. A 2-year-old's temper tantrum in a particular context—a specific variation in behavior—may be conveniently explained through reference to difficult temperament or insecure attachment. These are posited qualities that are projected onto the fussing child, and as such can be held to explain the particular (as well as many other) behavioral states of the toddler. This construction of causality is characteristic of nondevelopmental perspectives in psychology. As will be shown in Section

2.7, Assumptions of Causality, developmental approaches would replace such causality construction by different versions of systemic causality.

1.4 CULTURAL HISTORY OF PSYCHOLOGY AS (SOME KIND OF A) SCIENCE

Psychology as a science is necessarily embedded in the cultural history of any particular society. Hence, a critical question emerges: *How can psychology conceptualize a particular issue* (e.g., children's psychological development), *accepting at the same time that any such effort of conceptualization is itself guided by the cultural history of the given society?* As science, psychology needs to transcend this social guidance of its thought models (Valsiner, 1985a, 1994b). Yet, it cannot transcend that guidance, because the cultural history sets the stage for psychology's construction of knowledge. Psychology is a discipline that became differentiated from other social sciences when the cultural history of the European societies made this separation feasible in the 19th century. Since then, the discipline has been exported from Europe to other continents, where existing philosophical-religious belief systems have prepared the ground for their own culture-bound view of psychological issues (see Ho, 1995). Development of psychological ideas and research practices has been canalized by the various societies' systems of meanings and values.

1.4.1 Nonlinearity and Episodic Nature of Advancement of Science

Science develops through uneven spurts and periods of stagnation. Societies' periods of crisis and rapid social change have often given a boost to psychology. That was the case during the rapid industrialization in the United States at the end of the 19th century, and in Russia and Germany in the 1920s. Development of psychological knowledge—like any other science—is an international enterprise in which representatives of any single country cannot have an advantage over those of any other nation.

1.4.2 Heterogeneity of Psychology's Histories

Psychology has developed differently in different countries, given the sociomoral contexts to which it has been transplanted from its motherland—Germany. Also, a recipient society reacts differently to the social sciences and the physical sciences. For example, psychology and physical chemistry were imported into the United States at approximately the same time—the last two decades of the 19th century; yet, physical chemistry remained similar to its German parent discipline, whereas psychology became adjusted to the social conditions of North America (Dolby, 1977). The whole history of dissemination of gestalt psychology in the United States is a good example of selective reception of ideas by newly established psychology (Henle, 1977). Similar processes can be observed in Russian psychology (Joravsky, 1989; Kozulin, 1984). Psychologies often advance on the basis of social utopias that dominate the given society at the given time (Valsiner, 1996a). At that time, of course, it may not be clear that the dominating system of ideas is utopian; this designation takes place *post factum.*

1.4.3   Negotiations between Societies and Psychologies about the Nature of the Developmental Approach

The history of developmental thinking in psychology is particularly closely related to the social discourse about stability and change in societies as a whole. Developmental ideas entered European biological thought through the evolutionary perspectives of J.-B. Lamarck, A. Wallace, and C. Darwin, as well as through German natural philosophy and embryology (Cairns, 1983; Cairns & Ornstein, 1979). From these roots, biological thought expanded into issues of human development, most notably into issues of child development.

Issues of child development—like any issue pertaining to children—are of notable relevance in the social texture of a society. The basic fact that children develop and become adults rarely surprises anybody; however, specific issues of how different developmental outcomes are achieved, their differential valuation from some socioinstitutional standpoint, and efforts to insert goal direction into human development are usually complex ideological topics. Many such topics are taken for granted by laypersons. For instance, in our society, people want a child to walk independently as early as possible, and someone's desire to see the child walking as *late* as possible would seem intuitively awkward. It would not seem so for the Tuva, however, where the lateness of independent walking is believed to indicate a long life span for the child and is thus a desirable goal. Developmental child psychology may be a particularly complicated discipline, compared with developmental psychology of other animal species, because of the implicit assumptions about children that adults have constructed in their social worlds.

1.4.4   Developmental Ideas in the History of Psychology

The societal canalization by which the developmental perspective has been assimilated in the history of psychologies in different countries provides a fascinating web of versions of society–psychology relations. The decade of the 1890s was internationally a fertile time for developmental ideas being set forth in North America (Baldwin, Dewey, G.H. Mead, Thorndike), England (Morgan), Russia (Bekhterev, Pavlov), France (Janet, Binet), and Germany (Stern, Simmel, Wundt). This tendency became intensified in the 1920s in Russia under the catalytic conditions of Marxist thought and overall efforts to build a new society (Valsiner, 1988a). In parallel, the focus on development slowly disappeared from North American psychology in the 1920s and 1930s. The developmental focus similarly became deemphasized in German psychology in the 1930s, and remained so over many decades. In the 1970s and 1980s, an upsurge of developmental thought was observed in Spain—again in conjunction with social changes in the society. The *cognitive revolution* in American psychology that took place in the 1970s and 1980s freed psychology there from the terminological confines of behaviorist thought, allowing the language of "mentalese" to return. This revolution prepared the ground for acceptance of interpretationist directions (Bruner, 1990), which have traversed the intellectual landscape of European thought during the past century (Shanker, 1992). Similarly, a focus on development has been very slow in returning to psychology on the North American continent (Cairns et al., 1996). Perhaps this slowness of change in the interpretive and developmental directions has made cultural-historical perspectives in psychology useful in our present time.

1.5   TOWARD A CULTURAL–HISTORICAL DEVELOPMENTAL THEORY

To build a theoretical system that transcends these implicit assumptions, the nature of the assumptions needs to be made explicit. This application amounts to parallel elaboration of how children develop and how adults involved in their development assume they should, and do, develop. Such a theory can be viewed as belonging to the category of *cultural–historical* theories. The class of such theories is characterized by a focus on the specific cultural history of a society, and an analysis of how that is mediated through the personal psychological systems of individuals. History here plays a twofold role: First, the emergence of cultural niches within a society is a historical process; second, all actions of children within these cultural niches constitute their personal cultural history in the making. The context of children's mealtime has emerged in clearly specifiable ways in human history, which sets the stage for new children entering an already prestructured world of culturally meaningful objects. Specific cultural tools—feeding utensils, special chairs for children, and so on— have been around for centuries. In the context of living, people construct intra and extrasemiotically organized environments for themselves and their offspring (Lang, 1993). Cultural–historical theoretical perspectives focus simultaneously on the emergence of semiotic organization of both the history of context (e.g., settings of mealtimes) and the personal cultural history of the person in context.

1.5.1   Focus on Variability

The particular theory that is elaborated in this book is built on the assumption that *variability* within the phenomena of interest—in this case, the psychological functions of developing persons—*is the core of the issues* that need to be studied. Variability is not an error or an indication of disorder. Rather, it is a basis for constructive adaptation of the developing person to ever new and unpredictable life conditions, which afford different ranges of variability. Hence, the central notion of *constraining* of fields of variability is used in this theory.

Variability in psychological phenomena exists in three forms:

1. Actual variation of versions of a phenomenon within a person, observable over the course of irreversible time. This intraindividual variability may be both the outcome of the constraining processes and a part of further processes of development.

2. Actual variability between persons (interindividual variability), which is revealed by synchronic comparison of persons with other persons, within a sample from a population. This perspective is tantamount to the so-called individual differences research.

3. Potential variability in the actualization of the next developmental state of the individual. This variability in possibilities serves as the basis for any theory of development.

In this book, the intraindividual—both actual and potential—forms of variability are the focus of attention. The interindividual variability remains in the background of the generic theorizing and analyses of specific single cases. Single cases are the definitive source of evidence about development, yet an analysis of interindividual variability can provide a background framework within which the range of functioning of individuals can be located. (For an example in the area of memory development, see Cox, Ornstein, & Valsiner, 1991.)

1.5.2   Universality in Systemically Analyzed Single Cases

The theoretical system presented in this book treats the single case as the normative empirical evidence to accompany any theory, and rejects the notion of accumulation of data across cases (see Chapter 3). The usual narrative of the opposition between idiographic and nomothetic viewpoints (which equates the former with single-case analyses, and the latter with statistical inferences based on samples) is rejected here. The single case—analyzed systemically and in its context—is the basis for construction of *general* knowledge (further elaborated in Chapter 2).

The claim for the primacy of single (systemic) cases is not mere rhetoric asking for a return to examination of the complexity of the individual, who varies in time from context to context. This focus recognizes the person as the *system* that develops, locating the level of analysis in the individual, in contrast to adjacent levels of possible analysis. These other sites of analysis might be collective (seen in either an unstructured way—discourse about samples from populations—or a structured way—consideration of individuals as merely representatives of a social group or institution), or they might be subpersonal (e.g., cognitive functions within a person's psychological system).

1.5.3   Human Development: A Multilevel Integrated System

A cultural–historical theory of human development involves a set of integrated levels. Hence, hierarchy of the organization of the person is implied, and the question is how that hierarchy is organized, not whether it exits.

Multiple levels can be distinguished as: (a) those of current actions—the *action level;* (b) reflexivity on that action, including unity of feeling and thinking—the *semiotic level;* and (c) metalevel reflection on *both* the action and the semiotic levels—the *metareflexive level.*

The unity of the semiotic and action levels can be labeled the *domain of conduct.* Different ways of relating these levels can be conceptualized: mutual feed-in; unidirectional control of the action level by the semiotic level, or vice versa; parallel loose coupling, and so on. These relationships change dynamically and constitute a flexible system for which no general rules are applicable (e.g., a rule that the semiotic level always controls the action level, but not vice versa).

The hierarchical complexity is what governs the metareflexive level. In principle, an infinite number of metasemiotic levels—with each next level entailing an increase in abstraction from the conduct domain—can be built during a person's life course. However, in practice, the number of such metasemiotic levels is limited by the needs of the developing domain of conduct.

The conduct domain of a person is available for others on the side of the action level, and through the person's goal-oriented externalization of the semiotic and metasemiotic levels. This externalization leads to construction of states of intersubjectivity, and these constitute the basis for social negotiation of personal conduct domains (described in Chapter 8).

1.5.4 History as Transformation

In the most general sense, a cultural–historical theory uses the concept of transformation of structures (i.e., the basic notion involved in any developmental approach) while focusing on the semiotic (i.e., sign-mediated) nature of these transformations. By introducing signs into their making of personal futures (and presents), human beings transform themselves, and others, in ways that are personally unique, yet represent basic lawfulness of cultural development—the open-endedness of semiotic reconstruction of our reflection on ourselves and on the world.

1.6 UNITY OF THEORY, BASIC ASSUMPTIONS, PHENOMENA, AND METHODS IN PSYCHOLOGY

This book is organized around a notion of scientific methodology that has become lost in the flow of empiricism in contemporary psychology. The word *methodology* has de facto become a synonym of *method.* This is a major change, in contrast with the traditional continental European use of that term (Asendorpf & Valsiner, 1992, p. x).

Methodology as used here entails a systematic relationship among different components of the whole research process. Of crucial relevance is emphasis of the socially constructed (or constructively derived) status of any scientific knowledge. The theoretical—implicit or, preferably, explicit—structure of thought and practical actions of the investigator serve to channel the investigator's construction of knowledge. Theory determines the general direction in which any empirical work proceeds. At the same time, the theory itself is always incomplete. It can be modified both by empirical evidence and by alterations in the investigator's basic assumptions. Changes in these assumptions, in the ideal case, take place in conjunction with the investigator's experiencing of the phenomena. Contrary to the widespread received practices in psychology, the role of particular methods of study is always subservient to the relations among basic assumptions, theory, and phenomena. Methods do not possess independent status; they are merely tools in the wider process of construction of knowledge. The notion of methodology can be represented by a cyclical relationship (see Figure 1.1).

Methodology is the process of goal-oriented thinking and interventional procedures that is used by an investigator as he or she interacts with the investigated phenomena. The interaction leads to construction of new knowledge. Knowledge is constructed in a dynamic methodological cycle in which the researcher's general assumptions about the phenomena set constraints on theoretical constructions. The theoretical constructions set constraints on the construction of methods, in conjunction with the researcher's ability to access the phenomena in the research process. Finally, the interaction of the methods and the phenomena leads to the construction of the data. The data, in their turn, can constrain further construction of theories (jointly with general assumptions), and the revised or new theories may reorient the observer's view of the

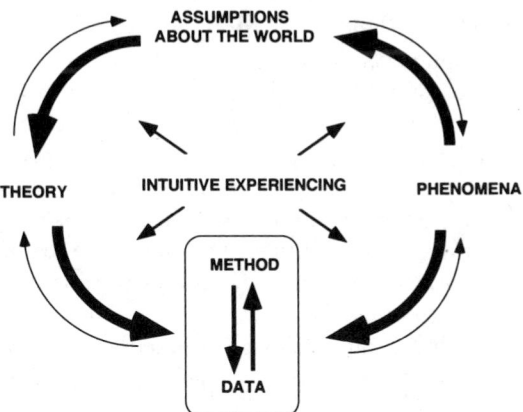

FIGURE 1.1.   The Methodology Circle that unites empirical and nonempirical sides of the research process (from Branco & Valsiner, 1997). Methodology is depicted as a circle (or cycle) that unites all sides of research, as well as the subjective world of the researcher (who intuitively experiences all of the sides). The relative strength of the arrows at each connection indicates the dominance of the role of one direction of inferential "movement" over its opposite counterpart.

world in general. Thus, the methodology cycle entails mutually constraining relations among assumptions, theories, methods, phenomena, and data. The data in this scheme do not occupy the singularly central place in the scientific enterprise, yet they are a crucially important part of the cycle as a whole.

1.6.1 Social Regulation of the Methodology Cycle

Psychology is an ideologically empirical science. The numerous claims made about its fact-based empirical status only elaborate its ideological nature. Any statements about empirical evidence are immediately fielded, within ideological discourses about issues relevant for science and psychology, as belonging to this reputable club (issues such as objectivity, quantifiability, nomothetic versus idiographic perspectives, and so on; see Chapters 2 and 3).

Much of psychology's construction of its research enterprise is based on negotiations with social institutions outside of science (Valsiner, 1988a, 1994a). These negotiations relate to assumptions about the world that have been promoted from some social institution's goal-oriented perspectives. The methodology wheel, Figure 1.1, is being constantly reworked by the goal-oriented canalization of social institutions. Thus, some phenomena are singled out for study and others are passed over. Some methods (e.g., standardized ones) are socially privileged over others, and the set of notions appropriate for constructing scientific theory often excludes some domains of meanings (e.g., no scientific theory in psychology would accept in its core the notion of ancestors' spirits, yet some theories can be built on selected versions of ancient Greek mythology; see Horton, 1967, for an analysis).

1.6.2 Social Reconstructions of the Methodology Wheel

Social regulation of the *methodology wheel* can become so restrictive that the integrity of the wheel is broken. For instance, it is not customary in contemporary psychology to make the researchers' basic assumptions explicit. Second, researchers' intuitive grasp of the phenomena under study is often ruled out as a valid basis for knowledge construction (e.g., cases in which researchers, with apologies, report anecdotal evidence that nevertheless is important for the investigators' thinking. The theory $\rightarrow$ methods connection often is viewed as disconnected: Theories become nominal umbrellas under which empirical work continues by its own consensual validation of separate methods through which the empirical work is supposed to contribute to the literature. The empiricist traditions of psychology have glorified the status of "the literature" (i.e., a semidefined corpus of empirical publications in one or another ill-defined content area). This emphasis fits with the notion of science that accepts the accumulation of empirical evidence as a crucial objective. In Thomas Kuhn's terminology, *normal science* is involved in accumulating evidence and hoping to weigh it by meta-analytic decision rules (see Van der Veer, Van IJzendoorn, & Valsiner, 1994), but this is not the goal of *revolutionary science* (Kuhn, 1970). However, revolutionary science is needed if psychology is to transcend a state that is close to alchemy and become a science comparable to chemistry.

1.6.3 Restoring the Methodology Wheel

Throughout this book, as is apparent from the theory construction involved, the explication of basic assumptions, the selection of the specific experiential domain for empirical work, the elaboration of the semiotic context, and the actual empirical analyses, the focus is on restoring the integrity of the methodology wheel and providing an example of a cultural–historical theory construction. Given the focus on the integrity of the wheel, the constructed theory could be labeled *relativistic*. What makes it relativistic is the conditionality of any aspect of the whole construction on other parts of that construction. Thus, the basic assumptions (Chapter 2) that are analyzed and explicated set up conditions for how to construct appropriate methods (Chapter 3), and the actual construction of those methods is further linked with the elaborated theory of *zones* in constraining processes (Chapter 5). The selection of the particular experiential domain—children's mealtimes—fits that set of mutually relativistic deductive constructions (Chapter 6). Finally, the theoretical system is claimed to be applicable not only in the case of children's actions but also in the realm of the internalized, personal cultural system of feeling and thinking in any life stage (Chapter 8; Valsiner, 1997a).

1.7 SUMMARY: DIRECTIONS FOR A CULTURAL–HISTORICAL THEORY OF DEVELOPMENT

This introductory chapter has set the stage for the material that follows in the rest of the book. The developmental approach has been explicated in contrast to its nondevelopmental counterpart. A strong claim has been made in favor of restoring the integrity of relations among the basic assumptions of psychologists' research, theories, phenomena, methods, and data. In the context of the relativity of these components of the general methodological process, substantive knowledge construction can take place.

Another influence on the construction of a cultural–historical theory of development is the inevitable cultural embeddedness of the theory constructor's acting and thinking. In a nonrelativistic approach, even if a theory is viewed as being independent of its cultural context, in the cultural–historical theory construction, it cannot be assumed to be free; rather, it emerges from the given cultural–historical context but is oriented toward representing the issues in general. Theory of this kind is a device to transfer our experiences from our familiar contexts to potentially extremely unfamiliar ones.

Recognition of the emergence of a cultural–historical theory from a specific social context leads to a need to make the historical and epistemological roots of the given theory explicit. Thus, it becomes possible to acknowledge the ways in which concepts used in child psychology (in contrast with developmental psychology) stem from axioms that are consensually accepted in a given society at a given time, rather than being universally true axioms. Empirical research acquires a new kind of importance in this context; its relevance becomes pointed to those aspects of theory $\leftrightarrows$ phenomena relations that are not obvious axiomatically, or ordinary in the sense of mere reiteration of everyday life events. Empirical work is relevant for obtaining crucial new evidence, rather than constituting a proof of the obvious. Through that circumscribed role, psychology may have a chance to escape from the trap of pseudoempiricism (Smedslund, 1994, 1995), within which it is currently caught in its own booming and buzzing conceptual confusion.

2

Basic Assumptions Underlying Psychological Research

Any effort to construct a relativistic theory of developmental psychology is embedded in a wider network of cultural and scientific knowledge. That knowledge base, which includes information about phenomena and about the ways by which further knowledge of them can be obtained, is based on some axiomatic (core) ideas. Those premises are accepted by investigators because they are either explicitly considered to be true, or they are followed implicitly as their truthfulness is felt to be beyond doubt. This chapter analyzes a number of such basic assumptions used in psychology. The aim of the analysis is to make explicit the assumptions that form the foundation of much empirical research in psychology as a whole, and in child psychology in particular.

2.1 PERSON/ENVIRONMENT SEPARATION AND RELATIONSHIPS

Psychology usually separates its object—persons and their psychological phenomena—from their surrounding environments. This has been accepted practice since the discipline gained its independent status (see Super & Harkness, 1981). The separation of the target (foreground, object) from its context (background) is perceptually a necessary step in the research process. It delineates the phenomena under study from others and allows investigators to concentrate on some, rather than all, of their aspects.

The person/environment separation in psychological research can be accomplished in different ways. The particular strategy used determines the kind of information about the object of research that will become available to the investigator as the result of the study. Differentiation is accomplished, first, in the form of *exclusive separation:* The phenomena are separated from their contexts, and the contexts, being irrelevant, are eliminated from any further consideration. This purified phenomenon is further studied as if it were independent of its context. Some of the principal analyses of phenomena in child psychology follow this strategy. Many psychologists have made efforts to separate cognitive development from its social counterpart. As a result, cognitive development is often explained as a process that is independent of the social environments within which children's thinking actually occurs. Causal explanations for cognitive development are found within that development itself, excluding the possibility that social experience participates in that process (see Valsiner, 1984a).

The second way to separate a phenomenon from its context is by *inclusive separation:* The target is differentiated from its context, but the context is retained in the subsequent analysis because it is considered to be interdependent with the phenomenon. Although the emphasis in research is on the object phenomenon, the relevance of its context is recognized in the investigation.

These two ways in which psychological phenomena can be studied parallel closely the distinction between open and closed systems (Bertalanffy, 1950), or between context-free and context-bound phenomena. The closed systems are systems that do not depend for their existence on exchange relationships with their environments. Any change in the system inevitably leads toward structural breakdown of the system. In contrast, open systems are dependent on exchange relationships with their environments, and their structural organization is maintained, or enhanced, by these relationships. If closed systems can be conceptualized as context-free, then open systems by definition are context-dependent. Biological, psychological, and social systems are open, and open (not closed) systems are capable of development. This important feature of developmental phenomena—their open systems nature—leads to the necessity for all developmental research to be systemic and ecological; it has to study the target object interdependently with its environment.

The development of open systems is characterized by the principle of equifinality—similar outcomes of development can result from developmental processes that can be vastly different from one another. In principle, it is impossible to predict the outcomes of the development of an open system from the starting state of that system because the system's interdependence with its environment and the possibility of different developmental trajectories keep the developing system open to adaptive changes most of the time. Because of the open system nature of development, it is not possible to conceptualize development as taking place along a fixed, unilinear trajectory. Instead, multiple trajectories of development can be expected theoretically and sought in empirical studies, even if the sets of these trajectories occur within a certain relatively common range. Unilinearity of development can be observed only at an abstract level—as it characterizes a family of different developmental trajectories—and not at the level of particular forms of developing systems (see Werner, 1957).

Some examples will help to clarify the distinction between the exclusive and inclusive separation types. Consider the widespread issue of *nature* and *nur-*

ture in human psychology. The controversy about these two abstract causal agents has been a constant theme in psychologists' discourse (Pastore, 1949; Teigen, 1984). Historically, it has emerged from the duality of thinking about God-given *natura* and this-lifely experience in the philosophies of the Middle Ages and Renaissance. The separation of these two agents is very much alive in contemporary psychology, irrespective of whether the nature–nurture controversy is a "hot topic" or a "dead issue" in psychological disputes of the time. For example, personality psychologists who build their study of human personality on the strong belief that personality traits are stable, and are potentially genetically programmed psychological entities, can use their measures to separate the true personality traits from the noisy everyday environmental settings where their subjects live. The data based on personality measures separate the particular material provided by the subjects (e.g., responses to questionnaires, or projective techniques) from their life environments, and eliminate any information about these environments by merely excluding them from the issues covered. Others, who believe in the environmental conditioning of personality, may undertake a similar effort, only in reverse. The environments can be measured in ways that exclude from consideration persons' actions within them, or their self-reports of such actions. In this case, the environment has become the object of investigation, and it has been separated from its context—the person's actions and subjective self-reports.

The *weak* version of the exclusive separation of the phenomena from their contexts is also often used. It would treat both the person and his or her environment as two separate, independently measurable phenomena. Both the persons' self-reports and their environments can be studied by separate sets of measures—following the belief that nature and nurture both affect the personality. The aim of such a study may be to measure the extent of that influence, using an additive model that treats personality as the sum of trait and environment effects. Such an approach still uses the exclusive separation of person and environment, while trying to reveal their mutually parallel effects on the same targets.

An investigator who starts from the premise that the human personality is context bound would study human personality through inclusive separation of the phenomenon and its environment. Although the domain of the target (person) and its background (environment) is differentiated, the investigator attempts to preserve the intrinsic connections between the two. These connections can then be studied directly if the researcher analyzes the process of person–environment interaction. For such researchers, personality is not a simple sum of a person's and an environment's characteristics, nor their formal (extrinsic) correlation. Instead, personality is the functioning of a person–environment system in which both constituents of the system are intrinsically related to each other—they are interdependent. The person cannot function without an environment, and the environment of the person would not be the same if the person were eliminated from it. An investigation of their relationships might not be fruitfully done through the use of linear models (Thorngate, 1986), and the axiom of additive elementarism (see 2.4) is inapplicable.

What, then, can substitute for the time-honored canons of basic theoretical psychology, which originate in classical physics? Instead of an emphasis on organism–environment correlations (i.e., formal, extrinsic relationships between the two), investigation of the interdependence (intrinsic) relationships can be carried out. The notion of interdependence follows directly from the open-system view of the world: Once the state of the organism and its change depend on exchange processes with its environment, the two are interdependent. The organism cannot function without its environment, and the environment requires the existence of the organism as part of its cycle of existence.

2.2   STATIC/DYNAMIC ASPECTS OF THE PHENOMENA

In the first chapter, the paradox of developmental psychology was mentioned: Research on issues of *change* is often performed with the help of methods that are designed to reveal *static* features of the issues studied. A psychologist interested in a certain psychological phenomenon makes a decision (often an implicit one) about the inclusion/exclusion of the dynamic side of the phenomenon in the study. For example, a decision to use a standardized personality test that has high test–retest reliability is a step toward elimination of the dynamic nature of personality, from a psychologist's theoretical view of the phenomenon. Aggregation of measures over time may further grant the stability of the measures, by reducing the role of dynamic aspects of personality in the aggregate. Underneath these practical aspects of research are hidden theoretical assumptions. As a practical step is taken to overlook the dynamic aspect of the phenomena studied, the elimination of that aspect in the investigator's thinking has taken place.

In contrast, a theoretical interest in change and development makes it possible to retain information about observable dynamics in the phenomenon. This perspective is based on the idea that the phenomenon changes over time. To observe the phenomenon, the investigator needs to follow its changes over time, retaining the original sequence of the observed changes in the process of analysis. Different states of the phenomenon in that sequence are not considered to be independent of one another. Instead, it is axiomatically accepted that a previous state of the phenomenon leads intrinsically to the subsequent states. The temporal order of the observed state sequence serves as data for learning about the processes of change. Any aggregation of the constituent states over the sequence into a total frequency count of states is geared toward goals that are diametrically opposite to the study of change. For example, consider a hypothetical sequence of behavioral states in the development of some phenomenon—$A \rightarrow B \rightarrow C \rightarrow A \rightarrow B \rightarrow C \rightarrow X$—where X constitutes an outcome (final state) of the developmental process in question. A simple aggregation of the frequencies of the behavioral states observed before the outcome would eliminate from consideration any information about the developmental sequence. Thus, the behavioral states A, B, and C are found to occur with equal frequency (2 times each) in that sequence. This information includes no knowledge about the temporal relationships among the states; from the frequency count that was made, it is impossible to retrieve whether A changed into B or vice versa. Frequency counts are ways to construct data that do not afford knowledge about the dynamic, developmental aspect of a phenomenon. In contrast, a data construction strategy that retains the temporal sequence present in the phenomenon (e.g., a strategy that decomposes the example into: The sequence A → B → C → occurred twice before the outcome X was obtained) is sensitive to the dynamic aspect of the phenomenon and may provide information about developmental issues.

If the study of change and development is the goal of an investigation, the researchers have to establish the domain of the phenomena in which the change is both expected and studied. An effort to study every possible aspect of a developing child at the same time may lead to an unlimited emphasis on the dynamic side of the phenomena in ways similar to Heraclitus's claim that one cannot step into the same river twice. Because every developmental process has its static outer limits, set by the context of the developing organism and the organism's own state, research on the dynamic aspect of further development of the organism may explicitly consider these (temporary) static constraints as a basis on which new development takes place. For instance, some intermediate outcome of development may serve as the static basis. A psychologist may study 8-year-olds' further cognitive development, starting from the static basis of observing that the children involved have already reached the stage of concrete operations. Or, likewise, the children's further cognitive progress (the dynamic, developmental aspect) may be studied on the basis of knowledge about the relatively stable state of the children's environment (e.g., the organization of their school environment: curriculum, discipline, and so on).

The selection of some stable aspects of the organism and its environment as the background, relative to which development is studied, does not deny the dynamic nature of the selected static background. It is a theoretical device that helps the investigator to avoid absolute dynamic relativism in empirical studies, where it is counterproductive. As long as the research interests are concentrated on a particular developmental issue, it can be studied by considering some related issues stable for the purpose of anchoring the developmental study. A good example here is the relationship between development of a child and development of a culture (Valsiner, 1983a). Cultural change takes place on a different time scale from change in the developing child. Something that a child may develop in the course of a few years, the culture may have needed centuries to develop (e.g., a child's development of writing skills and the culture's development of the same skills in history). Thus, if an investigator is interested in the empirical study of child development, the cultural environment in which the development takes place can be considered stable (i.e., unlikely to change at a pace comparable to the child's development) for practical purposes of research. However, that assumption of practical stability of the culture is only a heuristic device that helps the investigator to study the particular child development issues.

To summarize: It is usually accepted in psychology that issues under study (including issues of development) must reveal their stable facet if they are to be scientifically interesting. That basic assumption determines the range of issues that can be addressed, how these issues are addressed, and the range of possible findings that become accepted as valid psychological data. The use of this assumption necessarily guides the investigator toward addressing nondevelopmental research questions. For developmental psychologists, following this assumption may be highly counterproductive.

2.3 INTRACLASS UNIFORMITY VERSUS VARIABILITY

Similar to the static assumption underlying psychological research, the assumption of intraclass uniformity as the static basis for treatment of interindividual differences is often traceable in psychology. The first reaction of an empirical psychologist to impending knowledge about observed variability in the data from a group or class of subjects is to try to eliminate this variance from further theoretical consideration. This is an effort similar to reducing intraindividual change (variability) to the true static depiction of the individual. This reduction is applied synchronically to groups (classes) of individuals; interindividual variability within a class is often considered erroneous and is eliminated by averaging or prototyping (Valsiner, 1984b) that results in depiction of the modal case within the class as representative of the whole class.

The problems of variability are conceptualized in three ways in psychology. Historically, the first way has been to eliminate it from theoretical consideration. This can be accomplished through studying psychological phenomena, in which case the differences between individuals can a priori be considered minimal and inessential. Classical physics has provided thought models for that approach, and these models have been dominant in research on perception and psychophysics. Overlooking variability can also be illustrated through the work of an anatomist. An anatomist who studies the basic structure of the body of representatives of a certain species—humans, for example—legitimizes his or her lack of interest in individual differences between members of the species by arguing that the *basic* anatomy of every person is the same as that of every other person. The anatomist is certainly aware of substantial differences in many aspects (e.g., height, weight) of different bodies, but quite rightly argues that anthropometric interindividual differences are irrelevant to a study of basic anatomical aspects that are shared by all members of the species. This way of dealing with interindividual differences is realized by choosing those aspects of phenomena that are invariable across individual organisms. The choice, however, is made on theoretical rather than empirical grounds; an investigator starts his or her research by assuming that the interindividual differences in the phenomenon studied either are absent (i.e., sufficiently minimal) or constitute an error that obscures the actual true picture of the interindividually invariant phenomenon.

In many situations, the assumption of sufficiently minimal interindividual variability cannot be accepted. Again, the rejection of the assumption can be either axiomatic or inductive. An investigator may opt for making the issue of interindividual variability the object of investigation; he or she may accept a priori that this variability is not error that obscures some invariant truth, but a representation of many individually true states of affairs. On the empirical side of the study, interindividual variability also can easily be observed. This strategy of dealing with variability has given rise to the discipline of differential psychology, which from its very inception has been directly related to societal demands. For example, Binet's invention of mental tests was based on a direct practical need of the French educational system to classify and select school-children so as to fit subsamples of them into different institutional niches in the system. Francis Galton's pioneering efforts in anthropometric and psychometric measurements in Victorian England were cast in his utopian framework of eugenics, to which he attributed societal and religious functions (Buss, 1979; Galton, 1904). Likewise, the proliferation of psychological testing methods during World War I was based on the needs of societal institutions to select some individuals out of bigger populations. That interest was primarily pragmatic and practical, and led to no theoretical breakthroughs that could have explained how interindividual differences come into being.

An argument can be made that differential psychology has actually not considered variability in psychological phenomena at all, although this statement may seem counterintuitive and contrary to the claims of differential psychologists themselves. What differential psychology has accomplished is to accept the existence of interindividual variability *within populations,* but, at the same time, it has attempted to eliminate variability *within individuals* from its scope of interest (e.g., Bem & Allen, 1974; Bem & Funder, 1978). Instead of considering every individual in a population (class) to be similar to every other individual, differential psychology has recognized that there are stable differences between the "true" states of affairs of psychological phenomena (e.g., intelligence, personality, character, temperament). Any instability observed within an individual over time is an obstacle on the road toward empirical discovery of these true states of the particular individual. The ideal for differential psychology has seemed to be to discover the extent and nature of stable differences between individuals in a population, by assuming that any instability within the particular individuals is a result of error or noise due to unaccountable and irrelevant causes. This description makes clear that differential psychology's acceptance and study of interindividual variability within populations is antithetical to the study of development of the individuals in that population over time. The individuals are supposed to remain the same over their life course, although some individuals differ from others in a population by speci-fiable qualitative characteristics (e.g., individual-specific personality traits) and quantitative degrees of these characteristics (e.g., quantified amounts of certain personality characteristics).

The third strategy for dealing with variability (of both kinds: between and within individuals) is practically absent in contemporary psychology, although some calls for its legitimacy have been voiced thus far (Valsiner, 1984b; van Geert, 1983, 1984). It involves the idea that *generality is evidenced in variabil-ity, rather than in uniformity, of behavior and thinking.* Variability is not a source of error in the case of complex phenomena in psychology, but an indica-tor of psychological processes that can generate a variety of psychological out-comes, the function of which is both to adapt the organism to the environment and to accommodate the environment to the organism. In other words, observ-able uniformity in an organism's behavior over time (self-consistency in behavior) and similarity in behavior between organisms (populational consis-tency) are special cases of either psychological (in the individual's case) or evolutionary/sociological (in the case of a species, or a society) processes that generate intra- or interindividual variability in general. Uniformity in out-comes that results from these processes is a special case of the production of variability, as when the variability produced is narrowed down to very few possibilities, or even one particular outcome. Sometimes, such produced uni-formity may be adaptive (depending on the environmental conditions of the or-ganisms), but at other times it can be detrimental to the goals of adaptation. On the other hand, an organism's (or population's) variable nature may enhance its chance for adaptation when environmental conditions change. Processes that are capable of generating variable outcomes in populations or organisms thus can have adaptive advantages over others that can produce only unifor-mity of outcomes.

The implicit, culturally axiomatic nature of how variability is treated is particularly influential in the more applied areas of psychology in general, and child psychology in particular. Some ways of handling variability in child psy-chology lead necessarily to nondevelopmental research efforts. Others may guide an investigator toward the study of developmental processes that consis-tently generate inconsistencies in the organisms' behavior over time, and which may therefore facilitate their adaptation process.

2.4   ADDITIVE ELEMENTARISM VERSUS STRUCTURAL HOLISM

The surrounding world can be perceived in different ways. From one perspec-tive, it can be viewed as the sum of independent elements. In contrast, it can also appear as a system consisting of interdependent constituent parts that are united in some structural whole. The disagreement between these two—*atom-istic* and *holistic* worldviews— has been evident since the beginning of ancient

Greek philosophy. The basic assumption of *additive elementarism* is the model in which the world is thought of as classes of independent things that, if combined by simple summation, make up more complex things. In contrast, the assumption of *structural holism* presents the world in terms of the whole that consists of interdependent parts, which are necessary for the functioning of the whole. An illustration of structural holism is provided by Paul Weiss, one of the originators of the systems approach in contemporary biology:

> A living system is no more adequately characterized by an inventory of its material constituents, such as molecules, than the life of a city is described by the list of names and numbers in a telephone book. Only by virtue of their ordered interactions do molecules become partners in the living process; in other words, through their behaviour. And since this involves vast numbers of disparate compounds, all living phenomena consist of *group behaviour,* which offers aspects not evident in the members of the group when observed singly. (Weiss, 1969, p. 8)

In the history of Western science, the assumptions of additive elementarism and structural holism have existed in parallel since the beginning of the 17th century, when Francis Bacon explicitly formulated the canons of the scientific method on the basics of additive elementarism. In contrast, the development of the alternative scientific method on the basis of the structural–holistic assumption began almost 200 years later, and was wrought by the scientific endeavors of *Naturphilosophie*. Ordinarily, representatives of that school of thought have been characterized by value-laden descriptors that considered them *romanticists* who were, by the implication of that term, quite far from the exactness ideal of Baconian accumulation of facts. This popular and poetic image of *Naturphilosophen* is biased in the direction of presenting them as soft or nonrigorous thinkers and researchers. There is little substance behind such labeling efforts. Although the *Naturphilosophen* included some prominent poet-scientists (e.g., Johann Wolfgang Goethe) who may be more widely known in their culture for their literary role, there were also a number of representatives of the so-called hard science who adhered to the ideas of that school (e.g., Hans Christian Oersted, the discoverer of electromagnetism). In contrast, scientists from the Baconian school of thought were often involved in the mystical extension of their science (e.g., astronomers were also astrologers, chemists were also involved in alchemy); thus, the distinction between science and mystery was not strict in the past centuries, neither for Baconians nor for *Naturphilosophen*. Natural philosophers relied on some aspects of Immanuel Kant's multifaceted contribution to knowledge. On the foundation of Kantian ideas, *Naturphilosophie* began to build up a new, non-Baconian, scientific method, as Williams (1973, p. 17) has summarized:

> Kant and *Naturphilosophie* did produce a scientific method peculiar to *Naturphilosophie* and of obvious importance to the historian of nineteenth-century

science. But there was a final effect that deserves mention. Kant, and more particularly the *Naturphilosophen,* attempted to substitute a new cosmic metaphor. The world of the eighteenth-century *philosophie* was a machine; the *Naturphilosophen* insisted it was an organism. Its laws were laws of development; its basic theoretical paradigm was field theory in which connections between parts were as important as the parts themselves.

In psychology, the two alternative scientific methods have guided the thinking of investigators in different directions. The Baconian method has dominated psychology—especially in its nondevelopmental aspects. This method has also had a profound effect on child psychology. In contrast, traditions of gestalt psychology have promoted the holistic perspective on psychological phenomena. These two perspectives are the alternative methodological assumptions on which investigators' research is built. The issue of choice between these assumptions acquires particular relevance in the study of child development. The perspective of structural holism is undoubtedly better suited for the study of development, as long as the systemic whole is adequately and validly analyzed. The Baconian additive elementarism, in contrast, reduces that whole to the sum of its elements, which may suit the purpose of a nondevelopmental description of phenomena but is not capable of capturing the processes by which development is made possible. The additive elementarism of the Baconian scientific method was not a pure import from the hard physical sciences, as is sometimes assumed by psychologists. Instead, it constituted an effort to free facts from their theological-dogmatic contexts. W. Stanley Jevons explained the revolutionary role that Bacon's philosophy played in Bacon's time:

> Francis Bacon spread abroad the notion that to advance science we must begin by accumulating facts, and then draw from them, by a process of digestion, successive laws of higher and higher generality. In protesting against the false method of the scholastic logicians, he exaggerated a partially true philosophy, until it became as false as that which preceded it. His notion of scientific method was a kind of scientific bookeeping. Facts were to be indiscriminately gathered from every source, and posted in a ledger, from which would emerge in time a balance of truth. It is difficult to imagine a less likely way of arriving at great discoveries. The greater the array of facts, the less is the probability that they will by any routine system of classification disclose the laws of nature they embody. Exhaustive classification in all possible orders is out of the question, because the possible orders are practically infinite in number. (Jevons, 1873/1958, pp. 576–577)

This description of the nature of the Baconian scientific method would apply quite adequately to the state of affairs in contemporary child psychology. An ever-increasing number of facts is accumulated without explicit and systematic concern about the assumptions on which that kind of data construction is based, and efforts toward abstracting laws of child development from these masses of data either fail explicitly or use some hidden theoretical framework to make sense selectively of some of the existing facts. Because, as Jevons noted, the set of possible orders into which the large database can be imperfectly fitted at some level of approximation is practically infinite, many competing common-sense-based theories can gain support from some of the data (see Cairns & Valsiner, 1984). The Baconian ideology of the scientific method, as it is applied to developmental phenomena, leads inevitably to increasing theoretical confusion. Fashionable commonsense ideas of the given time are often used as theories in psychology. The progress of science cannot be based on the mass accumulation of facts, but is wrought by careful coordination of the investigators' theoretical activities with their empirical observations, where the activities influence the observations, and the observations, in their turn, correct the activities.

As an example of how additive elementarism has guided an area of psychological research away from addressing developmental issues, consider two approaches to the study of children's intelligence: the psychometric and the Piagetian. The traditional psychometric approach has utilized the additive elementarism of Baconian heritage *par excellence*. A child's intelligence is measured by counting the *sum* of test items that the child has answered correctly (from the psychologist's perspective). Interindividual differences in intelligence are conceptualized in a quantitative-additive fashion, and the psychological processes that were actually used by children to give their answers (both right and wrong) to the test items are left out of consideration. Furthermore, the development of intelligence of a particular child over time is viewed as quantitative gain: a developing child's IQ may increase as intelligence increases. The concept of intelligence in this framework of thought becomes an ideal substance that is assumed to be present in the child's mind, and the amount of the substance may change as the child grows. In its explanatory function, this conceptualization of intelligence bears remarkable similarity to explanations in other domains of human cognition (see Horton, 1967).

In contrast, Piaget's view of intelligence as a process of adaptation emphasizes the connection between the developing child and his or her environment, where the child's activity results in the construction of his or her cognitive development through a series of equilibrations and re-equilibrations (Piaget, 1977). The child's cognitive processes undergo a series of qualitative transformations, and once these transformations are accomplished, they afford the child new ways of thinking. Intelligence in Piaget's view is no longer a substance that is measured by summing up correct answers on a test, but a cognitive system that organizes the child's interaction with the environment.

Another example of the successful use of the structural–holistic perspective comes from neuropsychology. In patients with brain lesions, the systemic function of the whole brain is hard to overlook in the clinical research process. The lesion constitutes a static trauma to a particular area in the brain, but the whole structure of the brain is set to work toward attempting to overcome the adverse effects of the lesion. Luria (see Luria & Artemieva, 1970) has emphasized the systemic functioning of the brain in the context of suggesting *syndrome analysis* as the basic scientific research strategy for neuropsychology:

> The neuropsychological investigation is based on the assumption that any psychic activity constitutes a complex functional system that depends on the joint work of a whole complex of brain (and foremost—cortical) zones, and that every part of the brain carries its own, highly specific function that guarantees the factor which is important for the flow of complex forms of psychological activity. It can be thought, following that assumption, that damage to every part of the brain that eliminates that factor results in the immediate *primary defect,* which, in its turn, leads to a number of secondary or *systemic deficiencies,* which disturb the normal functioning of those psychological activities, for which that factor is necessary. (Luria & Artemieva, 1970, p. 106)

According to Luria, the neuropsychological syndrome analysis involves examining changes in the work of a brain that has been damaged in certain specific locations, while the whole organism continues to cope with the tasks that the brain system has to mediate. Localized brain damage alters certain functions directly and others by proxy, leaving many of the functions intact. An investigator who compares the impaired functions with the frame of intact ones analyzes the psychological syndrome structure of the brain lesion. Likewise, the idea of such systemic analysis can be directly applied to child development. For example, a new action emerges among the whole repertoire of a child's actions. This action immediately reorganizes the child's behavior—the new action becomes used in a particular situation, and its presence facilitates the development of some actions, while leaving others the way they were. In syndrome analysis, the issue of dynamic change in the phenomena is viewed in the context of its static aspects, relative to which change is observed.

The investigator's choice between additive elementarism and structural holism can be accomplished on different grounds. As long as the choice is based on the person's ideological preferences, it is possible to evidence efforts to study developmental phenomena on the basis of the elementaristic assumption. However, if the developmental nature of the phenomena is to be the basis of choice between these two axiomatic assumptions, then the selection of additive elementarism as one's foundation for empirical research is unproductive, given the investigator's goals. Development is a characteristic of structured biological, social, and psychological phenomena that depend on environments for their emergence, maintenance, change, and reproduction. Development is possible in open systems, and the structural–holistic assumption is therefore the only viable choice for an investigator who is truly interested in developmental research. Within the realm of different structural–holistic models of development, a wide variety of concrete ways of description and explanation can be constructed. However, the understanding that it is theoretically impossible to study development when the additive atomism assumption is accepted has only rarely been recognized in much of contemporary child psychology.

2.5   MAXIMIZATION OR SATISFICING

Psychological research is often based on the assumption that organisms tend to maximize their gains whenever possible, and to minimize their losses. Quite often, subjects in laboratory experiments are expected to demonstrate their maximal performance, triggered simply by the instruction of an experimenter. This assumption seems to be mediated by traditions of economic thought, which have developed within the Western industrialized cultures in conjunction with economic activities and the Protestant work ethic (Weber, 1930).

The idea of competitive comparison is closely intertwined with the economic thinking about maximization of action results. Positive value attributed to achievement is evident in psychologists' jargon used in talking about their data. For example, statements like "Boys were found to *do better* on test X than girls," or "Women *were found to be better* than men in Y" illustrate the implicitly coded cultural value of winning in a competition when different groups of subjects or individual subjects are compared with one another.

The axiom of maximization is often applied in a value-laden manner to different aspects of subjects' performance in psychological experiments. For example, in animal experimentation, an active organism (e.g., a rat that solves a Skinnerian box task by a series of trials and errors) may be considered to do better than a seemingly passive organism (e.g., an "insightful" rat that solves the problem by trying once), given that the former tries harder than the latter. This *maximization of effort* seems to be considered a prerequisite for success—in full accordance with the cultural value attached to the Protestant work ethic. Likewise, *maximization of outcomes* often gains positive connotational valence in psychology. The cultural–societal background of the maximization assumption has been quite extensively studied by historians and sociologists (e.g., Tawney, 1926; Weber, 1930).

An alternative assumption to the maximization-based worldview emerges from the work of Herbert Simon and takes the form of *satisficing*. Instead of maximizing the outcomes of one's decisions under conditions of incomplete information, one may opt for finding a course of action that is "good enough"— or, in other terms, set up the goal of satisficing for oneself (Simon, 1957, pp. 204–205). The conceptual difference between satisficing and maximizing is directly related to the assumption about the nature of the problem that the acting organism is trying to solve. Maximizing is possible when the problem is finite. This is the case when the set of its conditions, possible outcomes, and potentially usable courses of action is fixed (so that the organism can calculate the maximally useful strategy of action), and when all the information about the task is available to the problem solver. However, these conditions are only rarely present for problem-solving processes; usually the task situation is changeable over time. Partially because of the dynamic nature of the task, only rarely does the problem solver have access to all the aspects of the task situation. Furthermore, many tasks are performed in life under time constraints that render a thorough analysis of the whole situation impossible. Under these conditions of reality, satisficing becomes a more adequate assumption about organisms than maximizing can be. Or, in other words, maximizing is a special (boundary) case of satisficing—a case when an organism considers only "the best" solution to a problem to be good enough. This may be the case in those domains of life where competition is a legitimate aspect of the task, so that, for some of the competitors, winning is considered to be the task's only satisfactory solution. In other domains of life, however, competition plays only a small role, and the range of the solutions that are perceived to be sufficient can be wide. In fact, the majority of exchange processes between organisms and their environments are based on the regulation of the organism's state in ways that maintain it sufficiently above the conditions of the minimal threshold of necessity.

Psychology's frequent acceptance of the assumption of maximization in the efforts and outcomes of the behavior of subjects (animals or humans) may be unwarranted. For example, some studies in child psychology may point to the finding that mothers are better at taking care of infants than fathers. This finding follows from the emphasis on maximization—it is implicitly assumed that both categories of subjects (mothers and fathers) are trying their best to win, over the other, in competition that is judged by the investigator. This picture of parents' child-minding efforts being built around the idea of competition biases the discourse in psychology in ways that need not be warranted. Alternatively, mothers and fathers need not be in competition with each other (as an individual father and mother, or as the class of mothers against the class of fathers), but may play *complementary* and *supportive* roles. The mother may indeed be better than the father in the care of an infant, merely because she takes greater responsibility for the task, but the father can take over that task and perform it in ways that are good enough. Both the mother's and the father's ways of giving care to the infant are sufficient (although these ways are undoubtedly different). Thus, the comparison between the mother and the father along the lines of the maximization assumption can seriously bias child psychology's knowledge base about parenting. In fact, the question of mechanisms of parenting (shared by mothers and fathers, but implemented in different ways) is replaced by the question of outcomes (parental behavior) viewed in the context of implied mother–father competition or rivalry.

There may exist some psychological phenomena to which the assumption of maximization fits well. However, the application of that assumption to almost all phenomena in psychology, without considering the nature of the phenomena in the first place, leads psychology into a conceptual dead end where only a careful theoretical analysis can free psychologists' empirical inclinations.

As with other basic assumptions described in this chapter, the acceptance of one of the assumptions instead of the other, explicitly or implicitly, determines the kind of information that empirical research in the discipline can obtain about the given phenomena. It determines where and how psychologists try to find lawfulness in their empirical data, and where they find lawlessness instead.

2.6 CONCEPTUALIZATION OF LAWFULNESS

Dissatisfaction with the lawless nature of psychology surfaces in psychologists' thinking from time to time. It usually proceeds as follows: Psychology has not revealed any fundamental laws of behavior or thinking; its knowledge base contains a poorly ordered multitude of empirical facts, commonsensical concepts, and mediocre predictions of a statistical kind. Quite often, this unhappy picture is followed by a more positive note of reference to the infancy of the discipline (the underlying assumption seems to be that the science now in its infancy will some day grow up). Sometimes, the standard explanation (along the lines "We do not have enough data about X") is used as an apology for the shallowness of much of the scientific thinking in psychology.

Lack of data is always a factor in any scientific venture, the aims of which are the acquisition of new information and an arrival at new understanding. However, laws of psychology cannot be revealed by mere accumulation of data. These laws need to be actively constructed by scientists, for they are based on the empirical data, on the one hand, and on assumptions about what the law is and how to construct it, on the other. A scientific endeavor is always based on the interaction of the scientist's mind with the activities by which the empirical phenomenology of the particular branch of science is explored.

Kurt Lewin was one of the few theoretically minded psychologists of the past who worried about the lack of theoretical analysis of what is lawful in psychology. His analysis of the theoretical traditions of psychology led him to outline the implicit differences in what is considered lawful in psychology. Following the traditions stemming from medieval physics (which, in turn, originated in Aristotle's philosophy), psychology was seen by Lewin to follow the lead of physics in determining the meaning of lawful. Lewin (1931, p. 144) remarked:

> For Aristotle those things are lawful, conceptually intelligible, which occur *without exception.* Also, and this he emphasizes particularly, those are lawful which occur *frequently.* Excluded from the class of the conceptually intelligible as "mere chance" are those things that occur only *once,* individual events as such. Actually since the behavior of a thing is determined by its essential nature, and this essential nature is exactly the abstractly defined class (that is, the sum total of the common characteristics of a whole group of objects), it follows that each event, as a particular event, is chance, undetermined.

Contemporary child psychology has continued along Aristotelian lines in its conceptualization of lawfulness. Abstractly defined classes of individual subjects are often believed to be explained by the abstract essences that are used as the classification bases. Lewin's example (1931, p. 153) illustrates that operation of thought:

> The fact that three-year-old children are quite often negative is considered evidence that negativism is inherent in the nature of the three-year-olds, and the concept of a negativistic age or stage is then regarded as an explanation (though perhaps not a complete one) for the appearance of negativism in a given particular case! . . .
>
> The classificatory character of its concepts and the emphasis on frequency are indicated methodologically by the commanding significance of statistics in contemporary psychology. The statistical procedure, at least in its commonest application in psychology, is the most striking expression of this Aristotelian mode of thinking. In order to exhibit the common features of a given group of facts, the *average* is calculated. This average acquires a representative value, and is used to characterize (as "mental age") the properties of "the" two-year-old.

The use of essences of classes to establish the meaning of lawfulness in psychology has perhaps been the most widespread application, but by no means is it the only possible one. Lewin himself emphasized the need to transcend that Aristotelian notion through conceptualizing the relationships of a person and the environment in terms of field theory. His suggestion (see also Lewin, 1933, 1939) involves the recognition of lawfulness in the *single cases* of person–environment relationships, thus dissociating the concept of lawfulness from the idea of recurrence of the phenomena. Such treatment of lawfulness is inherently related to the structural–holistic assumption (see 2.4), as well as to the notion of systemic causality (see 2.7). The lawfulness of individual persons' psychological phenomena has been claimed by various psychologists over time (see Franck, 1982; Grossman, 1986, for overview). From the perspective of developmental psychology, the assumption of lawfulness has to proceed one step further and include the *newly emerging particular instances* of phenomena that result from the process of development of a given child.

2.7   ASSUMPTIONS OF CAUSALITY

The issue of what is lawful in psychology is closely connected with the conceptualization of causality in investigators' minds. Causality has been one of the most fiercely debated issues in the history of philosophy since the times of ancient Greece. The types of causality outlined by Aristotle have been intermittently used by people both in everyday life and in science. Several causes can function in parallel and at the same time. Aristotle outlines the *material* cause as being "that out of which a thing comes to be and which persists . . . e.g. the bronze of the statue, the silver of the bowl" (*Physica,* Book II, 194:25).

His treatment of the *formal* cause linked the outcome that is being caused to the essence of the class to which the outcome belongs. The *efficient* cause referred to "the primary source of the change or coming to rest; e.g. the man who gave advice is a cause, the father is the cause of the child, and generally what makes of what is made and what causes change of what is changed" (*Physica,* book II, 194:30). Finally, Aristotle emphasizes the *purpose* as the cause—acting "for the sake of" something is considered the cause of that thing (Hardie & Gaye, 1930).

Aristotle's conceptualization of the four different senses in which cause is thought of constitutes an effort to analyze causality into its constituents. However, he is not blind to the relationships between causes, and to the issue of presence versus absence of the causes:

> Some things cause each other reciprocally, e.g. hard work causes fitness and *vice versa,* but again not in the same way, but one as end, the other as the origin of change. Further the same thing is the cause of contrary results. For that which by its presence brings about one result is sometimes blamed for bringing about the contrary by its absence. Thus we ascribe the wreck of a ship to the absence of the pilot whose presence was the cause of its safety. (*Physica,* Book II, 195:10, quoted in Hardie & Gaye, 1930)

The different conceptualizations of causality that scientists adhere to serve as basic assumptions in their research. Like other basic assumptions outlined in this chapter, conceptualization of causality determines what kinds of empirical data are derived from reality in the course of scientific research. For example, a neuropsychologist may elect to use Aristotle's notion of the material cause as *the* meaning of cause in his empirical research. A cognitive psychologist studying similar phenomena may stick to defining causality in terms of Aristotle's formal cause. A positivist may solve the difficulty with defining causality by denying its existence at all. All these scientists, when narrowing down the meaning of causality to fit their respective inclinations, would easily deny the relevance of reciprocal causality in their research. Their research activities would then not result in empirical data that could retain information about reciprocal relationships present within the phenomenon under study.

The scientific meanings of causality are also dependent on the semantics of the ordinary language terms that are used in discourse (von Glasersfeld, 1974). Brown and Fish (1983) have demonstrated that causality is implied by verbs that point toward either the subject or the object in ordinary sentences. The implicit causality embedded in the semantic structure of language serves as the basis for building more explicit cognitive models of causality attributions.

In most general terms, scientists' basic assumptions about causality are of two kinds. Causality is considered to be either *elementaristic* or *systemic.* In the first case, a certain causal factor A is considered to cause an outcome B, under all circumstances. In the second case, the outcome B is considered to be a result of interaction of parts of the causal system A (designated as parts a1, a2, a3, etc.). When the assumption of elementaristic causality guides the investigator's thinking, explanation of an outcome is considered sufficient when the particular causal agent is specified. For example, a child's performance in mathematics at school can be attributed to the child's intelligence in general, or to a Q-factor in particular. Such an approach refrains from considering the interaction of the specified causal factor with other similar factors, or external conditions, and it implicitly accepts the assumption of elementaristic causality. Explanations through reference to a psychological term that serves as an explanatory principle (see Bateson, 1972—Metalogue: What Is Instinct?) are widespread in psychology.

In the history of occidental sciences, the canons of elementaristic causality can be traced back to David Hume. In *A Treatise on Human Nature* (first published in 1738, here cited in a concentrated form via Hume, 1854, pp. 221–223), Hume outlined the following rules, which have influenced scientists' discourse about causality since his time:

1. The cause and effect must be contiguous in space and time.

2. The cause must be prior to the effect.

3. There must be a constant union between the cause and effect.

4. The same cause always produces the same effect, and the same effect never arises but from the same cause.

5. Where several different objects produce the same effect, it must be by means of some quality that we discover to be common among them.

6. The difference in the effects of two resembling objects must proceed from that particular in which they differ.

7. When any object increases or diminishes with the increases or diminutions of its cause, it is to be regarded as a compounded effect, derived from the union of several different effects that arise from the several different parts of the cause. The absence or presence of one part of the cause is here supposed to be always attended with the absence or presence of a proportionable part of the effect. This constant conjunction sufficiently proves that the one part is the cause of the other.

8. An object that exists for any time in its full perfection without any effect is not the sole cause of that effect, but must be assisted by some other principle, which may forward its influence and operation.

It is evident that Hume's conceptualization of causality involves a basically static view of the world, where independent objects are constantly intertwined with one another in space and time ("constant conjunction"). The same cause always produces the same effect, and the latter can result only from the particular constant cause—which is immutable and would give rise to the same effect every time it occurs. Discussing the issue of constant cause–effect relationship, Hume (1854, p. 222) commented:

> The same cause always produces the same effect, and the same effect never arises but from the same cause. This principle we derive from experience, and is the source of most of our philosophical reasonings. For when by any clear experiment we have discovered the causes or effects of any phenomenon, we immediately extend our observation to every phenomenon of the same kind, without waiting for the constant repetition, from which the first idea of this relation is derived.

This quote illustrates Hume's acceptance of the idea of *homogeneous* classes—not only are cause–effect relationships constant, but once they are established in some cases (through "any clear experiment"), that finding can be extended to *all* cases of the given class (kind). Furthermore, Hume's conceptualization of causality involves additive elementarism (as described in 2.4), if we consider his Rule 7. Both the cause and the effect are separable into their parts (elements), so that if some of the cause elements are subtracted from the cause, the "proportionable" extent of effect is likewise altered. The contemporary thinking about decomposition of outcomes of some study into an additive conglomerate of their causes (as exemplified by the use of regression and analysis-of-variance methodology) follows faithfully the guidelines established by Hume, who, however, was aware of the limits of applicability of that idea. He cautioned against overly wide extension of Rule 7 (Hume, 1854, pp. 222–223):

> We must, however, beware not to draw such a conclusion [i.e., that absence or presence of a part of cause relates directly to absence or presence of the proportionable part of effect] from a few experiments. A certain degree of heat gives pleasure; but it does not follow that if you augment it beyond a certain degree, the pleasure will likewise augment; for we find that it degenerates into pain.

In contrast to the atomistic and static worldview inherent in Hume's thinking about causality, the conceptualization of *systemic* causality emphasizes the functional relationships between different parts of the causal system (Weiss, 1978). These relationships give rise to different outcomes. Thinking in terms of systemic causality has developed in conjunction with those areas of science in which the objects of investigation are sufficiently complex to render elementaristic notions of causality a priori inadequate—ecology (see Hutchinson, 1948), medicine (see Kuipers, 1984; Kuipers & Kassirer, 1984), economics and psychology (Bandura, 1983; Maruyama, 1963; Simon & Rescher, 1966).

Systemic causality can be either *circular* or *linear*. In the biological world, the overwhelming majority of causal mechanisms are circular or cyclic—that is, a series of biological or biochemical processes is organized in such a way as to form a closed circle of mutual transitions, the by-products of which lead to certain outcomes. In the case of such a cyclical arrangement of the relationships of the parts of the causal system (see Figure 2.1), it is not possible to attribute causality for the outcomes (X, Y, Z) of the system to any one (or few) of its parts (A, B, C, D, E) separately from the others. The whole cyclically arranged system causes the outcomes, not any single component of the system.

The linear form of systemic causality involves a sequence of factors (A, B, C, D) that are part of the causal system lead to a certain direct outcome (X), or to Y, which illustrates an outcome that is a by-product of the system:

$$A \rightarrow B \rightarrow C \rightarrow D \rightarrow \text{outcome X}$$
$$\downarrow$$
$$\text{outcome Y}$$

In the case of linear systemic causality, it is obviously possible for an investigator to limit the analysis of causality to the immediate predecessors of the outcomes (D for X, C for Y), and thus reduce the sequentially organized causal system to an emphasis on one of its constituents that is temporally the closest to the outcome. Many commonsense treatments of causality involve such reduction. Consider a hypothetical example of a person who explains her or his misbehavior under the influence of alcohol only through the effect of that substance. The person eliminates from the causal analysis certain factors in the chain of interrelated causal events that preceded the actual alcohol intake (e.g.,

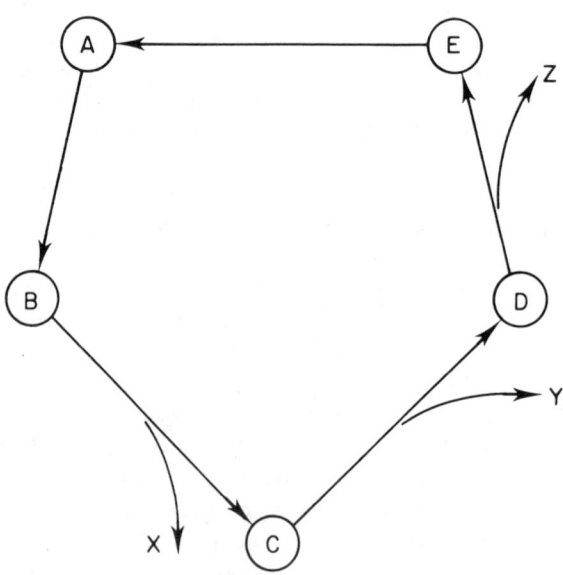

FIGURE 2.1. A schematic depiction of circular systemic causality.

frustration at home → need for company → meeting friends → their suggestion for having a drink → . . .). Only the immediate antecedent (drinking) is considered to be the cause of the outcome (misbehavior) in this reduction of the actual causal system to an elementaristic model of causality. The beginning part of the causal chain is dropped from consideration, and only the proximal (antecedent) event in the chain is attributed the status of the cause. This example need not illustrate the general rule in reduction of causality from its systemic–linear nature to an elementaristic attribution. In fact, any particular part, even in a sequence of the causal structure leading to an outcome, may be separated from its context and attributed the status of the cause. Some investigators subscribe to the cognitive explanation of an outcome of a long causal sequence of events through selecting an event close to the beginning of the sequence. The most vivid example of such reduction of a linear causal system to elementarist causality can be found in psychoanalytic explanation of adults' psychological problems by pointing to some events that took place in their early childhood. Causal inference from problems in infancy to those of adulthood is thus made, bypassing all the events of later childhood and adolescence that are the intermediate predecessors of the adults' psychological states.

Both the elementaristic and systemic causality as described here are context-free in their nature. The functioning of the causes and causal systems described thus far excludes reference to any contextual conditions that are necessary or that constrain the transition from causes to outcomes. The difference between *context-free* and *context-bound* conceptualizations of causality leads to the distribution of *direct* and *catalyzed* causality. The first of these two, as mentioned, is context-free: When that cognitive model is applied by a researcher to the research materials, no stipulation about external circumstances of its applicability is required. The second model—called here catalyzed causality (see Figure 2.2)—involves external conditions that do not participate in the causal process, but their presence is necessary for allowing the causal system to function. Both elementaristic and systemic causality models can be catalyzed. For example, to let an elementaristic causal connection A→X become actual, an additional catalytic condition C is necessary:

$$A \rightarrow X$$
$$\uparrow$$
$$C$$

The systemic-circular model of causality may be catalyzed as shown in Figure 2.2.

The notion of catalyzed causality introduces the role of the context that is necessary for the cause→effect relationships to be present. The catalyzing agents themselves do not produce the effects and are not direct parts of the causal system. Their presence, however, is necessary for the outcome to emerge as the result of the work of the causal system. An example of catalyzed

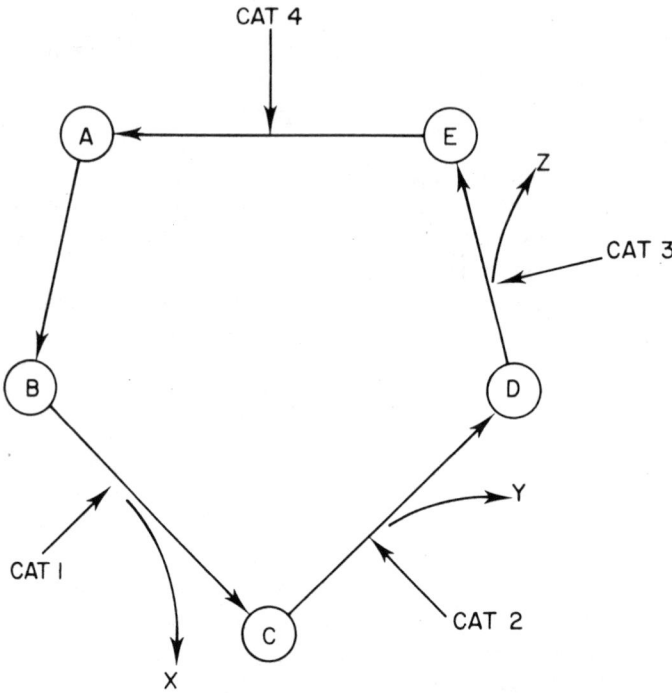

FIGURE 2.2.   A schematic depiction of the catalyzed version of circular systemic causality (CAT = catalyzing agent).

causality can be seen in the thinking of cancer researchers, who use the distinction between carcinogens (causes that produce cancer) and co-carcinogens (agents that do not produce the disease by themselves, but whose presence enables carcinogens to cause tumors). In psychology, part of the stock of basic knowledge of experimenters who condition animals in learning experiments is that the success of their conditioning efforts depends on some "incentive conditions"—circumstances of the setting and of the state of the animal—without which the animal's learning cannot be demonstrated.

Different perspectives on conceptualizing causality constitute the basic assumptions that lay the foundation for investigators' research efforts. Once a certain view of causality is accepted—implicitly or explicitly—it determines the outer range of possible interpretations that an investigator may devise by the end of an empirical study.

In sciences that are influenced by positivist thought, the issue of causality may be resolved through the denial of its existence, and through its replacement by the measurement of formal relationships between variables. However, the commonsense interest in the meaning of the data, conceptualized in terms of some form of causality, remains implicitly present in the thinking of the majority of psychologists (see Valsiner, 1986). The basic assumptions about causality constitute cognitive models that guide our thinking about psychological phenomena, both in psychology and in everyday life.

2.8   SCIENTIFIC BACKGROUND OF BASIC ASSUMPTIONS IN PSYCHOLOGY: COMMON SENSE AND CLASSICAL PHYSICS

Many scientists have demonstrated that psychology has taken its axioms from the "hard" science of classical physics. As shown above, psychology's concepts of lawfulness originate in Aristotle's metaphysics. This origin has produced a discrepancy in the discipline between psychological phenomena and psychology's knowledge base. Lewin (1931) advocated the replacement of Aristotelian physics with another classical-physical basis for psychology's thought models—that of Galileian physics. Haslerud (1979) and Brandt (1973) have likewise pointed to the classical-mechanics roots of psychology.

Without doubt, the majority of psychology's models of thought originated in classical physics. However, a powerful social choice mechanism seems to have been operational in the coining of psychology's models: the commonsense thinking of the laypersons who served as consumers of psychology's applied efforts in society. Ways of thinking *that resemble the style of physics* (a science with considerable social prestige in Western industrialized societies) *and that follow the content of commonsense ideas* (which are shared by laypersons within the culture) about human beings, their thinking and behavior, and the ways in which different events (conflicts, personnel selection, etc.) can be managed, became accepted as the basic assumptions underlying psychological research. The limiting role of commonsense thinking in selective acceptance of physics-based thought models in psychology has been demonstrated by Smedslund (1978, 1980) and Harré (1981). Harré conceptualizes psychological theories as social talk, which constitutes one of the many kinds of discourse in a society. His analysis of the content of some examples of contemporary theorizing in experimental social psychology leads him to characterize psychological talk in quite direct terms (Harré, 1981, pp. 219–220):

> In looking at psychological theories *as* talk, we are free to consider them as one among several possible contributions to the interpretation of what is going on, and to examine them for their display of "interests" and the uses of rhetorics to further those interests. It may be that a psychologist chooses a rhetoric because that is what he thinks is demanded of him by his professional colleagues and by the expressive demands of his social circle. By talking and writing in a certain way, he publicly displays himself as "rational" and presents himself as a "scientist." In a similar way, a [British] Trade Unionist may adopt a rhetoric for making television appearances which he would never use in everyday life, displaying himself as serious, committed, a mere servant of his Executive Committee, and so on.

The acceptance of ideas from classical physics into psychology has taken place under the mediation of the common sense of psychologists and the social expectations placed on psychologists by laypersons in society. The common sense—shared by psychologists and laypersons—contains a set of basic assumptions that are axiomatically and usually implicitly considered to hold true for psychological phenomena. The particular assumptions outlined above—separation of person from environment, emphasis on static aspects of phenomena over their dynamic side, assuming homogeneity within populations and individuals, tendency toward an additive elementarism in viewing psychological phenomena, considering psychology's subjects to be "maximizers rather than satisficers, feeling secure in the lawfulness of big numbers, and electing to look for some (rather than other) kinds of causality in the phenomena—all guide a psychologist's and layperson's efforts to make sense of psychological phenomena. When psychology lacks an emphasis toward self-analysis of the set of basic assumptions on which much of its empirical activity is based, no breakthrough in the basic knowledge can take place. Instead, the discipline is limited to the uncontrolled and implicit following of the fads and fashions in the society, where different basic assumptions may sometimes gain dominance in laypersons' minds, only to lose it after a while. Psychology's recurrent structure of general approaches to its phenomena (Buss, 1978; Flanagan, 1981) resonates with the fluctuations in the implicit social representations (see Moscovici, 1984) in the culture, and follows the latter.

2.9 SOCIAL CONSTRUCTION OF NARRATIVES OF SCIENCE

From the point of view of human existence, all scientific knowledge is encoded in different kinds of texts. Some texts, oral or written, are scientists' communications with themselves (for example, in a diary); others are meant for communication with a select group who share similar interests. Still others are created to persuade powerful rulers (or funding institutions) that a particular direction of research is worth economic support or constitutes symbolic value. Finally, the popularization of science leads to communication with an audience quite different from the communicator.

2.9.1 Basic Assumptions as Social Representations

Earlier sections (2.1–2.7) showed how psychological research is built on basic assumptions that are accepted without much reflection upon their validity. These assumptions have been made into social representations (in the sense of Moscovici, 1990, 1995; also see Wagner, 1994). Anchored within Durkheim's terminology of collective representations (see Némedi, 1995), Moscovici's theory of social representations has—slowly but surely—elaborated the complex nature of the core term. Moscovici considers social representations to entail *performative* and *constructive* functions. The representation prescribes a socially shared definition of a social situation, thus creating a basis for enabling a social group to communicate and maintain a sharedness of concepts and images (Moscovici, 1988, p. 230). Thus, social representations constitute a *theory-like* structure of *hierarchically organized propositions* forming a central core and a set of peripheral elements, as well as *metaphorical form as a figurative schema,* which results from objectification. Social representations carry the *function of anchoring new experiences,* and they are *collectively shared* (Wagner, 1994, pp. 212–213).

Basic assumptions can be viewed as complex social representations that channel the thinking and acting of scientists and lie at the foundation of knowledge construction (see Figure 1.1). Usually, that channeling purposefully excludes from consideration some possible aspect of phenomena. For example, the basic assumption of additive elementarism (see 2.4), once axiomatically accepted, leads psychologists to overlook the systemic and holistic nature of the phenomena, as well as to avoid the use of field-theoretic notions in theory construction. Use of concepts such as various "zones" (see Chapter 5) would be prohibited from theoretical discourse. In contrast, by axiomatic designation of structural holism as the root or basic assumption, not only are these zone concepts possible, but the view of the phenomena also entails acceptance of macrolevel descriptive entities. When contrasted in the domain of methods construction (see Figure 1.1), the opposing basic assumptions lead to diametrically opposite tactics. Whereas quantification is a natural part of data construction, given the additive elementarism, structural holism leads to analysis of specific complex structures as data that should adequately represent selected aspects of the phenomena. If quantification is exemplified in psychology by the endless number of standardized tests, structural holism supports the traditions of Piaget's empirical methods. (See the further discussion of data construction in Chapter 3.)

2.9.2   Basic Assumptions and Trade at Epistemic Markets

As general social representations, these basic assumptions are socially constructed and maintained semiotic mediational means. They regulate relationships between different epistemic markets (Rosa, 1994, 1996b; see also Bourdieu, 1988) and are thus open to social processes that organize scientific institutions in a given society at a given time. As Rosa explains:

> A look at the plurality of markets allows one to take into account the rules of the different markets, and to consider exchanges among neighbouring markets, their imports and exports. There are many different types of symbolic markets, but the ones which now interest me are the ones concerned with the production of epistemic products. There are, at least, as many "epistemic markets" as discursive formations, and each one has its own rules whose descriptions are of use for offering explanations of how epistemic products (texts) are produced, valued, distributed and consumed. (Rosa, 1996b, p. 399)

Basic assumptions serve as anchors within different epistemic markets; they also create contrastive opposition to the neighboring markets. To continue the example in the preceding section, the contrast between the epistemic market of psychometric empiricism in psychology and the knowledge-construction market of Piaget is anchored with the help of opposite basic assumptions (additive elementarism versus structural holism). Both markets create their own forms of discourse, which are mutually unintelligible—for example, psychometric talk about interaction, a technical term from analysis of variance (ANOVA) generalized to apply to the whole of human functioning, versus the Piagetian notion of the person relating to the task demands.

The social construction of divisions between epistemic markets, as well as their episodic unification, is part and parcel of the metascientific processes that regulate the given discipline. Certain barriers between epistemic markets are strictly held as bastions of identity of science. For instance, psychology as a whole maintains strict separation of its epistemic market from the market of religions, worlds of superstition, and parapsychological events (see analysis by Josephs, 1996a). At the same time, the boundaries of that epistemic market may be kept open for contact with discourses of physiology, physics, or (at times) cultural anthropology. Interestingly, relations with epistemic markets of certain other sciences—chemistry, for instance—have been left unclear. Some historically prominent relations with other markets—a good example is the relation with formal logic—have become distanced, yet not blocked.

Within psychology, a further differentiation of epistemic markets can be observed in ways that are organized by the axiomatic perspectives of the given orientations. Thus, psychometrically oriented personality psychology may create its epistemic market quite separately from that of psychoanalysis, while still allowing some discursive material to enter it. In the history of psychology in different countries, epistemic markets can at times merge, then become separated. Thus, in Soviet psychology of the 1920s, psychoanalytic and Marxist epistemic markets became unified, only to experience absolute separation by the 1930s—and the extinguishing of one of the two. This process may be reversed in Russian psychology of the 1990s, where the discourse of "Marxist psychology" is gradually moving to obscurity.

Despite its obvious 20th-century appeal, the talk about epistemic markets and their relations is another (in this case, meta-metascientific!) borrowing from society's self-organizing reflection. We use one social representation (market) to organize another (science). Borrowing from economics discourse of the present time, we superimpose the social representation of market on the domain of knowledge construction. If we were to substitute another kind of talk—for instance, borrowed from the feudal economic system—we might speak of the "kingdoms" or "grand duchies" of specific discourses rather than of "markets," and discuss "discourse wars" rather than "trade."

In any case, whether using the term markets or not, we arrive at a hierarchy of concepts:

Meta-metalevel: Epistemic markets (specified by discourses).

Metalevel: Basic assumptions (which organize discourses).

Science level: Theory construction, methods–phenomena–data relations, as channeled by basic assumptions (but not strictly determined in detail by them).

The story becomes more complicated when we look at the relations between epistemic markets and their nonepistemic counterparts in a society. Scientific knowledge, in whatever way it is constructed, enters these markets as a commodity and becomes an object in economic exchanges.

The result is intensified movement of ideas between sciences and societies. This process is more extensive for social sciences than for natural sciences. As scientific activities (which once enjoyed semi-isolated status) become integrated into the changing social fabric of society, the borrowing from the society, to form the basic assumptions of the science, becomes intensified. This intricate interdependence takes the form of adjusting scientists' social discourse (a) to the demands of either the lay public [in products such as "popular science" texts, or textbooks (Albury, 1983; Ravetz, 1971)] or functionaries of governmental or private research funding agencies, and (b) to the expectations of peers who have occupied different relevant positions in the social structure of various "review panels." The activities of scientists are surrounded by different kinds of dialogues with an array of social institutions (see examples in Gieryn, 1983; Yeo, 1986), and relevant pleas to these institutions for their support or approval of one or another scientific enterprise are commonplace.

Social institutions at times take upon themselves the role of arbiters of what constitutes "science" and its opponent—"pseudoscience." The history of science has many examples of such rulings. For instance, Copernicus's theory was banned by the Catholic Church in 1616 because it was considered pseudoscientific. In 1820, the reversal of the edict restored the theory to the symbolic status of science (Lakatos, 1978, pp. 6–7). Psychology, with its closeness to the sociomoral values of the society on which it depends, has provided many examples of how the texture of its principles has been guided by the socioinstitutional making (and remaking) of basic assumptions. In the 20th century, such canalization occurred in North America (Samelson, 1985); in pre-Soviet Russia and the Soviet Union, in conjunction with the building of "Marxist psychology" (see Joravsky, 1989; Valsiner, 1988); and, as evidenced in the National Socialist guidance of psychology, in Germany prior to World War II (see Geuter, 1984). In general, a socioinstitutional set goal (which may later turn out to be a utopian concept; see Valsiner, 1996) can lead the construction of a set of basic assumptions in psychology. In North American psychology of this century, much of the sociomoral background was revealed in the "mental hygiene" movement of the 1930s. The ideological agenda of the social institutions was encoded there in the form of "scientific objectivity." As Kingsley Davis observed,

> Mental hygiene hides its adherence behind a scientific facade, but the ethical premises reveal themselves on every hand, partly through a blindness to scientifically relevant facts. It cannot combine the prestige of science with the prestige of mores, for science and the mores unavoidably conflict at some point, and the point where they most readily conflict is precisely where "mental" (i.e., social) phenomena are concerned. We can say, in other words, that devotion to the mores entails an emotional faith in illusion. Devotion to science, on the other hand, *when social illusion constitutes the subject matter of that science, entails the skeptical attitude of an investigator rather than of the believer toward the illusion.* (Davis, 1938, p. 65, emphasis added)

Psychology is, in this respect, an impossible science. Its sociomoral premises either guide psychologists toward proliferating their beliefs under the facade of "objectivity" of research, or lead to their doubting these very sociomoral premises. This way, the general masochism of psychological research (and application) is guaranteed. When viewed from this angle, the pseudoempiricism that proliferates in psychology (see Chapter 1) is neither an oversight nor a mistake. Instead, it is socioinstitutionally set up to guarantee "scientific support" for social ideological actions concerning human beings. The general social representation of the objectivity of scientific research provides appropriate background for such actions.

2.9.3 Social Construction of "Objectivity"

In the history of science, three folk models can be identified as having guided scientists' ways of thinking about the objectivity of their activities. Historically, the oldest of the three is the *personal-perspectival objectivity* model, which emphasized the activity objectivity-constructing nature of specially educated persons, who are well acquainted with the phenomena and therefore can reach an understanding of how these phenomena function. The personal-perspectival model of objectivity prevailed in 18th-century and early 19th-century natural sciences (Daston, 1992). In psychology, it survived to the end of the 19th century, especially in introspection experiments where the authorship for the studies was legitimately attributed to the introspecting subjects (Danziger, 1985, 1990).

The acceptance of personal-perspectival objectivity coincided with the artisan or alchemist role of the scientist in the context of precapitalist societies. According to this model, objectivity is reachable exactly because a person is devoting his or her observational and inferential powers toward creating it. Undoubtedly, persons of this kind can come up with inadequate conceptualizations, and disputes among scientists are widespread—yet it is believed that the active person is the locus from which new understanding emerges.

By the second half of the 19th century, the second model, *aperspectival objectivity,* had become an accepted social norm in the natural sciences. Instead of communicability between specialists (i.e., disputes regarding personal perspectives of specialists), the commonality of perspectives became emphasized. It was as if science moved from an artisan's workshop to the factory floor of a manufacturer of objectivity:

> Aperspectival objectivity was the ethos of the interchangeable and therefore featureless observer—unmarked by nationality, by sensory dullness or acuity, by training or tradition, by quirky apparatus, by colorful writing style, or by any other idiosyncrasy that might interfere with the communication, comparison and accumulation of results. . . . Subjectivity became synonymous with the individual and solitude; objectivity, with the collective and conviviality. (Daston, 1992, p. 609)

Such collectivity needed to get rid of idiosyncrasies—both in the phenomena under study and in the minds of those who collectively and interchangeably study those phenomena. Averaging became the socially desired and glorified way of reducing heterogeneity to homogeneity.

In child psychology, the model of aperspectival objectivity is evoked every time researchers carefully train their so-called "blind observers" to apply their not-so-blind categorization systems to complex phenomena, demonstrate some conventionally accepted level of intercoder agreement (e.g., 70 or 80 percent or more) between the observers, and assume that this exercise of conformity training adds reliability to their substantive claims. Conversely, if the personal–perspectival objectivity model were to be evoked, the researchers would overcome their own blindness (about the blindness of trained observers), educate their observers to understand the theoretical perspective from which the object phenomenon is being analyzed, and *then proceed to look carefully* at the instances of interobserver *dis*agreements (i.e., the 30 or 20 percent or less of the cases), because a dialogue about disagreements would be heuristically valuable.

Finally, at the end of the 20th century, we can observe the spreading of the third type of models, *corporationistic objectivity* models. These models entail establishing control over the objectivity of scientific production by setting up specific generic "brand names" of quality, and operating at the level of comparison of such brand names (e.g., "Data from research group X are more adequate than those from research group Y"). A version of this kind of objectivity can be seen in presentations of results of research from well-established groups, which may include almost tachistoscopic presentations of data of any form on slides, without any explanation of their meaning. The function of such presentations is the same as that of TV commercials, where the value of a brand name is propagated in ways that purposefully limit access to the actual data, their methods of construction, and their actual explanations, while creating an illusion of public access to the objective data. The data presented by a representative of a research corporation are assumed to be objective because of the brand name; no critical insider in the corporation is allowed to question the data (and/or their construction methods), and relevant aspects of the data construction processes may even become legally protected against rival groups trying to replicate the studies. A precedent of the latter occurred around the Utah "cold fusion" case (Taylor, 1991), where rival institutions in varied scientific fields resorted to legal maneuvers to protect their respective control over the data and the procedures of their production.

By itself, none of the three folk models of objectivity can guarantee the adequacy of our empirically based and inventively generalized knowledge. Actual objectivity of research is always based on some perspective that is either implicit or explicit in the philosophical and theoretical systems of the scientists. These perspectives are undoubtedly *linked* with the wider sociocultural perspectives of the societies these scientists inhabit; yet, from that linkage, it is not necessary to assume that they are determined by the sociocultural backgrounds. Rather, the issue of objectivity is dialogically negotiated within two sets of processes. First, there is the negotiation of the activities of the scientists within the social role system of the given society. Different forms of narrative can be used to present the same findings of science to different recipients of the scientific products within the same society. This process of negotiation is not about the content of knowledge, but concerns the roles of the knowledge constructors. It is part of sociopolitical rhetoric, and not about science. Undoubtedly, this process has its implications for the actual construction of knowledge (e.g., consider how rhetoric turns toward the proliferation of "applied science" in a society, as a basis for administrative elimination of orientations toward "basic science"), yet it creates the context for actual processes of knowledge construction.

The second process of negotiation takes place within the cycle of scientists' knowledge construction process. Here, the "participants" are worldviews, theories, underlying assumptions, phenomena (as those are subjectively captured), methods (as those are constructed), and data (as those are derived from the phenomena). Our construction of explanatory understanding moves from the abstract to the concrete (i.e., from theoretical constructions to methodological access to the phenomena) in coordination with the move from the selection of the appropriate phenomena to adequate ways of translating them into data (see Chapter 3).

The story of the construction of objectivity tells us about the social embeddedness of science. At the end of the 20th century, science has become a commercially and legally socialized enterprise in which artisanship or small-scale data production has given way to "data factories" organized in imitation of large business corporations. Objectivity thus becomes a label that is applied to selected facets of the social activity of "research" by the public relations or marketing departments of the given enterprise, and ends up as rhetoric rather than as a descriptive device in communication within "the literature."

2.9.4   Social Organization of Science: Role-Based Institutional Negotiations of Sciences in Societies

Stories about science are constructed along the lines of goal-oriented actions by actively interested persons who represent some ideologically nonneutral social institution. Thus, when a chairperson of a governmental committee on science makes evaluative statements about "stagnation" in some area of science, and different scientists in that area make empathic statements about how wrong that chairperson is, we can observe a social negotiation process among social institutions, which is encoded into highly personalized forms. Such negotiations may be visible to outsiders or may occur behind closed doors. Publicity or secrecy of negotiations about the social role of a given science constitutes a mechanism of such negotiations. It barely needs to be stated that all such negotiations are extrascientific. Even if terms like "objectivity," "progress," or "contributions to society" are being used in these negotiations, the given science under question is used as an arena of social actions, and not as a domain of knowledge construction. For example, the roots of the notion of "progress" are in the religious discourse about "salvation" (see Wertheimer, 1985, p. 16). The notion of salvation was secularized into the notion of progress during the Enlightenment; hence, it is not surprising that stories about progress in science often are told with some semireligious fervor.

In the process of negotiations about science in a society, different forms of narratives (Gergen & Gergen, 1984; Valsiner, 1994a) are used for different purposes. For instance, the same scientist may create a nice progressive narrative for popular scientific communication channels, and while begging for funding from the financial powers may create a story of that discipline's being in danger (if not funded). Finally, the same person may tell his or her students a story of endless change of productive fashions in the discipline, yet, while interacting with selected peers, may pour out all the disappointments (e.g., "It is all the old stuff in this discipline; there is nothing new under the sun"). Such a hypothetical case demonstrates the relativity of the narrator's perspective to the different social roles the narrator assumes (a propagandist, a beggar, an educator, and a grumpy old peer of others). The person remains consistent in being role-relatedly inconsistent. All the narrated stories about the given discipline may be simultaneously true—when viewed from different vantage points.

The role of the recipients of the narratives about science is of no little relevance in that coconstruction process. The idea of an open society in which all different semiotic constructions of reality are included into a happily democratic polyphony is a carefully cherished social myth. The flow of communicative messages within any society includes constraints both on the outside of these messages (i.e., on the accessibility of different kinds of messages) and on the inside (i.e., the narrative forms and content metaphors that are used in the construction of the messages). Last, but not least, it is the recipients of the (externally and internally) constrained communication flow who transform the existing messages into their own knowledge bases. From this coconstructionist viewpoint follows the principal impossibility of "full sharing of knowledge" between scientists and laypersons, or among scientists from different realms of science, or between politicians and scientists. Even if scientists were to devote themselves fully to overcoming the semiotic boundaries that separate them from the lay public (effort of this kind can be found in "applied" psychology), the latter will reconstruct the scientists' intended messages in ways that fit their own goal orientations at the given time and in the current social context. The lay public would translate scientific knowledge into some kind of commonsense knowledge. Even as the latter is eventually changed through input from science, the initial orientation toward scientific knowledge may be rather mundane:

> [W]hat the general public appreciates in science is not what the scientists are doing. Rather, it can be classed under two headings: techniques and natural magic. The first is the collection of devices that make life easier to live, or the destruction of life more efficient. The second is the production of strange and wonderful effects without recourse to supernatural agents. Although the term "natural magic" fell into disuse some time ago, it is quite natural for this interpretation of science to persist. When a layman (child or adult) sees a demonstration of some astonishing effect, can he imagine the human endeavour and intricate technical work which led to its creation? No; it is the effect itself which captures the imagination, and produces wonder and delight: this is natural magic. Of course, the audience for the "wonders of science" is told that these achievements are simply the application of the laws of Nature, and that the creator of the effect is in no sense a magician. But since the audience cannot understand the laws of Nature that are relevant to the production of the effect, it is strange and wonderful (until it becomes a commonplace part of the environment) and so differs little from natural magic of the old sort. (Ravetz, 1971, p. 13)

The unity of perspectives of scientists and laypersons is thus an example of illusionary intersubjectivity. Scientists have their specific activities which, taken out of the knowledge construction process, are meaningless (or worse—can be viewed as either dangerous or idle activities) for the lay public. Yet it is exactly the lay public that at times benefits from scientists' achievements (and also their persistent failures). The "full view" of the inside of science is therefore not possible to communicate to outsiders because the scientists and the outsiders assume different social roles relative to the social institution of science. That difference of perspectives guarantees that the outsiders would reconstruct the insiders' messages in ways that are different from the intentions of the insiders. Thus, all the acts of communication between sciences and their outsiders (of different kinds) can be viewed as social regulation processes, rather than as mere "sharing" of knowledge, or purely altruistic efforts to "educate the public."

2.9.5 Narrative Forms

Different narrative forms can be viewed as cultural symbolic tools that make it possible to create the multivoiced texture of talk about a given science. Different narrative forms provide a framework for the sequence of a story that can be told about any object. Here I apply the typology of Gergen and Gergen (1984) to different stories about the history of psychology.

Gergen and Gergen (1984) discuss the following narrative forms:

Progressive–regressive (Figure 2.3a);

Stability (positive or negative; Figure 2.3b);

Tragic, comic (Figure 2.3c);

"Happily ever after" and, *"romantic saga"* (Figure 2.3d);

Dialectical (Figure 2.3e).

It is easy to see that all the narrative forms reflect some dynamic of evaluation (ranging, on a unilinear scale, from negative to positive) over time.

The progressive–regressive, stability, tragic, and happily-ever-after forms constitute a category of *monotonic change* accounts. Thus, in the case of stability, the narrative form suggests viewing of the next event, even in the described series of events, as continuing at the same evaluation level. For example, the following two possible statements about the continuity between "behaviorist" and "cognitivist" belief systems are equal (albeit different in evaluation) reflections of that form:

Example 1   "With the cognitive revolution, all the positive findings and methodology from the behaviorist era were integrated into a new direction that continues along the lines of objective study of the mind." (the *positive stability* narrative)

Example 2   "With the cognitive revolution, the unsolved problems of the behavioristic research became relabeled in mentalistic terms, but the problems remain unsolved, as before." (the *negative stability* narrative)

In describing scientific progress, the progressive narrative form of a linear progression over time is often used. The uses of that form are evident in the rhetoric of any psychologist who discourages doctoral students from reading articles published a few years ago, and instead enforces the rule of "being up-to-date" with the current literature.

The examples above can be rewritten easily in accordance with the progressive and regressive narrative forms:

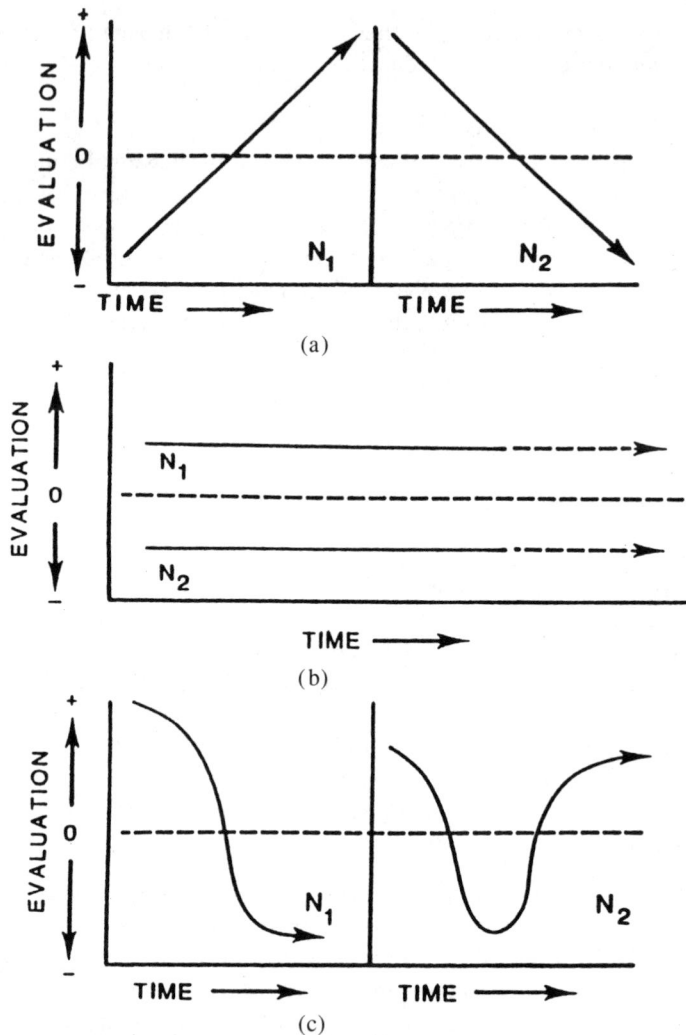

FIGURE 2.3.   Graphic depiction of various narrative forms (from Gergen & Gergen, 1984) (a) the *progressive* (left) and *regressive* (right) narratives; (b) two *stability* narratives (N1 = positive, N2 = negative); (c) *tragic* (N1) and *comic* (N2) narratives; (d) *"happily-ever-after"* (N1) and *"romantic saga"* (N2) narratives; (e) the *dialectical* narrative. Reproduced by permission.

Example 3   "Cognitive revolution has taken psychology above it previous behavioristic state, just like the behaviorist revolution took it above the previous Wundtian mentalistic state." (the *progressive* narrative)

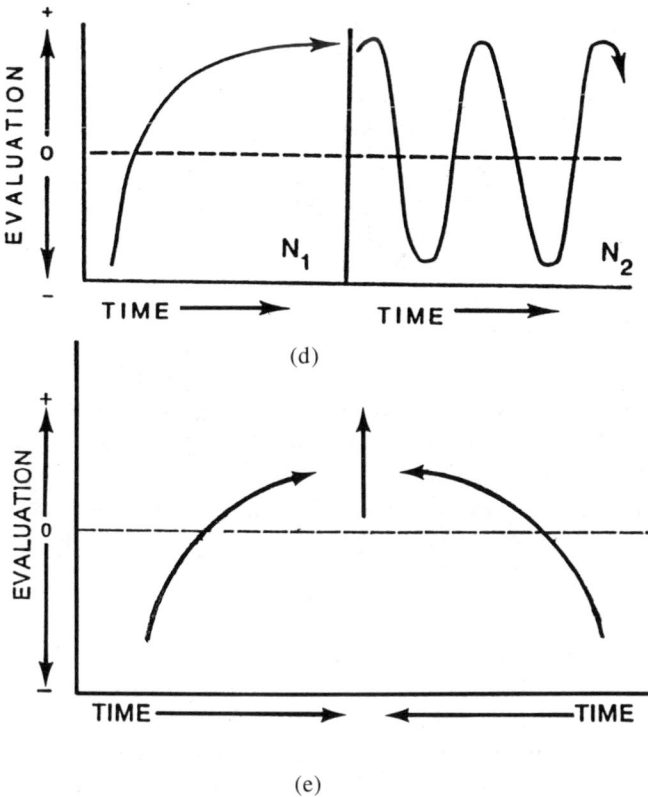

FIGURE 2.3.   *(Continued)*

Example 4   "Cognitive psychology has eliminated the rigor of behavioristic objectivity from science, in the same ways as the behavioristic turn in psychology eliminated theoretical sophistication
from psychology." (the *regressive* narrative)

The use of the progressive narrative form in thinking of the development of
science is commonplace in different disciplines. However, one might also find
some uses of regressive narrative form—for instance, a classics scholar who
claims that the history of our knowledge has experienced a continuous decline
since the ideal philosophies of Plato or Aristotle.

The main difference that separates the tragic narrative form from the regressive one (as illustrated in Example 4) is its assumption of the *dramatic
immediacy* of the regressive process, which is illustrated in Example 5. Furthermore, the reverse of the tragic narrative—the happily-ever-after kind—is
not different in its focus on "breakthrough" dramatism (Example 6).

Example 5   "John B. Watson's publication of the 'behaviorist manifesto' in 1913 led to the immediate downfall of the theoretical core of psychology, and its replacement by behaviorist dogmas." (the *tragic* narrative)

Example 6   "Psychology had been stagnating in its fruitless mentalistic discussions that were based on mere introspectionist methodology. But then, in 1913, Watson published his 'behaviorist manifesto,' after which the discipline achieved an objective basis for itself as science." (the *"happily-ever-after"* narrative)

The monotonic change type of narrative form may be too simple to characterize the complexity of changes depicted in the history of psychology. The more complex narrative forms described by the Gergens—comic, romantic saga, and dialectical narratives (see Figure 2.3 c–e)—may bring us closer to the complexities of organizing the quality and directions of change in psychology. Examples 7 through 9 describe possible applications of those forms.

Example 7   "Psychology had been in a sophisticated theoretical state at the turn of this century, with careful work going on also in making the introspective method applicable to a wide range of subjects and phenomena. But then, John B. Watson's publication of the 'behaviorist manifesto' in 1913 led to the immediate downfall of the theoretical core of psychology, and its replacement by behaviorist dogmas. However, the birth of modern cognitive psychology in 1956 rescued the discipline from behaviorism and restored the use of mentalistic theorizing and modern methods of self-study (e.g., thinking aloud protocols), so the positive state of our discipline is restored." (the *comic* narrative)

Example 8   "Psychology had been in a sophisticated theoretical state at the turn of this century, with careful work going on also in making the introspective method applicable to a wide range of subjects and phenomena. But then, John B. Watson's publication of the 'behaviorist manifesto' in 1913 led to the immediate downfall of the theoretical core of psychology, and its replacement by behaviorist dogmas. Fortunately, the influence of the behaviorist vice was largely confined to North America. In Germany, psychology was rescued by the activities of the gestalt school. The latter, however, lost its influence, and, in the post-World War II years, the behavioristic worldview dragged the discipline down to its swamp. However, the rediscovery of the works of Lev Vygotsky and of the activity-theoretic traditions that have dominated Soviet psychology has restored the value to psychologists' activities." (the *romantic saga* narrative)

Example 9   "Psychology had been in deep crisis at the turn of the 20th century, a fact that was recognized by psychologists of different persuasions. So, the behaviorists worked toward overcoming the mentalism and subjectivity of earlier psychology, and concentrated on objectively observable behaviors, analyzing them into their elementary constituents. In opposition, the gestalt school worked to preserve the holistic quality of complex psychological phenomena, and gave theoretical explanations that preserved the nature of the whole. Lev Vygotsky, however, created a new synthesis of studying complex mental phenomena of a developmental kind, based on both tendencies." (the *dialectical* narrative)

Undoubtedly, the set of possible narrative forms introduced by the Gergens in 1984 (primarily in the context of describing human life paths), and illustrated here, is not complete. Other forms can be invented or can be discovered in the stories that are told about sciences. The main reason for this exercise in the construction of possible texts is to indicate how different narrative forms promote one or another kind of communicative message about the science in question. The particular valuation of specific aspects of the science is provided by insertion of relevant key social representations ("objectivity," "subjectivity," "progress," etc.) and specific value-indicative descriptions (Example 9: "behaviorists worked toward *overcoming*"; Example 8: "the immediate *downfall*"; "the behavioristic worldview *dragged* the discipline *down* to its *swamp*"; Example 7: "*restored* the use of mentalistic theorizing"). Through the use of valuative implications of the specific meanings inserted into the narrative forms, the story about a particular science is told within a particular evaluative framework.

2.9.6   Meanings Inserted into Narrative Forms

The making of narratives about science entails communicative games based on the evocation of the implicit contrasts of the meanings used, as well as their connotations. Often, in the case of a particular scientific perspective, such evocations are taken into consideration. On some occasions, these are meant to create a boundary of a "new" perspective in contrast with an "old" one (e.g., "cognitive" psychology versus "mental" or "folk" psychology). On others, a name is invented for a theory that represents the given perspective, yet has the potential for being overextended far beyond its narrowly circumscribed original meaning (e.g., "catastrophe" theory; see Chapter 3). At the same time, specific constraints are placed on what meanings are not to be inserted into scientific or metascientific narratives. Any kind of personification of the entities involved in scientific talk is excluded (e.g., a person writing about a vector model is forced to avoid using expressions like "This vector lives in that space"), but other metaphoric extensions (e.g., "The computer is powerful") are allowed (see Chapter 3, on talk about "The Data").

Through the selection of particular language material into the narrative forms used, communicative messages about sciences and scientists are created. These messages often become integrated into larger units of messages—specific myths about the glory of some science (e.g., nuclear physics at the time of benevolent consideration of building nuclear power plants for heavily populated societies) or about particular scientists.

2.9.7 Construction and Function of Hero Myths in Metascientific Discourse

Although not construed as a magician, the scientist is usually presented to the lay public in the context of some narrative that creates a hero myth around his or her person. The myriad stories created around the person of Albert Einstein is probably the simplest example. The creation of such myths is of course not limited to the communication flowing from scientists to laypersons; it is likewise functional within the personal worlds of the scientists themselves.

Hero myths are abundant in metascientific discourse. In most cases, when careful historical analysis of the discovery process is made, the myths prove to be mere publicity devices beamed outward toward the lay public and inward for their creators' personal satisfaction. The construction of such myths belongs to the genre of *scientific hagiographies*. Scientists are presented as pious individuals who fight for the Truth of Nature and demonstrate superior visions. The scientist-hero is an agent who constantly is viewed as a participant in the progress of knowledge, rather than a victim of misunderstandings and preconceptions. That the reality of scientific activities is very different from this story of glory is well documented (Fuller, 1991; Mitroff, 1974; Shermer, 1990).

Thus, it turns out that Lavoisier (Bensaude-Vincent, 1983), Kekulé (Rocke, 1985), and Pasteur (Geison & Secord, 1988) were by far more interdependent with their immediate worlds and personal continuity of ideas than the existing scientific hagiographies presume. In psychology, Watson's behaviorist manifesto of 1913 did not really lead to a major qualitative breakthrough in American psychology; instead, it constituted a relatively lonely "voice" (the author of which was soon expelled from the ingroup of psychologists) which happened to be a suitable symbolic representation of a tendency that led to the social institutionalization of psychology in the United States during and after World War I (see Samelson, 1981). In a similar vein, the "pavlovization" of Soviet psychology in the early 1950s was a symbolic myth with not much substance behind it (Valsiner, 1988). Finally, our work on Vygotsky (Van der Veer & Valsiner, 1991) should put to rest the hero myth created around that interesting but highly intellectually interdependent thinker—a myth that considered Vygotsky to be "Mozart in psychology" (Toulmin, 1978).

The social dialogic (intermental) function of hero myths in constructing histories of science seems obvious from the analysis given above. The hagiographer fits the person-centered account of science to the lay public's expectations for such stories, hoping to negotiate some social objective (e.g., perceived value of the given science, images of its practical relevance, or—equally possible—stigmatizing some person or institution in the process). Thus, public institutions that supported (or refused to support) the person (or discipline) that is being sanctified as a "hero of science" in such texts can be expected to be evaluated by the recipients of the stories in some way. Thus, a scientific hero who is presented as an active fighter for social justice (under the constraints of a totalitarian social system that put obstacles in his way) enhances the depicted contrast between the "good" (i.e., the hero) and the "bad" (the opponents) forces in the given narrative plot. The hero myths and narratives about the history of a science then become united: *A hero myth provides a halo effect for the direction of thought that the hero represents,* and the specific narrative form supports the generation of the hero myth.

The connection of narrative forms and hero constructions by which scientists' public image is socially constructed—often, by relating the scientists' work with extrascientific social discourse of the society—provides evaluative directional flavor. Thus, the *positive* halo effect of Vygotsky's supposed relevance in Soviet psychology (narrated via the reference to his building of "new Marxist psychology") is in principle not different in its narrative construction mechanism from cases of negative halo effects. For the latter, one can look at later representations of the work of those German psychologists who aligned themselves with the National-Socialist belief system under the Nazi regime.

Different kinds of hero myths can be utilized in multiple ways in the metascientific communication process. First, such myths create symbolic currency in the communication between sciences and their surrounding societies. This currency may be similar to the uses of other personal images in social discourse—Einstein and St. Anthony may end up being used in similar functions.

Second, by taking advantage of these hero myths, it is possible for a person to project a humble image of self to other persons, while at the same time using that very image in the social dominance games that abound in the social groups of scientists. Hero myths afford self-presentation of the kind that identifies with glorious others. The socially constraining role of hero myths thus entails canalization of the scientists toward following, rather than transcending, the work of the hero-figures. In Thomas Kuhn's terminology, that would amount to the guidance of scientists' thinking toward doing "normal science." No surprise that during a historical period of relative stability, a discipline clings to some canonized hero-figures. Then, at times of attempted overturns of such periods, counter-heroes can be created and set up as opponents to the canonized hero-figures. Those involved in the renegotiations of the discipline are the present-day users.

Not infrequently, ardent followers of socially constructed hero-figures in psychology show greater evidence of rigid promotion of their heroes' incomplete ideas than the originators of such ideas ever wanted or expected. Psychology and education are filled with followers of Piaget and Vygotsky who often present the ideas of these two thinkers—who were, in many ways, close to each other—as irreconcilable images of two "opposing camps" (or football teams). Thus, construction of new knowledge becomes dissociated from the methodological cycle (as described in Chapter 1) and is replaced by the competitive comparison of the adequacy of "Piagetian" and "Vygotskian" "schools."

Following of hero images in any science may create intellectual self-blinders for the scientist, and a careful analysis of thinkers' ideas may reveal ways of possibly surpassing them. The actual contributions of leading scientists are valuable exactly as they are. They lead our thinking in promising new directions, and they give evidence of the intellectual *impasses* of the time. Ideas survive heroes, and displacement of the focus of interest from ideas to the personages of their constructors may inhibit intellectual search.

2.10 SOCIALLY CONSTRUCTED KNOWLEDGE IN PSYCHOLOGY, AND ITS INSTITUTIONAL USES

The hero myths and narratives about psychology are not part of psychology as a science. They contribute to the social regulation of psychology. Myths about psychology are semiotic mediating devices manipulated by social institutions for which basic knowledge about psychological issues is secondary to their own goal-oriented activities within a society. Thus, psychological knowhow and myths about psychology (and psychologists) can be used within a society in efforts to regulate conduct and reflections by its citizens (e.g., the uses of attachment theory in social-institutional efforts to keep mothers of young babies focused on mothering tasks), or to reorganize relations between institutions by revaluing one another's accepted hero myths (e.g., recurrent "discoveries" along the lines that "Freud was wrong" or "Vygotsky was right and Piaget was wrong" in regulating clinical or educational institutions). Further uses of psychology in service to institutions can be found in its extension beyond the contexts of its origin.

2.10.1 Psychology Exported: Missionary Spirit and Its Impacts

Histories of psychology in different countries provide ample evidence of tension between basic knowledge and the social utility of the discipline. The importation of psychology into the United States in the late 19th century led to a synthesis of psychology with basic sociomoral tendencies of the U.S. society. Historically, the widespread move toward applicability of psychology in the United States was a result of the sociohistorical turmoils of World War I and America's participation in it. Applied orientation in American psychology is well integrated with the missionary spirit that has characterized society in North America over a few centuries.

Psychology's recent export from the United States to other countries can be recognized as part of the sociopolitical relationships between the so-called "First" and "Third" World countries. Within these relationships, the takeover of North American (or Western European) cultural models for building psychology as if it were science has extrascientific undertones similar to those in the "donor" country (see Bloom, 1982; Enriquez, 1992; Joseph, Reddy, & Searle-Chatterjee, 1990; Montero, 1990; Nandy, 1974). Psychology's need for self-proliferation as science is undoubtedly linked with the construction of a scientistic utopia in the history of European societies (see Hakfoort, 1992). Furthermore, it has built up its normative conceptual system on the sociocultural domain of problems that have been surfacing in European-type societies (e.g., psychoanalysis emerging in the context of repression of sexuality in European bourgeois classes). When such extrascientific (applied) bases are hidden in the general theoretical schemes of a psychological theory, potential oversights of different forms of psychological phenomena can be overlooked when these schemes are exported to other societies (see Kurtz, 1992, for a re-analysis of psychoanalysis in the context of Indian society).

This situation in psychology is certainly shared with other social sciences. Thus, British social anthropology (and its North American counterpart, cultural anthropology) developed first as a companion (even if at times an oppositional one; Kuklick, 1991) to the colonial powers' social control efforts, and later as a culture-contact device between the societies "at home" and "overseas." The complicated nature of intersocietal dialogue is ongoing in sociology (Peirano, 1991) and has resulted in calls for authentic internationalization of the discourse in that discipline (Oommen, 1991).

2.10.2   Internationalization *of* Psychology or Colonization *by* Psychology?

Social propagation of one society's cultural heritage under the label of "science" necessarily leads to outcomes that, at best, are inconsequential for the recipient society. Propagation of psychology has a worse effect: It ends up debilitating both the application of psychology in the given country, and the general knowledge base of psychology. The problem is particularly complicated in the area of methodology, despite the criticisms of existing dominant sociopolitical practices in psychological methodology (Espiritu, 1989; Feliciano, 1989), as well as careful historical demonstrations of how psychology's methodology has become driven by social consensus (Danziger, 1990; Gigerenzer, 1993), which is guided by the social institutions that organize the discipline. Such social–institutional perseverance of normal science guarantees psychology's extensive self-proliferation within (as well as between) the societies of our time—a proliferation only rarely paralleled with intensive (substantive) development of the discipline. Psychology seems to be governed by waves of social fashions for the use of different explanatory metaphors, which are transformed into myths along the lines of social-institutional semiotic needs (Sarbin, 1990). Because those myths may repeat some collective-cultural beliefs, they may further amplify them—thus participating in the actual social organization of social processes.

Psychology's appeal and missionary self-presentation open the discipline for different fates in international communication. The usual pattern—that of proliferation of some fashionable tendencies ("revolutions") from one country to another without constructive modifications—is guaranteed to lead to subordination of the recipient country's psychology to that of the donor. We could observe a process of *de facto* colonization of the discipline in the recipient countries.

The mechanism of this process is relatively simple. The original "revolution" starts in country X, triggered by the dominance of a previous tendency in that country (e.g., the "cognitive" revolution in American psychology was a movement against "behaviorist" power orthodoxy). The tendency is then labeled in revolutionary terms and advertised worldwide. In country Y, the appeal of the label, and the efforts of advertising, do not remain unnoticed. Some psychologists (given their own social discourse around social relations within their institutions) will start to follow the new movement, and—with some latency—may succeed in making it central for psychology in country Y. However, the imported revolutionary fashion need not fit the cultural contexts (other than the academic, middle-class one), and by the time it has gained ground in country Y, a new revolution is in the making in country X. Thus, following fashionable tendencies from country X keeps psychology in country Y permanently one step behind the developments in country X, and away from at least some of the relevant psychological issues that may be of high relevance in country Y but are of almost no relevance in country X.

In contrast, the movement, between countries, of basic ideas (as distinguished from social fashions) in any science (including psychology) has been constructive. Science is by nature an international enterprise, and knowledge construction knows no country boundaries. Thus, it is at the level of concrete (but basic) ideas in psychology that international coconstruction of new knowledge takes place.

2.10.3   Inherent Guidance from Ordinary Language

Besides the social-institutional perseverance directed toward making psychology socially applicable, there exist epistemological limitations on innovation in psychology. Psychology is based on the shared semiotic codes of laypersons and psychologists, and in case that basis is borrowed from the collective-cultural meaning systems of some selected societies and turned into axiomatically assumed universal science, the universality of such science is always suspect. Even the culture-inclusive domain of psychology is largely ill at ease about its necessary reliance on some collective-cultural semiotic reflexivity of the common sense kind (Obeyesekere, 1990; Valsiner, 1985); or, it tries to overcome that insecurity by glorifying the richness and logic of common sense (Siegfried, 1994; Smedslund, 1982). Psychology's reliance on common language is ambivalent: On the one hand, the richness of common language can allow psychology a basis for sophisticated understanding; on the other hand, it limits psychological knowhow to those aspects that may be historico-cultural particulars of the investigator. Psychology, embedded in the common language as it is, needs to transcend the boundaries of that constraint system (Valsiner, 1985). Otherwise, it may remain part of the collective culture (of the persons acting in the role of "psychologists"), and, as such, may create different kinds of socially desirable myths under the halo effect of science.

2.11 SUMMARY: BASIC ASSUMPTIONS IN THE STUDY OF DEVELOPMENT, AND THEIR METASCIENTIFIC CULTURAL FRAMES

This chapter has made explicit a number of the social representations on which psychology has been built and which are products of cultural history. These representations—called basic assumptions in the chapter—form the axiomatic basis of psychology's knowledge structure. A number of these assumptions are antithetical to the study of developmental phenomena and are therefore better avoided by developmental psychologists. First, the exclusive separation of the person from the environment, which has been widely used in nondevelopmental psychology, makes it impossible to study developmental processes because the latter are open-systems phenomena. Development is possible only in the case of open systems, where the developing organism is intertwined with its environment and changes it in the process of development. This feature of development calls for inclusive separation of organism and environment, as outlined in the chapter.

Second, the nondevelopmental traditions in psychology have emphasized the static aspect of psychological phenomena, and have eliminated their dynamic side from consideration. This practice has been based on an assumption of the higher relevance of the "being" (ontological) side of phenomena as compared to their "becoming" or changing aspects. The inappropriateness of this basic assumption for developmental research was outlined—developmental processes cannot be studied via methods that eliminate the change in phenomena from consideration through an emphasis on "true" measures of the static being.

Other basic assumptions likewise direct psychological research in directions of thinking that are antithetical to the study of developmental processes. Psychological phenomena are often viewed from the perspective of additive elementarism, which eliminates from consideration the systemic relationships between different parts of an organism and the environment. Usually, this approach coincides with application of the cognitive model of elementaristic causality in the research process. Lawfulness is often considered from the standpoint of recurrence of specimens of phenomena that belong to the same class. This approach to psychological laws eliminates from the research process both the variability within a class, and dynamic changes in the particular phenomena from one to another instance of occurrence. The actions and thinking of human beings are often considered to work toward maximization of certain outcomes of their actions and thoughts, while mini-mizing others. This implicit cognitive model may be inadequate even for a few areas of nondevelopmental psychology, and may be a gross misrepresentation of developing organisms that may function on the basis of satisficing—solving particular issues encountered in their development in ways that are good enough, rather than resulting in maximum benefit of any sort. Developmental processes are characterized by high redundancy in potential routes of change, and complementarity in the functions of different factors that canalize develop-ment, rather than by highly "economic" and "cost-saving" strategies. Develop-ment, in its reality, is wasteful, whereas the majority of cognitive models on which psychological research on development is based include an assumption of rational economy of the process.

The chapter's brief analysis of the culture-bound axiomatic basis of much of psychology has served two functions: (a) it clarified the "blind spots" of psychological theory in general, and its conceptual difficulties, when it deals with developmental issues in particular, and (b) it outlined the notion of a rel-ativistic science of psychology, where the empirical data are located at the in-tersection of the investigator's axiomatic bases and the psychological reality, and where empirical results are meaningful only relative to the investigator's assumptions. The latter, of course, have to be made explicit in every case.

Beyond the basic assumptions, the whole construction of the scientific in-ference process needs explication. This entails an analysis of how empirical data are derived from the phenomena, how methods are constructed on theo-retical bases, and how formal models are constructed (e.g., the bottom part of Figure 1.1). Chapter 3 will describe the nature of "the data" and of different kinds of formal systems that are used to model development.

3

Crossroads of the Deductive and Inductive Lines of Knowledge Construction in Psychology

All knowledge construction entails *coordination* of two processes: (a) deduction (i.e., a move from basic assumptions and theoretical construction toward constructing data on the basis of phenomena), and (b) induction (an inferential process that moves from the constructed data to modify aspects of the theoretical system, or to change some of the basic assumptions). The deductive and inductive lines are equally important for creating our knowledge (as was described in Figure 1.1). Yet the actual coordination of these processes is often little known. Instead, psychologists can be observed in futile discourse about the "primacy" of one of those lines over the other. Instead, forms of coordination of the two produce novelty and are of importance for knowledge construction.

3.1 "COGNITIVE HEURISTICS" AS REPRESENTATION OF ABDUCTION PROCESSES

Since the early 1970s, the psychology of human reasoning has been obsessed by the simple fact that ordinary persons, in their everyday reasoning, violate the rules of statistical decision making. Psychologists' surprise—and sometimes their worry—that ordinary persons are "inadequate" reasoners constitutes a major oversight of the total field of reasoning. Statistical inference is only one of the many inferential systems that human minds have constructed. It is a system that belongs to the inductive line of inferential reasoning, and its applicability is limited to a very restricted area of the reasoning processes.

In fact, the "discovery" of "cognitive heuristics" (Kahneman, Slovic, & Tversky, 1982; Tversky & Kahneman, 1974), and disputes about the contexts where they are used (Gigerenzer, 1991; Sovran, 1992), constitutes a return to phenomena of the construction of novelty (or qualitative leaps) in human reasoning which, since the 19th century, have been known under the label *abductive reasoning.*

Deduction constructs the world as it *must be,* induction helps to reveal how it *actually is,* and abduction allows us to consider how it *may be.* For developmental perspectives, abduction is thus the main linkage between the inductive and deductive lines. A future state of a system cannot be deduced from general premises, nor can it be extrapolated from inductive inference about past experiences. Both deduction and induction lack the moment of construction of novelty, and hence are not fit for explanation of developmental processes.

The notion of abduction was developed within the philosophy of sign construction and use by Charles Sanders Peirce. In his efforts to build a logic that would reflect on reality of reasoning—rather than prescribe its "correct forms"—he saw the "leaps" that occur in human hypothesis setting:

> The first starting of a hypothesis and the entertaining of it, whether as a simple interrogation or with any degree of confidence, is an inferential step which I propose to call *abduction.* This will include a preference for any one hypothesis over others which would equally explain the facts, so long as this preference is not based upon any previous knowledge bearing upon the truth of the hypotheses, nor any testing of any of the hypotheses, after having admitted them on probation. (Peirce, 1935, p. 358 [6.525])

Abductive inference is *the* main process of reasoning—given time and the information limitations of the cognitive process—and is paralleled by the satisficing strategy in real-life decision processes (see 2.5). Any human reasoning (and action) process takes place under inevitable limits set by the irreversibility of time, moving from the past to the future. Because the conditions under which this move takes place always include uncertainty, the use of only the deductive line may lead to inadequacies of adaptation, while the information obtained via inductive inference is never conclusive for specific future applications. The happenings of the past need not be repeated in the same way in the future.

Abduction allows qualitative leaps in our reasoning, beyond its present confines. Such leaps are made possible by processes of disequilibration (see also Chapter 4). Peirce was perceptive of the moments at which novelty becomes created:

> Everybody knows that the long continuance of a routine or habit makes us lethargic, while a succession of surprises wonderfully brightens the ideas. Where there is motion, where history is a-making, there is the focus of mental activity, and it has been said that the arts and sciences reside within the temple of Janus, waking when that is open, but slumbering when it is closed. Few psychologists have perceived how fundamental a fact this is. A portion of mind

abundantly commissured to other portions works almost mechanically. It sinks to the condition of a railway junction. But a portion of mind almost isolated, a spiritual peninsula, or *cul-de-sac,* is like a railway terminus. Now mental commissures are habits. Where they abound, originality is not needed and is not found; but where they are in defect, spontaneity is set free. (Peirce, 1893, p. 187)

Peirce's simile, comparing the operation of railway connections to the different kinds of mental processes, brings out the focus on the linkage of abductive inference with *history in the making.* His focus on the role of "defect" in the established connections ("spontaneity is set free") was later echoed by Lev Vygotsky in his efforts to explain emotional synthesis as being similar to "electric discharge" (Vygotsky, 1925/1971). Abduction and dialectical synthesis are notions that allow for consideration of novelty within the contexts of familiarity.

3.2 PSYCHOLOGY'S CONSENSUAL INFERENTIAL DISCOURSE

Psychology's conceptual apparatus has been largely essentialistic. Thus, statements about direct linear causation (see 2.7) have been rampant—and probably on the increase in recent decades (Gigerenzer et al., 1989). Thus, talk about "cultural effects" on "cognition" (or vice versa: "effects" of "cognitive models" on "culture"), or about "accounting for variance" by way of "variables," abounds in the literature, yet we have rather few insights into the *processes* that are involved in such implied causal effects. Only rarely are models of systemic causality being created in psychology. Instead, we usually see efforts that apply the notion of maximization to the activity of linking the inductive and deductive lines of inference. Regarding contemporary cognitive science, Francis Crick has expressed his astonishment about such received practice:

> In cognitive science the usual procedure is to isolate some psychological phenomenon, make a theoretical model of the postulated mental processes, and then test the model, by computer simulation, to make sure it works as the author thought it would. If it fits at least some of the psychological facts it is then thought to be a useful model. The fact that it is rather unlikely to be the correct one seems to disturb nobody. (Crick, 1988, pp. 149–150)

Crick captures a very general problem of psychology at large—the belief that a consensually sufficient fit of theoretical models to reality is also a real fit between the two. A biological scientist looking at psychology as an outsider certainly can see this belief as a serious limitation that has rendered psychology rich in published papers but poor in actual understanding. The concept of "usefulness" of partly fitting models is often invoked to stop further inquiry. Psychology is in the habit of creating "black box" explanations—consensually agreed-on acceptance that a certain concept (or formal model) provides an adequate account of the phenomena of interest. This is the result of the discipline's closeness to the commonsense encoding of knowledge. Based on the commonsense expectations, it is not difficult for psychologists to agree (among themselves, as well as in their dialogue with laypersons) that "secure attachment of child to parent" leads to "positive outcomes in life." The notion that harmony leads to harmony (and conflict to conflict) may dominate the commonsense view of the desirable (or just) state of affairs in the world. Once translated into psychological discourse, it allows for pseudoempiricism that pretends to "discover" in the empirical evidence what is already known by virtue of the meanings in ordinary language (Smedslund, 1994, 1995).

3.3 VARIABLES AS "BLACK BOXES"

Psychology's usual logic of inference has begun with outcomes (products of some psychological processes) and explained the causes for these outcomes. The latter are usually—in an Aristotelian way—viewed as static essences. Or, if they are declared not to be viewed that way, they nevertheless become "black boxes" that include processes that psychologists consensually agree not to tear open. The "black box" construction is further facilitated by the inference, from a difference between phenomena, of the hypothetical causal agent that stands behind that difference.

3.3.1 A Generic Example: "Culture" as a "Black Box"

Convenient labels that describe a technical aspect of psychologists' empirical work can easily be turned into complex "black-box" pseudoexplanatory terms. Psychology is filled with such terms: "gender," "at-risk" status, and so on. Let me consider here the uses of the notion of "culture" that are habitual in cross-cultural psychology (Valsiner, 1989b).

An investigator who is interested in knowing how culture organizes human psychological phenomena (i.e., starting along a deductive path, "culture" is *assumed* to have *some* organizational role) moves to the domain of empirical study and selects two (or more) groups of people (claiming at times that they are "sampled randomly"). These groups—or "samples" from a "population"—*become labeled* as culture X and culture Y. The term "culture" is used descriptively, yet behind that use is a carryover from the assumptions in the deductive line. Because each person in the "sample" is assumed to belong to the "population" of either culture X or culture Y, and because culture is assumed to have some organizational role for psychological processes, then each person in the "sample" is assumed to show that role (and the sample is assumed to represent that role for the population). It may be accepted (as it usually is) that individuals differ *in the extent* to which they "share the given culture." When that happens, the investigator has constructed—deductively—a model of cultures as homogeneous essences. All persons in culture X *have in them* the essence of culture X, and all persons in culture Y have in them the essence of culture Y.

Where the two groups of people were initially merely labeled by the culture term, the label now projects an essentialistic quality for each member of the group. The quality is assumed to be present in each and every member of the group (i.e., the "population" is assumed to be a homogeneous class *in terms of the quality*), but the quantity of the essence present in each individual is assumed to vary from one person to the next.

This deductive separation of quality and quantity becomes linked with the received belief in the "law of large numbers"—that individual idiosyncrasies of persons cancel one another out if a sufficient number of persons are studied as a sample. With this linkage established, the door is open for efforts to discover the nature of the essences (of culture X and culture Y), through their comparison with sample averages (or prototypical cases). Thus, a statistically significant difference between samples of culture X and culture Y (again, a purely descriptive denotation here) becomes interpretable as a substantive difference between the assumed homogeneous essences of culture X and culture Y. In the latter use of the terms, the Aristotelian homogeneity of the causal essences is established. The investigator may even claim that he or she has "hard empirical evidence" that culture X entails characteristics A, B, and C, while culture Y evidences the opposites of these characteristics (non-A, non-B, non-C; or a, b, c). This claim is not empirical; it is pseudoempirical (in Smedslund's sense) because the move from a descriptive to a prescriptive function of the term *culture* was the investigator's deductively inserted action in the knowledge construction process. It is preconstructed as a static essence, and then projected into the empirical contrast.

An interesting demonstration of this deductive construction of a homogeneous essentialistic notion of culture would appear in those cross-cultural investigations that are aimed at proving the universality of human psychological functions in terms of their invulnerability to "effects" of local phenomena (labeled *culture*). Here, the desirable goal is to demonstrate *lack of differences between samples* (e.g., culture X and culture Y). However, within the inductive inferential framework of statistical methods, *lack* of differences between samples cannot be inferred from the nondiscovery of a statistically significant difference between averages. Nevertheless, it is tempting, given the deductively set goal, so different quasi-interpretations in terms of cultural universality are constructed after failing to find intersample differences (e.g., "The fact that no differences between cultures X and Y were found *may* indicate that human psychology is universal and possible cross-cultural differences constitute merely a special case"). The game rule of statistical inference is clear: Nondiscovery of statistically significant differences is not interpretable as sameness of the averages. Researchers' interpretations, however, make the abductive leap in the direction of violating that rule, through vaguely worded interpretations that, on the one hand, do not claim the discovery of universality but, on the other hand, imply it anyway.

Furthermore, inferential "leaps" similar to the generic example that I elaborated here are not limited to those directions in cross-cultural psychology that adhere to the use of quantitative methods. An exactly similar inferential issue is present in the case of qualitatively oriented cross-cultural research, where structured prototypes of specific psychological processes are being compared across societies. For example, empirical efforts to demonstrate that highly developed (dialectical) forms of reasoning about human nature are present in a number of societies (Oerter, Oerter, Agostiani, Kim, & Wibwo, 1996) have led to elucidation of the same inferential problem (Minoura, 1996; Oerter, 1996).

The example of cross-cultural comparisons is no special case in psychology's inferential impasses, although what happens in cross-cultural psychology is perhaps a more visible example than similar ones in other areas. (Inference about the role of gender in human psychological functioning entails a similar process.) This highlights the domain of psychology's knowledge construction that has been left without proper attention in the discipline's methodology: How do investigators use abductive processes in their construction of knowledge, given their assumptions, their constructed data, and the phenomena that the data are expected to represent?

3.3.2   "Index Variables" Treated *as if* "Independent Variables"

Psychology's "variables" are usually symbolic constructs that acquire a life of their own in the course of research practices. Elaborating the example above, labels of the (supposedly) shared essentialistic features of a phenomenon (i.e., features that cannot be changed by the investigator) are treated *as if* they were "independent variables" [e.g., sex, age, socioeconomic status, culture (as ethnic group membership)]. *De facto* "index variables" are treated as independent variables.

Again, cross-cultural psychology's use of the term "culture" is an example. The usual tradition in research is to treat it as being equivalent to a label that is appropriately applicable to a sample of subjects (e.g., the comparisons of German culture versus Zulu culture). As such, the notion of culture performs the role of an index variable: Each person in the given sample is "indexed" as belonging to this or another society. Surely no investigator assumes that such an index could entail the possibility of an investigator's varying the state of affairs at his or her will (i.e., the possibility of an investigator's transforming a particular German into a Zulu would be left to the realm of magicians in traditional folklore texts, where frogs become princes, and vice versa).

Nevertheless, the notion of such magical transformation becomes *de facto* assumed, once the investigator begins to treat index variables in *post factum* data analyses as if they were independent variables. Again, this transformation may start from a shorthand descriptive labeling (e.g., shorthand designations of terminology while using ANOVA packages). Yet, in the following interpretation of an index as if it were an independent variable, the transformatory power of the investigator becomes assumed.

Interestingly, there exist cultural phenomena that do entail situations close to the treatment of culture as an actual independent variable. These phenomena are of various kinds: people migrating from one society to another, either temporarily and in circumscribed roles [such as tourists (Shi-xu, 1995) or students in "study abroad" programs], or more permanently (émigrés, guest workers). Thus, it would be a perfectly direct application of the meaning complex covered by the independent variable notion if cross-cultural psychologists were to study such persons in transition between societies. Thus, investigation of how German *Gastarbeiter* would psychologically adjust themselves when migrating to Zululand would make use of the naturally occurring migration processes in terms similar to psychologists' desire to "control" and "vary" their "variables."

3.4   ALTERNATIVES TO VARIABLES-ORIENTED APPROACHES

All in all, the variables-oriented methodology has created a stalemate in psychology's knowledge construction. It has decomposed complex (gestalt) phenomena into separate components, and has replaced the inherent linkedness of these components with an investigation of formal (usually statistical) relations between the supposedly independent components.

An alternative view focuses on the person-centered analytic look at variables (Magnusson, 1988). This entails a return to the focus that was brought into psychology by William Stern in his personalistic philosophy and differential psychology (Stern, 1911). From the point of view of development, the developing person's active role in the environment determines which facets of the environment enter into functional relations with the developing characteristics of the organism. The investigator's designation of some of these facets as variables (which can be manipulated at will by the investigator) overlooks both the possible relevance of the given facet, as well as its nature as a changeable quantitative variable. From a person-centered viewpoint, what is (or is not) an impacting factor—a qualitative condition or variable, in the sense of having potentially changeable quantitative parameters—is set up by the person who relates to the given environment. The person can effectively disable many of the factors of the environment (and those would cease to be variables, even if a researcher had designated them as such), or turn a neutral feature of the environment into a personally significant one. (More on semiotic meaning construction appears in Chapter 8.)

3.5   PATHWAYS TO METHODOLOGY: SEEING THE WORLD
BEYOND "THE DATA"

Much of the existing empirical investigative effort in psychology has been hampered by research conventions that have rendered the systemic analysis of psychological processes unresearchable.

First, the preponderance of associationist summative inference strategies—the most widespread of which are analysis of variance models—has guided our understanding further away from systemic causal analyses. As Gigerenzer has pointed out:

> [Analysis of variance] entered psychology in the mid-1930s and, after World War II, became the most used research "tool" in experimental psychology. This statistical model has been used in psychology as if it were the battlehorse of Claude Bernard's determinism: (1) Analysis of variance, it was assumed, can answer the question whether a *causal* relationship exists between variables. However, influenced by David Hume, psychologists of this century were somewhat reluctant to speak of causes in print. Instead one spoke of "effects" only, of the effect of X on Y, or of "conditions," an expression well chosen for its ambiguity without damaging the idea of necessity. In the terminology of analysis of variance, causes and effects were replaced by "independent" and "dependent" variables. (2) Analysis of variance was based on the principles of *isolation* (of a few "independent" variables and the "dependent" variable), and *control* (of other relevant variables), and (3) it was used in accordance with the *nomothetic* ideal, that is, treating individual differences simply as the "error term." What was considered as psychologically important were mean values only; distributions and dispersions were viewed as reflecting some technical "assumptions" concerning the applicability of the instrument. Psychological theories were not about those "assumptions." (Gigerenzer, 1987, p. 16)

Second, the "quantophrenic" obsessions of psychologists (see Sorokin, 1956) have further obscured the investigators' field of vision. Psychologists' deep belief in the act of quantification as a guarantee of the scientific nature of their discipline has led to a situation where the structured nature of most psychological phenomena is eliminated at the very beginning of the research process. Fascination with quantification as the first step toward deriving data from phenomena has both blinded psychology's research practices with respect to many complex phenomena (which defy quantification, or for which quantification is unreasonable) and created immense quantities of empirical data that no longer adequately represent the phenomena that they claim to explain.

Third, in human psychology, the meanings that research participants construct in the process of a study have been viewed as inevitable nuisances rather than as features of reality that can be utilized for methodological purposes. Through the meaning construction process, the actual psychological phenomena (of the research participant) may overcome the designated data-collection strategies.

3.5.1 Psychologists' New Deity: "The Data"

Psychologists like to talk about "The Data," and when they do, their identities become formed, ingroup/outgroup relationships are being set up, and time is being filled in. In this process, the data acquire an almost omnipotent role as the Final Judge of all claims in the science of psychology. In this role, the *de facto* deified data acquire personalized characteristics, as can be observed in the discourse of psychologists, who can be heard or observed to talk in some (or all) of the following ways:

"The data *show* [or *demonstrate,* or *prove,* or (verb X)] that [Y] . . . ."

"*According to* the data, [X] is [Y]."

"The data *do not allow* us to conclude that [Y] . . . ."

"We *must consult* the data in order to [X]."

The data are assumed to have a capacity for speech, and well-established agency:

"Let the data *speak for themselves!*"

Like any other personified entity, the data become an object of adoration, pride, jealousy, and desire for possession:

"[Colleague X] *has better* data than [Colleague Y]."

"Our data *are by far the best* that exist in the literature."

"We need some *hard* data, *not merely anecdotal evidence!*"

"The data are *objective* . . . ."

"We must *have more* [or *better*] data before we dare to say [X]."

"*It is not possible to trust* the data of [study X]."

"I want *to play with* the data."

"*We must collect more* data."

The humanized character of the data may be also rather complex:

"My data *have given me a hard time* to make sense of them."

"*I don't know what to do* with my data; they resist all efforts of analysis."

Psychologists have constructed for themselves an *alter ego,* a significant other, or an imaginary companion in their pursuits—the data. The whole range of human characteristics can be projected into that significant other, thereafter presentable as the very convenient and consensually accepted supporter for any statement the author of a study may decide to utter. The data are the God of Objectivity in contemporary psychology!

Nevertheless, it may be worth a careful study as to how that God of Objectivity is evoked in psychological discourse, and how a turn to the data in different locations, in such discursive practices, may actually guide the construction of knowledge. Yet, objectivity in psychological research is not created by the data. Following the line of argument advanced in the previous chapters, the data are constructed in accordance with the conceptualization of objectivity as that notion is socially set up in a given discipline at the given time.

3.5.2 Meanings of "The Data"

If we were to examine what has become labeled as the data in contemporary psychology, we would be faced with a myriad of forms. Yet the notion of the data goes undefined, and becomes a side product of explanations of the notion of "measurement," as the following explanation (aimed at American undergraduate students) reflects:

> The process of attaching meaning to numbers is known as *measurement,* and numbers that have meaning are often called *data.* (Thorndike, 1982, p. 9)

But how does this process of "attaching meaning" proceed? In other words, how are the data constructed? That it is a process of construction of meaningful symbols follows from the claim above, but how does that construction process take place?

The claim that data are symbolic representations is not new in psychology. Since the times of Helmholz, and up to those of S.S. Stevens (i.e., until the 1950s and 1960s), the question of how the data represent the phenomena has been an important theme (Michell, 1986; Nunnally, 1967, chapter 1), which led to caution in the selection of data-analytic strategies. If the data were of a quantitative kind, the nature of their scaling properties—whether they would fit a nominal, ordinal, interval, or ratio scale—was to be determined. The result of this diagnosis would lead to rules of "permissible" operations to be performed with the data in the course of data analyses. Analytic schemes were expected to honor the properties of the original scale, rather than transfer numeric depictions from one scale to another (e.g., treating ordinal scales as if they were interval scales, and so on).

In contrast, the borrowing of the operationism of Percy Bridgman (1927) from physics led to the proliferation of an "anything goes" kind of quantification in psychology. Stevens's representational view of measurement entailed limits on the permissible ways of handling the measurements so that their representational value (of whatever phenomena these measurements reflected) was not to be lost. The operationism fused the distinction of the data and the phenomena, and glorified the process of data construction *as if* that process itself equaled knowledge [e.g., Bridgman's claim that "the concept is synonimous with the corresponding set of operations," (1927, p. 5)].

Psychologists—who, by the 1950s, had become believers in empiricism as science and had accepted the illusionary unity of "the statistical method" (see

Gigerenzer, 1993; Gigerenzer et al., 1989)—found this kind of operationism a welcome solution to their theoretical problems. Operationism allowed them not to bother about defining their concepts, but just to measure whatever they claimed to study. From a representationist perspective, the often-used statement, "Intelligence is what intelligence tests measure," would be utter nonsense—or an example of magical thinking (along the lines discussed by Horton, 1967). Not so from the operationist viewpoint; it would be a sufficient definition of "intelligence" as it is exemplified by the operation of its measurement.

In more general terms, the two perspectives can be contrasted in their look at how quantification works in psychological measurement:

> [Representationist and operationist perspectives] agree that measurement involves making numerical assignments to things. However, according to the representational theory, the numbers represent an empirical relational system, which is thought of as an objective structure existing quite independent of our operations. Numbers are used as a convenience and are, in principle, dispensable. This is not so, according to operationism. According to it, numbers do not point beyond themselves to a scale-free realm. Rather, the data on which measurement is based are inherently numerical. They are numerical because the operations involved produce numbers. For the strict operationist, science is simply the study of our operations and not the study of a reality that is thought to lie beyond them. (Michell, 1986, p. 404)

At the end of the 1930s, operationism was taken over by psychology as a cargo-cult phenomenon from physics (Allport, 1940). Since that time, and particularly in the 1960s, the colonization of psychology by operationist legitimizations of the data has taken place, and the core of worries has moved to the pervasive question of how to analyze them.

The explosive growth of operationism was a convenient excuse for psychologists to keep doing whatever they had been doing in their empirical work and to stop worrying about major theoretical issues. Together with that worry, the question of what the data represent disappeared into oblivion. The question itself was carefully avoided and was replaced by technical questions regarding how to operate using the data (i.e., how to handle and analyze them). The "empire of chance" had succeeded in colonizing psychology's empirical enterprise (Gigerenzer et al., 1989). The meaning of the data had become a nonquestion for psychology, and the socialized quest for ever more and increasingly conventionalized kinds of data has dominated ever since.

3.5.3   Construction of *Symbolic Remove:* Levels of Data Reconstruction

When we look at data as semiotic constructions (based on some access to the reality of phenomena), we can immediately address the issue that each new operation in the process of data construction and analysis (= reconstruction) entails construction of new meanings. Thus, by each next step in operating with the data, we may build up a symbolic remove of the constructed meanings from the original phenomena. Each new step adds to the previously constructed meanings—hopefully, in ways that help to construct general knowledge, always on the basis of particular data. This sequence of symbolic remove can be described by a hierarchy of levels: from Level 0 (phenomena) we move to Level 1 (data), from there to Level 2 (some version of data aggregation), followed by Level 3 (data analyses) and Level 4 (interpretation of the results, or some version of meta-analysis). Each level may entail its own technical language where specific terms are constrained to be used in specific defined ways. Semantic extensions occur when the same terminology becomes used at an adjacent level (e.g., transfer of the term "effect" from ANOVA language at Level 3 to use in interpretation at Level 4). The additional set of meanings that emerges at the transition of discourse to the next level entails possibilities for a greater variety of interpretations. Not all of those are substantiated by the previous level (even as they may be possible ones), and some are promoted by mental heuristics or by sociopolitical or sociomoral assumptions that the interpreting person uses, implicitly or explicitly. The greater the symbolic remove of the data-handling work from its origins, the greater is the possibility for *both* innovative and ideologies-affirming generalizations. Psychology's recurrent problem is the absence of ways to make distinctions between the latter. In contrast, psychology's appropriation of operationistic thinking has led to the construction of a number of rules for actions at the medium levels (Levels 2 and 3) of the symbolic remove.

3.5.3.1   Consensual Regulation of Data Construction and Analyses.   Operationism led to another preoccupation in psychology—the construction of social rules for how to operate with singular data points in order to actually be able to make statements about the data. Each step in the process of "handling" the data points entails some kind of symbolic remove relative to the phenomena these data are to represent. This is important only if a representationist view of the data is used; for the operationist view, that is not an issue.

Figure 3.1 depicts different possible conceptualizations of the symbolic remove. All these conceptualizations are social conventions, but, as such, they are based on different epistemological and philosophical premises. Thus, in Figure 3.1(a), we can observe a "naïve realist" model, in which the data equal phenomena (albeit in some selected aspect), and data analyses lead to direct interpretability of the data for the sake of accumulation of knowledge. This model can be viewed as bearing some semblance to Gibsonian "direct perception" as applied to the construction of the meaning of the data. The issues of transitions from phenomena (denoted by ?) to interpretation are not addressed in this model, or are only mentioned if "obstacles" are assumed to exist on the way of direct interpretation. Here belongs the widespread slogan: "Let the data speak for themselves!"

In Figure 3.1(b), a model that could be called "progressivist" is described. The power of knowledge construction is believed to be enhanced by specific

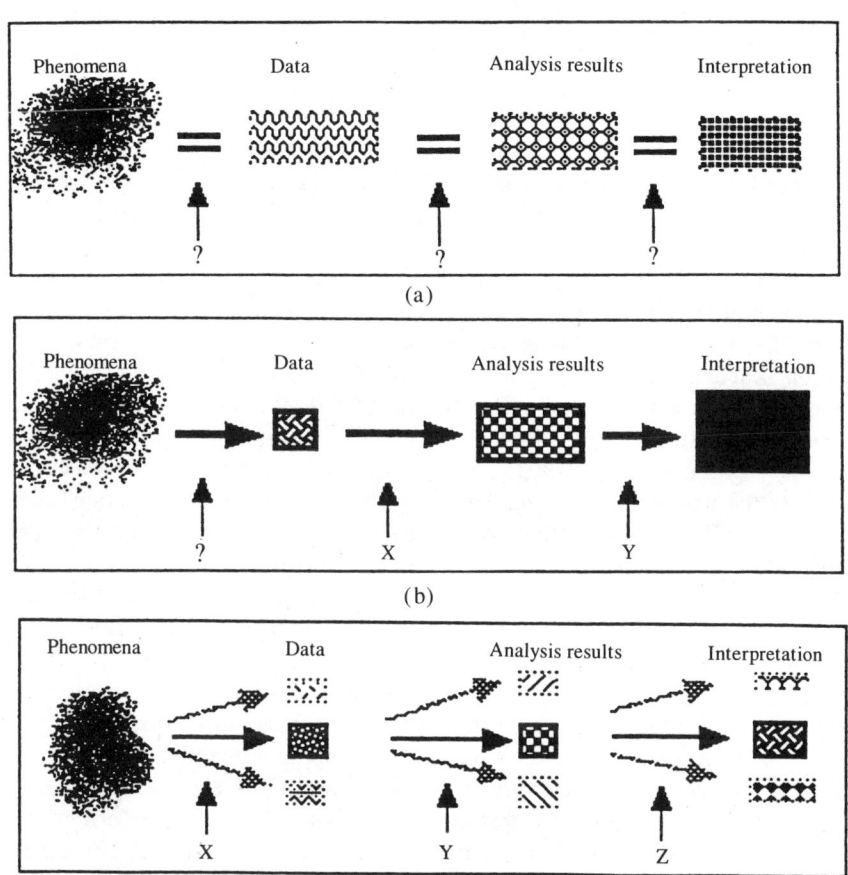

FIGURE 3.1.   Models of symbolic remove in data construction (a) the "naïve realist" model; (b) the "progressivist" model; (c) the "skeptic constructionist" model.

data analysis techniques (X) and following the rules of interpretation of the results of the analysis (Y). Notice, though, that the process of transformation of phenomena to the data (represented by ?) remains unquestioned. The data are the starting point for scientific inference through the ever-complex and sophisticated data analysis techniques. A psychologist who endorses this model will be easily persuaded to move from F-tests to those of ANOVA, and from there to MANOVA; or to find LISREL techniques believably superior to those of other kinds of factor analysis, often without any knowledge of what happens with the data in the process of their analyses.

The model in Figure 3.1(c) has been labeled "skeptic constructivist." Each transformation of the "symbolic capital" [or the "cultural capital" (Bourdieu, 1991)] from phenomena to the interpretation of analyzed data is viewed as a constructive step, where different routes of transformation would lead to different constructions of the issues, and where each further step of symbolic remove (relative to the phenomena) at least potentially increases the difficulties of interpretation. Thus, a psychologist who assumes this perspective is not ready to believe in the "new possibilities" afforded by some newly advertised (and consensually accepted) statistical data analysis scheme, but would like to figure out the ways in which that scheme fits with the aims of making sense of the issue under investigation.

It has never been a secret, in the history of data analysis methods in psychology, that potential skepticism about the methods produced for the "market" of empirical psychology has been promoted at the level of persuasion, rather than through deductive proof. The halo effects of these (quantitative) methods belonging to mathematics (the pure gemstone of science), together with presentation of the statistical method as a uniform objectivity-granting device [which it is not (Gigerenzer, 1991, 1993)], have been successful strategies for proliferation of the use of ever-new methods. As a market-oriented production enterprise, socially institutionalized forms (corporations) necessarily do their best to guide psychologists' thinking in the direction of their most favorable model [the progressivist model in Figure 3.1(b)]. In some ways, scientists' adoption of the naïve realist model in Figure 3.1(a) may be a reaction to the ever-increasing changes in language usage that accompany the progressivist model. By way of social conventions, new data analysis methods introduce new terminology, which becomes loosely related with common-language terms (see 3.2), sometimes in ways that facilitate retranslation of the data analysis discourse into everyday discourse. For instance, a psychologist can talk about having found a "gender effect" after using F-test, ANOVA, or MANOVA (where "effect" has its specific technical meaning), and move to interpret it in terms of ordinary language terms (i.e., causally). Smedslund's (1988, 1994) criticism of psychologists' work as often being "pseudo-empirical" is worth serious consideration in this context. If a MANOVA or a LISREL application to some data produces results that could be derived from the (causalistic) implications of ordinary language terms, the whole exercise of complicated data analysis can be considered futile. The empirical efforts in this case are simply misdirected. *Instead of leading to some knowledge that is new* (relative to what is encoded in our language), these efforts—through unsystematic historical encoding of meanings in language—merely reify what we knew anyway.

3.5.4 Consensual Ignoring of Scale Types

Even as the meanings of the four scale types—(a) nominal, (b) ordinal, (c) interval, and (d) ratio—have been emphasized in psychology (Stevens, 1946), it has become a socially conventionalized rule to ignore the scale type and "feed" the data into analytic procedures that seem subjectively convenient, socially fashionable, or conformity-demanding. The process by which such ignoring takes place is of interest. It often involves strategies that actively circumvent the primary meaning. The researcher knows that a particular scale cannot be transformed into another one, and the general reasons why this is not possible, but then discounts this knowledge and performs the transformation anyway. Such overcoming of the specific constraints on action that have been set by meanings is claimed to be a universal feature of human dialogical communication (Josephs & Valsiner, 1996), and provides the syncretic nature of human meaning-making. Researchers' actions with the data may be a good example of such syncretism.

Often, one aspect of the phenomena is substituted for another involved in the process of data transformation. Consider the depiction in Figure 3.2, where we can view that process step-by-step. In the rectangles, we can see the accumulation of detected similarly categorized specimens of data. Each rectangle is classifiable, even if its particular nature (indicated by different inner textures) remains unique. Each assignment of a specimen to a class of rectangles maintains the specimens as nominal-scale phenomena.

However, what becomes accumulated over time is the frequency of these rectangles (the summary column in Figure 3.2). A frequency count of specimens in an assigned category has an ambiguous status. On the one hand, it remains a descriptive summary of the nominal-scale data. On the other hand, the frequency is easily treated *as if* it were a ratio-scale phenomenon. By all criteria, that treatment is possible: A "true zero" (an absence of the observations) exists for such a scale, and the intervals between the scale values are defined in terms of equality because *each observed instance is assumed to be the same.* Thus, each increase of +1 in the frequency count can be assumed to be equal to each and

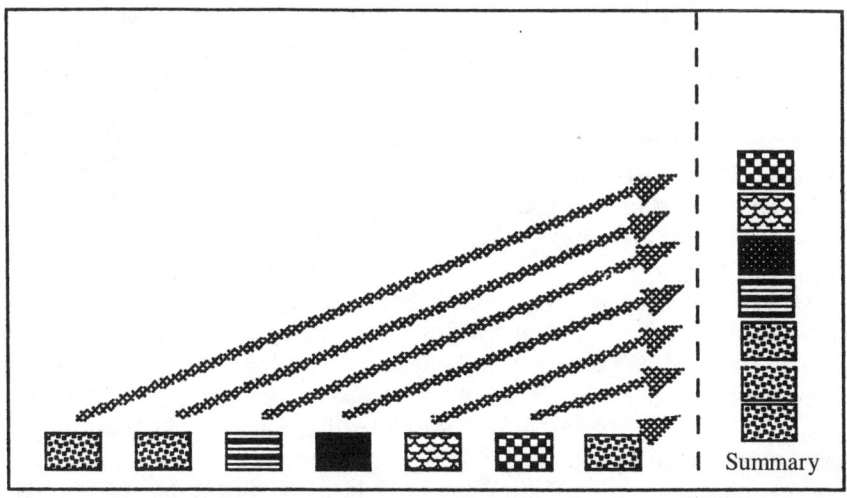

Time ⟶

FIGURE 3.2. Accumulation of nominal-scale data units over time.

every other increase of a similar kind. Negative values are not possible. There cannot be any "collection" of frequencies of instances of "antispecimens"; the frequency count builds up only positive values. For instance, a frequency of −3 specimens in some *observable* category is not possible. Finally, the criterion of invariance over transformations (the scale remains the same when multiplied by a constant) is also satisfied. Thus, frequency counts, by all formal criteria, can be further submitted to various kinds of analyses that presume properties of interval scale or ratio scale. Given this dual nature of frequency phenomena, and the consensus of psychologists that quantification is the basis for any scientific approach, it is very simple to ignore the original (nominal)-scale properties of the observed phenomena as those are transformed into data.

3.5.5 How Quality and Quantity Are Separated: Implications for Developmental Investigation

Even if by formal criteria the frequency count as a nominal-scale summary can be transferred to the realm of ratio-scale (further) operations, *on substantive grounds such a move entails a substitution of what is being investigated.* The focus of investigation becomes shifted from the detection (and labeling) of the target object in its ontological state (i.e., presence, or absence, at the given time) to treating the *recurrence* of the target object as if it were the property of the object under investigation. It is no longer the detected nature of each specimen (a rectangle in Figure 3.2) that is of interest. Instead, the focus is shifted to whether (and how often) the detected specimens can be found again, at a later time during the observation. The frequency becomes the nature of the specimens, rather than their quality (e.g., the form of a rectangle vs. a triangle, or the internal contents). The Aristotelian separation of quality from quantity (see Chapter 1) is accomplished by such substitution; the quality (rectangle-ness in Figure 3.2) has been established by the nominal-scale assignment, and the quantity becomes established by unitizing the nominal existence of a specimen (frequency of 1; accumulated over time) as if the *event* of occurrence constitutes the quantitative unit of the quality. The ambiguity of frequency of nominal-scale units—they can be mapped onto both nominal-scale and ratio-scale conceptual fields—makes the Aristotelian separation of quality and quantity possible.

From a consistently developmental perspective, the possibility of such a substantive turn from nominal-scale to ratio-scale operations in the inductive accumulation of data constitutes a nonpermissible step. The focus of a developmental approach is twofold: to investigate (a) the *emergence* of the new phenomenon, and (b) its *further transformations* into novel states. Thus, instead of accumulation of the rectangles in Figure 3.2 over time (construction of frequency count), the target of investigation is the period antecedent to the emergence of the first detected specimen, until its detected existence. In terms of Figure 3.2, that period amounts to the move from a frequency of 0 to a frequency of 1. That transformation process cannot be reconstructed from the outcome (which is detected only as the first specimen becomes available). It can be investigated only through the observation of the emergence process itself. Furthermore, the transitions from the first to the second, and on to the third and later occurrences of the specimens constitute *qualitative transformations of the emerged phenomena* (e.g., the rectangles in Figure 3.2 change their internal texture, while remaining detectable as belonging to the class of rectangles). From this perspective, the frequency of the phenomenon (after emergence) remains the same (1), and the emerged phenomenon is viewed not as accumulating its quantity, but as transforming its quality over time. *Developmental investigation deals with transformed qualities of nominal-scale data over time.* The more (or less) frequent occurrence of the specimens remains merely a background fact that may help in the process of investigation of these transformations.

An example from the history of developmental psychology, where ratio-scale substitution for nominal-scale interpretation of the data was denied, may elaborate the explanation above. Jean Piaget's youthful deconstruction of the psychometric research practice (c. 1919–1920) is a good example. In the practice of intelligence testing, the recurrence of "correct"-designated answers was consensually made to be a measure of a child's intelligence (in Chapter 2 of Chapman, 1988). Piaget, in defiance of his superiors, refused to accept that assumption. Instead, he charted out the specific intelligence test item as a task environment. *Each individual item poses a problem for the child's intelligence,* and irrespective of whether the child ends up solving the task in "correct" or "incorrect" ways, that intelligence has been put to concrete practice. Thus, that intelligence can be studied through looking at the process of such practice. Recurrence of the use of intelligence in other tasks does not automatically add any new features to that intelligence. It may—if the task provides new challenges—or it need not, yet in both cases the child's intelligence cannot be represented by a frequency count of answers designated as correct by adult test-makers.

3.6   ANALYTIC LEVELS AND PARSIMONY IN INVESTIGATION

Most of the discourse in modern psychology has been struggling with the problem of analytic levels of the phenomena most useful for knowledge construction, and with the issue of relations between these levels. The empirically observable phenomena (from which data are derived) are accessible only at a specific microlevel—their immediate context of occurrence. Yet, the integration of psychological functions does not take place in these immediate ("situated activity") contexts, but somehow transcends them. In other words, the actual psychological development—based on the microlevel experiential foundation—takes place in ways that cannot be immediately accessed by researchers (i.e., at some macrolevel; in contrast to the microlevel, however defined).

All issues of relationship of the levels, where human mental functions are in collective-cultural contexts, are thus systemic (see 2.7). There exists limited indeterminacy between the micro- and macrolevels. Under some conditions (at some time) the input from one to the other leads to a reconstruction of the latter (with feedback to the former), but a very similar input at another time (and in other conditions) is ineffective.

A simple solution to the micro/macrolevels problem in psychology would be an outright a priori denial of the specificity of different levels. Even if the latter may be observable as being apparently different, a psychologist may claim that one level of complexity actually can be reduced to another. Such reductionism has been widespread in different psychologies; usually, it entails reduction of the more complex levels of analysis to more elementary ones (e.g., physiological, biological, or genetic reductionism). However, it is also possible to observe cases of reduction of psychological functions to more complex levels (e.g., sociological reductionism—viewing of psychological functions as mere reflections of discourse, rhetoric, or "collective representations"). Finally, psychologies have been active in proliferating horizontal reductionism—translating explanations in one theoretical language into another, at the same level of complexity. Thus, by replacing behavioristic terms by mentalistic ones, a contemporary "cognitive revolution" has succeeded in the trick of relabeling the issues and reattributing their locus, yet keeping out of investigative focus the psychological processes that make cognitive functions available.

3.6.1 "Morgan's Canon" and Its Transformation

In the history of the comparative psychology of species, similar kinds of reductionism can be traced. The intellectual capacities of *Homo sapiens* have been viewed, at times, as not different from those of the nearest other species, or the capabilities of those other species have been elevated to the level of humans. Controversies about the evaluation of differences of levels led C. Lloyd Morgan to the formulation of his famous canon:

> In no case may we interpret an action as the outcome of the exercise of a higher psychical faculty if it can be interpreted as the outcome of the exercise of one which stands lower in the psychological scale. (Morgan, 1894, p. 53)

Morgan's law of parsimony has often been used as a legitimization for downward-oriented reductionism. "Downward" here presumes a certain hierarchical set of levels of investigation. Thus, psychological phenomena of thinking may be considered to be higher than those of instincts or habits, which, in turn, are higher than the physiological basis that makes them available. Furthermore, the physiological basis can be seen as higher relative to the genetic basis. If the canon is followed in light of this interpretation, reduction of all psychological phenomena to their physiological and genetic bases is a prescribed scientific credo. In the history of psychology, such interpretation of the credo has been tried out in many forms (behavioristic and reflexologistic reductions of psychological phenomena to physiological ones). This makes psychology as a discipline obsolete (which is a question of sociology of science); more importantly, it creates a guarantee that complex psychological functions can never be explained.

Morgan introduced the law in the context of argument with any kinds of reductionism, and in contrast with the commonsense interpretations of animal intellect, which glossed over the issues for investigation. Morgan had a clearcut emphasis on development of psychological functions toward higher levels of complexity, and in order to be able to provide an adequate account of the emergence of the new levels, a certain rule of thumb (in the form of the canon) was necessary.

A developmental reformulation would restore the focus of the canon on the process of emergence of psychological levels of different complexity:

> If we assume development to be a multi-level probabilistically epigenetic process, in no case may we interpret an observable (i.e., emerged) outcome as being caused by a unitary lower level process (within the hierarchical network of processes), but always as a result of causal systemic processes that operate between levels. Attribution of causality to a singular-level ("higher," or "lower") causal system is possible *only and only if* we have ruled out any possible regulatory impacts from adjacent levels, especially by a process at the next higher level in the hierarchy. (Valsiner, 1997b)

This reformulation of Morgan's canon sets up a sequence of investigative activities in ways that at first require examination of the lack of between-levels ties. If that examination rules out such ties, the construction of causal explanations (of a systemic kind) within the given level is possible. If that examination fails to rule out possible ties between levels, then the construction of explanatory frameworks needs to retain the hierarchical (between-levels) nature of the phenomena under study, at least to the extent of immediate next levels of hierarchy.

3.7 LOOKING FOR DEVELOPMENTALLY APPROPRIATE FORMAL MODELS: AN EXCURSION TO BIOLOGICAL, LINGUISTIC, AND ECONOMIC DOMAINS

Surely the criticism of the received data construction practices is but a starting point for a fresh look at formal models that could be adequate for the study of development. As the developmental approach has been underdeveloped within psychology, and as the latter has been colonized by the "empire of chance" (Gigerenzer et al., 1989), that discipline does not seem to be a fruitful area of such search. However, there exist numerous efforts in other disciplines that are worth an inquiry, especially in the area of developmental biology. After all, the closest discipline to developmental psychology is not the rest of psychology, but its historical parent discipline of embryology.

However, in the realm of biology, the importation of formal devices from different branches of mathematics has its own complications, as has been observed:

> Very often efforts in mathematical biology depend upon existing mathematics and try to make the biology fit these existing theories. But the biology is the real world, and the models must fit it rather than the reverse. (Guckenheimer, 1978, p. 38)

The same is true for psychology. Importation of new forms of mathematics because they have gained some popularity (e.g., chaos theory) is not sufficient for a productive reconstruction of psychology's conceptual apparatus. This issue becomes particularly crucial if we look for adequate systems of mathematics for modeling development.

3.7.1   The Closed Nature of Mathematics and the Open Nature of Development

Development entails constant innovation in form and function. In this sense, developmental processes are open-ended, so that it is impossible to predict the exact form and final state of the developing system. In contrast, formal mathematical systems are closed and incapable of developing themselves without the intervention of their creators. Pankow has contrasted the closedness of mathematics to the openness of philosophy:

> By definition, formal languages are incapable of recognizing themselves and . . . are therefore also incapable of recognizing any other position. Thus, a formal language does not link positions, but constitutes itself a fixed position. It is not, like philosophy, an open eye to the outer world, but a closed eye which may also be called a logically isolated eye. (Pankow, 1976, p. 22).

The status of "logically isolated eye," attributed to formal mathematical systems, is crucial for any psychological application of the rigor of mathematics. *Every mathematical system carries with it its axiomatic basis. Its nature is firmly fixed on that basis. When applied to the phenomena of a particular field of science, the system's axiomatic basis sets the conditions that guide what kinds of data can be derived from the phenomena by the given mathematical system.* These conditions determine the outcomes of the application effort *prior to* the effort itself, rather than provide for any postapplication empirical decision about the adequacy of the given system for the target phenomena. Thus, an empirical discovery of "goodness of fit" between a formal model of a phenomenon and its empirical characteristics does not prove the conceptual adequacy of the model in general.

All mathematical systems are embedded in their philosophical frameworks, and it is the latter that make the application of a particular system potentially adequate for a certain class of phenomena. This stipulation is particularly important to bear in mind in the case of developmental biology and developmental psychology. The majority of available formal systems are based on assumptions that exclude development from their focus. Therefore, it would be impossible to apply such systems to the study of development, because such application necessarily leads to a nondevelopmental description of the object of investigation.

The picture is even more complicated because different formal mathematical models (e.g., geometric, logical, game-theoretic) belong to different subdisciplines of mathematics and may have few if any connections between them. All this has contributed toward making the effort to apply mathematics to the description of structured phenomena and their change highly compartmentalized and domain-specific. The application of mathematics for its own sake cannot help developmental sciences, but the application of *adequate* mathematics for the sake of understanding how developmental processes work may lead us to a better understanding of the structured complexity of development.

What is meant by "adequate mathematics" in this context depends on the abstract-philosophical analysis of the research questions requiring empirical investigation in psychology. Contrary to the widespread emphasis on quantitative methodology as almost synonymous with "mathematical" in contemporary psychology, present-day mathematics is a highly heterogeneous discipline that includes a variety of nonquantitative domains. Nigel Howard has emphatically illustrated the misunderstanding between mathematicians and others:

> Non-mathematicians often think that mathematics is primarily concerned with numbers. That is not so today. In fact, while twentieth-century social scientists have tried desperately to become more quantitative in the belief that this would make them more mathematical, twentieth-century mathematicians have become increasingly nonquantitative. . . . The idea that mathematics is the science of quantity is a nineteenth-century notion, and social scientists who pursue it are immersing themselves in dead ideas. (Howard, 1971, p. 2)

However, even among qualitative mathematical systems of this century, examples of immediate applicability to developmental phenomena are very rare. The following short overviews of some of these domains will bring the theoretical separation of developmental from nondevelopmental ideas again into the center of attention.

3.7.2 Space Structures and the Geometries of Contour Change

Some structures of phenomena can be described as spaces that are limited by their outer closed contours, and the change of these space structures may be reflected in the change of the contours. The geometric description of such cases interested D'Arcy Thompson (1942), who offered mathematical solutions to both the description of such spaces and their transformation. Largely, the methods he suggested involved finding formal systems to describe biological forms that undergo transformation during development. For example, methods introduced by Thompson have been useful in the prediction of human craniofacial growth in two-dimensional (Mark, Todd, & Shaw, 1981; Todd & Mark, 1981; Todd, Mark, Shaw, & Pittenger, 1980) as well as three-dimensional versions (Mark & Todd, 1983). The relevance of different geometries to characterize the perceptual and action space of organisms is likewise important for theoretical issues in ecological psychology (Shaw & Pittenger, 1977).

Despite the success in the application of different geometries to describe the growth of biological forms, the geometric formal descriptions provide little for the task of explaining the developmental processes involved in children's acting and thinking. These formal geometries may fit particularly well for description of those biological forms the growth of which is relatively strictly genetically determined, rather than a result of organism–environment epigenetic process. Without doubt, the structural development of the human cranium is a good example of such forms. In contrast, the main aspect of children's psychological development involves constructive acting by the children that transforms their environment, which is set up for them by "social others." The mathematical description of the space within which the social agents act may be useful but cannot serve as the definitive formal model for all aspects of development.

3.7.3 Syntactic Models: Chomsky's Application of Context-Free Grammars in Linguistics

Describing the form and function of human language and explaining its development, in both ontogeny and cultural history, provides a difficult and as yet unsolved set of problems. These problems are partly due to the fact that language is structured interdependently within its syntactic, semantic, and pragmatic aspects. Historically, the syntactic aspect has been of primary concern to linguists and philosophers because the questions of language grammar have been held to be of relevance by language users.

The contribution of Noam Chomsky toward the formal analysis of language has been a much disputed system over the past three decades. It has been the subject of fierce attack by its opponents and equally fierce defense by its proponents. Active discussion of Chomsky's program of formal analysis has largely been based on extrascientific and epistemological issues that have become the foreground of societal discourse in conjunction with the active exposure of Chomsky's methods and ideas to the public. Because Chomsky's contributions to societal discourse cover a wide area, ranging from computer science through linguistics and philosophy to social politics, the discussions of his ideas have often borrowed from one aspect of that range to concentrate on another.

From the perspective of developmental psychology, Chomsky's philosophy and formal models constitute a "fascinating mix of geneticism and Cartesianism" (Piaget, 1970b, p. 87). Chomsky's geneticism is reflected in his effort to provide a formal description of the generation of language performance as it functions in the case of the "idealized speaker-bearer." This abstract person is constantly involved in the *creative production of new sentences,* or, in other terms, the construction of performance (actual speech) on the basis of competence (implicit language knowledge). Chomsky states:

> The most striking aspect of linguistic competence is what we may call the "creativity of language," that is, the speaker's ability to produce new sentences, sentences that are immediately understood by other speakers although they bear no physical resemblance to sentences which are "familiar." . . . Normal use of language involves the production and interpretation of sentences that are similar to sentences that have been heard before only in that they are generated by the rules of the same grammar, and thus the only sentences that can in any serious sense be called "familiar" are clichés or fixed formulas of one sort or another. (Chomsky, 1966, p. 11)

As is evident from this quote, Chomsky's emphasis on the microgenesis of speech (the production of sentences) involves the notion of construction (novel sentences are constructed by the speaker), which is based on the fixed generation mechanism. The fixity of the latter constitutes the nondevelopmental basis of Chomsky's linguistic thinking, which is most explicitly evident in his arguments about the ontogeny of language. His conceptualization of the ontogenetic side of language is built on a belief in an innate and genetically determined "language faculty," which specifies the class of "humanly accessible grammars" (Chomsky, 1980a). Chomsky's use of exclusive separation of the organism and its environment leads to the denial of interactionist viewpoints in the explanation of development (Chomsky, 1976, 1980b) and to genetic preformationism as the only alternative explanation that would fit his assumption of the static nature of the kernel of linguistic competence.

Chomsky's nondevelopmental theoretical perspective is also evident in his efforts to formalize the rules by which language competence can be turned into language performance. The fundamental idea of Chomsky's "transformational generative grammar" is that surface structures are formed through the application of at least two types of rules. The base rules generate an abstract phrase structure representation, and the transformational rules move elements and otherwise rearrange structures so that those become acceptable language sentences, and only such sentences. Because the adequacy of a formal grammar is determined on the basis of the fit of its output to the reality, the sequence in which different rewriting rules of the formal system are applied in order to generate sentences is irrelevant. Different sequences of rule application can produce the same (fully adequate) outcome, but these sequences themselves need not be adequate descriptions of the actual sentence-generation processes that the speaker uses to produce the sentence. In contrast, developmental research has its goal to *adequately represent the reality of the generation process* for the microgenetic and ontogenetic phenomena in psychology or biology. Instead of reaching satisfaction in finding a formal system that accurately describes all the possible outcomes of a productive (i.e., outcome-generating) psychological process, the goal of developmental research is to describe all the possible versions of the time-dependent (sequential) structure of the process itself—even in cases when the process produces in some sense "deficient" outcomes. Furthermore, developmental research includes the option that the set of different versions of the process is not finite, and new versions of the process can emerge in the course of development. Contrasting these characteristics of developmental research with Chomsky's thinking, it becomes evident that Chomsky's "generative grammar" is a formal description of little or no value for the study of development. It is true that Chomsky's emphasis on linguistic creativity looks, at first glance, developmental (in its microgenetic aspect). However, in reality, it represents a nondevelopmental view on the production of performance, given the static limits of the competence. In that "generative process," the *outcomes* of the production process are the actual object of the study. The actual production process is of no relevance in the course of formal model building.

3.7.4   Context-Sensitive Grammars and the Description of Structure

The formalisms involved in Chomsky's application of the transformational generative grammar to linguistic analyses represent the *context-free type* (Type 2) of formal grammars. The productions (application of rewriting rules to symbols) are not dependent on their context and take the general form of [a → b]. In contrast, the Type 1 formal grammars include a dependence on the context of the symbols. These *context-sensitive grammars* differ from their context-free counterparts in how the context is taken into account in the description of transformations, which involves the form of the rewriting rules of symbols used to depict transformations. The rewriting rules of context-sensitive grammars take the form $[x/a/y \to x/b/y]$ where a and b are symbols, and x and y represent the context (Fu, 1974, p. 28). In the case of context-sensitive grammars, the rewriting of a symbol by another $(a \to b)$ can take place only in the appropriate context (x/y), and in no other context.

Incidentally, the distinction between context-free and context-sensitive grammars was introduced into the theory of formal languages by Chomsky (1959), who then proceeded to concentrate on the application of the context-free type to linguistic material. Context-sensitive formal grammars have remained largely underdeveloped mathematically but are potentially useful formal descriptive systems. As long as the ethos in most of the scientific enterprise has been to generate context-free abstract knowledge about the objects of investigation, the ideas of context-sensitive formal systems may have been found superfluous to the goals of science. The few efforts to discuss context-sensitive formal languages have been largely confined to the realm of computer languages and pattern recognition (Fu, 1974; Kasai, 1970; Rosenkrantz, 1969).

From the developmental perspective, context-sensitive grammars fit the inevitably context-dependent nature of developing systems, for they take into account the contextual conditions under which a structural change (rewriting in a symbol structure) can take place. This constitutes a clear advance over the context-free grammars. The environmental embeddedness of context-sensitive grammars does not yet make them adequate developmental models as such, because the open-endedness (innovation) of developmental processes is not included in the version of existing grammars of that kind. If a context-sensitive grammar is developed so that it specifies the *contextual conditions under which the grammar would generate new rules within itself* that would restructure the grammar and its relationships with the environment, only then does the possibility arise that context-sensitive grammars can become adequate formal models of developmental processes.

3.7.5   Automations in Describing Structure and Its Change

Contemporary automata theory has developed its own tentative answers to the question of how to model change in a system. Not surprisingly, the efforts to develop mathematical models of such change grew out of learning theory in psychology (Bush & Mosteller, 1955). The theory of learning automation (Fu, 1970; Narendra & Thathachar, 1974) is aimed at specifying a formal system that (a) involves a stochastic automation nested in an exchange relationship with the environment, and (b) changes as a result of that exchange relationship. The basic operation carried out by a learning automation is the updating of its action probabilities, depending on the feedback from the environment. The environment (as it is defined by the feedback regime that it provides for the learning automation) can be conceptualized as either stationary or nonstationary. The environmental feedback regime has usually been conceptualized using the ideas of reward and punishment, which are highly familiar among psychologists. Usually, the probability distributions of reward versus penalty, which the environment feeds back into the automation following its particular actions, are the core data on which the automation's learning is based. Traditionally, binary probability distributions (probability of the reward $= p$, and of the penalty $= 1 - p$) have been used by the learning automation theorists to characterize the environment, but some applications have also experimented with continuous probability distributions (e.g., Fu & McLaren, 1965, cited via Narendra and Thathachar, 1974, p. 332). The resemblance of this way of describing the learner's environment to the traditions of learning theory's use of probabilistic reinforcement schedules is quite obvious. That resemblance brings into learning automation theory the strengths and weaknesses of psychological learning theories. Among the former, the emphasis on learning as reorganization of the learner should be mentioned. This emphasis brings learning automation theory closer to the needs of developmental psychology. On the other side, however, the assumption of *inevitable* and *direct* feedback to the learner from the environment—which learning automation theory seems to have implicitly taken over from behavioristic learning theories— may limit the applicability of the learning automations as potential formal models of actual developmental processes. This point requires explanation. The assumption of "inevitable feedback" includes the belief that whenever the organism/automation acts in manner *x,* it will elicit from the environment either a reward [with probability $p(x)$] or a penalty [probability $1 - p(x)$; e.g., Lakshmivarahan & Thathachar, 1973], while any other outcome is excluded. In real-life learning outside Skinner boxes, however, the third option of *receiving no feedback* is always possible, and is very often the case. The environmental feedback to the learner (organism or formal automation) is better characterized by conditional dependence on the situation at a given time. That aspect of environmental feedback makes the assumption of a stationary environment highly unrealistic for any reality-linked advancement of learning automation theory.

The assumption of "direct feedback" from the environment relates to learning theory's acceptance of the assumption that causality is *elementaristic* in its nature (see 2.7). Both the reward and the penalty are considered to cause change in the organism (learner) in a direct manner. In contrast, many aspects of the learning process are in reality *catalyzed* by the simultaneous presence of other conditions, either in the learner or in the environment.

It is easy to see that learning automations with stationary environments— where the probability distribution of the environmental feedback options remains constant over the time during which the automations are studied— constitute the simplest possible case that does not fit developmental phenomena. The assumption of stationariness of the environment (as its basic nature) is unwarranted for all open systems, and thus for all systems that undergo development. This does not rule out the possibility that a developing system's environment is stationary for a limited period of time, but this is a special case of no-change of a dynamic environment, rather than the normal state of the environment.

Learning automation theory has provided advancements that go beyond the environmental stationariness assumption and allow learning phenomena to be dealt with in ways that are closer to reality. First, the environments have been conceptualized as switching between different stationary states. Second, environments have been considered to vary in a periodic fashion. Third, the environments can be thought of as "slowly-varying" (Narendra & Thathachar, 1974, p. 331). The direction of considering nonperiodically (but not necessarily slowly) varying environments would bring the learning automation theory closest to becoming useful for the developmental sciences.

Another aspect of developmental relevance that contemporary learning automation theorists have attempted to formalize is the hierarchical nature of organized and developing systems. This is accomplished by constructing a multilevel system of automations, where each action of an automation at a certain level triggers automations at the next lower level. The basic problem to be solved in the formal analysis of such a hierarchical system is to find an algorithm suitable for each level that ensures the coordination of the whole structure in the optimal action (Thathachar & Ramakrishnan, 1981a, 1981b). The issue of the coordination of the whole structure in the process of development is indeed important for developmental psychology to which learning automation theory may have relevance. However, until the theory of learning automation with changing environments is applied directly to developmental phenomena, it remains unclear exactly what it can offer to the developmental sciences in terms of any new understanding of the process of development.

3.7.6 Modeling the Growth of Multicellular Structures: L-Systems

Lindenmayer-systems (abbreviated as L-systems) are a special family of formal descriptions of the development of multicellular patterns of biological phenomena. In mathematics, the theory of L-systems belongs in the realms of automation theory and the theory of formal languages (cf. Lindenmayer & Rozenberg, 1976).

The introduction of L-systems into developmental biology was related to the empirical question of how to model the growth of branching plants in botany (Lindenmayer, 1968, 1975). The phenomenology of filamentous growth processes in botany constitutes an empirical domain where the abstract modeling efforts can be verified against the observation of the actual growth process of plants. Furthermore, the L-systems theory was constructed to fit the structured (multicellular) nature of developing botanical structures. The growing filament is not homogeneous but is made up of a multitude of cells, some of which are immediate "neighbors" of others. Furthermore, the whole structure—a tree-leaf, for example—grows to take a final general form that is invariant for the leaves of the given tree species, although variability exists in the exact outer contour forms that individual leaves may have. The structured nature of the growth of multicellular plants requires the use of mathematical formalisms in any description that considers the structural aspects of that growth. Lindenmayer (1978, p. 38) contrasted his formalisms with preceding efforts to model growth:

> As frameworks for the description of growth and morphogenesis in time and space mathematical formalisms have been borrowed from mechanics and dynamics, primarily based on differential equations, which are suitable for changes of form of homogeneous objects like crystals or clouds, but are entirely unsuitable for complex heterogeneous systems like developing organisms. Precisely the cellular aspect is missing from most of these models. In terms of the above formalisms the description of a multicellular growing body would require at least as many separate differential equations as there are cells in it. Since the number of cells, or whatever other units one might choose, increases in the course of development, sometimes without limit, this

would imply a mathematical description with increasing numbers of differential equations. Systems described in this way cannot be handled with any presently available analytical method.

L-systems, like generative grammars, can be *context-free* or *context-sensitive*. In context-free L-systems (OL-systems, also called zero-sided or informationless Lindenmayer systems), the growth of the multicellular organism depends only on the lineages of its constituent cells, which are independent of their neighboring cells. The growing biological structure goes through a series of changes (modeled by the rules of the OL-systems) where the growth at the next time interval depends solely on the cells in the previous interval. At each step (time interval), each of the cells in the structure can either change its state (or remain in the same state) or disappear from the structure ("die").

Lindenmayer (1975) demonstrated that context-free (OL) systems are, in principle, incapable of generating complex forms that could fit the majority of biological species. For example, sets of adult forms of tree-leaves with three or more equal-size lobes cannot be produced by OL-systems, and require taking the intercellular interaction into account. This limitation of the context-free L-systems leads to the necessity of modeling processes of growth in ways that are context-sensitive. The context in the particular case of L-systems constitutes taking the status of a cell's neighboring cells into account when modeling its developmental course. A context-sensitive L-system consists of a set of states of the cells, a set of transition rules, and the starting structure. The transition rules specify, for each state of a cell and each combination of its neighboring cells, what the state of the given cell during the next time interval would be. Both context-free and context-sensitive L-systems can be either deterministic or probabilistic. The deterministic L-systems assume that any transition rule used in modeling the growth process is either applicable with full certainty or not applicable at all. Deterministic OL-systems (called "DOL-systems" in the literature on L-systems) use fully determinate application of transition rules independent of the simultaneous context of the given cell. Probabilistic OL-systems (POL-systems) include the application of transition rules independently of the simultaneous structural context on the basis of the probabilities of the application of these rules (e.g., Jürgensen, 1976). The deterministic context-sensitive L-systems include absolute (probability = 1) conditions for application of transition rules, given the required state of the complex of the neighboring cells. Probabilistic context-sensitive L-systems add to that aspect the probabilities of the application of different rules, given the particular context.

Because the purpose of this chapter is to analyze the most general aspects of different mathematical systems with claims to usefulness in modeling development, the specific formalisms and examples of the L-systems are not given here. The interested reader may want to study Lindenmayer's original work (Lindenmayer, 1968, 1975, 1978) or its introductory and simplified presentation (MacDonald, 1983, Chapters 18 & 19). Of relevance in the present context is the question of what novel opportunities for formal modeling of developmental processes the L-systems afford. Because the L-systems were constructed starting from the empirical problem of understanding the principles of multicellular organisms, their applicability in other developmental sciences (aside from the study of botanical growth) can be expected to be relatively straightforward. The L-systems framework also provides the rare proof that the growth of complex structured organisms cannot be modeled by context-free formal systems (Lindenmayer, 1975). On the other hand, the use of context-sensitive L-systems can be complicated when applied to developmental phenomena that are not characterized by a relatively stable pattern of units (like a multicellular anatomical structure) where the neighborhood of the units in the pattern cannot be simply determined. For example, psychological structures involved in child development (either motor action patterns or cognitive schemata) may be difficult to model with L-systems because the "neighborhood" of different action patterns and the contexts in which they are applied cannot be described by straightforward mapping, as is possible in the case of a growing tree-leaf. However, despite these limitations, the context-sensitive probabilistic Lindenmayer-systems are potentially the closest to the task of modeling epigenetic developmental processes. The difficulty that may still appear insurmountable is how to determine the origin of the probability values that get entered into such formal models. If the aim is to use the formal model for better understanding of the reality, then the probabilities cannot be assigned to transition rules *ad hoc,* but have to be based on some aspects of the reality. There exist many different empirical possibilities of finding the probabilities on empirical grounds and some (or all) are dependent on the particular investigator's often implicit assumption of what probability is.

3.7.7 Catastrophe Theory and the Explanation of Development

René Thom's topological catastrophe theory was developed explicitly for the purpose of formalizing morphogenesis, a process of qualitative change from a previous form to a new morphological state. It is aimed at the construction of "an abstract, purely geometrical theory of morphogenesis, *independent of the substrate of forms and the nature of the forces that create them*" (Thom, 1975, p. 8). As has often happened with abstract theoretical systems in the history of science, the dissemination of knowledge about Thom's catastrophe theory led to selective retention of the nondevelopmental aspects of his originally developmentally oriented system. For example, Gilmore's (1981) overview of catastrophe theory and its applications in science makes no mention of the theory's explicit historical conceptual roots in problems of embryology. Morphogenesis is not even included in the subject index of the book! A similar fate has followed the application of catastrophe theory in psychology. The majority of efforts to apply it, *and* its active critics (e.g., Zahler & Sussmann, 1977), have been similarly nondevelopmental in their emphasis. The application of catastrophe theory in psychology is an example of the recurrent situations where an originally developmentally oriented abstract system of thought is turned into a nondevelopmental basis for local "theories," which are subsequently discounted because they may be found not to provide "better predictions" (a cliché used widely in psychology, often in an indeterminate way) of behavior.

Thom's definition of catastrophe in the context of the "morphology of a process" involves the observation of forms created by the location of points in a four-dimensional time–space structure:

> Suppose that a natural process, of any kind whatsoever, takes place in a box B; we then consider $B \times T$ (where T is the time axis) as the domain on which the process is defined. Also suppose that the observer has at his disposal probes or other means to allow him to investigate the neighborhood of each point x of $B \times T$. As a first classification of points of $B \times T$ we have the following: if the observer can see nothing remarkable in the neighborhood of a point x of $B \times T$, that is, if x does not differ in kind from its neighboring points, then x is a *regular point* of the process. By definition the regular points form an open set in $B \times T$, and the complementary closed set K of points in $B \times T$ is the set of *catastrophe points*, the points with some discontinuity in every neighborhood; "something happens" in every ball with center c where c belongs to K. The set K and the description of the singularities at each of its points constitute the *morphology* of the process. (Thom, 1975, p. 38)

The emphasis in Thom's formal system is clearly on how to describe structural–dynamic processes that take place in space.and time. This constitutes the aspect of catastrophe theory that is of primary relevance for developmental biology and psychology. On the other hand, the catastrophe theory was also based on the typological (static) worldview. It is fundamentally a classificatory theory, the predictive power of which (as with other similar theories) is weak. It includes a typology of different elementary catastrophes that can be described topologically and are found to fit different morphological phenomena in nature and society (Thom, 1973). The actual complexity of the biological phenomena has made it necessary for catastrophe theorists to go beyond the types of elementary catastrophes (Thom, 1973; Zeeman, 1977) and to provide mathematical descriptions of their form. That typology-based descriptive application of the theory is nondevelopmental in nature and therefore is largely irrelevant for developmental sciences. In other terms: A sophisticated mathematical description of a biological form that fits any of the list of elementary catastrophes need not yet constitute an explanation of its development. For example, knowing that a certain form can be characterized as a version of the "cusp catastrophe" does not allow us to consider the formal mathematical description of the cusp the explanation of that form. Even less adequate would be any consideration that the formal description is an explanation of its development.

The developmental relevance of catastrophe theory is similar to that of geometric efforts at describing changing forms (see 3.7.2)—both kinds of formalisms can provide adequate descriptions of complex static and even dynamic (changing) forms; but as abstract descriptive systems, they need not be sufficient for explanation of the development of particular structured biological or psychological phenomena. Guckenheimer's cautious criticism of the catastrophe theory is worth mentioning here:

> Without a better understanding of *both* the geometry of morphogenesis and the answers to a variety of mathematical questions, the relevance of catastrophe theory to problems of development will remain an open issue. Moreover, it is not clear that catastrophe theory can ever provide strong evidence for the correctness of any explanation of development. It may be limited to suggestive analogies between the mathematical theory and reality. (Guckenheimer, 1978, p. 15)

Thom himself has admitted that catastrophe theory has turned out to be of little use for modeling living systems. He argues that catastrophe theory "at least . . . does not dissociate the genesis of a system (and its death) from its adult behavior, as do all existing schemes" (Thom, 1976, p. 252). This emphasis on nondissociation of development from static (albeit structural) being may actually be the reason why the theory does not easily afford explanation of development. Thom consistently intermingles developmental and nondevelopmental approaches in his epistemology (e.g., see Piaget, 1980; Thom, 1980).

Perhaps the key to a productive integration of catastrophe theory with developmental sciences lies in the presence of empirical developmental research issues. In its beginning, Thom's theory was explicitly developed (see Thom, 1975, p. xxiii) to provide formalization of Waddington's ideas of epigenesis and the chreod, which were introduced into biology within the framework of a developmental approach. Thom's mathematical formalization of the concepts of chreod (p. 114) and his discussion of the process of canalization (pp. 142–143) provide formalized leads toward further advancement of the developmental side of catastrophe theory. Likewise, Zeeman's (1974) analysis of the primary and secondary waves in cases of biological growth may provide interesting leads for formalizing the development of boundaries and the structure of real developing organisms. Last (but not least), the introduction of catastrophe-theoretic ideas to linguistics in the framework of gestalt linguistics (Wildgen, 1984) may provide a more sophisticated and a more suitable formal method than has been available in linguistics thus far. The direction taken in gestalt linguistics has relevance from the standpoint of the theory espoused in this book. The catastrophe-theoretic semantics is based on the axiomatic assumption that the meanings of propositions are vague, and semantic theories that do not take the user and his or her social context into account are nonsensical (Wildgen, 1981). The basic vagueness of the phenomena and their context-dependence are also the cornerstones of the present theory. In gestalt semantics and in the theory presented in this book, catastrophe-theoretic thinking may prove to be useful for the analysis of boundaries between different zones involved in the microgenesis of children's actions or word meanings (Wildgen, 1983).

3.7.8   Game Theory and Problems of Development

In various social sciences, the use of game-theoretic ideas has become widespread. Perhaps that has been due to the fact that the game-theoretic branch of mathematics has been constructed in analogy with phenomena in society and individual psychology that are of primary interest to social scientists. Among the topics in the study of which game-theoretic thinking has been used are the understanding of conflicts and ways of their resolution, individual and collective interests and moral decisions, the formation of coalitions, and ideas of economic processes and rationality involved in economic decision making. Many of these central problems of social life include developmental aspects. For instance, conflict *resolution* is a process that covers (ideally) the movement of a system from a conflict state to a nonconflict state. Likewise, any moral decision outcome that involves the process of economic decision making leads to one or another economic outcome. On the other hand, all real-life phenomena to which the game theory has any links can (and most often are) also be thought of in static, nondevelopmental terms.

3.7.8.1   Traditional Emphases in Game Theory.   Beginning with the real-life analog of a game where different players make certain choices among the options that are available to them, and where certain specific goals are sought, the traditional game theory has proceeded to formalize gamelike phenomena in their abstract form. The historical starting point of these ideas was the nature of strategies used in economic decision making and their "rationality" (Von Neumann & Morgenstern, 1944). This guaranteed the inclusion of the complexity of the participants' motivation in the analyzed phenomena from the very beginning of the game theory. Economics may be the most complex of human inventions, but its importance is too central for it to be disregarded or brushed aside as "too messy" to study. On the other hand, the specific nature of economic processes (often based on the idea of obligatory maximization of benefits in relation to costs—see also 2.5) may set the stage for game-theoretic applications in social sciences outside economics, in ways that may be inadequate for the phenomena.

Psychological application of game-theoretic ideas has varied from one of its branches to another. Game theory has been quite widespread in some areas, such as social psychology (particularly in the fields of small group studies and interpersonal processes). At the same time, it has been virtually unused in others (e.g., in child psychology), with the exception of some use of game-theoretic experimental situations with school-age children (Graves & Graves, 1978). There are two major ways in which game theory is applicable in psychology.

First, it can be used as *a means* for the study of different psychological phenomena. In this case, the game theory is applied as a part of the independent-variables complex. Social psychology experiments that are conducted in laboratory settings usually reflect the use of game theory as a means to some end. Experimental subjects are given "payoff" matrices and asked to "play the game" under different experimentally manipulated conditions. The latter are often made up so as to fit the requirements of the game-theoretic thinking, rather than reflect the ultimately more complex conditions of persons' interaction in real life. In such experimental settings, different extra-game "variables" (e.g., the subjects' "competition" or "cooperation") are studied with the help of the game-theory-based experimental manipulations. The game itself does not function as a model of the inherent psychological processes involved in interpersonal transaction in these experimental situations. Instead, it creates the conditions for specific ways of interaction between the subjects to which the participants are expected to conform, at least during the experiment.

The second way of using game-theoretic thinking in psychology involves the modeling of psychological phenomena. Here, the game theory is used as part of the dependent-variables complex: The particular phenomenon is studied using other methods, and the results of that study are used in the attempt to reveal which of the different formal models best fits the reality. In such applications, game theory is part of the end goal of establishing the formal model of the phenomenon.

It could be argued that the second type of application is closer to the philosophical goals of mathematics. Paradoxically, the first kind of use has been widespread in psychology, despite the difficulties of inference from the laboratory game tasks to the reality of daily life and experience. In the game theory, a number of abstract assumptions (constraints) were developed under which its formalizations are applicable. These constraints on conditions under which an abstract game is assumed to be played determine the domains of reality to which the particular game-theoretic formalizations are applicable. For example, consider the widespread use of ideas from traditional game theory in the practice of social-psychological experiments where two previously unacquainted subjects are instructed to make choices between given (and immutable) action options based on a given payoff matrix. The subjects' choices are supposed to be made independently of each other and at the same time, after which the outcome (determined on the basis of the payoff matrix) of the conjunction of their choices is established by the experimenter and made known to the subjects. As the experimental game progresses, the partners may shift their choices of strategies (e.g., from the cooperative to the competitive domain, or vice versa, as determined by the payoff matrix). However, the partners are constrained by the way the game conditions are set up—they cannot construct a new action option, or change the payoff matrix during the game, and neither of them can delay making a choice until the other's choice has become known. Such constraining conditions effectively limit the applicability of game-theoretic formalisms to real-life domains where such constraints do not apply.

The Prisoner's Dilemma Game (e.g., Rapoport, 1974) is a good example of the constraints set up for a widely popular type of game used in many investigations, particularly in the late 1960s. Two prisoners who are kept in separate cells are accused of the same crime. They both—independently of each other and on the basis of their own rational decision—have to choose whether to confess or not. If both confess, both receive a medium-severity sentence. If one confesses and the other does not, the first one is freed and the second one gets a high-severity sentence. If neither of the prisoners confesses, they both get a minimal sentence.

In the prisoner's dilemma situation, two kinds of advantages for the decision makers are set against each other because of the limitation of communication opportunities between players. The *individual* advantage ("I had better confess, since there is a chance that he will not") and the *cooperative* advantage ("If we *both* do not confess, then we *both* get the minimal sentence") are in contradiction under these circumstances. They do not allow any modification of the situation on behalf of the prisoners, who must choose between two courses of action, and cannot make up a new action option. In fact, the prisoners are not playing *their* game; they are trapped by the law enforcement system, which tries to make them confess by eliminating the most adequate (from the prisoners' standpoint) option of communicating between themselves, and thus preventing cooperation while making their choices.

In other terms, the Prisoner's Dilemma Game may indeed reveal psychological issues that are applicable to the real-life domain of prisoners' dilemmas, but *not* to psychological phenomena outside prisons or to prisoner–law–accomplice relationships where the two (or more) sides caught in such dilemmas can establish information-gathering systems and communicate in negotiations about possible actions. The proliferation of different kinds of espionage to counteract the limits of access to relevant information, and the extension of negotiations about real-life decisions over lengthy time periods, illustrate the freedom of preparatory actions that people outside prisonlike situations use to avoid getting trapped in the Prisoner's Dilemma Game.

Many of the traditional assumptions of the classical game theory have served as effective limits to the adequacy of its application in different real-life contexts. First, the players in real-life "games" are usually not limited in their communication during the decision process that leads to their choices. The traditional game theory is not adequate as a model of phenomena where limitations on communication are not enforced. Second, the set of options for people "playing games" in real life includes the possibility of *constructing new action strategies,* which can usually include the choice of *no action* under the given circumstances, or of moving away from the situation that requires action. The games in real life are constructed (and reconstructed) in all of their aspects—the set of strategies, payoffs, conditions of decision making, rules of acting, recruitment of arbiters, and so on—all of which can be reorganized. In other terms, games in real life are embedded in processes of change and development (psychological, social, cultural) and are thus open-ended, whereas the formal models of any kind of game theory are necessarily closed and therefore always of limited rather than universal applicability (see 3.7.1).

Some contemporary developments in game theory have moved the formalization efforts closer to fitting real-life problems completely. Not surprisingly, efforts of this kind have mostly taken place in conjunction with applied problems of conflict resolution in politics and industrial relations (e.g., Bennett & Dando, 1979; Fraser & Hipel, 1979; Howard, 1971; Kuhn, Hipel, & Fraser, 1983). Two extensions of the traditional game theory are noteworthy—the metagame and hypergame theories.

3.7.8.2   The Metagame Theory.   The metagame theory, advanced particularly by Nigel Howard (1971, 1974), takes its beginning in Von Neumann and Morgenstern's (1944, p. 100) conceptualization of the *minorant* and *majorant* games. The conditions of these games eliminate the constraint of simultaneous independence of the players' actions. In the minorant game, Player 2 acts after gaining knowledge of Player 1's action. In the majorant game, Player 2 has to make a choice before Player 1 acts. The minorant/majorant games introduce temporal reciprocity to the players' actions in the game. The metagame concept involves the notion of metalevel reflections used to guide one's reactions to the other player's actions:

> If G is a game in normal form, and if k is a player in G, the (first-level) metagame KG . . . is the normal-form game that would exist if player k chose his strategy in G in knowledge of the other players' strategies (in G).
>
> Hence, by recursion, the second-level metagame jkG, where j and k are players, is the game in which j chooses his strategy (in kG) in knowledge of the other's strategies (in KG); in terms of strategies in G, it is a game in which j reacts (a) to k's reactions to the actions of the players other than k; (b) to the actions of the players other than j and k. (Howard, 1974, p. 261)

The metagame approach makes its application more suitable to those real-life phenomena which have action/reaction reciprocity at their core. However, it assumes that the outcomes of the players' actions (which, of course, are decided by their partners' previous choices) are stable, even if the information about these outcomes is imperfect (i.e., includes probabilistic information).

As a rule, the game theory has avoided modeling reality where information is incomplete. Gaps in information are an inevitable part of the reality. These gaps usually get interpreted in game theory as an indication of *imperfect rather than incomplete* information. Incompleteness is theoretically deemphasized by the assumption that the information is, in principle, complete, although it may be imperfect (Harsanyi, 1982, p. 215). Avoiding the fact that information is incomplete may be a crucial feature of both the traditional and metagame theories in that it reduces their usefulness as formal systems in modeling processes of development. Development necessarily involves incomplete information about the outcomes of different events that occur as it proceeds. A game-theoretical formal system that can be assumed to fit developmental phenomena has to take the open-endedness into account. Hypergames have features that seem to satisfy this requirement better than other game types that have been discussed thus far.

3.7.8.3   Hypergames and the Requirements for Game Theories That Would Be Adequate for Developmental Phenomena.   Hypergames are games where one or more players are not fully aware of the nature of the game situation. This unawareness may include lack of knowledge of the consequences of their own and other players' different choices. The players may have an inaccurate understanding of the preferences of others or may lack full and correct information on the range of options available to them and to other players. Furthermore, they may be unaware of the identities of all the players involved in the game (Fraser & Hipel, 1979, p. 811).

The existing few efforts to analyze complex phenomena have concentrated on the understanding of the process of decision making in political or military situations (Bennett & Dando, 1979; Berresford & Dando, 1978; Fraser & Hipel, 1979; Kuhn, Hipel, & Fraser, 1983). Usually, these applications cover a series of events within a specified time frame, rather than conceptualize event sequences over a longer time period. An example of the limited time frame of hypergame modeling is the study of the fall of France to Germany in 1940 (Bennett & Dando, 1979). It covered events that led to the decision to have the German troops attack via a route (in the Ardennes) that the Allied leadership had discounted as an option. The hypergame modeling of that short period in the history of World War II provided *emphasis on the difference* in the perception of the situation by the two sides. However, the hypergame model covered only the static rationale that led to the outcome (choice of an attack route); it did not provide a dynamic analysis of the process by which that outcome was reached. In this sense, the hypergame theory in its present form is not applicable directly as a model of developmental phenomena. Although its premises include the highly relevant feature of incomplete information about the game, it excludes some aspects that are relevant for capturing development. Hypergame theory still assumes that the players' options are stable, rather than emerging or disappearing. It likewise excludes the fact that the whole payoff matrix can be in flux, so that its stable state cannot be determined.

What, then, are the conditions under which a game-theoretic formal model can be considered to fit the developmental nature of phenomena? First, it should share the assumption of incomplete knowledge by the participants with the hypergame theory. Beyond that, it should emphasize the context-bound nature of the strategies used. It also should allow the conceptual restructuring of the whole game *at each action* of a player. Every move by a player, whether choosing an already existing action option, refusing to act (which is included with the set of existing options), or making up a new option, restructures the whole game. *The game is thus constructed by the participants rather than played as provided for the players.* Game-theoretic endeavors that incorporate these issues seem to be absent in that branch of mathematics at the present time, although the issues of dynamic game theory have captured the attention of mathematicians (e.g., Basar & Oldser, 1982). A developmentally relevant game theory may integrate the irreversibility of developmental processes (see 3.7.9) with the notion of the constructive role of the agents who create themselves in their transaction with the environment.

3.7.9 Modeling Nonequilibrium-Based Changes of Form

Among the physical sciences, the field of nonequilibrium thermodynamics has been closest to the study of developmental phenomena in nature. That domain of physics and chemistry deals at the present time with problems of how quantitative fluctuations in the system give rise to qualitatively new structures of the phenomena. The theoretical interest concentrates on how to model such qualitative change stemming from fluctuations. This task is diametrically opposite to the modeling efforts in the social sciences, which have traditionally depended on believing in the *law of large numbers.* In fact, the emergence of new structures as a result of disequilibration is an issue that the traditional statistical worldview cannot explain because of its emphasis on averaging as a means to the end of obtaining "true" information (cf. Valsiner, 1984b). The "order-through-fluctuation" approach *depends on the breakdown of the law of large numbers. During the emergence of a new form, the fluctuations that take place far from the average of the system are instrumental in the qualitative transition* (Nicolis & Prigogine, 1977, p. 9). For Quetelet's "social physics," the average served as an ideal toward which all phenomena strive. From the standpoint of the order-through-fluctuation school of thought, the development of a system due to far-from-average fluctuations constitutes the nature of the system.

The other crucial feature by which contemporary thermodynamics has enriched science is the emphasis on the time dimension. The *irreversible* nature of thermodynamic changes under conditions that are far from equilibrium should make clear the obvious aspect of all developing phenomena—*all developmental processes take place in irreversible time.* Shotter has pointed to a lesson that scientists who study development should learn from contemporary thermodynamics:

> . . . organic structures (processes) only exist (live) in a state of exchange with their surroundings—they are "rooted" in them. And in the course of such exchanges, they transform themselves from simple individuals into richly structured ones—without having to wait, so to speak, to be "switched on" to act once the "last part" is in its place. They live and grow as individuals from the moment of their "birth." They grow in such a way that their "parts" at any one

moment owe, not just their character, but their very existence both to one an-other, *and* to what the "parts" of the system were at some earlier moment in time—that is, if it is legitimate at all to call the different regions in each phase of a temporarily evolving process its "parts," for there is never a moment at which they cease their growth. Thus they are always in the process of becoming *other than* what at any moment they already are. Their growth is an essential and irreducible aspect of nature; it cannot be partialled out and "added in" later, when convenient. Temporal processes cannot be made up from parts themselves devoid of temporality. Truly temporal processes are *continuous* or *indivisible* in the sense that, the very process of differentiating them into phases of *before* and *after* serves, not to separate them into a "patchwork of disjoined parts" . . . but . . . to relate their phases of aspects of the same dynamic unity. It is a unity which is perceived as a unity, and not in spite of its novelty in every moment, but because of it; for while clearly changing in one sense, like a swirl or eddy in a stream, it remains recognizable in another sense as continually the same. (Re-produced with permission from Shotter, 1983, p. 21)

The time dimension, which has been of little relevance in classical physics, becomes an integral part of dynamic processes studied in contemporary physics and chemistry. This change requires theoretical rethinking of the concept of "sameness" (as is attempted by Shotter in the quote above), and the development of new formalisms to capture the dynamic aspects of thermodynamic change.

The kinds of formal models that are used by investigators who apply the order-through-fluctuation theoretical framework to social science stem from the traditions of thermodynamics that use different kinds of equations to de-scribe the laws inherent in the phenomena. The kinds of equations used are nonlinear in nature. In a nonlinear system, the whole system is not given by the simple sum of its parts. The nonlinear character of equations used in research that is based on the philosophy of nonequilibrium thermodynamics is thus, in principle, suitable for solving the historically long-ranging conflict in psychol-ogy between the investigators who reduce the phenomena to their elementary constituents, and others who follow the gestalt-psychology-based ideas of the nature of psychological phenomena (see 2.4).

Different formalisms used in the paradigm of dissipative structures are not always connected with one another (see Jantsch, 1980, for an effort of unifica-tion). Thus, applications of the disequilibration paradigm to different empiri-cal domains in the biological and social sciences may include formal descriptions that need not resemble one another, although they all may be built on the idea of disequilibration as the process that creates novel structures.

In the social sciences, the efforts to model economic and social systems like those of urban areas (Allen, 1981, 1982; Allen & Sanglier, 1980), or eco-nomic analysis (Berry & Andresen, 1982), have emerged in the framework of contemporary disequilibrium thermodynamics. Urban units (towns, cities) il-lustrate the kinds of problems that dissipative structure modeling can afford. The emergence, development, and maintenance of a town are part of a process within which the input and output flows (e.g., food, building materials, and capital brought into the town, and waste, products, and so on, brought out of the town) between the town and its surroundings are of decisive character. The interdependence of these input/output flows illustrates how the developing town is treated as being an open system. Among the different formal systems with claims to capturing laws of development that have been overviewed in this chapter, only the disequilibration approach treats its objects of investigation consistently as open systems.

The input–output flow in the town is a quantifiable process that leads to qualitative outcomes in the form of the structural development of the town. A step-by-step illustration of the development of a town can be easily constructed. An entrepreneur with capital (input flow) constructs a road through a forest. Once that road is completed, the forest will never be the same—its structure is irreversibly altered by the road. The completion of the road makes it possible for another businessman to build a fuel station somewhere along the road, which again leads to irreversible alteration of the existing structure. However, the decision to build the station may depend on the flow of drivers along the new road. If the number of drivers is sufficiently high, the construction of the station is economically profitable. The personnel of the station may decide to build houses nearby, and in conjunction with their residence there, a need for shops emerges. Once a shopping center is constructed, the people living in the locality may provide profitable labor for an industry to set up a plant nearby. After many qualitative changes in the locality, a small town emerges, which may become a bigger town, and so on. However, if the services/products that the people in the town provide/produce (i.e., the output flow) become noncompetitive in the outside markets, the companies that have set up their plants in the town may decide to close them, introducing another new (regressive) development into the structure of the system. Allen's (1982) simulation of the development of the urban system formalizes exactly such processes of growth and regression—starting from the formal equations, it is possible after every iterative step to determine the particular structure of the urban system, and to observe dramatic (catastrophic) changes wrought by the quantitative changes in the exchange of the urban system with its wider environment.

The efforts to model dynamic processes, treating them as leading to a new order through fluctuations, has also slowly entered psychology (Kugler, Turvey, & Shaw, 1982). The empirical domain in which formal modeling of this kind has occurred has been the area of motor functioning and motor development (e.g., Kelso, Holt, Rubin, & Kugler, 1981; Kugler, Kelso, & Turvey, 1982). The disequilibration approach to modeling developmental phenomena is also unique among the formalisms described in this chapter, in its acceptance of the systemic version of causality (see 2.7). The factors that instigate the system's development involve a multiplicity of cycles or loops between its parts. These cyclic relations lead to development of a system that is dependent on its exchange with the environment. The use of "morphogenetic causal loop models" (see Maruyama, 1982) makes this framework more suitable for the study of developmental phenomena than is afforded by other formal systems that either reject systemic causality or avoid the issue of causality.

Disequilibration-based formal models, if applied in developmental psychology, will have a difficulty similar to that which emerges in the application of L-systems. If, in the case of L-systems, the difficulty was related to the specificity of the nature of the suitable objects of modeling (multipart structures that can be directly represented by a topographic map), then, in the present case, problems emerge on the opposite side of high generality of the basic ideas behind the equations that fit the phenomena. For example, the development of a toddler's acting within his or her environment includes both qualitative change and some quantitative aspect (e.g., frequency or time spent in a certain activity) that could be modeled through such equations. However, the basic parameters by which the general input–output exchange relationships of the toddler (as the system) can be conceptualized leave a wide range of open possibilities for the modeling-oriented child psychologist, only some of which may be adequate as far as the reality of children's action development is concerned.

3.7.10 Possibilities and Limitations of Formal Models of Development

This chapter seeks to show that borrowing formal descriptive systems from mathematics for developmental psychology is a complicated enterprise of fitting the nature of formal systems with the nature of developmental phenomena. Given the structured nature of developing children and their environments, currently widespread quantitative strategies for deriving data from the original phenomena are quite inappropriate. Furthermore, different currently existing branches of qualitative mathematics tend to be specific to the domains in conjunction with which they have emerged (e.g., L-systems, nonequilibrium thermodynamic formalisms, and so on). Developmental sciences need their own kind of mathematics that starts from the essentials of development (e.g., its open-systems nature, and time dependency) at its axioms, and constructs particular formal models for developmental processes *per se*. The mathematics used in developmental psychology must fit the developmental phenomena, and not the other way around.

Mathematics is essentially a conglomerate of different kinds of philosophies that are turned into formal systems within which statements can be deductively proven. However, the axioms these systems use are often selected on some *ad hoc* basis stemming from the psychology of the particular mathematician as a philosopher. It is exactly in the realm of these axioms where the usefulness (or principal uselessness) of a mathematical system for the purposes of a scientific discipline is determined. Once the axioms of a mathematical domain fit the basic characteristics of the phenomena under study, then that particular mathematical system may be valuable for furthering our understanding of the phenomena. Likewise, if there is no fit between the two, or if there is a basic discrepancy between the characteristics of the phenomena and the axioms of the mathematical system, then the application of that mathematical formalism is likely to lead only to an illusion of greater precision, or the "Type III error" described by Mitroff and Featheringham (1974).

Developmental psychology has been particularly ill-served by the mismatch between the phenomena of development and efforts to make the study of child psychology more mathematical, in the mistaken belief that this will lead to a more scientific psychology. Usually, the mathematical tools that have filtered into developmental psychology have been outgrowths from linear statistical models that originated in the mathematics of the last century. The linear model itself is ill-suited for psychological phenomena (see Thorngate, 1986).

Unfortunately, the alternative mathematical approaches that could be of value in developmental psychology are either absent or insufficiently developed. They are often deployed in the service of very specific tasks (mostly within developmental biology) and the design and construction of computer systems that can learn new information. The systems that have been briefly examined here illustrate the gap between developmental thinking and existing mathematics. This gap is not surprising; developmental questions have rarely been posed in different sciences. In this sense, biology is not much better off than psychology. Curiously, it is in the framework of contemporary physics and chemistry that the need for adequate formal descriptions of qualitative (structural) change has emerged.

Of the different formal systems considered, none was found to fit the needs of developmental psychology directly. Nonequilibrium thermodynamics is closest to capturing the general nature of development, but its actual use in developmental psychology is complicated because of the high fluidity of the structures observable in the empirical research on children. The mixing of developmental and nondevelopmental approaches in catastrophe theory renders it of doubtful value—despite the fact that it originated in an attempt to solve the basic developmental problem of epigenetic canalization. The static assumptions involved in most versions of game theory were also found to be unpromising, with the possible exception of the hypergame theory. The latter, however, is a relatively new line of theorizing within game theory, and has so far not been applied to the study of developmental phenomena. The Lindenmayer systems were developed for the modeling of a specific developmental issue (growth of filament structures in botany) and they are difficult to apply to more heterogeneously structured phenomena. Learning automation theory deals with modeling of complex organismic learning, but its assumptions of the environmental structure of the learning automations are much too simplified to fit the reality of ontogeny in their present form. Finally, Chomsky's widely known philosophy of generative grammar captures the important issue of what the formal models of development should allow (i.e., the generation of all possible cases of the class of phenomena), but fails to capture the context-sensitive open-systems nature not only of psychological but also of linguistic phenomena.

3.8   FRAMES OF REFERENCE IN PSYCHOLOGY

The basic cultural–cognitive axioms that have shaped human thought and the science of psychology have created a situation where very few empirically oriented investigators study developmental processes. Indeed, even fewer psychologists have tried to deal with the theoretical issues of development. The purpose of this section is to analyze those attempts at theoretical explanation of development that have been made and that serve as the historical predecessors of the present theory.

Any theoretical or empirical stance in developmental psychology is embedded in a reference frame of thought, which in turn comes from investigators' cultural backgrounds. A reference frame guides investigators' thinking toward some (rather than other) theoretical and empirical research issues and strategies. Different studies of child development have been conducted within different reference frames. Very often, the difference of these frames makes it impossible to relate different studies or makes certain kinds of data irrelevant for some theories.

The reference frames studied here are: (a) intraindividual, (b) interindividual, (c) individual–ecological, and (d) individual–socioecological.

3.8.1   The Intraindividual Frame of Reference

This reference frame treats all issues of an individual's psychological organization as results of some processes (or their interaction) *within* the individual person. The majority of personality theories are phrased within the intraindividual reference frame. As an example, consider Freud's reconstruction of personality using the concepts of id, ego, and superego. All of these components of personality are located within the person, and their functional relationships determine how the person exists as a personality. The personality is decontextualized and is explained fully in terms of its intrinsic organization.

In developmental psychology, any theoretical approach that explains development by reference to either elementaristic traits or systemic mechanisms that are supposed to locate strictly inside the organism uses the intraindividual reference frame. Very often, psychologists who use this reference frame model their thinking along the lines of traditional genetics; they posit the existence of psychological analogs of genes that are supposed to cause temporal unfolding of predetermined developmental sequences of phenomena. For example, the widespread acceptance of Piaget's stage-account of cognitive development without a simultaneous emphasis on his theory of equilibration is built on such predeterministic ideology. Children are considered to progress through the predetermined sequence of stages *because* that is believed to be the normative sequence of development. Tautological explanations (e.g., "John, who is 14 years old, can use formal operations *because* he is at the formal-operational stage") are rampant in such use of Piaget's stage-account.

The stage is treated as a concept that supposedly explains the phenomena described by it. Such black-box explanations (see Bateson, 1972, pp. 39–40) serve the function of stopping researchers from accomplishing the task of disentangling the contents of the black box.

Invariably, all maturational accounts of individual organisms' development make use of the intraindividual frame of reference. The use of that framework may be adequate in some domains of developmental biology (e.g., explanation of metamorphosis in insects), but its extension to other species whose ontogenetic existence depends more evenly on both genetic and environmental factors can be unwarranted. Even in modern genetics, a number of issues (e.g., the principles of the formation of the tertial structure of protein; see Stent, 1981) cannot be explained by straightforward pointing to its genetic code as its intrinsic cause. The ideas of probabilistic epigenesis (Gottlieb, 1976), which constitute an interactive perspective on development, are gradually becoming more widely acceptable in developmental biology. The intraindividual frame of reference is of limited use in the explanation of development, because development is a central characteristic of open systems—the definition of which involves an emphasis on organism–environment relationships. To explain open-systems phenomena by attributing causality to the system and failing to mention interdependence with the environment equals eliminating the open-systems nature of the phenomena.

3.8.2 The Interindividual Frame of Reference

This frame of reference is by far the most widely used in psychology at large. It involves comparison of an individual organism (or samples of organisms) with other individuals (samples), in order to determine the standing of these subjects relative to one another. For example, any comparison of two (or more) persons with one another, resulting in statements like "Jimmy is better than Johnny and Mary in reading and writing, but worse than the other kids in arithmetic," involves thinking within the interindividual frame of reference. A quick introspective scanning of our everyday activities and thinking may reveal that this frame of reference is very often used, particularly on occasions where interindividual competition is required and emphasized. An emphasis on competition between individuals necessarily results in taking into account differences between those individuals. In that emphasis, the interindividual frame of reference differs cardinally from the intraindividual one, which disregards interindividual variability. In contrast, the interindividual frame of reference promotes the search for differences between individuals in the causal mechanisms underlying their acting and thinking, or at least in the quantitatively variable outcomes produced by qualitatively similar mechanisms that are shared by individuals in a population.

The interindividual reference frame is also used to compare groups of persons. In this case, groups (samples) serve as the basis for reconstructing the modal or average individual—the prototype for the whole sample (Valsiner, 1984b). For example, a comparison of two samples of subjects—e.g., boys and girls—on some measure that leads to a statement about a difference (or lack of it) between the samples uses this frame of reference. In psychological research literature, we often come across statements like "The experimental group was *found to do better* than the control group" in an experiment. In these comparisons, both samples—boys and girls; the experimental group and the control group—are dealt with as if they are individuals who are being compared with each other. This is similar to a comparison between Johnny and Jimmy, where a parent of one of them may state, "Jimmy does better than Johnny in X, Y, or Z."

In nondevelopmental psychology, the interindividual frame of reference has guided the *normative* ["populometric" or "parametric," as these terms were used in Raymond B. Cattell (1944)] tradition of psychological measurement. In that reference frame, the environmental context in which individuals function is excluded from consideration as a part of the particular issue. This feature of the interindividual frame is similar to the intraindividual reference frame: Both explain their phenomena without including their context in the explanation. For example, finding out that Jimmy's IQ score is 115 can lead a psychologist to compare it with the average for a population (100), and to make relative statements such as that "Jimmy has above-average IQ." However, Jimmy's particular environmental context in the process of testing his IQ—the test materials, Jimmy's conceptualization of the tasks involved, his motivation to pass the test at the level of his maximum performance at the testing time, and so on—all these aspects are fully and irreversibly eliminated from the psychologist's information base about Jimmy's intelligence. The interindividual frame of reference leads to decontextualized knowledge, which in turn leads to attribution-based explanation of the psychological phenomena in question (see Valsiner, 1984a, for further analysis of that aspect). As outlined in Chapter 2, psychology's theoretical mainstream emphasizes decontextualization of individual psychological phenomena. From that perspective, the use of the interindividual frame of reference is very natural. However, its effect on the advancement of psychological knowledge may divert psychologists from theoretical explanations of the issues that the empirical data represent. This danger was nicely described by Cattell (1944, p. 300):

> If individuals can be given a score simply from putting them in rank order—and people can be put in rank order for anything under the sun—there is very little incentive to find the exact nature of the thing with respect to which they are being put in rank order. The facility with which IQ or percentile scores can be used in educational and placement problems has apparently obscured interest, for example, in the problem of the nature of intelligence at different age levels . . . while the readiness with which interests can be ranked . . . seems to have made it superfluous to ask "What is interest?"

The use of the interindividual reference frame in developmental psychology has led the discipline away from the study of developmental processes (see McCall, 1977). This frame of reference is the one in which the use of statistical methods and their epistemological basis fits in most with the scientific goals of the discipline. The emphasis on the use of statistical methods leads developmental investigators *de facto* into the realm of nondevelopmental empirical questions. The use of correlational techniques applied to longitudinal data from some sample of developing organisms is aimed at detecting interage *stability* in the *relative standing* of the individuals within the sample, and does not reveal any information about either the individuals' development or the development of the sample as a group. McCall has provided an illuminating figurative description of this problem:

> Relying solely on an individual difference approach to establish the validity of infant tests or to learn about mental development is rather like concentrating on predicting a 10-foot height difference in mature giant sequoia trees from the size of seedlings while completely ignoring the issue of how all the trees eventually grow to be over 300 feet tall. (McCall, 1977, p. 338)

Both the intraindividual and interindividual reference frames, aided by the use of statistical methods, are unfit for the tasks of developmental psychology because of their axiomatic background of decontextualization of phenomena. The interindividual reference frame cannot capture the generative and creative aspects of development. *Generativity* (as it is defined by Sandor Brent) implies that "each structure in a developmental series is not merely the predecessor in time but is an active agent in the process by which its successors come into being" (Brent, 1984, p. 156). An interindividual comparison of children at a certain developmental level does not afford explanation of how the given psychological phenomenon that a particular child demonstrates has developed from (and with the help of) its predecessors. A teacher who compares Johnny with other children in the class and labels him as "the most difficult child in the class" has shed no light on the developmental question of how Johnny has developed to be difficult.

In a similar vein, the interindividual reference frame is unsuitable for explaining the *creativity* of development. Brent (1984, p. 156) defines creativity as the process "by which new forms and new information can be acquired or produced," which "integrate with a previously existing generative process." Continuing our hypothetical example, the teacher who has labeled Johnny difficult on the grounds of comparing him with other children in the class has no way of explaining how Johnny might in the future either become a delinquent, or improve and cease to be difficult. From interindividual comparisons, no *individual* prediction that is based on explanatory theories dealing with the functioning of the individual can follow (see Allport, 1942). The interindividual frame of reference may attempt to predict the constancy of the relative positioning of individuals in a sample over time, but is insensitive to the functioning of a causal system that generates change in these relative positions of the individual in the group.

3.8.3 The Individual–Ecological Frame of Reference

The individual–ecological frame of reference considers an individual person (or a social group—a "collective" individual) as it acts on its environment to solve some problem, created at the given time by the given structure of the environment and by the individual's goals. The person's (or group's) actions are viewed in the context of problem-solving situations that emerge in interaction with the environment. Questions asked about these actions concentrate on the issue of *how* (in what ways) a person solves the given problem. Whether he or she is better or worse at that than other persons are is unimportant.

The individual–ecological reference frame includes the context of action in its sphere of study, making that frame of reference suitable for developmental research. The individual–ecological reference frame is most notably present in Piaget's developmental theory. It is also evident in a number of other research directions of microgenetic kinds (Anzai & Simon, 1979; Duncker, 1945; Köhler, 1925; Werner, 1937, 1957). This frame of reference emphasizes the individual's confrontation with life tasks through which individuals become participants in their own development (see Lerner & Busch-Rossnagel, 1981). However, the individual–ecological frame excludes the purposeful actions of other organisms around the person, who may set up task situations with different socially defined end goals in mind. To take the social and purposeful organization of individuals' task environments into account, an additional frame of reference is outlined.

3.8.4 The Individual–Socioecological Frame of Reference

The individual–socioecological frame of reference differs from the individual–ecological frame because of the presence of *assistance from another individual* (or individuals, groups, etc.) in the process of individual–environment transaction. Within this reference frame, an individual's actions and thinking to solve a problem that has emerged in the person–environment transaction is not a solitary, but a social event. A person who is confronted with a problem may ask for help from someone else, who may be more experienced in solving that kind of problem. For example, for quite a long time in ontogeny, a child depends on others for help in acquiring culturally appropriate and successful ways of solving problems in his or her world. Help can also be sought from another person who has less experience with the given problem, but who, by being related to the problem solver, can be used as a "social other" whose presence helps the problem solver to deal with the problem. An example of the latter case is a young mother of a 2-year-old child, whose husband has deserted her. The child, and the mother's feeling of responsibility toward the child, may help her to cope with the psychologically traumatic event of desertion.

In any species where parent–offspring contact is relatively long and where the adult organisms carry out the task of teaching (explicitly, or by example) their young some important survival skills, the application of the individual–socioecological frame of reference in psychological research is warranted. In developmental psychology, the use of that reference frame is exemplified by Vygotsky's theoretical contributions to the discipline. Not only does child development take place within structured task settings that the child masters in action and thinking, but these settings are purposefully set up to aid the child in the process of development and to offer guidance toward becoming an adult who has, in the course of growing up within a culture, constructed an internalized knowledge base that is sufficient for life within that (and perhaps some other) culture.

3.8.5   Independence and Mixing of Reference Frames in Psychology

Admittedly, the four reference frames described above occur in an unevenly distributed fashion across different domains of psychology. Some of these reference frames are more usual in some areas than in others. For example, the intraindividual reference frame is usually applied in psychodynamically oriented settings of research and clinical practice, where the goal is to treat the psychological issues of individual clients. The interindividual reference system is that which the majority of psychologists of quantitative inclination continue to use. It is the framework most suited for solving applied problems that involve the selection, relatively quickly and on a large scale if necessary, of some individuals from a population for a particular task, without much worry about the causality of the phenomena used in the interindividual comparisons. Only some areas in psychology—particularly in the cognitive domain—have adopted the individual–ecological reference frame. The individual–socioecological frame of reference is rare in contemporary psychology, although the renewed interest in Vygotsky's psychological heritage may perhaps lead more investigators to adopt it. It is adequate for many problems in developmental psychology, where psychological phenomena undergo changes that are guided by "social others." For example, a psychological analysis of children's accidents and their prevention may benefit from the latter reference frame (Gärling & Valsiner, 1985).

In accordance with the uneven presence of these reference frames in psychological research traditions, methods of inductive inference in psychology have been invented, mostly to fit the interindividual frame. Within this frame, statistical methodology has been put to extensive use—sometimes up to the point where its use becomes a goal in itself for some psychologists' research games! The application of statistical methodology in research conducted within the intraindividual reference frame is rare but is possible (see A. L. Baldwin, 1940, 1942, 1946; Kelly, 1995). In contrast, the two ecologically oriented reference frames exclude the use of traditional statistical methodology from the research process because their basic assumptions and those of the statistical worldview do not match one another. (See 3.7 for a discussion of existing formal methods of modeling the development of systems.)

It is necessary to stress here that the actual adoption of one of the four reference systems depends on the psychologist's general perspective. The scientific value of adopting any of the four is determined by the adequacy of the reference frame to the phenomena under study and the investigator's goals. There is always the possibility that any of the four frames of reference can be combined with others. In psychology, the interindividual and intraindividual reference frames have traditionally been linked together. The majority of empirical studies in psychology are conducted within the interindividual frame of reference but are interpreted within the intraindividual frame. This switching of frames is often unwarranted (see Valsiner, 1986). Likewise, makers of the computerized control systems not only bear in mind the task that the new program must perform, but also depend heavily on the structure of the hardware (intraindividual reference frame) and, in addition, consider the new program's chances of success within the interindividual reference frame of the competitive marketplace. In a similar vein, parents of children, who teach the children new skills (which the children develop within their individual–socioecological reference frameworks), are eager to find out from a psychologist "how my child is doing" as compared with other children in the given age group. The parents also hope that the knowledge and skills that they have helped their children to develop will be used by the children individually in situations where parental presence and guidance are not available (within individual–ecological contexts). The education of children for facing different life situations in their future illustrates the combination of the individual–socioecological and individual–ecological frames.

The possibility of combining the four reference frames does not make it desirable for psychologists to mix them in with their research and practice. Although every psychological phenomenon can be simultaneously considered within each of these frames, different research goals of psychologists may make it necessary to consider them separately. A conscious and explicit decision by a psychologist not to use a particular frame of reference on theoretical grounds (despite the fact that its use is possible in practice) may help the psychologist to reach particular scientific goals. The four frames of reference, although combinable, provide science with distinctly different kinds of knowledge, each of which may have its place somewhere in the knowledge structure of psychology.

The two ecological reference frames are at the center of attention of the research program of the studies of children's action development that is described in this book. Other developmental theories have used these ecological reference frames in the past. The theoretical perspective represented in this book is an attempt to integrate a few of the older, well-known, but often incompletely understood, theories in psychology.

3.9   FORMAL MODELS AND STUDY OF PROCESSES OF EMERGENCE

Methodological imperatives of traditional psychology do not fit the goals of making sense of development, which is the process of emergence (Lightfoot & Folds-Bennett, 1992). Therefore, the developmental perspective in psychology becomes a desirable methodological norm. It entails the study of the process of *movement from "chaotic"* (or "fluid," and hence categorically difficult to describe) *phenomena to the emergence of clear forms* (Basov, 1991).

In this focus, the study of emergence entails consideration of a process of differentiation, de-differentiation, and re-differentiation of structures. A schematic outline of this process is given in Figure 3.3.

Figure 3.3 describes a time sequence of differentiation and de-differentiation (move from time units 1–9 to 10–18) and re-differentiation (move on to time units 20–31) of a hypothetical structure. It is important to stress that the developmental process takes place exactly in that phase of the observable process which is most difficult to observe (i.e., the interobserver agreement while observing tends toward 0%, rather than toward 100%, which may be the case both before and after the crucial de- and re-differentiation process).

The difficulty with developmental analyses is that the real action of development takes place at times and in ways that are difficult to observe or invade. Figure 3.4 magnifies the de-differentiation phase of Figure 3.3, on which a researcher's efforts are graphically superimposed.

The investigator may try to focus on some *seemingly organized part* of the de-differentiated "mess" (e.g., indicated by A). However, the fact that this location seems better organized than the rest of the phenomenon does not necessarily mean that its role in the actual differentiation process is relevant. This may become empirically provable if the researcher hypothesizes that, if at time unit 1 an intervention occurred at A, then there will be a consequent emergence of *any* of the forms {B, C, D, and possibly a totally novel form, here denoted by ?} and not some other forms that can be specified in terms of the opposites of the expected ones {non-B, non-C, non-D, non-?}. This claim is consistent with the bounded indeterminacy notion outlined in this book. The set of {B, C, D, ?} constitutes the range of possible outcomes of the intervention (A), but which one of the items of that set actually emerges is not predictable. Nevertheless, the general direction of the process is predictable; hence, the set of opposites {non-B, non-C, non-D, non-?} is predicted *not* to emerge when A takes place.

The form ? (and its opposite, non-?) in the explications here denotes the possible openness of the developmental process—a novel form that has never been observed in a *similar* version before, *can* emerge. Such forms could not be predicted by the researcher's previous understanding, yet that novel form does not undermine that understanding. The impossibility of predicting such

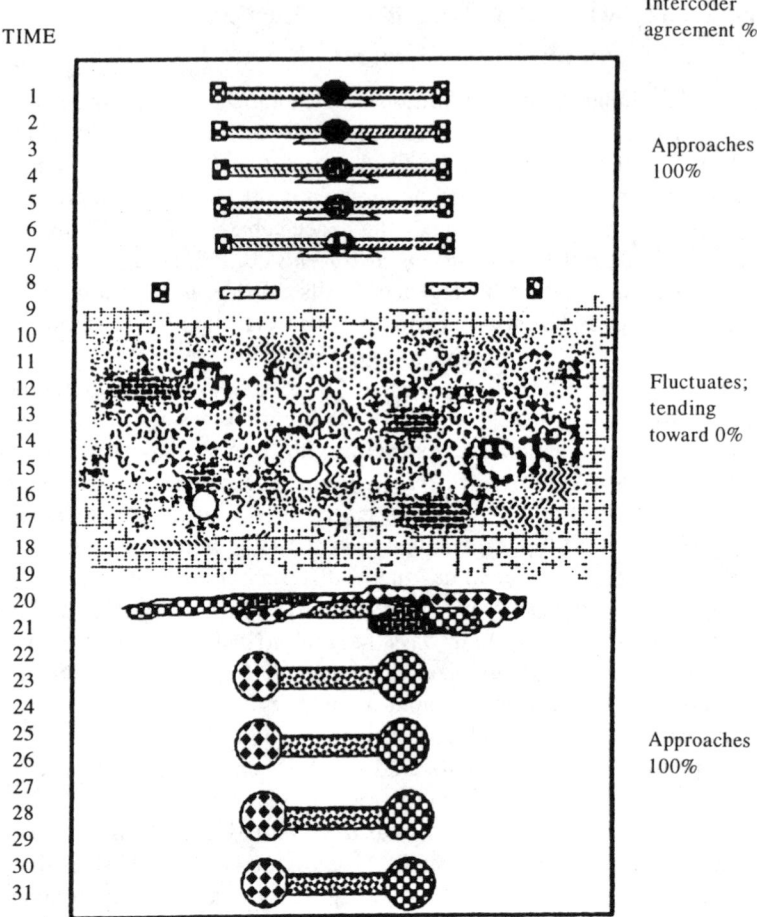

FIGURE 3.3.   Development depicted (and detected) as a process of differentiation, de-differentiation, and re-differentiation.

forms is already present in the biophysical world of irreversible chemical reactions (as described in 3.7.9).

3.9.1   What Kinds of Hypotheses Can Be Set When Studying Emergence?

The explication of formal models and methods-construction strategies in this chapter leads to the question of *discourse about hypotheses* that are tested in empirical research. It must be emphasized that psychologists' ordinary talk about appropriate hypotheses belongs to the realm of social discourse, rather than to scientific linkage of the deductive and inductive sides of the research.

TIME

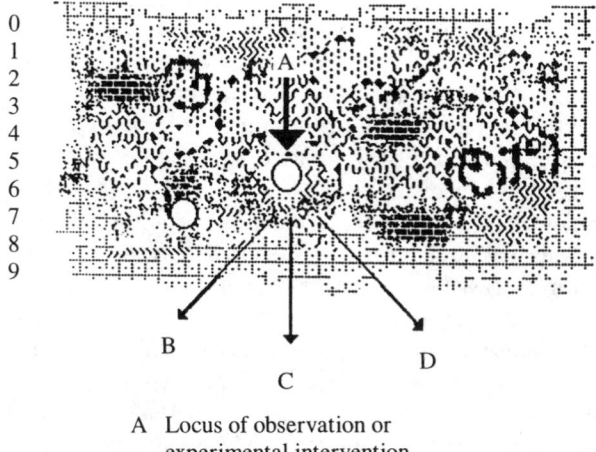

A   Locus of observation or
    experimental intervention

B ⎫
C ⎬— Set of expected emergent forms
D ⎭

FIGURE 3.4.   A microgenetic example of the study of the developmental process.

Through the setting of hypotheses, and their actual testing, the grounds for abductive inference are set up.

This claim, however, leads to two interesting and crucial points. The first is the social-discursive nature of psychologists' talk about hypotheses. The dominance of the use of the interindividual frame of reference in nondevelopmental psychology has led to the social (rather than substantive) expectation that hypotheses are to be set up in terms of some comparison of samples—directly, or under some experimental intervention conditions. Surely this practice is inapplicable for the study of development within the individual–socioecological reference frame. It is also inappropriate for the application of schemes of systemic causality. The consensually accepted talk of psychologists about the hypotheses is therefore an example of metascientific social canalization of research practices (see Chapter 2). Thus, a reconciliatory talk usually occurs when the issue of "hypothesis-testing" versus "hypothesis-generating" kinds of research is being discussed (Minoura, 1996; Oerter, 1996). It is usually assumed that the latter is open to a variety of ways of looking at the phenomena (while transforming them into data), but the "real" scientific enterprise follows when the generated hypotheses are then subsequently "molded" into "right" testable form (for intersample comparisons). This privileging of one discourse (hypothesis-testing) over the other (hypothesis-generating) is a phenomenon of metascientific discourse. In the actual scientific discourse, hypotheses are generated and tested intermittently. It is another issue whether these hypotheses are made explicit (which is often not the case in empirical psychological work), and *how* the hypotheses of one or another form can be tested. All hypotheses that can be set within the individual–ecological or individual–socioecological reference frames need testing on the basis of individual cases and in ways that recognize the limited indeterminacy of developmental phenomena.

Second, the whole nature of hypothesis "testing" acquires a different flavor, if viewed as a set-up road to abductive inference. No longer is it important to prove that the set hypothesis was empirically right (or that its invented imaginary opposite—the null-hypothesis—was wrong). This kind of proof does not add anything to the deductive line of inference because it does not allow the empirical evidence to correct any aspects of the deductive construction (refer back to Francis Crick's observation on cognitive science, in 3.2). Thus, paradoxically, an imperative that emphasizes the importance of the inductive (empirical) side of psychological research by requiring rigorous testing of preset hypotheses (and clear decisions about their rejection of acceptance) *de facto* supports the projection, via data, of psychologists' general presuppositions onto the phenomena. The empirical evidence is "allowed to say" only that "this is right" or "this is wrong," but it cannot lead to *constructive modifications* of the deductively derived hypotheses. In contrast, the focus on hypothesis testing as an abductive process renders the role of empirical evidence constructively relevant for creating new knowledge. From that position, all set hypotheses will be partially wrong—in the sense that they are *approximate and abstracted schematic representations* of what might be happening in the realm of the phenomena under study. Empirical evidence about their partial "wrongness" allows the investigator to modify these schematic representations and to use them again in the empirical "testing" phase. The hypothesis becomes the central semiotic mediating device in the researcher's abductive knowledge construction. As such, the reconstructed hypothesis necessarily goes "beyond the data" (in an abductive leap), to be further questioned by re-inserting it into the empirical study process. This can be considered the hermeneutic role of the hypothesis: It is constantly being abductively reconstituted, and therefore correcting the specifics of the theoretical (deductive) construction of the knowledge system.

Following the focus on emergence, as outlined above, the kinds of hypotheses that are possible in developmental science take a very different form from those in nondevelopmental psychology. To continue in terms of the example depicted in Figure 3.4, the form could be the following:

Hypothesis: Given the developmental process of the kind observed in time units 0–9, and the theoretical system that proposes intervention in space location A, the emergent forms can be any of the kind {B, C, D, ?}, but cannot be of the kind {not-B, not-C, not-D}.

Criteria of Proof: Emergence of B, C, D, or ?.

Criteria of Disproof: Emergence of any of the opposites of B, C, or D.

Abductive Results:

1. If one of the predefined forms (B, C, or D) emerges, it feeds into modi-
    fication of the estimation of further possible re-emergences of similar
    forms, yet it does not reduce the whole set of possibilities. From here it
    becomes possible to estimate the probabilistic structure of the set (or
    the membership functions of the items, if the full set is considered to be
    a fuzzy set).

2. If a completely novel from (denoted by ?) emerges, then it leads to the
    description and denotation of the form, and is considered a new defined
    item in the set. The set becomes modified: {B, C, D, E [previous ?], and
    ?}. Note that each modification of the set includes the preservation of
    the "dummy" denotation for further openness (?). The presence of such
    denotations is obligatory is a claim about the potential emergence of to-
    tally novel forms is theoretically made.

3. If any of the three disproof-indicating forms {not-B, not-C, not-D}
    emerges, the theoretical system from which the hypothesis was derived
    must be modified.

In this elaboration of hypothesis testing, some very traditional notions are
being woven into the developmental methodology cycle. First, *conditions of fal-
sifiability* (Abductive result 3) of the theoretical system are indicated—not the
system as a whole, but those parts of the system from which the hypothesis was
deduced. Second, it allows consideration of the notion of multilinearity of development—the proof that the hypothesis is accepted in B, or C, or D, or ? actually emerged. Third, it maintains the constructive nature of knowledge, as well
as the openness of the new hypothesis to developmental novelty (via Abductive
result 2). Last (but not least), Abductive result 1 integrates the traditional focus
on estimating probabilities from observed frequencies (obviously a nondevelopmental operation) into the domain of a "landscape" of a possible preference
structure of the set of emerging forms. However, even as the preference structure becomes inductively established—for instance, if the form B becomes observed in 80 percent of the emergences of novel forms—this information is no
more than a probabilistic estimate of the relative occurrence of the members of
the set, while the probability of any new emerging form under similar circumstances is determined by the size of the set {B, C, D, & ?} and provides for
equal probability. It may be here that Gordon Allport's focus on morphogenic
science—treating any concrete phenomenon as lawful—acquires appropriate
substantive context:

A murderer seldom commits more than one murder. Therefore, we cannot reason from his previous behavior that when conditions are thus and so, he will

commit murder. The act is a one-time happening. Although no frequencies are involved, the deed is *determined* and scientifically speaking, lawful. It should then be predictable. (Allport, 1942, p. 158)

In other terms, information accumulated from the past (in the form of frequencies, which may be at some moment relabeled probabilities) are merely orientational, not explanatory, for the study of the emerging new case. The hypothesis notion as constructed here includes such orienting information, but denies its central relevance for the study of emergence.

3.9.2 Methods to Study Emergence

It becomes obvious that the emergence of novel psychological phenomena is embedded in the fuzzy nature of persons' concrete interaction with a context. This general worldview needs to be translated into appropriate methods of empirical analysis (see 1.6.3 on the imperative of integrity of methodology). The first step in this direction is taken by a consistent proliferation of longitudinal research designs (Cairns, Elder, & Costello, 1996). In fact, it is almost a trivial statement to call for longitudinal designs in the study of development, because development becomes available for study only when viewed over time. Again, the takeover of psychology's inferential system by the nondevelopmental worldview, and the inductive logic of statistics, makes repeated calls of this kind necessary.

However, once the longitudinal research design is accepted and put into practice, more problems are created than are solved. The longitudinal approach can be sculpted to take different time spans into account—from life-span studies extending over decades, to the studies of new percepts of tachistoscopically presented pictures in a laboratory. Surely these specifications of the time span allow researchers to address different issues. These different issues are distributed along the lines of microgenetic and ontogenetic research questions.

In the microgenetic case, the process of emergence can be approached through a focus on the specific construction of an answer to the posed problem (Catán, 1986; Saada-Robert, 1994, 1995; Siegler & Crowley, 1991). Any "measurement" of the process of emergence here captures the time-based move from a fuzzy preliminary state of affairs to the emergence of discernible forms. In other words, the microgenetic orientation entails the study of genesis of actuality (*Aktualgenese* was its original name), and has had a venerable tradition in the history of psychology. For example, Vygotsky's "method of double stimulation" (see Valsiner, 1989a, Chapter 3) constituted an effort to directly observe (and trigger) the emergence of novel psychological phenomena.

In a similar vein, contemporary applications of discourse analysis (Edwards & Potter, 1992), protocol analysis of thought processes (Ericsson & Simon, 1993), and analyses of the dialectic and multivoiced nature of the construction of psychological phenomena in dialogue (Markova, 1990, 1993; Smolka, 1993) all lead research practices toward discovering specific cases of emergence of novelty. Different hermeneutics-labeled approaches are of a similar kind. In the hermeneutic process of knowledge construction in researcher ⟷ subject relationships, there may be moments of sudden mutual divergence of communication where the relevant phenomena are discovered (see Hermans, 1991, 1996; Hermans & Hermans-Jansen, 1995; Hermans & Kempen, 1993). The person who takes the role of a subject in the research process is constantly creating novelty on the basis of his or her previous state of relationship with the world. In the process of research, the roles of subject and investigator are constantly in the process of modification, based on their dialogical integration (Markova, 1993).

3.9.3   Units of Analysis

Any method that is utilized for developmental research has to preserve the time as a directional vector in the unit of analysis. The first decision involves extension of the time vector (the duration) that is to be constructed as the basis for a unit. This decision is guided by the basic assumptions → theory → method line on the one hand, and the phenomena → methods line on the other (Figure 1.1).

The second decision entails the extension of the unit to include specific actions by specific persons in the unit. When the individual–socioecological frame of reference is used, inclusion of the regulating efforts of the "social other" is necessary to maintain consistency between the theoretical and empirical sides of the investigation. However, decisions need to be made regarding how such a regulating role is concretely conceptualized. Because the social other can entail a multitude of persons and of culturally organized (semiotically encoded) environmental settings (see analysis of mealtime contexts, in 6.4), the specific "detection lens" of the selected side of such phenomena is to be set up.

In their general form, the units of analysis cover the following:

1. A time sequence (at least in its minimal form, of t1→t2 transition) must be retained within the unit.
2. The relation between the developing person and the environment must be specified as transforming over time.
3. The directions of regulatory actions of the other must be specified—in the context and/or over time.

In formal terms, such a unit is given by a 2×3 table:

t1   a R b1   w R (a R b1)
t2   a R b2   w R (a R b2)

where t is time, a is the developing person, b is the state of the environment, w is the other, and R denotes the relationship. This formal unit includes two relationships in a linked form: (a) that of the person and the environment (a R b) and (b) that of the other *with the relation* of person and environment [w R (a R b)].

To simplify, consider the following example of a transaction involving a mother and child:

t1   The child is reaching toward an object.   Mother: "No!"

t2   The child abandons the effort.   Mother: "Good!"

This example is very close to the three-step units of analysis of dialogical processes suggested by Markova (1990). In her notion of units, a particular opposition between parts in the same whole at time 1 (e.g., "a and non-a") leads to a new form of the previous opposition at time 2 (e.g., "b and non-b"). In the example above, the two relations (child to object; mother to child and object) emerged to be in opposition, which led to a new structure of the whole relationship at time 2.

However, the simplicity of this example is deceiving, because it is built on an *assumption of clearly detectable events* in the flow of ongoing actions (of mother and child). In reality, such clarity may be episodic. Undoubtedly, there exist clear examples of when a child reaches for an object, and the mother stops the activity. But these facts need not be the full story. It is more realistic to assume uncertainty in the phenomena. Thus, the simple example above might be rewritten in the following way:

Time 1: The child is doing something that *might be interpretable* (by the mother, or an observer) as *being about to* reach for an object, yet it is not clear that the child is actually reaching toward the object. The mother *pre-emptively interprets minimal signs* of the child's actions that *might* indicate reaching the object, and says, "No."

Time 2: The child indeed *stops displaying the features of action that could be interpretable* as reaching. The mother *detects the cessation of these minimal signs,* and says, "Good."

This elaboration of the example shows that the units of developmental (in this case, microgenetic) analysis need to consider the present relationship of the actors (a person and a social other) versus the set of possible next states in the relations in the unit. Hence, the formal structure of the unit becomes more complicated:

t1   a R b1   w R (a R b1) and w R {possible a R b2}

t2   a R b2   w R (a R b2) and w R {possible a R b3}

where the symbols remain the same and a set of anticipated immediate future relations *{possible a R b (t + 1)}* is added.

Let us consider a new hypothetical example that is an elaboration of the previous one, but in the direction of greater closeness to relevant everyday reality:

Mother and child (the latter estimated to be 2 to 3 years of age) are walking on a pavement of a busy street in a city, the mother holding the child by the hand. For a moment, the mother releases the child's hand, paying attention to the charms of the street vendor, or the products he is selling. The child wanders toward the road, on which a large bus is approaching at a high speed. The mother abandons the chat with the vendor, rushes after the child, drags him by the arm back from the edge of the pavement, pushes him in the direction of the other side of the pavement (the no-traffic side), and hits his arm. The child toddles toward the entrance of a house. The mother goes after him, catches his ear, and twists it. The child cries.

This narrative description indicates that consideration of the immediate future possibilities in mother–child interaction takes place in real time—and therefore always under some (often extreme) time pressure. The consequences of such consideration may be various; the example here is an extreme case, where such consideration may make the difference between the life or death of the child. Other cases may be less extreme (e.g., the scenario of the child reaching for an object), yet of similar underlying structure.

Let us explicate the *possible* set of anticipated possible future relations (i.e., the w R {possible a R b2} part of the unit). There is no way to have access to the full set of possibilities as the described mother may have actually considered them. However, my goal here is to make explicit the centrality of the component of our analytic unit that relates the perceived present setting with the possible future.

The mother in this example cannot be expected to be a rational decision maker who considers all the possibilities in the set of anticipated future states, relates those to her personal goal-orientations or belief-orientations system (see Valsiner, Branco, & Melo Dantas, 1997), and then decides on the best solution for her action (i.e., maximizing strategy). In critical situations, a satisficing strategy considers a minimal subset of options, under the particular assumed situation definition (e.g., "danger" versus "educational experience"). Thus, let us assume that the full set of anticipated possible future relations in this case can be given by the following (phrased as if these are the mother's intrapsychological explanations):

w R {possible a R b2}:

1. {"My child may be run over by the bus"}
2. {"Seeing the bus rush by may help my child to avoid dangers"}
3. {"My child has the right to learn about the world"}
4. {"My child must not leave my side"}
5. {"How awful!"}
6. {Anything else}

It is easy to see that the five hypothetical constructs for the set of anticipated possible future relations are phrased on the basis of very different backgrounds: emotional generic construction (5), parent's demands (4), child's rights (3), parent's education (2), or fatal danger construction (1). All of those relate the present with the future in terms of possibilities for what might (but, equally, need not) happen with the child (e.g., the rushing bus might indeed pass by the child at a close distance, causing no accident—but *this cannot be preknown at the moment* of the mother's action).

If we now assume that the mother may consider one (or more) of the items in this hypothetical set, it becomes possible to see how the immediate action can be mediated by these items. Let us assume that the mother marks the situation by defining it as "dangerous." In this case, items (1), (4), and (5) of the set— singularly or in combination with one another—would lead to the immediate reaction of intervention (as described in the example). However, if items (2) or (3) flash through the intrapsychological evaluation system of the mother, the intervention need not happen. If that is the case, the accident may occur (the mother may then forever accuse herself for not acting at the right time), or not. In the latter case, the mother may construe the near-accident but nonintervention situation as an "educational experience" for the child. *Both* of these scenarios for the aftermath of the traffic situation event are *post-factum* constructions, from which no reconstruction of the actual psychological mechanisms (of action or nonaction in the situation) is possible. James Mark Baldwin's "positive postulate" for developmental science—that development cannot be *pre*dicted or *post*dicted (see Chapter 4)—is illustrated by this example.

This example also indicates how a whole realm of relevant everyday phenomena—those of accident prevention—can be conceptualized using developmental assumptions and matching units of analysis (see Gärling & Valsiner, 1985). Accidents are classified only as *post-factum* events, but *all* efforts to *prevent* accidents from happening are necessarily actions and ways of thinking that take place *pre-factum*. Therefore, any accident prevention effort—be it microgenetic (as in the example given here) or ontogenetic (e.g., planning educational programs for children, to protect them from having dangerous situations turn into accidents)—necessarily needs a developmental theoretical system and a matching analytic unit.

3.10   SUMMARY: ABDUCTIVE CONSTRUCTION OF SCIENTIFIC KNOWLEDGE

In this chapter, the move from basic assumptions (described in Chapter 2) to the linkage among theory, methods, and the construction of "the data" was outlined. It was demonstrated that science is an abductive process that takes place at the intersection of deductive and inductive reasoning processes. Abductive processes, the invention of appropriate systems of abstract formal analysis of issues, are helpful, if they retain linkage with those aspects of the phenomena that are of interest for the given area of investigation. The latter, in this book, include issues of emergence of novel forms in human actions and reflection, and processes of development in general.

It was demonstrated that there exist different mathematical systems—many of which belong to the domain of qualitative mathematics—that can be used for modeling developing systems. However, the specific nature of human development—reiterative transformation of persons' relation with the environment, and its regulation by other persons—sets up new requirements for formal modeling systems, hypothesis generating and testing, and the construction of specific methods. Traditions of nondevelopmental psychology, especially the kinds of quantification (transformation of nominal-scale data into ratio-scale constructions) that pass the methodological orientation of developmental investigation by, cannot be considered as appropriate for the purposes of the study of development.

4

Theoretical Bases for a Theory of "Bounded Indeterminacy" of Development

The theoretical system that is set forth in this book (and elaborated in Chapter 5) is based on a number of developmental perspectives that have been present in the history of psychology and biology. Any developmental perspective necessarily requires the adoption of either the individual–ecological or individual–socioecological perspective. Hence, the theoretical roots of the present system can be located within the genetic epistemology framework of Jean Piaget and the field-theoretic thinking of Kurt Lewin, both of whom worked within the individual–ecological reference frame. Likewise, the perspective is based on the individual–socioecological frame that led the thinking of James Mark Baldwin, Heinz Werner, and Lev Vygotsky. In developmental biology, the work of Conrad H. Waddington shows similarities with the present perspective.

All these historical linkages are presented in this book as evidence for the historical nature of our construction of understanding. Yet no following of any of the analyzed theoretical systems is claimed—in the sense of declarations of identification. The present theory cannot be labeled "Vygotskian," "Piagetian," "Lewinian," "Wernerian," or "Waddingtonian," yet it attempts to constructively borrow ideas from all of these directions and to set those ideas up in a novel form and in new contexts. Given this focus, only selective coverage of the ideas of particular theorists is given here. An analysis of their full contributions is not attempted, as this has been accomplished elsewhere (e.g., for Baldwin—Valsiner, 1994c; Valsiner & Van der Veer, 1997; for Piaget—Chapman, 1988; for Werner—Langer, 1970; for Vygotsky—Van der Veer & Valsiner, 1991; for Waddington—Gilbert, 1991).

Historically, James Mark Baldwin stands out as the forerunner of both Piaget's genetic epistemology and Vygotsky's cultural–historical approach. Baldwin created an elaborate system of a consistently developmental perspective, much of which has remained out of the focus of the cohorts of researchers who came later.

4.1 JAMES MARK BALDWIN'S EPISTEMOLOGY FOR DEVELOPMENTAL SCIENCE

Baldwin's contribution to the theoretical side of understanding development is based on the natural philosophical and dialectical thought of the 19th century. It antedates Piaget's theoretical system in its emphasis on the active–constructive role of the developing child in his or her environment, and in its use of the concepts of assimilation and accommodation to explain how the development proceeds (Wozniak, 1982). Likewise, Baldwin's emphasis on the dialectical person–society relationships is a forerunner of the dialectical perspective that was later developed by Vygotsky in the framework of the cultural–historical school of thought in psychology.

A number of theoretical points that Baldwin introduced into psychology are of relevance from the perspective of the present theory. These include: (a) an emphasis on organism–environment relationships and on the interactionist perspective in thinking about the evolutionary process; (b) the role of self–other relationships in ontogenetic socialization; and (c) concerns about how to construct research methodology for psychology so that it cannot violate the nature of psychological phenomena.

4.1.1 Baldwin's Conceptualization of Development

Baldwin's emerging dialectical and philosophical viewpoint made it possible for him to overcome the heredity–environment dualism in thinking and to replace it with an interactionist perspective that views these two working together (e.g., Baldwin, 1902, pp. 76–77; see also Baldwin, 1930). Baldwin's interactionist perspective led him to be one of the forebears of the feedback principle, which he first described while reporting his empirical observations on the development of voluntary movements in his infant daughter (Baldwin, 1892b). The feedback principle, extended to both ontogeny and phylogeny, made it possible for Baldwin to introduce the concept of "circular reaction" and to let that concept play an important role in his theory of "organic selection":

There is a characteristic antithesis between movements always. Healthy, overflowing, favorable, outreaching, expansive, vital effects are associated with pleasure; and the contrary, the withdrawing, depressive, contractive, decreasing, vital effects are associated with pain. This is exactly the state of things which a theory of the selection of movements from overproduced movements requires, i.e., that increased vitality, represented by pleasure, should give excess movements, from which new adaptations are selected; and that decreased vitality represented by pain should do the reverse—draw off energy and suppress movements.

If, therefore, we say that here is a type of reaction which all vitality shows, we may give it a general descriptive name, i.e., the "Circular Reaction," in that its significance for evolution is that it is not a random response in movement to all stimulations alike, but that it distinguishes in its very form and amount between stimulations which are vitally good and those that are vitally bad, tending to retain the good stimulations and to draw away from and so suppress the bad. *The term "circular" is used to emphasize the way such a reaction tends to keep itself going, over and over, by reproducing the conditions of its own stimulation. It represents habit, since it tends to keep up old movements; but it secures new adaptations, since it provides for the over-production of movement-variations for the operation of selection.* This kind of selection, since it requires the direct cooperation of the organism itself, I have called "Organic Selection." It might be called "motor" or even "psychic" selection, since the part of consciousness, in the form of pleasure and pain, and later on experience generally, intelligence, etc. is so prominent. (Baldwin, 1896, p. 304, italics added)

It is not surprising that Baldwin could bring into the thinking about evolution the psychological factors that serve as criteria in the individual's selective retention of his or her actions in the environment. Baldwin was first and foremost a psychologist whose primary interest was turned toward the question of understanding how ontogeny is organized (see Baldwin, 1930, pp. 6–7).

4.1.2 Baldwin's Concepts of Imitation

Baldwin's conceptualization of imitation entails different forms, organized in a hierarchical order. At a low level of development, Baldwin recognized the realm of *pre-imitative suggestions,* which covered much of the involuntary phenomena in the child–environment relationships. At that level:

[W]e find many *Subconscious* and *Physiological* Suggestions akin to the subliminal suggestive reactions in recent hypnotic reports. Especially do suggestions of sleep, and of the personality of the mother, nurse, etc., take early hold upon the child. An important source of subconscious suggestion to the child is its dreams. Another class of suggestive influences in the pre-imitation period, we may call *Deliberative* Suggestions: cases in which two or more motor suggestions come into conflict. For example, the suggestion of a forbidden act and the memory of the pain of punishment give rise to apparent deliberation which is merely the balance of motor tendencies. (Baldwin, 1892a, p. 49)

The active role of the child is not evident at the level of pre-imitative phenomena. The world of pre-imitative kind is filled with numerous *influences on* the person, to which the person reacts (rather than acts on).

In contrast, the phenomena of "imitative suggestion"—subdivided by Baldwin into *simple imitation* and *persistent imitation*—go beyond the here-

and-now reactivity of the organism to the external influences. For Baldwin, ". . . an imitative reaction is one which *tends normally to maintain or repeat its stimulating process*" (Baldwin, 1895, p. 350, italics added for emphasis).

4.1.2.1   The Meaning of "Simple Imitation."   For Baldwin, simple imitation amounted to "sensori-motor or ideo-motor suggestion which tends to keep itself going by reinstating its own stimulation" (1895, p. 352). His efforts to explain the meaning of this version of imitation may be more understandable:

> The child imitates a word, gets it wrong, and repeats its own mistake over and over. Physiologically we have a "circular activity"; the stimulus starts a nervous process which tends to reproduce both the stimulus and the process again. In Simple Imitation *the channels of association are sufficient for the discharge, and there is no effort.* (Baldwin, 1892a, p. 50, italics added)

This kind of simple imitation is in fact equivalent to what both common sense and post-Baldwinian psychology have habitually considered imitation to be (i.e., a version of the external model is replicated, in full or in some less-than-accurate form, in a child's behavior, where it may persist). In contrast, for Baldwin, this form of imitation was clearly of secondary importance, because *simple imitation is incapable of producing novelty beyond the model,* which is provided externally. It is reproductive (in contrast with productive) and automatic (i.e., effortless), and it lacks future orientation (it can be explained by past associative links). After the first act of imitation of the external copy, the "circular process" of simple imitation enters a loop of repetitive *status quo.*

4.1.2.2   The Meaning of Persistent Imitation.   As Baldwin described the persistent imitation process, it involves the "trying, and trying again" phenomenon of experimenting with the features of the model. In terms of contrast, the persistent imitation entails increasing experimentation with different aspects of the model, and going beyond the model as given—producing imitations that deliberately modify the model.

Persistent imitation leads to a hierarchical organization of psychological mechanisms, and control of the voluntary actions is then given over to the higher psychological functions (e.g., see Baldwin, 1895, p. 379). Furthermore, the function of persistent imitation is oriented toward future encounters with the world:

> Imitation to the intelligent and earnest imitator is never slavish, never mere repetition; it is, on the contrary, *a means for further ends,* a method of absorbing what is present in others and of making it over in forms peculiar to one's own temper and valuable to one's own genius. (Baldwin, 1911b, p. 22)

Simple imitation is a special case of the more general persistent imitation; it is a special case in which the constructive nature of the subsequent imitations is limited to the exact replication of the model. If that fixation (or perseverance) is overcome, the imitative process returns to its normal (i.e., persistent) mode. Furthermore, it becomes clear that persistent imitation is the mechanism by which individual uniqueness is constructed under conditions of uncertainty in the environment.

4.1.3 Heterogeneity of the Social Environment, and Emergence of Person–World Duality

The social world of the developing person is variable, particularly because of the personal constructions of the individuals who constitute that social world. There is sufficient regularity, but the endless encounter with changes forces the person to be constantly ready for new challenges. As Baldwin remarked:

> ... the child begins to learn in addition the fact that persons are in a measure individual in their treatment of him, and hence that individuality has elements of uncertainty or *irregularity* about it. This growing sense is very clear to one who watches an infant in its second half-year. Sometimes the mother gives a biscuit, but sometimes she does not. Sometimes the father smiles and tosses the child; sometimes he does not. And the child looks for signs of these varying moods and methods of treatment. Its new pains of disappointment arise directly on the basis of that former sense of regular personal presence upon which its expectancy went forth. (Baldwin, 1894, p. 277; also Baldwin, 1895, p. 123)

This principal unpredictability of the specific events in one's life-world leads to the differentiation of the person from the world:

> From the start, the growing individual finds himself bound constantly more and more tightly in the bonds of the actual; his actual self makes constant effort and finds constant resistance in the actual world. The two domains, "inner" and "outer," grow harder and more opposed one to the other, as his life adjustments proceed. The dualism of substances grows fixed and rigid. His release from this tension, this very serious business, is found in play, in fancy, in illusion, in fiction—in short, in semblance or make-believe of all kinds. Here he has a sense of freedom, of don't-have-to, of detachment; he plays with symbols, erects fancies, lives the hero, the pauper, the prince, at his own sweet will. In play, as a child or man, he remakes the world, mixing himself with other persons and with things in a delightful chaos; similarly, in art the man and artist again remake the world having in view only his own creation of something—anything—within the possibilities of the ideal reconstruction that the materials allow. (Baldwin, 1930, p. 20)

Baldwin was a "dualist," in the sense that he defended the *inclusive* separation of the person and the social world (see Chapter 2). Duality of integrated phenomena—the "inner" and the "outer," or the self and the society—constituted the field worth analysis of how the opposing-yet-united parts of a duality actually relate with each other.

4.1.4   Human Development as a Socially Organized Process

Baldwin's emphasis on the social nature of individual–psychological phenomena can be viewed as a historical predecessor to Vygotsky's cultural–historical thinking. For example:

> Man is not a person who stands up in his isolated majesty, meanness, passion, or humility, and sees, hits, worships, fights, or overcomes, another man, who does the opposite things to him, each preserving his isolated majesty, meanness, passion, humility, all the while, so that he can be considered a "unit" for the compounding processes of social speculation. On the contrary, *a man is a social outcome rather than a social unit.* He is always, in his greatest part, also someone else. Social acts of his—that is, acts that may not prove anti-social— are his *because they are society's first;* otherwise he would not have learned them nor have had any tendency to do them. (Baldwin, 1902, p. 96)

The point about the primacy of society over the individual in ontogeny is the forerunner of Vygotsky's concept of internalization of higher psychological functions. Baldwin's thinking includes conceptualization of the individual person's inevitable dependence on society during the developmental period. Individual persons differ, but all of them have developed in the web of their society, and, in this sense, all are dependent on their culture. Baldwin's thinking about the individual–society relationship is similar to the concept of "dependent independence," which is outlined in a later chapter (see 5.4).

4.1.5   Personal Constructivity in "Inner" ↔ "Outer" Relations: Play and Art

The dynamics of "inner" ↔ "outer" relationships led Baldwin to two other relevant phenomena: play and art. In the process of make-believe play, Baldwin saw a setting where one can observe the coordination of previous experiences (via memory) with suggestions from the objects in the present moment (Baldwin, 1906, Chapter 6).

Play was viewed by Baldwin as having the function of "education of the individual for his life-work in a network of social relationships" (Baldwin, 1897, p. 148). Like Vygotsky in later years, Baldwin relied heavily on the work of Karl Groos on play.

In role play, "inner" (memory-based) experiences are brought together with the present external situation. The constructive nature of imitation transforms immediately available objects into functionally different ones. The persistent form of imitation makes play available. The roles in the play can be reconstructed at every moment, yet while the particular play is taking place, roles have temporal continuity (Oliveira & Rossetti-Ferreira, 1996).

However, there are limits to the constructivity in play. Some aspects of the "outer" reality can be made into insurmountable obstacles for functional redefinition [e.g., a child telling another child, "You cannot be an earthworm, you have too many legs" (Baldwin, 1906, p. 114)]. The possibilities available for play are definable via limits on the range of such possibilities.

4.1.5.1   Centrality of Empathy (Sembling).   In the realm of discussing play and art, Baldwin relates his theorizing with the issue of *Einfühlung,* as presented by Theodor Lipps. Baldwin's translation of that term into English is a good example of his liking for terminological inventions. He translated it as *sembling* ["to semble" = to make alike by imitation (Baldwin, 1906, p. 122)]. This was an alternative English synonym for *empathy,* which gained wide usage in psychology later on.

Originally focusing on "feeling into" an object, Baldwin's version of sembling translates *Einfühlung* into his imitation-centered conceptual system:

> Broadly understood, the process of Sembling consists in the *reading-into the object of a sort of psychic life of its own,* in such a way that the movement, act, or character by which it is interpreted is thought of *as springing from its own inner life.* (Baldwin, 1906, p. 124, italics added)

Sembling thus entails psychological persistent imitation. The person actively "populates" the object with his or her own intrapsychological subjective material, and thus reconstructs the outer object as if it were an inner one. Sembling was claimed to be relevant in both play and art. It is based on anticipatory imagination, which is oriented toward possible future events. Baldwin emphasized the person's affective orientation toward the future, while being embedded in the social world in the present:

> [T]he sort of meaning known as ideal, due to an imaginative *feeling-forward,* has an essential place in the development of the affective life. The entire movement of cognition and feeling alike has not only the interest and intent to conserve its data and preserve its habits, but also the interest and intent to achieve, to learn, to adapt, to acquire, to *feel-forward.* (Baldwin, 1911a, p. 125)

4.1.6   Baldwin's Methodological Revolution

Baldwin's theoretical ideas about development were out of tune with events in the social history of psychology in North America at that time (first decade of the 20th century). The advent of the pragmatism-based social movement of behaviorism coincided with Baldwin's understanding that developmental methodology must move in a direction almost opposite to the "study of behavior." Although Baldwin had been instrumental in setting up experimental psychology laboratories in various North American universities, he moved increasingly away from his colleagues in his efforts to create his full theoretical and methodological system. This system was published in three volumes titled *Thought and Things* (Baldwin, 1906, 1908, 1911a), and in a fourth, *Genetic Theory of Reality* (Baldwin, 1915). These volumes constitute the high point of Baldwin's theoretical and methodological synthesis. Because his work (and his person) were mavericks among the rest of American academia by the time of the volumes' completion, little concrete work has been done to make sense of his philosophical arguments and his suggestions for a "genetic [i.e., developmental] logic." Baldwin's methodological claims were revolutionary for his time, and would remain so in the context of contemporary developmental psychology.

4.1.6.1   Rejection of the Quantitative Method.   Baldwin understood the necessity to overcome socially constructed norms in science when those are misfits for the goals of investigation. This was (and is; see Chapter 3) a crucial issue in developmental research. In his autobiographical retrospect, Baldwin explained the reasons why developmental psychology needs to overcome traditional methodology:

> The Spencerian or quantitative method, brought over into psychology from the exact sciences, physics and chemistry, must be discarded; for its ideal consisted in reducing the more complex to the more simple, the whole to its parts, the later-evolved to the earlier-existent, *thus denying or eliminating just the factor which constituted or revealed what was truly genetic.* Newer modes of manifestation cannot be stated in atomic terms without doing violence to the more synthetic modes which observation reveals. The qualities of flower and fruit, for example, cannot be accounted for, much less predicted, from the chemical formulas of processes going on in the tissue of the fruit tree.
>
> A method is therefore called for which will take account of this something left "over and above" the quantitative, something which presents new phases as the genetic progression advances. This something reveals itself in a series of qualitative aspects . . . . (1930, pp. 7–8; italics added)

Baldwin's emphasis on analyzing the *series of qualitative transformations* of the developing phenomena was a predecessor to Vygotsky's work toward developing nonreductionist and qualitative methodology for psychology. Baldwin was perhaps the first developmental psychologist to understand that the canons of the scientific method may fit the study of static aspects of phenomena, but they are counterproductive for the study of their dynamic aspects.

4.1.6.2   Elaboration of Developmental Logic.   As an alternative, Baldwin elaborated a system of logic that would take into account processes of transformation. This system took the general form of "axioms" and "postulates" (see Valsiner, 1994c, 1995; Valsiner & Van der Veer, 1997). His four "axioms" of genetic science (1902, p. 323; 1906, p. 20), emphasized the irreducibility of the developmentally more complex phenomena to their preceding (less complex) counterparts:

> [Axiom 1]. . . . the phenomena of science at each higher level show a form of synthesis that is not accounted for by the formulations which are adequate for

the phenomena of the next lower level. ["Lower" here denotes a developmental antecedent, "higher," an emerging subsequent.]

[Axiom 2]. . . . the formulations of any lower science are not invalidated in the next higher, even in cases in which new formulations are necessary for the formal synthesis which characterizes the genetic mode of the higher.

[Axiom 3]. . . . the generalizations and classifications of each science, representing a particular genetic mode, are peculiar to that mode and cannot be constructed in analogy to, or *a fortiori* on the basis of, the corresponding generalizations or classifications of the lower mode.

[Axiom 4]. . . . no formula for progress from mode to mode, that is, no *strictly genetic* formula in evolution or in development, is possible except by direct observation of the facts of the series which the formulation aims to cover or by the interpretation of other series which represent the same or parallel modes. (Baldwin, 1906, p. 20)

Following these axioms, specific elaborations of methodology of the developmental science were in order. Baldwin specified two "postulates of method." The first (or "negative") postulate emphasized the irreversibility of time in development:

> *The logic of genesis is not expressed in convertible propositions.* Genetically, A = (that is, *becomes,* for which the sign ((is now used) B; but it does not follow that B = (becomes, (() A. (Baldwin, 1906, p. 21)

The first postulate specified the realm of possible relations that are allowable among the formulas of "genetic logic"—namely, each proposition includes a temporal directionality vector. Thus, the reversal (i.e., B ((A) is not implied by the notion of A becoming B. If we were to use better known terminology (from Piaget's talk about operations, for example) Baldwin's genetic logic is set up using nonoperational terminology. The symmetry of transformation between A and B is broken by the irreversibility of time and of the transformation itself.

The symmetry-breaking process (see also 3.7.9) leads to the question of *loci of accessibility* to developmental phenomena for Baldwin's designated "developmental science." These loci were charted in the second (so-called "positive") postulate:

> [T]hat series of events is truly genetic which cannot be constructed before it has happened, and which cannot be exhausted backwards, after it has happened. (Baldwin, 1906, p. 21)

The "positive" nature of this postulate emerges in the study of development with a focus on the *unfolding novel processes,* rather than their prediction or a retrospective explanation of them. The phenomena of *emergence, becoming,* and *transformation* become the objects of investigation—an investigation that entails *preserving the irreversible time sequence* in the data. Baldwin's developmental logic leads to the study of emergence processes through microgenetic (see 3.9.2) or analogous time-preserving methods.

Baldwin's sociopersonal constructionist perspective can be viewed as the common parent of the constructionist (Piaget) and social (Vygotsky) directions in subsequent psychology. In his focus on transformation of forms, Baldwin was akin to Heinz Werner's line of thought. His efforts to develop genetic logic have largely remained without elaborations (but see Herbst, 1995).

4.2 JEAN PIAGET'S EPISTEMOLOGY OF DEVELOPMENT

Piaget's contributions to psychology are constantly discussed, and most of those discussions emphasize the nondevelopmental aspect of his work—the stage account (see 1.1.3). Piaget was primarily a biologist who moved into the area of child studies, carrying the best of his observational skills into this new field (Chapman, 1988). His theoretical elaborations followed suit with some latency, covering all of his life span.

In most general terms, Piaget's emphasis on *dynamic structuralism,* which involves the subject's *active interaction* with the changing environment in a *process of equilibration* that leads to *restructured knowledge,* serves as the main theoretical linkage of his theory to the one presented here.

4.2.1 Dynamic Structuralism

Piaget's dynamic structuralism was an implicit part of his thinking even in his earliest writings, thus antedating by far the social fashion for structuralist thought in France after World War II (see Kurzweil, 1980, for an overview of the French structuralist movement). However, the social discourse in France about structuralism motivated Piaget to make *his* kind of structuralist thinking explicit (Piaget, 1970b).

Historically, Piaget followed the lead of his predecessors in gestalt psychology and biology in his refusal to reduce the phenomena of the world to constituent elements that are void of structural wholeness. In this emphasis, Piaget's roots were in the *Naturphilosophie* of the 19th century, mediated via the thinking of J. M. Baldwin and E. Claparède. His conceptualization of "structure" involved three key ideas: (a) *wholeness,* (b) *transformation,* and (c) *self-regulation* (Piaget, 1970b, p. 5). The last two ideas were crucial in making Piaget's brand of structuralism developmental in nature. Structures (in the natural world, as well as in action and thinking) are wholes that are constantly being transformed from one state to another via self-regulatory processes taking place at the intersection of the organism and its environment. Piaget's emphasis on transformation as an operation that changes one state of a structure into another has been largely left without further elaboration (see Vuyk, 1981, p. 55). The concept of "self-regulation" entails self-maintenance and "closure" by the structure. In parallel with the distinction of open and closed systems, Piaget introduced his notion of open versus closed structures (Piaget, 1970b, pp. 14–16 and 44–51). He described closed structures as closed systems:

> the transformations inherent in a structure never lead beyond the system but always engender elements that belong to it and preserve its laws. Again an example will help to clarify: In adding or subtracting any two whole numbers, another whole number is obtained, and one which satisfies the laws of the "additive group" of whole numbers. It is in this sense that a structure is "closed," a notion perfectly compatible with the structure's being considered a substructure of a larger one; but in being treated as a substructure, a structure does not lose its own boundaries; the larger structure does not "annex" the substructure; if anything we have a confederation, so that the laws of the substructure are not altered but conserved and the intervening change is an enrichment rather than an impoverishment. (Piaget, 1970b, p. 14)

The "conserved" nature of the closed structure involves the presence of "perfect" regulations within these structures, which are possible in the case of decontextualized systems. (A "substructure" functions in "confederation" with a larger structure, in ways that do not alter the former's laws of functioning.) From the perspective of the present theoretical system, the paradox in Piaget's developmental theory is embedded in the conjunction of his emphasis on organisms' active role in interaction with the environment on the one hand, and the preferred status allotted in his epistemology to context-free logicomathematical structures on the other. This paradoxical nature of Piaget's theory seems to be a historical outgrowth from the efforts evident in the occidental sciences to separate the ideal logical forms of thinking from the complexity of culturally devised and changeable meanings (e.g., Boole, 1854).

Piaget did not deny the existence of other structures, which (in parallel with open systems) he called "open structures":

> [T]here is, of course, an immense class of structures which are not strictly logical or mathematical, that is, whose transformations unfold in time: linguistic structures, sociological structures, psychological structures, and so on. Such transformations are governed by laws ("regulations" in the cybernetic sense of the word) which are not in the strict sense "operations," because they are not entirely reversible (in the sense in which multiplication is reversible by division or addition by subtraction). Transformation laws of this kind depend upon the interplay of anticipation and correction (feedback). (Piaget, 1970b, pp. 15–16)

Although Piaget recognized the existence of a wide variety of open structures, he nevertheless followed his implicit assumption that, developmentally, such structures are directed toward reduction of their openness. Vuyk traced the background of this assumption:

Though Piaget came to agree with Bertalanffy that every structure of [the open] type is open to the environment with interactions between the two, he did add an important restriction. According to Piaget the system always strives for closure. This is due to the fact that an open system *is threatened* by the environment: lack of food, sex, cognitive stimulation, etc. Therefore the organism tries to extend its mastery of the environment, biologically by, for example, the extension of its territory, and cognitively by extending its knowledge of the environment. . . . If the organism could succeed in closing the system this would mean a restriction of the organism's action to a circumscribed field in such a way *that the exchanges would guarantee the conservation of the system.* Seen in this way the closure of the system is no more than a limit that is never attained. (Vuyk, 1981, p. 57; italics added)

Vuyk's analysis of Piaget's axiomatic background brings out the conservative stance that the open structures assume in respect to potential change: These structures are threatened by their environments and tend toward a state where restricted interdependence with the environment makes it possible for those structures to restrict themselves to self-conservation. In the case of "open structures," Piaget introduced the notion of *cyclic order,* which in many ways parallels the issues of systemic causality (discussed in 2.7). Piaget's cyclic order both expresses the stable (conserved) structure and, simultaneously, "represents an opening to the environment as a source of ailment" (Piaget, 1971b, p. 156).

Piaget's cyclic closure of a structure involves a set of "dynamic elements" (A, B, C, . . . Z) of the structure and a corresponding set of "energetic elements" (A', B', C', . . . Z') that are necessary for the maintenance of the former. The cyclic closure of the system is organized by system–environment interaction, as is evident in a schematic description provided by Piaget (1971b, p. 156):

$$(A \times A') \to (B \times B') \to (C \times C') \to \dots$$

$$\dots \to (Z \times Z') \to (A \times A') \to \text{etc.}$$

At the start, A interacts with A' and results in B. The next step involves the interaction of B with B', which results in C, and so on, until the interaction of Z with Z' closes the cycle as it results in A. The cycle maintains itself through the transformations—A to Z to A, etc.—due to the interaction with the environment, whereas at the same time the system itself stays in a "steady state." Piaget's explanation of the closure of the open structure interdependently with the environment illustrates how complex structures can be maintained, but does not yet offer an explanation for their development. Development is integrated into this descriptive system when the whole process cycle (A . . . Z . . . A) assimilates new input information into its structure with a simultaneous accommodation of the structure to the incoming information.

4.2.2 Equilibration of Reequilibration as Mechanisms of Development

Development in Piaget's theoretical system is explained through the process of equilibration and reequilibration. For Piaget, equilibration involves the *process* that is aimed at elimination of disequilibrium by either a return to a previously present state, or a progression to a qualitatively new equilibrium:

> We can observe a process (hence the term "equilibration") leading from certain states of equilibrium to others, qualitatively different, and passing through multiple "nonbalances" and reequilibrations. Thus the problems to be solved involve various forms of equilibrium, the reasons for nonbalance, and above all the causal mechanisms, or methods, of equilibrations and reequilibrations. It is especially important to stress from the very beginning the fact that, in certain cases, the reequilibrations merely form returns to previous equilibriums; however, those that are fundamental for development consist, on the contrary, in the formations not only of new equilibriums but also in general of better equilibriums. We can, therefore, speak of "increasing equilibrations," and raise the question of self-organization. (Piaget, 1977, pp. 3–4)

This quote from Piaget reflects the bifurcational nature of his understanding of the process of equilibration. Under some conditions, a disequilibrium situation is resolved by a return to a previous (or similar to previous) equilibrium state; but under other circumstances, the process of equilibration can lead to the establishment of a new equilibrium state. The qualitative "break" between the return to the previous state and advancement to a new state captures the qualitative nature of development. The process of progressing equilibration" [compare also Vuyk's term (1981, p. 68), "improving equilibrium" for Piaget's "equilibration majorante"—see Inhelder, Garcia, & Voneche (1976, pp. 39–42); Piaget (1977, part 6)] constitutes the theoretical explanation that captures the open-ended nature of development.

Piaget viewed equilibration as existing in three forms. At the beginning of subject–object interaction, there is the equilibration between the assimilation of action schemes and their accommodation of the objects of action. The second form of equilibration involves mutual relationships between schemes. Finally, Piaget (1977, pp. 8–9) outlined the importance of the progressive equilibrium between differentiation and integration of the organism—involving relations of the schemes to the totality that includes them as its constituents.

4.2.3 Complementary Processes in Development: Assimilation and Accommodation

Piaget's developmental theory is built on the role that assimilation and accommodation *interdependently* play in the organism's *process of adaptation* to its environment. As soon as the environment changes, the adaptation process begins as well. Because the environments of living systems are in constant flux, the process of adaptation cannot end as long as the organisms are alive. In the case of humans, adaptation involves also purposeful action on environment, with the goal of reaching a new state of the organism itself.

Assimilation and accommodation "are not two separate functions but the two functional poles, set in opposition to each other, of any adaptation" (Piaget, 1971b, p. 173). There is no assimilation (integration of new elements to an existing scheme or schema) without its corresponding accommodation (the change of the scheme/schema to fit the conditions of the environment). The interdependence (rather than independent coexistence) of assimilation and accommodation constitutes the mechanism of adaptation, so when these concepts are used to explain development, that interdependence must be explicitly outlined (see Figure 4.1).

The assimilation–accommodation relationship is one of Piaget's concepts that has been consistently misrepresented in many didactic efforts to teach beginning psychology students about Piaget. Very often, the two concepts are presented in textbooks as if they were separate adaptation mechanisms that are applicable independently. That basic misunderstanding of Piaget's central concepts involved in adaptation continued beyond the teaching contexts, and triggered Piaget himself to emphasize the gravity of that misunderstanding (Piaget, 1970a, 1971b).

4.2.4 Piaget and Nonequilibrium Thermodynamics in Explanation of Development

The bifurcational idea of the process of development has been influential—indeed, it has revolutionized scientific thinking—in contemporary physical and biological sciences over recent decades (see Bohm, 1980; Pattee, 1973; Polanyi,

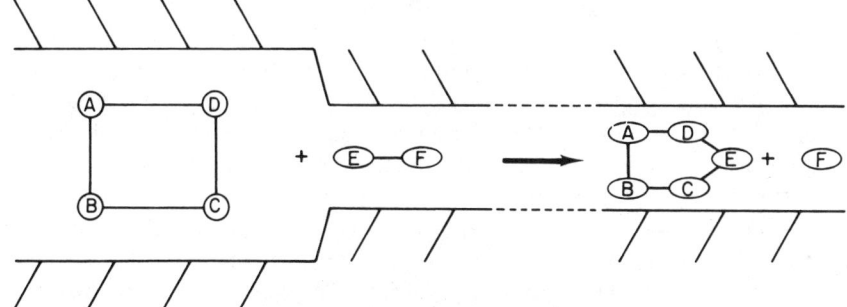

FIGURE 4.1.   A schematic depiction of the interdependence of assimilation and accommodation in Piaget's equilibration theory. The original structure ABCD that exists in the "wide area" of the environment receives an input from the environment in the form of structure EF, while moving into the "narrow area" of the environment. Element E from the input structure is assimilated into the original structure, at the same time as the new structure accommodates to the environment (by shrinking its size), and the form of the components of all of the structural units. (The latter change is depicted in the transformation of the circles into ellipses.)

1958; Prigogine, 1973, 1976b; Weiss, 1969). Yet, in psychology, this idea has been largely overlooked, despite its availability (London, 1979; London & Thorngate, 1981).

There exists, however, a difference between Piaget's conceptualization of development in terms of equilibration and that of contemporary nonequilibrium thermodynamics (Prigogine, 1976a, 1982). Differing from Piaget, the latter perspective emphasizes the role of *increasing disequilibration* in the development of new structures. This process of the development of new structures through amplification of fluctuations in biological systems was described by Prigogine and Nicolis (1971, p. 113):

> [A] new structure or organization . . . is always the result of an instability. It originates in a fluctuation, i.e., in a fundamentally stochastic element. A fluctuation is usually followed by a response that brings the system back to the original state and which is a perfectly deterministic process. It is only at the point of formation of a new structure that fluctuations are amplified, reach a macroscopic level, and finally stabilize to a new regime representative of the structure arising beyond instability. Once this effect is allowed by the boundary conditions imposed on the system, it will happen with probability one, provided the fluctuation is created initially by some mechanism.

The difference in emphasis (Piaget—on the tendency toward equilibrium; Prigogine and Nicolis—toward increased disequilibrium) parallels the contrast outlined above (4.2.1) between Piaget's conceptualization of the tendency toward the closure of open structures and the theory of open systems. In both cases, Piaget's thinking was based on the idea that structures strive toward greater stability (equilibrium) and independence from the environment (closure), even if he accepted that they can never practically achieve those end states. Both the open-systems perspective of Bertalanffy (1950, 1960, 1981) and the theoretical framework of contemporary nonequilibrium thermodynamics emphasize the opposite. The development of new structures is possible once an old structure is moved far from its previous equilibrium, and the interdependence of the system and its environment is the inseparable aspect of the life of the system. At first glance, the distinction between these axiomatic positions may look like the old cognitive problem that one encounters with a half-filled glass of water: Is the glass half-full or half-empty? However, the theoretical repercussions of the differences between Piaget's approach and open-systems approaches at that highly abstract level are considerable, and are worth explication.

To summarize, both in contemporary biological and physical sciences, and in Piaget's theory of psychological development, the process of emergence of new structures (biological or cognitive) involves the overcoming of some disequilibrium state in the organism's relationship with the environment. This overcoming takes the form of either restoration of the previous state of affairs, or, if the disequilibrium is beyond a certain threshold condition, development of a qualitatively new state. Such a bifurcational nature of development is an important aspect that this author's theoretical system borrows from Piaget and the contemporary thermodynamic thinking, leaving aside disagreements between them. Piaget's dynamic structuralism leads to consideration of how novel action structures develop when a child is acting on structurally organized environments, and is under structured efforts by the caregivers to guide that transaction. Piaget's developmental theory of equilibration served as one of the bases of the present theoretical system because it was aimed to overcome the static nature of the majority of structuralist accounts of the world on the one hand, and the unstructured nature of most of the dynamic perspectives in psychology on the other.

4.3 WILLIAM STERN'S PERSONOLOGICAL APPROACH

Stern can be considered a contemporary of Baldwin and a creator of developmental ideas that were parallel to those of Piaget and Vygotsky. His personalistic philosophy was developed in the first two decades of the 20th century and was outlined in various publications (Stern, 1906, 1911, 1918, 1919).

Stern's major focus was on person–world relations, but his multifaceted work has mostly led to his being recognized as the founder of differential psychology and the inventor of the IQ notion. His fame on the latter ground is quite unfortunate because it marks Stern's work as if it belonged in total to the realm of that intellectual *impasse* in psychology that is called "intelligence testing" and is at times brought to the center of postmodern public attention via speculation about bell curves and lay genetics. Despite the eminent availability of Stern's theoretical work in English translation (Stern, 1938) and its explanations by Stern himself (Stern, 1930) as well as by others (Hardesty, 1976; Kreppner, 1992; Lamiell, 1991), his theoretical efforts have remained beyond postmodern psychologists' attention span.

4.3.1 Persons and Contexts in *Spaltung* and *Spannung* Relations

Stern's perspective is clearly person-centered, yet it entails inclusive separation of the person and the context, and a focus on their relations. From the beginning of the development of his personological worldview, Stern emphasized the *contradictory unity* of persons and things (Stern, 1906, p. 16). According to him, the person—a multifaceted, functioning whole *(unitas multiplex)*—is spontaneously active relative to surrounding things; yet the organization of both the person and the things has structure, which is constantly in the process of reorganization (by the goal-orientedness of the active person).

The focus on goal-orientedness makes Stern's theoretical system process-oriented, as is reflected in his *hierarchy and convergence principles* (Stern, 1919, pp. 8–10). The person is constantly living through (experiencing) relations with the external world, which entail simultaneously separation *(Spaltung)* of, and tension *(Spannung)* between, different facets of the total wholeness of experience (Stern, 1935, p. 103). This process is very similar to Piaget's reliance on the unity of assimilation and accommodation (see 4.2.3), but in Stern's personalism the process is given in the context of a heterogeneous totality of person ↔ world relations, rather than in relation to information coming into the cognitive system.

4.3.2 Differentiation of Personal Worlds

According to Stern, each person has a "personal [person-relevant] world"—a world of the person's own construction (Stern, 1935, p. 126). That world is constructed by two parallel processes in person ↔ world relations: (a) participation in the world (the centrifugal direction: spontaneous actions guided by the material nature of the world; Stern, 1938, p. 388), and (b) the world's impression on the person (the centripetal direction: reactions of the person to the demand characteristics of the world). The personal world differentiates itself from the surrounding world and serves as a further guide in development. It leads to the emergence of novelty:

> However great the power exerted by the world to make the individual fall in with its trend, he nevertheless continues to be a "person" and can react to its influence only as a person, thereby modifying and deflecting its very tendency. And vice versa, however strikingly novel and penetrating the effect of the impress by which the genius of an artist, the founder of a religion, a statesman, puts a new face upon the world; since this modified world has no creative genius, it can absorb novelty only in a diluted, simplified form; and since it meanwhile follows its own laws and is subject to other influences, it perforce modifies all acquisitions. (Stern, 1938, p. 90)

This notion of person ↔ world differentiation is similar to Baldwin's ideas (see 4.1.3). Differentiation processes produce novelty. It remains unclear how the tension between centrifugal and centripetal processes actually function to produce novelty. Baldwin's elaboration of persistent imitation, and Piaget's assimilation–accommodation mechanisms might be productively brought to explain Stern's differentiation notion.

Stern's personalistic theory was a basis for Heinz Werner's systematic and pervasive emphasis on the differentiation notion. It also gave important input for Gordon Allport's efforts to construct a theory of personality. Stern's notions about the role of environment were close to those of Lev Vygotsky. All in all, William Stern was a crucial figure in the advancement of developmental perspectives in psychology during the 20th century.

4.4 HEINZ WERNER'S DIFFERENTIATION AND DE-DIFFERENTIATION PERSPECTIVE

Heinz Werner's legacy in developmental psychology is curious. On the one hand, it has been widely noted (e.g., Langer, 1970; Lerner, 1979, 1986; Wapner

& Demick, 1997); on the other hand, it has been easily dismissed as misfitting with the prevailing social ethos of developmental psychology. Because Werner's ideas have clear parallels to Piaget's, an interesting historical (and scientific-sociological) question can be posed: Why did the fashion for Piaget proliferate in North American psychology in the 1960s and 1970s, while similar ideas initiated by Werner in the 1950s and 1960s, at Clark University, were relevant for only a relatively small group of developmentalists?

Werner's focus on development came to maturity in the 1920s, when he was William Stern's assistant. At that time, Stern's institute in Hamburg was an active center of developmental and ecological psychology. Aside from Stern's own role, the presence there of philosopher Ernst Cassirer and of biologist Johann Jakob von Uexküll was notable. From its original realm of embryology, the differentiation idea was carried forth in Hamburg by multiple theoreticians (Raikov, 1961; von Baer, 1828).

4.4.1   The "Orthogenetic Principle" and Its Implications

Werner has been usually noted for his general developmental principle, which is a transposition of the idea of differentiation from developmental biology to developmental psychology:

> Developmental psychology postulates one regulative principle of development; it is an orthogenetic principle which states that wherever development occurs it proceeds from a state of relative globality and lack of differentiation to a state of increasing differentiation, articulation, and hierarchical integration. (Werner, 1957, p. 126)

Usually, this quote is presented without elaboration, to give readers a glimpse of Werner's thinking. However, some elaborations make Werner's ideas applicable in the methodology cycle (see Figure 1.1) of consistently developmental research.

Werner's own elaborations of the idea of differentiation are helpful here. He concentrated on the emergence of the polarity (= differentiation) of the subject (of action) and its object:

> [I]ncreasing subject–object differentiation involves the corollary that the organism becomes increasingly less dominated by the immediate concrete situation; the person is less stimulus-bound and less impelled by his own alternative states. A consequence of this freedom is the clearer understanding of goals, the possibility of employing substitutive means and alternative ends. There is hence a greater capacity for delay and planned action. The person is better able to exercise choice and willfully rearrange a situation. In short, he can manipulate the environment rather than passively respond to the environment. This freedom from the domination of the immediate situation also permits a more accurate assessment of others. (Werner, 1957, p. 127)

This focus on increased person–environment differentiation reflects Baldwin's and Stern's earlier claims that it is the person's relative autonomy from the context that grows out of the interdependency with the context.

The orthogenetic law was not meant to be a unilinearity-prescribing principle at the level of concrete developmental phenomena. In actuality, Werner recognized the multilinearity of developmental trajectories (1957, p. 137) as well as the need to include de-differentiation as the complementary process to differentiation.

Werner's principle also included a focus on emergence of qualitative novelty. Hierarchical integration involves qualitative reorganization of the "lower" (i.e., previously established) levels of organization, when the higher levels emerge in their specificity:

> [D]evelopment . . . tends towards stabilization. Once a certain stable level of integration is reached, the possibility of further development must depend on whether or not the behavioral patterns have become so automatized that they cannot take part in reorganization . . . . The individual, for instance, builds up sensorimotor schemata . . . these are the goal of early learning at first, but later on become instruments or apparatuses for handling the environment. Since no two situations in which an organism finds itself are alike, the usefulness of these schemata in adaptive behavior will depend on their stability as well as on their pliability (a paradoxical "stable flexibility").
>
> . . . if one assumes that the emergence of higher levels of operations involves hierarchic integration, it follows that lower-level operations will have to be reorganized in terms of their functional nature so that they become subservient to higher functioning. A clear example of this is the change of the functional nature of imagery from a stage where images serve only memory, fantasy, and concrete conceptualization, to a stage where images have been transformed to schematic symbols of abstract concepts and thought. (Werner, 1957, pp. 139–140)

The parallels between Werner's theory and the thought of Piaget should become clear when the question of equilibration is considered. Like Piaget, Werner emphasized the emergence of new structures. However, Werner's search for symbolic mediating devices that would emerge from subject–object differentiation brings his perspective closer to Vygotsky's.

4.4.2 Mediating Devices

In Werner's terms, these mediating devices emerge in the differentiation process:

> Development from a lower to a higher type of action—in terms of differentiation—is marked by the appearance of circuitous approaches, that is, means of action, instruments of mediation. On the level of the most primitive action, object (stimulus) and subject (response) are not separated by the devices of mediation; that is, the interaction is *immediate*. Development in the mode of

action is further determined by a growing specificity of the personal and sub-jective as against the objective aspect of the action involved. The growth and differentiation of the personal factor in action are demonstrated in the emer-gence of a specifically personal *motivation*. The growing recognition of a self-dependent objectivity is reflected in the development of *planful behavior*. (Werner, 1940, p. 191)

Werner's inclusion of *motivation* among his set of emerging mediating de-vices serves as an example of the theoretical alleys in psychology that have been suggested and then have been forgotten. Persons, as builders of their own motivation (via construction of cultural meanings), allow ever-new forms of self-regulation to emerge in ontogeny, and they permit innovation of cultural meaning systems (as well as differentiation of language forms, such as metaphoric devices; Werner & Kaplan, 1963) to occur in human history.

4.4.3   The Problem of Hierarchy

A crucial feature of Werner's thought was his recognition of the hierarchical nature of human psychological organization. Development entails the creation (and constant recreation) of hierarchical order. However, in hierarchical order, some parts of the system under consideration are superior to others, even if such superiority is only transitory. Had it been applied to intramental func-tions—for example, claims that "higher psychological functions," in the sense of Lev Vygotsky, are superior to, and are regulating, the "lower psychological functions" (voluntary processes control involuntary ones; symbolic forms orga-nize our emotional flow), the hierarchical organization notion might have been acceptable to psychologists. But it has led to serious "boundary negotiations" between social sciences and their background ideological institutions.

A distinction between "primitive" (lower) and "civilized" (higher) forms of thinking (e.g., see Werner & Kaplan, 1956) was common in cognitive psy-chology of the 1920s and 1930s. Lev Vygotsky explicitly accepted that notion (Van der Veer, 1996a), and so did significant other contributors to our knowl-edge of development (e.g., Goldstein, 1971). The distinction made between "primitive" and "civilized" thought processes was a carryover from the colo-nialist term, accepted in European societies, which referred to the colonized "primitive societies."

In the context of the 20th century, the social ideologies underlying social sciences have guided the latter away from assuming "lower" or "higher" dis-tinctions among societies, nations, and social-ethnic groups. Hence, Werner's or Vygotsky's focus on a hierarchical organization of the human psychologi-cal system has limited possibilities for flourishing in contexts where social sciences pre-assume equality of different forms of cultural organization of human life. An ideological commitment to a position of "cultural relativism" makes it complicated for many social scientists to espouse the notion of a hi-erarchical organization in any area of psychology that is linked with some kind of social concept. Surely, developmental psychology, when it emphasizes the notion that human development is social, comes to this area of ideological canalization.

Yet, such ideological canalization is highly selective. Simultaneously with the rejection of the contrast between "higher" and "lower" psychological functions in Vygotsky's thought (which are based on an ethnological/anthropological contrast of "primitive" and "civilized" societies; see Nicolopoulou & Weintraub, 1996; Van der Veer, 1996a, 1996b), there is no difficulty with accepting a similar hierarchical order in the case of intramentalistic stage accounts. Thus, Piaget's formal-operational stage may be viewed as superior to that of concrete operations, without any worry about the "primitive/civilized" contrast (which *de facto* is present in any occidental contrast between adult and child). Thus, Werner's hierarchical integration notion may be in the ambivalent domain of a social need to reject hierarchies (on the basis of some social representation of "modern democratic society") while at the same time there may be a need to accept the hierarchy as part of ontogenesis. After all, the age-graded nature of existing educational institutions offers a perfect example of hierarchical organization (tenth graders are expected to be superior to eighth graders in academic performance) and of promotion of such hierarchy (by limiting students' access to advanced degrees). Hierarchy is an inevitable—yet socially de-emphasized—part of any society. The social de-emphasis filters into social sciences to render their focus equally unfocused on the hierarchical side of their phenomena.

4.4.4 Teleology in Development and Multilinearity of Trajectories

Werner was explicit about the *directiveness* of developmental processes (see Werner, 1957, p. 126 footnote). This focus was similar to Stern's, and would be inevitably entailed in any stage account of development.

Developmental psychology needs a concept of directiveness in its core. Werner's focus on differentiation entails such generic teleological moment that, whenever development takes place, it is *oriented toward* construction of increasingly more complex psychological forms, even if at times the corresponding reverse process of de-differentiation can be present.

By being *oriented toward* (in contrast with *determined by*) a future state, the teleological emphasis is allowed to maintain directionality (e.g., oriented in direction B, C, or D, but not in the opposite counterparts; see 3.9), while at the same time not assuming that development has a pregiven "final point." Instead, the actual courses of individual development are unique, and mostly unpredictable, except for their general direction. This focus links Werner's ideas directly with the present theory of "bounded indeterminacy."

The multiplicity of trajectories of individuals' development can be highly complex in their organization. Contemporary research in developmental biology of organisms whose structural (cellular) development takes place in shorter time frames than in the case of human children has revealed great complexity of ongoing developmental changes in simple organisms (Lewin, 1984).

In the domain of children's motor development, Trettien (1900) demonstrated that infants progress through different sequences of motor skill attainment: Some progress from a stationary position to bipedal locomotion via the crawling/creeping intermediate state, but others bypass that state and begin walking independently after getting up from a sitting position. Werner's "orthogenetic principle" does not contradict such multilinearity of development, because it is formulated at a highly abstract level, as Werner himself pointed out. The multiplicity of developmental routes to the same end state is one of the characteristics of the open systems (Bertalanffy, 1950). Werner's orthogenetic principle is applicable only to open systems (closed systems are incapable of development, i.e. differentiation and hierarchical integration).

Werner's contribution to the study of development is relevant in the context of this book, in two respects. First, his orthogenetic principle when interpreted as allowing for different developmental courses that lead to similar outcomes, constitutes the basis of the explanation of ontogenetic development of children's action structures. Second, his emphasis on hierarchical reorganization of differentiating organisms makes it possible to conceptualize the emergence of qualitatively new parts of developing structures. It is largely (but not exclusively) that idea that links with Vygotsky's emphasis on the "cultural" development of children. Werner's earlier work served as a direct source for Vygotsky's thinking on child development.

4.5   LEV VYGOTSKY'S CULTURAL–HISTORICAL APPROACH

Vygotsky's approach was based on his systematic interest in questions of psychological synthesis (Van der Veer & Valsiner, 1991), which in its case was farmed by the organismic–dialectical philosophical traditions of the 19th century. Because the newly adopted Soviet ideology in the 1920s claimed that it followed the philosophical traditions of Marx and Engels, the actual philosophical heritage that Vygotsky used, and his surrounding societal talk about Marxism, seemed to fit with each other quite well. Still, that fit was more apparent than real (Van der Veer, 1996a; Van der Veer & Valsiner, 1991), and Vygotsky's synthesis of various ideas, from very different backgrounds, into one persistently developmental scheme continues to fascinate us.

Thorough analysis of Vygotsky's theory can be found in many sources (Davydov & Radzikhovskii, 1980, 1981; Kozulin, 1984, 1990; Van der Veer, 1984, 1996a, 1996b; Van der Veer & Valsiner, 1991; Van IJzendoorn & Van der Veer, 1984; Wertsch, 1981, 1985). Here, I concentrate only on the basic notions from Vygotsky's complex heritage that are of importance for the theory outlined in this book.

4.5.1   Development of Novel Complexity in Irreversible Time

The central issue in Vygotsky's theoretical thinking is the *development of qualitatively novel ("higher") psychological functions in the history of cultures and ontogeny of children in the process of organisms' (i.e., culture, or child) goal-directed acting on their environments.* In child development, the developing child and the cultural environment of the child are intrinsically related. The cultural environment is organized by active members of the culture who belong to the generations older than the child. That environment itself guides the child toward the personal (but socially assisted) invention of culture. Furthermore, the "social others" of the child may assist in child development directly, by becoming involved in the instruction (Russian: *obuchenie*) process.

The theoretical framework in which the children's relationships with their environments (and with other human beings) are cast has been called by Vygotsky *zona blizaishego razvitia* in a figurative way. That concept has been translated into English usually as *Zone of Proximal Development* (ZPD; see Rogoff & Wertsch, 1984; Vygotsky, 1962, 1978), or, alternatively, as *Zone of Potential Development* (Vygotsky, 1963).

The basic theoretical feature of the ZPD concept, for Vygotsky, was the interdependence of the process of child development and the socially provided resources of that development. That interdependence was conceptualized by Vygotsky in structural–dynamic terms, following the lead of his contemporary gestalt psychology. Vygotsky (1960, pp. 440–441) gave credit to Koffka in overcoming both the preformationist and environmentalist perspectives on the relationship of the learning and instruction. The preformationist (hereditary determinist) view on the issue reduced the relationship to the dominance of the biological development of the organism. The child was considered to be ready for instruction when the processes (the intended object of instruction) were ready in their mature form. Vygotsky characterized this perspective in terms of "instruction drags after development, the development always is ahead of instruction" (p. 439). Indeed, when causality for child development is fully attributed to maturational (genetically predetermined) course, then thinking about the role of instruction in that development would be viewed as superfluous by definition. The opposite of the maturationist view—the environmentalist perspective on child development—performed a similar (but opposite) extreme reduction of the issue to one of its sides. For an extreme environmentalist (the Watsonian or Pavlovian kind), instruction (teaching) is equated with child development, and the child's contribution to it is reduced drastically. In this case, as Vygotsky figuratively remarked, "Development follows instruction, like shadow follows the object of which it is a shadow" (p. 440).

In contrast, Koffka's view of learning and instruction emphasized the interdependence of the two processes, linking development to the general influence of instruction that makes it possible for the organism to transfer what is learned in one setting into another. Vygotsky, however, proceeded in his thinking beyond Koffka, by asking: At which developmental stage of the emergency of some new psychological function would instruction be most appropriate? That question was answered by him: By locating the most appropriate time for linking instruction with learning, the time when new functions are *beginning* to emerge but have not unfolded yet. Likewise, the instruction would have no effect on learning if the novel psychological function is beyond the current biological capacity of the organism. It is within the range between the "already begun, but not yet developed" and the "fully developed" state of a function in child development. Vygotsky stated:

> The crucial characteristic of instruction is the fact that instruction creates the zone of proximal development, i.e. elicits in the child, promotes, and brings to movement a number of internal developmental processes, which at the present time are available for the child only in the sphere of relations with the people around and in joint action with peers, but which later, undergoing [an] internal course of development, become then the internal property of the child himself. (Vygotsky, 1960, p. 450)

However, according to Vygotsky, ZPD can also be constructed without the direct efforts at instruction on behalf of adults. It can be constructed by simple organization of the child's environment, for example. Vygotsky's discussion of child development at the preschool age illustrates that case:

> The experience of child-rearing in the family shows that a child, who is surrounded by books, on the sixth year of life acquires reading without any teaching. The experiences of kindergartens shows that learning to read has its place in a preschool institution. One of the important moments which is important for the definition of the linkages of the programme, consists of what could be called embryonal instruction or preteaching . . . . (Vygotsky, 1956, p. 437)

Finally, the developing child can construct the ZPD for himself or herself in the process of play. Vygotsky viewed the crucial role of children's play in the construction of their future development through ZPD:

> The play creates the zone of proximal development of the child. In the play the child is always above his average age, above his usual everyday behavior; in play he is as if head-high above himself. The play contains in a condensed way, like in the focus of a magnifying glass, all tendencies of development; in play the child tries as if to accomplish a jump above the level of his ordinary behavior. (Vygotsky, 1966, p. 74)

Vygotsky's specification of two different kinds of trajectories in the construction of ZPD—(a) socially assisted and (b) personal—indicates the redundancy involved in the process of development. The child can develop (usually) under the social suggestions emanating from real-life social others. Yet, when the latter are absent or are not involved in the actual instruction efforts, the child can develop through reconstruction (in play) of novel versions of adult activity models. By acting in an *as if* fashion in play, the child becomes his or her own instructor, which is sufficient for development. The actual development is usually not only redundantly compensable, but actually redundantly overdetermined. The child is at times involved in active teaching/learning tasks, with goal-oriented involvement by the instructor; or, the child is a participant in or observer of the activities of others, and uses play as a way to reconstruct these experiences. And, at other times, the child is involved in solitary or peer play. In each instance, *the child is the person whose ZPD is constructed*—with or without assistance from other persons.

The ZPD concept faces the possible immediate futures of the developmental process in all their relative indeterminacy; it entails efforts to reflect the *present* process of emergence of new psychological functions, which will become discernible *in the near future*. Thus, from the point of view of detection (or *measurement*, a word more often used by psychologists), the ZPD concept is necessarily ephemeral, because it is impossible to detect (i.e., match with a model of established form) a form that is only presently in the process of becoming. The axiom of sociogenetic primacy (i.e., that psychological functions first emerge in the interpsychological sphere and subsequently become established intrapsychologically) has been invoked to support the use of teaching experiments, in the hope of gaining access to the emerging psychological functions at the given present. If, in a teaching experiment (i.e., under conditions of social goal-directed input), the person can be led to arrive at a form of psychological function that, in the individual's own autonomous psychological functioning, is not yet demonstrable, it is taken to be an indication that this specific function has been within the ZPD. The rationale of this argument entails a translation of the present-pointed acceleration efforts to the possible future (see Figure 4.2).

If a particular function e, not yet detectable at the present, can be brought to be detectable in a microgenetic teaching/learning encounter, it is viewed as being "within" the ZPD at the given present. Conversely, if a particular function (not detectable at present) is not made detectable in the microgenetic teaching/learning experiment, it is viewed as *not* being within the ZPD at the given present. From the results of intervention at the *microgenetic* level, we can infer an ontological "diagnosis" of the *ontogenetic* future states. A microgenetic account of development becomes projected onto the ontogenetic future.

4.5.1.1   An Ignored Basic Problem: Relations of Ontogenesis and Microgenesis.
Studying ZPD through microgenetic teaching/learning experiments eliminates the open-endedness (constructivity) of development from the study. What is (and is not) projected into the ZPD depends on the success (or luck) of the microgenetic intervention, and on the process of encounter between the social other and the developing person.

Theoretically, it cannot be assumed that all microgenetically emerging (i.e., assistable) psychological phenomena carry over from that context to lead the person into a new phase of ontogenetic advancement. This issue has been worked through in evolutionary epistemology by A. Severtsov, who suggested a distinction between *idioadaptations* (adaptations to the local environmental demands that disappear, together with the actual disappearance of those demands), and *aromorphosis* (transition of the species from a lower to a higher

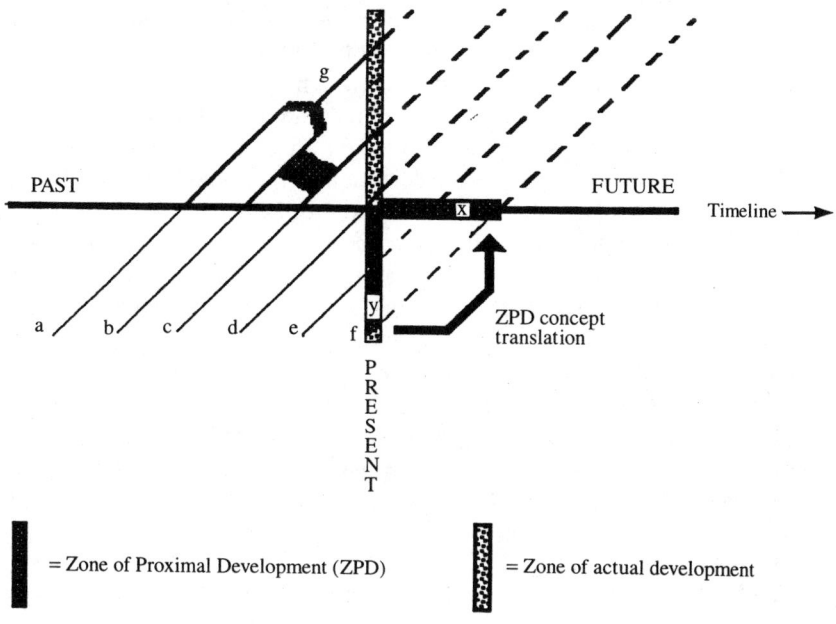

FIGURE 4.2.   Inferential projection from present to future in discussion of the Zone of Proximal Development (ZPD).

organizational level under environmental demands; Sewertzoff, 1929). If each teaching/learning-setting-based new psychological phenomenon was to be accurately projected into ontogenesis, we would operate with a model that includes only aromorphosis, and no idioadaptations. In terms of educational efforts, any success of a teaching/learning process is assumed to be retained, and no psychological acquisitions by the person are ever lost. Surely, this is an unreasonable proposition: Many successful educational tasks never transfer over to ontogenetic progress, and many can be lost when not in use (see Tulviste, 1991, on the loss of literacy in rural Kirghiz villages). *Only under some conditions are microgenetic demonstrated developmental successes transferable into key roles in ontogenesis.* Developmental science has thus far failed to study which conditions these are, and what kinds of microgenetic emergent functions transfer to ontogenesis.

Consider again Figure 3.4 (page 117). In terms of microgenetic intervention, the efforts of the social other are necessarily blind (or semiblind) in their locus of impact (A, in Figure 3.4). In the semideterminate context of emerging psychological functions, a microgenetic intervention by a social other cannot have clearly determined guidelines. It may catch on to specific seemingly organized phenomena in the total flow (e.g., a seemingly structured action effort of a toddler, *interpreted* by the adult and guided in the direction *assumed* to be productive by the latter). However, because actual development is jointly constructed by the teacher and the learner, the actual direction of further development of the semistructured form (i.e., which of the directions—B, C, or D in Figure 3.4—is taken) remains uncertain at the time of impact. Let us assume that C is the form (psychological function) that emerges from the microgenetic encounter. By the rules of the detection of functions within ZPD, it is thus argued that because C did emerge, it (and B or D, which *did not*) is within the ZPD at the given present. Furthermore, because C emerged, it is not possible to say anything about B or D either being or not being within the ZPD at the time of the beginning of the intervention A. The ZPD concept is a theoretical term to cover the set of immediate next possibilities, of which only one can become actualized. From that singular outcome, it is not possible to get knowledge of the full set of possibilities that was there at the beginning of the process that led to the particular outcome. Thus, the ZPD concept is poorly fitted for being "empirically operationalizable" because, for Vygotsky, it was merely a general metaphorical device to spur teachers, in their art of educating, to provide children with opportunities that are slightly beyond their assumed level of actual abilities (Valsiner & Van der Veer, 1993). The term was not meant to be used as a central theoretical concept. Traditional psychology's discourse about motivation has also included a focus on the relevance of "moderate novelty."

4.5.1.2   How to Study the Phenomena of ZPD.   An alternative to *measurement of ZPD* is actual investigation of the process of emergence of the singular potentiality that does become actualized. The emergence of C in Figure 3.4 was actually a result of the negotiated actions between the teacher and learner; under other conditions of such negotiation, B or D could have resulted as well (but did not). The feature of negotiatedness of actions in any present context retains the open-endedness of developmental processes, and creates an impossibility of inferring with full certainty what is (or is not) within the ZPD at a given moment in time. Hence, microgenetic intervention results are projected onto ontogenetic developmental course results when transforming the ZPD concept from a concept intended to reflect development, to another concept that reflects a subset of outcomes of present teachability/learnability. In other words, the full range of functions within ZPD cannot be measured because of the constructivity of development within irreversible time and in negotiation with other organisms. Thus, the use of the ZPD concept in contemporary developmental psychology is a theoretical impasse, because it eliminates exactly those phenomena (of emergence) that it was to emphasize (in Vygotsky's uses) in generic terms.

4.5.2   Vygotsky's Emphasis on Interiorization (Internalization)
Observations of children's development give ample evidence about psychological phenomena that first emerge in child–adult interaction and are subsequently

carried over to the sphere of the intraindividual psychological functions of the child. Such transition of phenomena from person–environment relationships to the inner psychological organization of the person is labeled internalization. For developmental psychology, it is the process of internalization that needs to be described and explained.

Vygotsky's emphasis on internalization (interiorization) is another issue in which he relied constructively on the world psychology of his time. Its roots are embedded in the thinking of Janet, Baldwin, Stern, and Piaget. At the same time, the idea of internalization, borrowed from other psychologists, was considered by Vygotsky to develop further Marx's basic idea of human psychology as a system of social relationships. He conceptualized internalization as a "set of social relationships, transposed inside and having become functions of personality and the forms of its structure" (Vygotsky, 1960, pp. 198–199). In disagreement with Piaget's concept of egocentric speech, Vygotsky formulated his major principle of development:

> The actual course of the process of development of the child's thinking takes place not in the direction going from the individual to the socialized state, but starting from the social and proceeding to the individual—such is the main result of both theoretical as well as experimental investigation of the problem that interests us. (Vygotsky, 1956, p. 89)

Vygotsky's indebtedness to Janet in formulating the general law of internalization in human psychological development is clearly evident in his writings. For example:

> The history of the development of signs brings us, however, to a far more general law that directs the development of behaviour. Janet calls it the fundamental law in psychology. The essence of that law is that the child in the process of development begins to apply to himself the very same forms of behaviour which others applied to him prior to that. The child himself acquires the social forms of behaviour and transposes those onto himself. (Vygotsky, 1960, p. 192)

The idea that words that are originally commands for others develop into means of regulating oneself (see also Vygotsky, 1960, p. 194) is one of the cornerstones of Vygotsky's explanation of the ontogeny of speech and thinking. The issues of speech and thinking are special topics within the general domain of children's cultural development. In more general terms, Vygotsky formulated a "general genetic law" of cultural development:

> We could formulate the general genetic law of cultural development in the following way: every function in the cultural development of the child comes onto the stage twice, in two respects; first—in the social, later—in the psychological, first in relations between people as an interpsychological category, afterwards within the child as an intrapsychological category. . . .

All higher psychological functions are internalized relationships of the social kind, and constitute the social structure of personality. Their composition, genetic structure, ways of functioning—in one word—all their nature is social. Even when they have become psychological processes, their nature remains quasi-social. The human being who is alone also retains the functions of interaction. (Vygotsky, 1960, pp. 197–198)

The closeness of this general perspective to that of Baldwin (see above) is quite evident in this quote. In its generality, Vygotsky's "general law" is similar to Werner's "orthogenetic principle." Vygotsky's thinking about internalization resulted from his constructive development of ideas that had occurred previously in the work of Janet, Baldwin, Piaget, Bühler, Kretschmer, and Marx. Vygotsky did not invent the idea of internalization anew. Instead, he integrated different existing viewpoints creatively into a new general principle.

The idea of internalization of social experience was analyzed by Vygotsky in different empirical contexts. Consider his example of the process of development of indicatory "gesture" in the child's mind:

When the mother comes to the aid of the child and comprehends his/her movement as an indicator, the situation changes in an essential way. The indicatory gesture becomes a gesture for others. In response to the child's unsuccessful grasping movement, a response emerges not on the part of the object, but on the part of another human. Thus, other people introduce the primary sense into this unsuccessful grasping movement. And only afterward, owing to the fact they have already connected the unsuccessful grasping movement with the whole objective situation, do children themselves begin to use the movement as an indication. The functions of the movement itself have undergone a change here; from a movement directed toward an object it has become a movement directed towards another human being. The grasping is converted into an indication. Thanks to this, the movement is reduced and abbreviated, and the form of the indicatory gesture is elaborated. We can now say that it is a gesture for oneself. However, his movement does not become a gesture for oneself except by first being an indication, i.e., functioning objectively as an indication and gesture for others, being comprehended and understood by surrounding people as an indicator. Thus, the child is the last to become conscious of his/her gesture. Its significance and functions first are created by the objective situation and then by the people surrounding the child. The indicatory gesture initially relies on a movement to point to what others understand and only later becomes an indicator for the child. (Reproduced with permission from Vygotsky, 1981, p. 161; original: Vygotsky, 1960, p. 196)

This example illustrates the dependence of the particular internalization process on the context of the child's relationship to the environment, which is regulated (by the adult caregiver's responding to the child's effort, and later gesture) by the social others surrounding the child. Only some parts of this process take place under conditions of immediate interaction of the child with the adult. Once a gesture has begun its relocation in the inside direction, the presence of interaction may perform only a supportive function in the internalization process. The cultural structure of the child's environment then serves as a field that sets up external limits for the child's acting and—eventually—for the direction of what becomes internalized.

The sequence in which the child's gesture becomes interpreted by the parent, is responded to as such, and then leads to the child's pointing to self in his or her mind, is a good example of underestimation of Vygotsky's intellectual interdependence with his predecessors. The example was borrowed from Wilhelm Wundt, and it was used by Vygotsky and by George Herbert Mead in their parallel development of ideas of internalization (Valsiner & Van der Veer, 1996).

4.5.2.1 Contemporary Elaborations. The issue of internalization (and its counterpart—externalization) became a topic of theoretical arguments in sociocultural psychology during the 1980s and 1990s. The main theoretical issue has been the feasibility of using a basic assumption that differentiates the "inner" and "outer" domains of human psychological functioning. Authors who would view the dangers of dualism in the inner/outer distinction would argue that the concept of internalization is better replaced by that of appropriation. Those who see no such conceptual dangers can assume the distinction, and thus make the use of the internalization concept feasible (Lawrence & Valsiner, 1993; Valsiner & Lawrence, 1996).

4.5.3   The Role of Meanings in Human Psychological Development

The meaning of signs in a culture can arise from the multitude of particular and idiosyncratic uses of the signs in social communication. At this point of theorizing, Vygotsky's emphasis (following Paulhan, 1928) on the difference between "meaning" and "sense" may be worthwhile mentioning. Vygotsky states:

> The sense of a word . . . is the sum of all the psychological events aroused in our consciousness by the word. It is a dynamic, fluid, complex whole, which has several zones of unequal stability. Meaning is only one of the zones of sense, the most stable and precise zone. A word acquires its sense from the context in which it appears in different contexts, it changes its sense. Meaning remains stable throughout the changes of sense. (Vygotsky, 1962, p. 146)

The developing child is, from the very beginning, embedded in the context of meanings, as these are defined within the culture [e.g., meaning of childbearing, indigenous understanding of conception and pregnancy (see Monberg, 1975); meaning of abilities of children at different ages (see Harkness & Super, 1983)]. In the immediate social environment of a developing child in any culture, these meanings guide child development by providing a framework for parental understanding of child-rearing goals and methods, as well as by creating a basis for organization of children's everyday environments. In addition, these cultural meanings help the parents to interpret the development of their children, and they constitute the context of child development with which any behavioral events in children's lives are interdependent.

On the other hand, the *personal sense* of a sign develops in the course of the individual child's ontogeny, and with assistance from the social environment. However, although the development of sense is aided by that environment, it is not determined by it. This constrained indeterminacy in the children's sense development guarantees the open-ended nature of cultural change, which is wrought by individuals' transactions with their cultural environments. New meanings can emerge in a culture as a result of convergence of the personal senses of different individuals. Meaning, thus, is not a pre-given and immutable ideal entity, but a byproduct of social transaction that is used to regulate person–environment relationships. Meanings are thus dynamic—they emerge, develop, and dissipate in their cultural contexts, interdependently with changes in the personal sense of the members of the culture. On the other hand, cultural meanings themselves are constantly undergoing change, part of which is due to the innovations that children introduce into their (and their parents') senses during their development. The children's environments are structured by the cultural–historical meanings that they include. These meanings are coded into objects and events of the particular child's environment through the actions of the people who surround the child and on the basis of their personalized senses derived from the meanings. Within such culturally structured (meaningful) and personalized ("sense-ful") environments, developing children invent (or reinvent, by imitation) novel ways of acting and thinking, out of which only those that end up being accepted by the child *and* his social environment might be retained. Baldwin's "circular reactions" in the actions of the developing child are embedded in the culturally structured environments that (rather than in the child's "pleasure" or "pain") guide the process of child development. That guidance, however, is accomplished within the total structure of the life environment of the developing child, rather than in only some of its aspects.

4.5.4 The Nature of Human Environment in Relation to the Person

Vygotsky was very close to William Stern in his emphasis on the particular forms of linkage of the same sociophysical environment with the personal perspectives of different children at different levels of development. Thus, in his analysis of an alcoholic mother, he outlined the different positions of the children relative to the everyday phenomena these children would experience:

> We are dealing with three children, brought to us from one family. The external situation in this family is the same for all three children . . . . The mother drinks and, as a result, apparently suffers from several nervous and psychological disorders. . . . When drunk, and during these breakdowns, the mother had once attempted to throw one of the children out of the window and she regularly beat them or threw them on the floor . . . .

As far as the youngest of these children is concerned . . . , he reacts to the situation by developing a number of neurotic symptoms, . . . of a defensive nature. He is simply overwhelmed by the horror of what is happening to him. As a result, he develops attacks of terror, enuresis, and he develops a stammer, sometimes being unable to speak at all as he loses his voice . . . .

The second child is developing an extremely agonizing condition, what is called a state of inner conflict, which is a condition [that] . . . we have called ambivalent attitude. On the one hand, from the child's point of view, the mother is an object of painful attachment, and on the other, she represents a source of all kinds of terrors and terrible emotional experiences for the child . . . .

Finally, at first glance, the third and elder child presented us with a completely unexpected picture. The child had a limited mental ability but, at the same time, showed signs of precautions, maturity, seriousness, and solicitude. . . . He understood that their mother was ill and pitied her . . . . And he had a special role. He must calm his mother down, make certain that she is prevented from harming the little ones and comfort them. Quite simply, he has become the senior member of the family, the only one whose duty it was to look after everyone else. (Vygotsky, 1935/1994, pp. 340–341)

This case description is a rare glimpse into Vygotsky's treatment of "the data"; in his work, his own empirical evidence was almost completely absent. This clinical description indicates that different persons (because of their age-related developmental level) relate to the same external environment from their personal positions. Any social environment is centered around the developing person in his or her present developmental state, which itself is constantly anticipating its own future. The three children in Vygotsky's clinical case represent three personal trajectories that are differentiated from one another exactly because of their sharing of an otherwise similar environment. The social role of the oldest child can lead him to develop caregiving capacities of high resiliency. The second child is working out a trajectory of "ambivalent attachment," and the youngest child can be viewed as avoidant.

The social world within which a person develops was, for Vygotsky, a total whole rather than a system of separate "variables." Within that total field, the person situates his or her subjective world, becomes interdependent with the social field, and is guided by the latter (and yet preserves and develops a personal autonomy). Vygotsky's metaphorical talk of "zones"—those of "nearest development," or "meaning as a zone of sense"—indicates his commitment to holistic ways of making sense of the phenomena of emergence. Whether the person is a reader of a short story, or a child in a context of teaching/learning, or an adult who tries to make sense of another person (or of the world at large)—in all these cases, novel synthesis (of feeling, or of new knowledge) occurs where the personal–psychological field intersects with the social surroundings. Specific features are at times differentiated out from these holistic fields, and a description of the particular relation of the person and the world is then possible. This brings Vygotsky's general perspective close to the field-theoretical conceptualizations of Kurt Lewin.

4.6   KURT LEWIN'S FIELD THEORY

Kurt Lewin "is recognized as a great psychologist, but the nature of his great-ness seems not to be clearly understood" (Henle, 1978, p. 237). Lewin's theo-retical perspective developed within the web of gestalt psychology on the one hand, and on the basis of his own personal experiences during World War I on the other (see Lewin, 1917). His interest in overcoming the person-versus-environment dualism in psychology led him to propose new ways for psychol-ogy to view the lawfulness of psychological phenomena (see 2.6). Lewin's major concern was improvement of the scientific nature of the psychological theories of his time, which were hopelessly built onto culture-specific implicit assumptions. In this sense, the state of affairs in theorizing in psychology has not changed since Lewin's times (see Benigni & Valsiner, 1985).

Lewin's theoretical system went through different stages in its develop-ment. After starting from the issues of connection among action, will, and emotion (see, for example, an overview by Zeigarnik, 1981), his interests proceeded toward finding adequate qualitative-structural formalisms to de-scribe the structure and events in the "psychological space" (Lewin, 1933, 1935a, 1938). After his topological and vector concepts were introduced, Lewin turned again to the issues of how these concepts can capture the dy-namic aspect of the person–environment system, and investigated a number of issues pertaining to children (Barker, Dembo, & Lewin, 1941; Lewin, 1939, 1942) and adults (Lewin, 1948, 1951; Lewin, Lippitt, & White, 1939). Two aspects of Lewin's theoretical heritage contribute to the foundation of the pre-sent theory: (a) qualitative-structural analysis of the person–environment fields; and (b) emphasis on the dynamic nature of the field, and the descrip-tion of how the field is transformed.

4.6.1   The Structure of the Person–Environment Field

Lewin's theory may be best understood by thinking of contemporary empiri-cally minded psychologists as that of a metatheorist (Henle, 1978). Lewin himself noted the metatheoretical nature of his field theory:

> Field theory . . . can hardly be called correct or incorrect in the same way as a theory in the usual sense of the term. *Field theory is probably best character-ized as a method:* namely, a method of *analyzing causal relations and of build-ing scientific constructs.* This method of analyzing causal relations can be expressed in the form of certain general statements about the "nature" of the conditions of change. (Lewin, 1943a, p. 294)

Lewin's widely known general formula (Behavior = Function of Person and the Environment) constitutes the core of his field theory. Interpretations of that formula have sometimes overlooked the *interdependent rather than corre-lational* nature of the link between the Person (P) and the Environment (E).

For Lewin, the intrinsic (rather than formal-statistical) nature of the conjunction between P and E was of central theoretical importance. He explained:

> In this formula for behaviour the state of the person (P) and that of his environment (E) are not independent of each other. How a child sees a given physical setting (for instance, whether the frozen pond looks dangerous to him or not) depends upon the developmental state and the character of that child and upon his ideology. The worlds in which the newborn, the one-year-old child, and the ten-year-old child live are different even in identical physical or social surroundings. This holds also for the same child when it is hungry or satiated, full of energy or fatigued. In other words, $E = F(P)$. The reverse is also true: the state of the person depends upon his environment, $P = F(E)$. The state of the person after encouragement is different from that after discouragement, that in an area of sympathy or security from that in an area of tension, that in a democratic group atmosphere from that in an autocratic atmosphere. . . .
>
> In summary, one can say that behavior and development depend upon the state of the person and his environment, $B = F(P,E)$. In this equation the person (P) and his environment (E) have to be viewed as variables which are mutually dependent upon each other. In other words, to understand or to predict behavior, the person and his environment have to be considered as *one* constellation of interdependent factors. (Reproduced with permission from Lewin, 1951, pp. 239–240)

Lewin's analysis of the person–environment field led him to introduce the concepts of "barrier," "boundary," and "boundary zone" to characterize the structure of the field. It also facilitated a description of the field in terms of its demand character ("valence") and the different "forces" that reflect the person's locomotions in the process of restructuring the field. Although Lewin was careful not to extend his field notions to include absolutely every aspect of P–E relationships in the past, present, and future, he still included the "psychological past" and "psychological future" alongside the "psychological present" in the field, in cases where these concepts could be exactly determined (e.g., Lewin, 1943a; Lewin, Lippitt, & Escalona, 1940, p. 36).

Lewin's goal of building up psychology's formal-theoretical system so that it could represent science of the Galilean kind (see Lewin, 1931) led him to juggle different areas of mathematics that could, in principle, provide the formal basis for that new psychology (e.g., Lewin, 1936a, 1938). These formalizations of Lewin's basic organismic thinking are less important in the context of the present book than is emphasis on the *structured nature of person–environment relationships* and his efforts to analyze these relationships in ways that retain it, rather than eliminate it for the sake of the traditions of psychological methodology. Lewin's insistence on building a psychology that would resemble Galilean physics was largely a theoretical endeavor where the ideal psychological "laws" would follow the closed-systems axioms of classical physics, rather than the open-systems basic assumptions of organismic phenomena that are capable of development. The paradoxical nature of Lewin's theorizing is somewhat similar to the nature of Piaget's. Lewin, like Piaget, had the ideal of developing psychological theory along the Galilean lines of closed systems, and abstracting general formal laws from complex reality. In practice, though, Lewin's descriptions are close-to-reality structural maps of the life space and of "forces" that remain far from the Galilean ideal of the analog of "frictionless spaces" for psychology. Lewin's use of formalisms in his field-theoretical descriptions was more reality-bound than mathematical (see London, 1944; Sorokin, 1956). Nevertheless, or perhaps because of that, Lewin's field descriptions of psychological phenomena provide a picture of thorough understanding of the complexities involved, which no other theoretical system in psychology after Lewin has managed to do.

4.6.2 Field Dynamics and Lewin's Conceptualization of Development

The dynamic nature of the field structure is an idea that is inseparable from Lewin's concept of the field. However, Lewin's (and his students') empirical interests concentrated largely on issues that required microgenetic rather than ontogenetic perspectives, even when Lewin studied children or wrote about them. Thus, among the problems studied empirically by investigators in the "Lewin group" were issues of the effect of unfinished activity on memory (Zeigarnik, 1927), change in the aspiration levels under conditions of failure (Hoppe, 1930), relationships of frustration and regression in children (Barker, Dembo, & Lewin, 1941), prospects for cultural reconstruction in postwar Germany (Lewin, 1943b, 1943c), culture change in general (Lewin, 1948), and adolescent (Lewin, 1939) and marital conflicts (Lewin, 1948). Lewin's interest in the dynamics of social groups (Lewin, 1951; Lewin, Lippitt, & White, 1939) bears marks of a similar microgenetic emphasis. Although he occasionally talked about ontogeny (in the context of the transformation of the psychological field over time), Lewin never studied it over any considerable length of time.

Lewin comes close to dealing with issues of development from two perspectives. His efforts to reformulate the concept of learning from the position of field theory necessarily involved some explanation of development (Lewin, 1942). In this context, Lewin emphasized the change of meanings in the cognitive structure of the field, once the field has undergone transformation:

> Learning, as a change in cognitive structure, has to deal with practically every field of behaviour. Whenever we speak of a change in meaning, a change of such cognitive structure has occurred. New connections or separations, differentiations or de-differentiations of psychological areas have taken place. The "meaning" of an event in psychology may be said to be known if its psychological position and its psychological direction are determined. In Mark Twain's *Life on the Mississippi,* the passengers on the boat enjoy the "scenery," but for the pilot the U-shape of the two hills, which a passenger admires, means a signal to turn

sharply, and the beautiful waves in the middle of the river mean dangerous rocks. The psychological connection of these "stimuli" with actions has changed, and therefore the meaning has changed. (Lewin, 1942, pp. 228–229)

Lewin's more explicit effort to conceptualize development is present in a monograph on frustration and regression in children (Barker, Dembo, & Lewin, 1941). He emphasized the widening of the child's space of free movement in ontogeny. In his description of the developmental processes in general, Lewin followed largely the line of thought shared by Werner and the gestalt tradition of emphasizing differentiation-and-integration as the basic characteristic of development (Barker, Dembo, & Lewin, 1941, pp. 18–20). Lewin saw the person–environment field ("life space") as becoming gradually more differentiated and integrated as the child develops. The child becomes increasingly more able to organize parts of the physical and social environments as means to reach some end. The growing child tries increasingly to organize the environment so that the satisfaction of his or her needs is not left to chance.

To summarize, Lewin's theoretical emphasis was developmental (dynamic) mostly in respect to the changes in the field structure over shorter periods of time. This emphasis can be summarized by the term *microgenetic,* which, in accordance with its narrower German term of origin (*Aktualgenese;* see Draguns, 1984) has been used in psychology in a very specific sense in the context of perceptogenesis. However, the English term may be fruitfully used to denote any restructuring of a psychological structure in the course of a limited period of time. Lewin's field-theoretical thinking emphasized the dynamic, microgenetic aspect of psychological process. However, Lewin's thinking was not outrightly developmental in its nature. For example, he was not much interested in the developmental question of how children's life spaces develop over longer time periods, although he recognized the question as one of scientific importance and provided some general ideas about it from the position of his field theory.

4.7   MIKHAIL BASOV'S DEVELOPMENTAL STRUCTURALISM

Basov's work has become available to a modern readership (Basov, 1991), yet its functional role for developmental psychology has not been made clear. The origins of Basov's dynamic structuralism are in the realm of gestalt psychology and its unification with developmental principles (in Chapter 5, Valsiner, 1988). Furthermore, Basov emerged from the historical tradition of V.M. Bekhterev's reflexology and A. Lazurskii's focus on "natural experiments." Basov's research group provided Vygotsky with a number of relevant empirical materials for the development of the notion of a "method of double stimulation." Vygotsky succeeded Basov in his lectures on pedology in Leningrad, after Basov's death in 1931.

4.7.1   The Hierarchically Structured Nature of Environments

The principle of the structured nature of children's environments was first formulated extensively by Basov, whose considerable contribution to developmental psychology has been almost fully unnoticed [despite its international
availability (see Basov, 1929; Valsiner, 1988)]. Basov emphasized the relational
nature of the concept of environment—it is always definable as "environment of
X," rather than "environment" in any absolute sense:

> *The coordinated factors in the case of the concept of environment are the organ-
> ism, and some portion of the rest of its world—that part of it which is in certain
> relationships with the given organism. . . .* No single organism, including man,
> is related to the *whole* world in such a way that is obligatory for considering the
> *whole* world its environment. Every organism has its limits in establishing rela-
> tions with its world; for some organisms that limit is very small, for others im-
> perceivably large. Starting from that, it can be said that the segment of reality
> in connection with which the given organism practically exists, constitutes its
> environment. (Basov, 1931, pp. 69–70)

Basov addressed the question of the nature of organization of the environment, recognizing the implications carried by different possible answers to
that question. Accepting that the whole world is characterized by interdependence of parts within their whole, Basov addressed the issue at the level of
particular environments of people:

> Let us consider that question [of the nature of environment] only as it appears in
> the case of humans. Consequently, here we talk about the environments of some
> specific individual who lives at a specific time, belongs to a particular human
> society and social class, etc. What is the environment of such X like in its struc-
> ture? Is it some kind of a holistic system in which phenomena are related to one
> another, or is it a simple sum, a conglomerate, of their mechanical grouping?
> This question is very important because, in accordance with one or the other
> view on the structure of human environment, our practical relation to it would
> vary. If the environment is a set of separate factors that are totally unrelated to
> one another, then our relation to it is determined. Every factor will in this case
> be evaluated in itself—today one, tomorrow another—and after such account of
> all the separate factors ends we have accounted for all the environment, so that
> nothing is left over. If the environment is a holistically organized system of phe-
> nomena, then, obviously, our practical relation with it must take that into ac-
> count. The separation of independent elements in that case will not give the same
> result as in the first condition, since the organized whole is always larger than
> the sum of its elements, and—its most important aspect is that quality is some-
> thing else than a simple conglomerate of elements. (Basov, 1931, p. 73)

The influence of gestalt psychology's emphasis—the primacy of the whole
over the sum of its parts—on Basov's thinking about human environments is
obvious in this quote. Differently from those gestalt psychologists of his time

who came closest to addressing developmental issues (e.g., Koffka), Basov emphasized the gestalt-like nature of both the organism's actions and the environments in which these actions take place. The question—posed in the quote above—of the nature of particular environments of developing humans was largely rhetorical as Basov asked it, and his theoretical background made it possible to answer it only in the structuralist direction:

> [E]lements of environment do not exist separately from one another, but in a mutual relationship and in the unity of the whole. While examining one of the relations [in that whole], we drag behind it a long chain of relations that do not exist without one another. This is because all these phenomena emerge from some shared origin and therefore are related to one another by cause-consequent relationships. And since it is so, it means that these relations can be ordered in a hierarchical way. (Basov, 1931, pp. 74–75)

The principle of hierarchical organization—the core of Heinz Werner's "ontogenetic principle" that applies to *organisms*—was applied to their *environments* by Basov. His emphasis on the inequality among different parts of the environment from the standpoint of the environment as a whole (albeit that of a particular individual) renders all efforts toward quantitative measurement of children's environments largely groundless.

Instead, the main question of developmental research involves dynamic structuralism: How are persons' actions emerging in their own hierarchical structural form, given that the environment itself has some hierarchical order? This question is close in spirit to the thought of Jean Piaget, as well as to that of Heinz Werner. Its methodological focus is on the actual study of the emerging structural forms (in accordance with Baldwin's "second postulate," above).

4.7.2 Structural Forms of Action

Basov tried to demonstrate the emergence of novel differentiated structures through the use of three increasingly complex forms (and "transitional forms" between them) that are constructed in ontogeny (Basov, 1929, 1931):

1. The *temporal chain of acts* is a form where actions follow one another without specific connections in time. These actions are triggered by a given situation at a given time. Neither past experiences nor expectations for the future are involved in this flow of context-specific behaving. An example of this form may be taken from the erratic sequence of activities of a toddler, who may toddle from one area to another and be involved with a sequence of separate activities, without linkages from one to another.

2. The *associatively determined process* is a structural form of behavior that operates on the basis of associations between the present state and past experiences. This differentiated structure entails continuity in time from past to present (e.g., our contemporary modeling efforts to temporal

processes through Markovian analyses, and other forms of time-series analyses, are axiomatically limited to detect this form of differentiation à la Basov). However, the differentiation of form here does not include any orientation toward the future; hence, it cannot be viewed as the ultimate result of differentiation.

3. The *apperceptively determined process* constitutes the unification of the past-to-present and present-to-expected-future linkages. The expectations for the future—the apperceptive focus—provide the structure of action in any given moment of focus. This is used to integrate selected associative ties with past experiences into the structure, which then is instrumental in bringing about *a* future.

Each of the forms could occur concurrently in the conduct of a person, once they have ontogenetically emerged. Hence, one often sees intermediate or transitory forms, and quick dynamic shifts from complex to simple forms (and vice versa). The crucial breakthrough in human action is the emergence of the apperceptively determined process. This form allows for goals-oriented actions and anticipation of the future.

4.8 NOTIONS OF CANALIZATION IN EXPLAINING DEVELOPMENT

The notion of canalization was introduced to developmental biology by Waddington (1942, 1966, 1968, 1970), who used it in discussing genotype–phenotype relationships. The term *canalization* describes an epigenetic mechanism that leads to definite outcomes: "The main thesis is that developmental reactions, *as they occur in organisms submitted to natural selection,* are in general canalized. That is to say, they are adjusted so as to bring about one definite end-result regardless of minor variations in conditions during the course of the reaction" (Waddington, 1942, p. 563).

Waddington's concept of a "chreod," a buffered developmental pathway, illustrates the notion of the structured nature of the organism and its environment. According to Waddington's formulation, the genome's interaction with the environment results in conditions that define the set of further possible pathways of change (cf. Waddington, 1966, pp. 109–111). The chreods (or necessary pathways) are structurally organized on the plane of an "epigenetic landscape" (see Figure 4.3).

The developmental pathways are constructed to possess self-stabilizing characteristics that restrain the variation of the organism–environment system as it changes over time (Waddington, 1970, pp. 185–186). By restraining the further development of the organism, the chreods mediate the process of development via *canalization* (gradual guidance and direction). The notion of canalization is of theoretical importance for developmental biology and psychology because it illustrates the bounded character of developmental processes. Development is

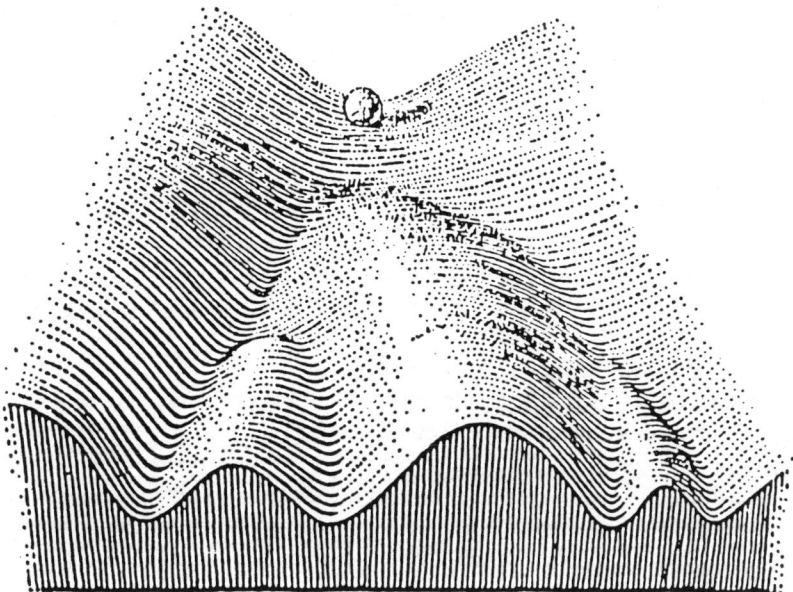

FIGURE 4.3.   An example of an epigenetic landscape.

canalized in the direction of the organism's adult state by a system of constraints that leave the *particular* individual organism's developmental route largely indeterminate (and therefore adaptable to unexpected changes in the environment) in the sense of *exact* prediction of its future. However, the *principle direction* of development in general terms is predictable from constraints that constitute the canalizing system.

Pathways (chreods) defined by the biological system determine the developmental course over time, although the homeorhetic (self-stabilizing) nature of developmental processes within a pathway can be compensated by switching to another pathway within which a similar canalization takes place.

Waddington's version of the epigenetic landscape was a conceptual effort to depict rather than explain (see Waddington, 1966) the joint functioning of genetic and environmental aspects of development over time. Waddington himself was careful not to overextend the use of his epigenetic landscape image. He hesitated to use it at all toward the end of his career (Gilbert, 1991).

Waddington's concept of canalization cannot be carried over from its original context to the present one without some modifications. Two important changes are necessary. First, the set of constraints that are present in human socialization are not present in a static form during the whole period of childhood (e.g., like the "valleys" on Waddington's epigenetic landscape). Instead, the particular constraints are set up by the relationships within the Caregiver(s) ⟷ (Child ⟷ Environment) system. The constraint structure is not "just there" for the child to develop by. It is made up by purposefully acting participants who take the child's current developmental state into account in one or another way.

Second, the child can actively constrain its own development—in the immediate (short) term or by feed-forward preparation of constraints a longer term ahead. In either case, the child participates actively in its own development by altering its constraining structure. Canalization as the general mechanism of children's action and cognitive development is a gradual process in which earlier child–environment structures guide the child's subsequent development in the direction of new structures, which, in turn, canalize the child's progress further.

In its application to human development, the canalization image needs to be complemented by the active role of the developing persons in constructing a path toward some future objective. The channels by which to proceed are provided to the person only in their general form, but the exact pathway of development is worked out in life through that general form, and the person's active efforts to choose one channel over another, and to construct new pathways, often meet resistance from the pregiven structure of possible pathways. This view is more appropriate for a coconstructionist perspective, where an actual pathway of development is *jointly constructed* by the person and the surrounding world.

Thus, instead of the schematic image of a ball rolling down a mountain into pregiven valleys (as in Figure 4.3), the imagery of a mountain climber is more appropriate for the present theoretical transformation of Waddington's epigenetic landscape. The mountain climber has set the goal of reaching a particular mountain peak. The climber faces the mountain and has a way to estimate which climbing route might be appropriate to take. However, each step on the selected route can lead to modifications of the structure: blocking of previously promising directions, or revelation of new possibilities. The structure of the landscape is constantly being altered by the actions of the goal-oriented climber. Furthermore, specific technical devices to alter the landscape (ranging from axes and spades to bulldozers and dynamite) can be invented preemptively to make arrival at the goal easier. Technical inventions might emerge that would open new pathways to the same goal, fully bypassing the previous structure (e.g., a tourist might arrive at the mountaintop by helicopter before many of the mountain climbers had reached the top by the surface route).

4.9 SUMMARY: CONVERGENCE OF IDEAS ABOUT THE STRUCTURED NATURE OF DEVELOPMENTAL PROCESSES

All the theoretical predecessors of the present theoretical system converge on a basic issue: Development entails emergence of *structural* novelty. That structural novelty may be viewed as a phenomenon of the developing person or (also) of the environment. In all cases, it is a novel form that comes into existence through person–environment relationships, in irreversible time. The historical predecessors of the present theory-building effort were consistent with the open-system nature of developmental phenomena, even if they did not use systems-theoretic framing of their thoughts.

Different theorists invented their own terminologies for modeling that process of emergence. The role of the social world was made explicit by some (Vygotsky, Basov, Baldwin), and was deemphasized—yet not denied—by others (Lewin, Stern, Werner, Piaget). The persisting question—How do we make sense of the emergence of such novelty?—remained largely unanswered until our present time. Nice labels—"dialectical synthesis" (Vygotsky) or "hierarchical integration" (Werner), not to speak of Baldwin's "persistent imitation"—need to be decomposed into their subprocesses, so that the emergence of novelty becomes conceptually focused.

The next chapter outlines the theoretical system that was developed for the purpose of understanding human development in structurally organized cultural environments. The system has specifiable linkages with the thought of the theorists whose work has been discussed in this chapter. However, it also selectively rejects some aspects of the previous theories, and fails to relate to many contemporary theoretical efforts in sociocultural developmental psychology.

5

The Theoretical System

The theoretical system presented here constitutes an attempt to conceptualize three aspects of human development. First, there is the issue of *organization of person–environment relationships in the contexts of everyday actions.* The developing person is constantly involved with dynamically changing environmental contexts in ways that are oriented toward transcending the structure of the context-at-the-time. The contexts are set up by human actions and are transformed by further actions, thus guiding human actions toward their transformation, and so on. In that process, different facets are turned into goal orientations—both by the developing person and by others who attempt to direct that development. These goal orientations temporarily organize actions, and lead to the emergence of structures of actions, within larger frameworks that are often labeled "activities." These larger structured frameworks, set up around the necessities of organizing everyday life tasks, constitute a culturally constructed relationship structure of persons (and *by* persons) with the specific "niches" of environment.

The second aspect that is being conceptualized here is the *relation between the person's actions and reflection upon those actions* in their process. This theme entails the development of an intrapersonal psychological (personal) world that can exist because of the human-species-based possibility for semiotic mediation of personal relations with one's own (and others') actions within the world. In the context of acting upon environment, not only is that external environment reorganized (by actions), but the intrapsychological domain of the acting person entails emergence of mediational structures that make it possible to *transcend any concrete activity context through semiotically mediated reflection.* Here, constructive internalization and externalization processes create a relative autonomy of the person from any "here-and-now" context.

The third aspect covered by this theoretical system includes the question of how experiences by the developing person in any here-and-now setting can *transfer to the general life-course development of the person.*

There exist four levels of developmental phenomena:

1. Microgenesis (emergence of novel structures in a here-and-now context).

2. Ontogenesis (emergence of new functional structures in the organism's conduct; in humans, the domains of actions and feeling/thinking that remain relatively stable organizers of the person's psychological functions).

3. Culture-genesis (in humans, emergence of collective cultural frameworks for regulating person–environment encounters).

4. Phylogenesis (emergence of biological structures that make species' development possible).

The issue of development requires analysis of the relationships among these levels, from the standpoint of biology as well as of cultural psychology (Gottlieb, 1992; Gould, 1984; Oyama, 1992). The question of relation among these levels in the irreversible time of experiencing is crucial for our understanding of mechanisms of development (see Cole, 1995). Human beings operate within their life courses, and participate in the alteration of the adjacent levels of the phenomena.

Therefore, the third focus of the theory is one of specific conceptualization of the coordination of microgenetic processes with those of ontogenesis, under the conditions of specific culture-genetic setup backgrounds. This focus entails an assumption of the individual–socioecological reference frame. The *person* actively constructs his or her own next psychological organizational state (in actions and internalized psychological functions) by way of encounters with culture-genetically set everyday life contexts, and under the impact of efforts by other persons to guide his or her ontogenetic course. Through microgenetic processes, ontogenesis is regulated—under the influence of culture-genesis, and on the basis of the species-specific developed biological organism that has emerged in phylogenesis.

The present standpoint eliminates the usual exclusively disjunctive view of the determinism–indeterminism issue, and replaces it with a conjunctive axiom. Thus, developmental process is at the same time both deterministic and indeterministic. To avoid getting lost in any pseudo-dialectical verbiage that can easily follow the acceptance of this axiom, it is necessary to explain the perspectives from which these two views are united in the same whole. The process of development is considered deterministic in the sense that it is always guided by some set of constraints (in psychology: external and physical, or internal and cognitive/emotional) that organizes the development in some (rather than another) future direction. However, the *exact* future state (i.e., within the general direction provided by constraints) of the developing organism is necessarily indeterministic (unpredictable in any exact ways from some previous state). A closer analysis of the basic assumptions of the theory would clarify the rationale for solving the determinism–indeterminism issue by seeing the two views united within the whole of a developing organism.

5.1 BASIC ASSUMPTIONS OF THE PROPOSED THEORY

The basic assumptions of any theory establish its build-up possibilities. These assumptions are deductively set axioms that can be either accepted or rejected, and that remain outside of any empirical (inductive) claim in the given science. The following basic assumptions are accepted here:

1. The environment of the developing person is structurally organized in some form (including dissociation of structure as a structural form) in any present moment.

2. There exists a personal world of lived-through experiences that is centered on the person and is available directly only to the person in his or her personal subjective constructions.

3. The domain of personal lived-through experiences is constantly being culturally structured by the person, through the construction and use of semiotic mediational devices (signs).

4. Each person's semiotic mediation of his or her personal psychological functions is prestructured by the sign systems that exist in the given society, and leads to further construction of meaning structures, both in the personal subjective world and in the domain of the person's actions in the social world.

5. The process of structural construction of the domains of actions (and reflection on actions) takes place in irreversible time; no event in psychological development is ever repeated as the "same" as a previous one. There is only *similarity*—established by way of semiotic mediation (category construction) that can be described as if it "exists" over time.

6. Psychological and environmental structures are to be conceptualized in terms of the outer limits that distinguish between processes that are included in the structure and processes that are not. The central theoretical notion of the theory is *constraint*—a partition of a field.

7. All psychological structures are processual in their nature—they are transitory organizational forms that can vanish, or transform into other forms during development.

8. Development is an open-system process that entails construction of novelty, and therefore cannot be modeled by formal systems that presuppose finality.

9. Development entails redundancy, equifinality as a form of multifinality, and simultaneous organization at different levels of regulation (action, feeling/thinking, and so on).

The theory that is built on these axiomatic bases is expected to be applicable to human development in general, even if the empirical extensions in this book remain concentrated on early childhood phenomena.

5.2 ELABORATION OF THE STRUCTURE: CHILDREN'S ACTIONS AND ENVIRONMENT

The dynamic interactionism of the present theory is explicitly structuralistic—it emphasizes the obvious fact that both the developing child and his or her environment are structurally organized. That structured nature of the child and the environment is not static and immutable, but is dynamically transformed both microgenetically (as the child and/or caregivers act within the environment) and ontogenetically (as the child develops in transaction with the environment). A number of basic notions on which this theory is built must be made explicit before the theory is outlined in detail. From the time of conception onward, the developing organism—embryo, fetus, and neonate—goes through a series of structural–anatomical transformations that provide the basis for all the behavior that can be observed in the newborn. The structural organization of a newborn's anatomy and physiological functioning sets constraints on the range of behaviors that the baby displays. These constraints likewise determine the boundaries of the set of new behaviors that the baby can learn at a given time under social circumstances that promote their acquisition. Only a limited subset of what the baby can learn at the time ends up being acquired, and the newly acquired capabilities widen the set of potentially learnable skills at the next period of development. By actualizing some of the potentially learnable skills at a given time, the child actively participates in the construction of its future potential development. However, that participation is always constrained by the child's physical, emotional, and cognitive constraints, which are structurally organized at any time in development. For example, the increase in infants' body weight beyond the capacity of their muscle strength in the middle of their first year of life may lead to the disappearance of the newborn "walking reflex" in the usual environmental conditions (Thelen, 1983). However, such a "regress" is not to be the case for long—the developing cognitive capacities and haptic exploration lead the infant to progress further from quadrupedal to bipedal mode of locomotion. That progress is made available by the neurophysiological system of coordination of the muscles of the body that participate in bipedal locomotion. Once an infant masters walking independently, quick access to different areas in the environment is facilitated, which, in turn, leads to further psychological development by the new encounters with the environment made available to the child through the new skill.

The child's current psychological organization determines the ways in which the child can act. Thus, a 2-year-old who is beginning to use verbal commands to control his or her own behavior is engaged in limiting the latter via the help of the former. Or, an adolescent may use an emotional involvement with a referent group or person to abandon some rational ways of thinking and acting. The connection among emotions, cognition, and action *within* the person's psychology and behavior constitutes a system in which different components are connected in complex qualitative ways. That system cannot be reduced to the sum of its parts. Any reduction of such systemic complexity to a conglomerate of "quantitative measures" of each of the supposed components would eliminate the systemic nature of the person's functioning from consideration at the outset of the psychological study. No linear equation with the factors of *action, emotion,* and *cognition* neatly displayed in it makes it possible to explain the structural organization of the whole that exists due to the interaction of these three as its parts.

5.3   THE ENVIRONMENT AS A DYNAMIC STRUCTURE

The newborn child inherits not only its biological (genetic) background, but also the structural organization of the environment into which it is born (West & King, 1985). The child's behavior is interdependent with the possibilities that the environment provides, and the latter is structurally organized all through ontogeny. As the newborn develops, its actions begin to reorganize the structure of the environment. Likewise, the people around the child purposefully re-arrange the structure of the child's environment so that it can eliminate dangers (e.g., taking away dangerous objects) and promote socially relevant goals (e.g., the integration of young children into the family's subsistence activities and their participation in social rituals). The people in the child's environment guide the child's development in accordance with their personal goals and on the basis of their interpretations of cultural expectations (cf. Newson, 1974; Newson & Newson, 1968, 1975, 1976).

Thus, we can advance a general *principle of the structured nature of environment:* At all times in the course of life, the child's environment provides a structured framework in which development takes place. During development, that framework undergoes a number of transformations. In one extreme, some of these are wrought by the actions of the developing child. On the other side, some transformations are caused by factors in the environment that are beyond the child's control. However, the majority of transformations are controlled simultaneously by both the child and the environment (including other persons who may reorganize the environment for the child). Whatever the roles of the child, other people, and environmental factors in transforming the environment, the latter is never in a random or unstructured organizational state.

5.4   STRUCTURING PERSON IN CONSTANTLY
RESTRUCTURED ENVIRONMENT: THE CASE
OF "DEPENDENT INDEPENDENCE"

As was emphasized above, *both* the developing organism and its environment are organized in a structural way. Both constitute physical, psychological, and cultural structures. All of the life of the organism takes place within its environment—thus, the structural nature of the organism's behavior has to relate to the structure of the environment in some way.

The nature of that relationship becomes particularly complicated in human ontogeny, where children gradually come to act in ways that go beyond the immediately available environmental conditions. They learn to change their environment, often pursuing some longer- or shorter-term objective, and thus participate in their own further development. Often, the direction in which child development is perceived to move is characterized as a transition from dependence to independence. Such a description, however, overlooks the basic interdependence of the child and the environment.

Instead of thinking of the concepts of dependence and independence as opposites, it is possible to see them as characteristics that are embedded in the same whole. Taking the organism–environment system as that whole, the interdependence of these concepts can be helpful in explaining how children develop in ways that are simultaneously dependent and independent of the environment. For example, child development can be described as proceeding through different states of *independent dependence* (rather than independence). This alternative concept (Valsiner, 1984a) illustrates quite well the difference between the common-sense and scientific terminology. From the perspective of common sense, a child (or an adult) who behaves or thinks "on his own" and is not seen to be influenced by others, is considered to be independent, in our everyday discourse. However, from the perspective of the developmental sciences (which rely on the axiom that only open systems are capable of development), the child can never be independent from the environment. In the present context, we can think of an independent (in our common sense) child as actually being independently dependent. If we look at the child's immediate action, it seems to be unconstrained by any factors, and any efforts to introduce constraints may be actively blocked (e.g., a 2-year-old showing a temper tantrum in a public place). However, if we consider the phenomenon more carefully, it becomes evident that the seemingly independent action has emerged in the context of the child's dependence on its environment and social interaction partners. The latter may facilitate the emergence of the notion of independence as part of the child's emerging cognitive system. Consider an observation of a mother and her 3.5-month-old daughter interacting. The mother tries to get the infant to pull herself up from the prone position to sitting, and then to standing. She manages to get the infant to hold on to a ring, and pulls the child up to stand, commenting: "You are a big girl! You did it all by yourself!" The task described could be accomplished only by the mother–infant joint efforts, where the mother played the leading role. Nevertheless, after the task was accomplished, she discounted her own role in it and attributed the responsibility fully to the child's action— all by *yourself!* This, of course, happened when the observer (who shared the mother's cultural background) was present, and thus the other's verbal comment obviously played a communicative role in the mother's showing herself and her daughter to the observer from the *culturally expected angle* of doing one's best for a baby whose early independence is promoted. On the one hand, the mother's verbal commentary about the child's behavior constituted early exposure of the child to the use of language in making self-attributions in situations where the child depends on cooperation for accomplishing some task. On the other hand, the mother demonstrated her own independent dependence by sending to the observer the message that was prescribed by her own background socialization.

The concept of independent dependence was introduced in a context (Valsiner, 1984c) of efforts to make sense of curious features of human personality. Many people claim that their thoughts and actions are completely independent, whereas in actuality they may—*on their own initiative*—follow the rules that somebody else has set up for their acting and thinking. Child-rearing ideologies often put an emphasis on developing independent dependence of children in relation to their culture as an important educational goal. Thus, the explicit emphasis on "conscious discipline" that is evident in the pedagogical writings of a well-known Soviet educationalist, Anton Makarenko, illustrates the social context of that general goal. According to him:

> [The model Soviet citizen] is expected not only to appreciate to what end and why it is necessary for him to carry out this or that command, but also actively to endeavour to carry it out to the very best of his ability. Yet that is still not everything. Our citizens are expected to do their duty at any moment of their lives without waiting for instructions or orders, they are expected to be ready to take the initiative and be possessed of creative will. It is hoped at the same time that they will only do what is really useful and necessary for our society and our country and that in this work they will not be deterred by any difficulties and obstacles. . . . In respect of our common enemies it is demanded of every individual that he resolutely obstruct their activities and be constantly vigilant whatever unpleasantnesses and dangers might ensue. (Kumarin, 1976, p. 246)

The statement of the goal of *arriving at conscious discipline as a result of education* matches educational and child socialization goals in principle in any culture, although the particulars of how the socialized person is expected to act obviously vary. In a way, the common sense concept of independence can be viewed as the successful result of cultural socialization within Western industrialized cultures. That concept has been socialized in conjunction with Protestant religious belief systems. That belief itself is an example of independent dependence—individuals are socialized within the culture (case of dependence) to believe that they are independent of their environment and "free" to act in any way (idea of independence). The belief in one's independence is thus dependent on the culture within which one is socialized.

In the present context, the meaning of independent dependence is defined in ways that include organism–environment relationships. In terms of the *boundaries that define the range of possibilities* of behavior, any organism is fully *dependent* on both its own structure and the structure of the environment. At the same time, *within* the boundaries of the set of possibilities, an organism may (but need not always) have the opportunity of choice between different ways of behaving, or of constructing new ways of acting which are possible, given the particular coupling of the organism and the environment.

The concept of independent dependence is closely linked with the ecological approach in psychology where the person–environment interdependence is turned into the object of investigation (Valsiner & Benigni, 1986). The structures of the person and the environment specify the dependence of the person on the environment, and that dependence makes it possible for the person to act independently (but within limits) upon the environment in an effort to restructure it. When the environment is transformed, its relationship with the person is changed, and this change guides the person's development.

5.5 SEMIOTIC MEDIATION IN ACTION: CONSTRUCTED MEANINGFULNESS OF PERSON AND ENVIRONMENT

A human child is born not only into a physically structured environment (like the offspring of all species), but also into one that is meaningfully organized. Places, objects within places, and different actions that can be performed with objects either have culturally specified meanings for people, or develop them in accordance with the culture's folk model of meanings at the given time (Holy & Stuchlik, 1981).

The inevitability of the development of meaningfulness of environments stems from humans' use of signs in controlling their environments and themselves (Vygotsky, 1978; Vygotsky & Luria, 1930). The adults and older children either have developed their own personal understanding of the world around them (system of personal senses), or are on their way to establishing such a system. In contrast, the newborn is at the very beginning of that developmental course. An advance along these lines involves strong reliance on the personal senses of people around him or her, in the form of intersubjectivity (Trevarthen, 1977, 1979a, 1979b, 1982). In the context of intersubjective processes of child–others interaction, the child constructs his or her own personal sense system under the guidance of other people: parents and other adult relatives, older siblings, peers, and even younger siblings. The developing child is a coconstructor of the cultural meaning system, a target of his caregivers' purposeful and culturally organized actions. However, the child's input into the cultural meaning system is mediated by the personal sense systems of his or her caregivers. The cultural meanings are not transmitted from society to the child's parents and from them to the child in an immutable form. Instead, each participant in this social communication process is a coconstructor of the cultural meanings. Thus, the parents develop their personal sense system on the basis of *their* interpretation of cultural rules and expectancies. The part of their personal sense system that is relevant for their child's development involves their meaningful organization of the home environment (to be shared by the children), and their thinking about child-rearing goals and practices. The multitude of different objects in adults' homes that are part of their personal culture is noteworthy (see Czikszentmihaly & Rochberg-Halton, 1981). As the children develop, they act within the personalized environment of the parents, and acquire information about their meaningfulness by parental counteractions to their actions. The children develop their versions of the cultural meaning system as a result of their social interaction with others. These versions are constructed by the children and do not constitute a simple copy of the parents' sense systems. Children's versions build in innovative ways on the structure of the culturally organized information that they experience in interaction with others and in their exploration of the man-made physical environment. The children grow up in meaningfully structured home environments that they inherit socially (by the mere fact of being born to *their* families), and these environments guide them toward construction of their own personal sense systems.

5.6   CONCEPTUALIZING THE *POSSIBLE* AND THE *ACTUAL* IN DEVELOPING SYSTEMS

A consistently developmental perspective requires an assumption of nonrepeatability of experiences (basic assumption 5, above). This focuses the whole investigation not on phenomena that already exist, but on the realm of *how, from a set of possibilities* $P = \{a, b, c, d, e\&f\&g, h\&b, and ?\}$—which is semi-open due to unknown or emerging members (?) and includes mutually bound structures ($e\&f\&g$ and $h\&b$)—*the actual event* is being constructed.

Traditional modes of thinking in psychology have been particularly ineffective in dealing with events that *could, but need not, happen*. This is the distinction between the *possible* and the *actual*. Conceptual traditions in psychology have offered many ways for describing and explaining what actually happens, while leaving largely unanalyzed the relationships with what is possible. In cognitive psychology, efforts to reconstruct knowledge about a person's possibilities frequently take the form of looking for "competence" in the person, rather than in a person–environment relationship. The need to examine these relationships is particularly important in developmental psychology. Development constitutes the process of transformation of what is possible at an earlier stage of an organism's life, into what is actual at a later stage. The later stage, in turn, provides the organism with new possibilities, some of which become actualized and serve as a basis for still further development.

Usually, the prediction of the *actual* future occurrence of psychological phenomena, rather than their *possible* occurrence, has been attempted in psychology. Because the prior performance can be only a small (actualized) aspect of the total set of possibilities of an organism within a given environment, and because the realm of possibility may change over time, the prediction of subsequent performance is unlikely to be accurate. Furthermore, even if it happens to be adequate, it does not explain the processes by which the subsequent performance came into being. The explanation of psychological development through a prediction of future performance based on some earlier performance, without an analysis of the organism–environment interdependence that generates the performances, is not feasible on epistemological grounds. Historically, it originates in psychology's traditional emphasis on decontextualization of its phenomena, which has been the reason for much of psychology's inefficiency in explaining its phenomena.

5.6.1   How Can the Emerging Actuality Be Investigated in Human Development?

Research activities of developmental psychology are clearly directed by a focus on emergence of the actual from the possible. This focus has been felt in the history and the present status of the discipline—different versions of the Zone of Proximal Development (ZPD) concept (see 4.5.1) indicate a recognition that conceptualizations of such emergence are necessary for the discipline. Yet these conceptualizations are slow to emerge; the appropriate versions of formal mathematical systems (see Chapter 3) remain segregated from the knowledge base of developmental scientists.

What follows from all the deductive theoretical line above is that human development of actuality out of potentialities cannot be explained by a competence-versus-performance distinction. That distinction assumes a fixed pool of possibilities (labeled "competence"), which, under some conditions, are actualized in the form that they are given in the pool. (Performance reflects isomorphically the specific underlying competence. A child succeeds on task A and is therefore "diagnosed" to "have" competence for A, or a generalized *competence a.*)

The argument along the lines of competence versus performance is a good example of a nondevelopmental solution to the possibilities-to-actuality problem. There is no posited connection from a specific performance (actuality) to the set of possibilities (competence); the latter are not remodeled, given a particular performance. In contrast, in the present theoretical perspective, any particular actualized possibility (observable in terms of *performing*—as ongoing action—rather than entified *performance*) may (but need not) reorganize the set of possibilities for the next developmental actualization of possibilities.

In practical terms, a microgenetic study of how the set of possibilities is turned into actuality entails a focus on the efforts that do *not* succeed in the given action sequence (within the context), prior to the success of some other efforts. Let us assume the formal example of the set of possibilities given above:

$$P = \{a, b, c, d, e\&f\&g, h\&b, \text{ and } ?\}$$

Let us further assume that this is a set of directly observable action possibilities. In this case, in some structured context, the following time sequence may emerge:

$$b \rightarrow h\&b \rightarrow b \rightarrow a \rightarrow a \rightarrow a \rightarrow \ldots$$

The person, after brief efforts to use a subset P (namely, {b, h&b}) ends up with turning a into the actualized part of the set P. However, evidence about the efforts to actualize the other members of the set—those that fail—is informative for a microgenetic study of emergence. In terms of the competence-versus-performance distinction (which is a nondevelopmental distinction), the *pre*performance (rather than the actual performance) can be informative. This refocusing also makes it clear why microgenetic methods are the ones that fit developmental study: *The task for the investigator is to make the preperformance processes sufficiently observable,* by purposeful complications entered into the context of study in order to *slow down the processes* that may end up with an actual performance. Therefore, the tachistoscopic methods of microgenetic study of percept formation (Draguns, 1984) or time-structure analyses of problem-solving tasks (Duncker, 1945) satisfy the methodological demands of developmental science—with the additional feature that the actualized possibility needs to be considered as reorganizing the set of possibilities:

$$P(t+1)/(\text{given } a(t)) = \{b, c, d, e\&f\&g, h\&b, i, j, \text{ and } ?\}$$

The latter consideration is again a theoretical (deductive) step, after the inductive (empirical) knowledge of the actualization of a becoming available. The situation is further complicated if we construct models of processes (rather than discrete members of the set of possibilities and actuality).

5.7   PROCESS DESCRIPTIONS OF THE PHENOMENA: DAVID BOHM'S "WORLD TUBE"

Living organisms operate in terms of interdependent processes, rather than through entified parts of causal systems (see systemic causality in 2.7). Even when we may use labels of formal description of the processes, the labels designate a flow of bounded processes, rather than "things."

For the focus on processes in models, science is indebted to William James's (1890) talk about "stream of consciousness." David Bohm has expressed the notion of process thinking in physics:

> What is needed in a relativistic theory is to give up altogether the notion that the world is constituted of basic objects or "building blocks." Rather, one has to view the world in terms of universal flux of events and processes. Thus . . . instead of thinking of a particle, one is to think of a "world tube."

This world tube represents an infinitely complex process of a structure in movement and development which is centered in a region indicated by the boundaries of the tube. . . . One can perhaps illustrate what is meant here by considering the "stream of consciousness." This flux of awareness is not precisely definable, and yet it is evidently prior to the definable forms of thoughts and ideas which can be seen to form and dissolve in the flux, like ripples, waves, and vorticles in a flowing stream. As happens with such patterns of movement in a stream, some thoughts recur and persist in a more or less stable way, while others are evanescent. (Reproduced with permission from Bohm, 1980, pp. 9–11)

Bohm's concept of the "world tube" is illustrated by the schematic drawings in Figure 5.1.

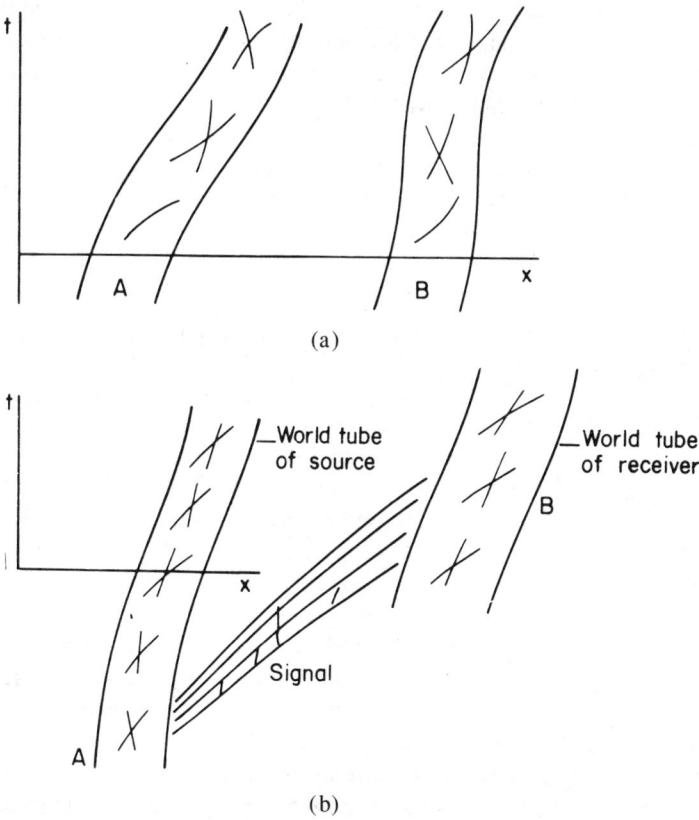

FIGURE 5.1.   The world according to Bohm: (a) description of processes as "world tubes"; (b) communication between two "world tubes." (Combined from Bohm, 1980: (a), p. 10; (b), p. 136; reproduced with permission.)

The constraint-oriented approach affords the study of the possibility of events. The actual position of phenomena in either of the two world tubes [A and B in Figure 5.1(a)] can be located in any place within the tube at the given time. Furthermore, over time, the phenomenon may move to another location within the tube. There exists a wide variety of possible trajectories of the examples of the phenomenon within the world tube, *all of which inevitably come to the range specified by the boundaries of the tube.* Communication between two processes [world tubes A and B in Figure 5.1(b)] can be conceptualized as a connection that is set up between the tubes with the help of constraints that channel the signal process from tube A to tube B.

However, there is an important distinction between the physical and the biological worlds—the latter involves active participation by organisms in the construction of their development, whereas the former does not. This difference seems to be lost in Bohm's example. In nature and society, the limits of what is possible develop together with the organism's active efforts to change its relationship with its environment. Organisms do not experience their environments passively; they construct (and reconstruct) their environments and, through those, themselves (Baldwin, 1892a; Lewontin, 1978, 1981). Thus, when a system, functioning within its current boundary conditions, develops into a qualitatively new state, *new* boundary conditions are set up for the further development of the system. These new constraints guide the system toward the possibility of developing into another new qualitative state, which, in turn, would bring along a new set of constraints, and so on, until the organism ceases to exist.

5.8   THE NOTION OF CONSTRAINT AS A LIMIT ON THE FLOW OF PROCESSES

In the present terminology, a *constraint* is a regulator of the move from the present to the immediate future state of the developing organism–environment system, which delimits the full set of possible ways of that move, thus enabling the developing organism to construct the actual move under a reduced set of possibilities.

Webster's *Third New International Dictionary* (1981, p. 489) provides a set of meanings for the term *constraint* that originates from a combination of two Latin words: *con* + *stringere* (to draw tight). Constraint is (a) the act or action of using force to prevent or condition an action; (b) the quality or state of being checked, restricted, or compelled to avoid or perform some action; (c) compulsion by circumstances, the force of necessity; (d) control over one's own feelings, behavior, or actions, which is exercised either to feign or repress; and (e) the sense of being constrained, checked, or inhibited. These different meanings of the term converge on the notion of control of action. The use of the term *constraint* in science is rooted in the common language. In the Western cultural meaning systems, the emotional connotation of the term often includes an implicit reference to the control of actions against the actor's wishes or well-being. This negative connotation of the term in our common sense is not to be taken over when constraint is used in psychological discourse.

The term *constraint* has been used in a similarly neutral manner in other sciences. For example, Pattee has described its use in physics:

> In common language the concept of constraint is a kind of forceful confinement which limits our freedom. The same general concept may also hold in physical systems where the constraint is a fixed boundary, like the box which confines the molecules of a gas. . . . In other words, constraints are most easily explained as the invention of the physicist who sees a new way of looking at a problem which is much simpler or more useful than taking into account all degrees of freedom with equal detail. (Pattee, 1971, pp. 260–261)

> Constraints, unlike laws of nature, must be the consequence of what we call some form of material structure, such as molecules, membranes, typewriters, or table tops; these structures may be static or time-dependent, but in either case it is important to realize that they are made up of matter which at all times obeys the fundamental laws of nature in addition to behaving as a constraint. (Pattee, 1972, p. 250)

It is easy to see that the physical definition of constraint covers only a narrow area of the semantic field of the term as it can be used in psychology.

As a scientific term, *constraint* is value-free—*it indicates a specific partition of a field.* The only conceivable case of absence of some constraint is a fully homogeneous field. Any distinction within a field, any separation of a figure from the ground, is possible only through the creation of constraints. As is later claimed, constraints delimit different areas of the field (zones), and these zones are specifiable via constraints.

5.8.1 Constraints as Dynamic Regulators

The term *constraint* denotes a dynamic temporary regulator of development (a device to partition the field of possibilities), which may, under some conditions, become statically represented in the environment or within the person's psychological system (e.g., fixed ideas, relatively stable personal senses). Constraint in this theoretical system is a *primarily dynamic, and secondarily (potentially) relatively stable,* organizational device. It is a means of differentiation (in the sense of Werner's "orthogenetic principle"; see 4.4). Constraints emerge (and vanish) together with the domains that they delimit, and the delimited domains are differentiated with the help of constraints (Herbst, 1995).

Some constraints can become structurally fixed entities; they may become encoded in some fixed form in the environment of the developing person. Even these constraints are maintained in a dynamic steady state, rather than being "fixed" in terms of becoming "things." The dynamicity of such constraints may be particularly clear when their *form* becomes materially fixed (e.g., the building of the Berlin Wall in the middle of a world capital, or equivalent social-institutional belief systems internalized by persons, perhaps as ingroup/outgroup feelings). Yet the function of such materialized constraints is maintained by dynamic semiotic processes, and once the latter undergo the breaking of their status quo in the psychological systems of persons and the social discourses of social institutions, the materially fixed constraints can be broken and turned into symbolic tokens for tourists or collectors (e.g., there is symbolic value to possessing pieces of the former Berlin Wall), and will vanish from the sociocultural material worlds.

5.8.2   Constraints as Viewed in Human Development

In human development, constraints are coconstructed both externally (parents' attempts to regulate children's actions, given goal orientations, and children's actions toward these efforts) and, in parallel, internally (persons' self-constraining of acting, feeling, or thinking, in dialogue with different meanings). If they are encoded in the fixed aspects of the environment (e.g., architectural forms of buildings of symbolic relevance—churches, temples) or in constantly maintained semiotic forms, then their organizational roles can be passed on over generations—with appropriate reconstructions according to the internalization/externalization process.

In the analysis of child development, we may have examples of physical constraints in early childhood (playpens, safety latches, baby-gates) that indeed limit the degrees of freedom of the child's actions. However, when the child develops further, the physical constraints give way to internalized psychological phenomena (e.g., beliefs, rules of logic, social norms) that continue to serve the function of constraining the person's degrees of freedom of acting, feeling, and thinking. Many people are actively seeking ways to construct such constraints within themselves—often by initially establishing a set of external constraints, which are gradually transformed into a set of intrapersonal psychological constraints. Psychology's conceptual knowhow, which should afford explanation of such phenomena, is still largely underdeveloped. Very real phenomena—for instance, joining the army, or a religious cult; or aligning personal acting and thinking with the propagated ideas of a social institution—are only rarely described (Festinger, Riecken, & Schachter, 1956) and are even less effectively explained. Fortunately, newly developed ways of analyzing personality organization in relation to its control over the environment may help to overcome this conceptual weakness of traditional psychology (see the concepts of secondary and primary control introduced by Rothbaum, Weisz, & Snyder, 1982).

The majority of psychological phenomena that are the results of socialization processes—norms of acting in different settings, moral beliefs, sociopolitical or religious convictions—constitute cases of internalized (cognitive and emotional) sets of constraints. These constraints cannot be studied by an analysis of the person's external environment; they require, as their database, a combination of observation of the person's actions within an environmental setting, and his or her own thinking about these actions. Although in this book the concept of constraint is used mostly in ways that apply to physically or behaviorally verifiable limitations set on children's actions, this more restricted empirical application of the term should not obscure its internalized nature in middle and later childhood and adolescence, as well as in adulthood. Constraints organize both interindividual and intraindividual aspects of psychological processes. Only in the early years of child development can they be analyzed as basically external. In later years, they become internalized from the children's external experience, and constructed by children internally in their minds.

An intrapsychological realm—one that entails the interdependent fields of feeling and thinking—needs to be assumed in any consistent theory of human development. Here, it is assumed that the notion of constraining is applicable to both intrapsychological and interpsychological processes.

5.8.3   Constraints as Borrowed from Kurt Lewin's Field Theory

The terminology of constraining in psychology emerged via Kurt Lewin's transposition of the notion of environmentally fixed constraints ("barriers") to the realm of the psychological life space. In the bounded indeterminacy view on development, Lewin's notion of barriers (as relatively static organizers of the life space) was extended in the dynamic direction, with an emphasis on the temporary functional and constructed nature of these regulational devices. Aside from constraints, we encounter notions of boundary and barrier in Lewin's thinking. It is interesting that Lewin did little to elaborate on the meanings of these terms, whereas his treatment of other concepts of the field theory is extensive (e.g., Lewin, 1936a, 1938). He defined the boundary of a psychological region as "those points of a region for which there is no surrounding that lies entirely within the region" (1936a, p. 118). Bringing in more specific examples where boundaries are involved, Lewin had little difficulty in finding instances of domains within which the boundary concept is intuitively feasible. For example, Lewin illustrated his definition of boundary by analyzing how it structures the person's locomotion:

> In carrying out a locomotion the experience of crossing a boundary is often a clear one. This is for instance the case when one climbs over a fence or enters a strange house for the first time; or, to use an example of a quasi-social locomotion, if one is admitted to membership in a club by some special ceremony. Thereby the position of the boundary is quite accurately determined. However, there are cases in which one can establish with certainty that the locomotion has proceeded from one region into another one, although the crossing of the boundary does not become evident as a special event during locomotion. For instance, one can gradually pass from one circle into another. A path may lead from the mountains into lower hills and on to a plain, or from a great city through more and more open suburbs into the country and it may be impossible to describe definite boundaries between these regions. The same is true for all gradual transitions between two regions. For instance, it can happen in conversation that one is not even aware of a "gradual transition." That the person has

passed the boundary can then be inferred only indirectly from the fact that he is in another region. In these cases it even remains doubtful how many boundaries and intermediate regions the locomotion has crossed. (Lewin, 1936a, p. 119)

Lewin's passing interest in the nature of different kinds of boundaries may be explained by his overwhelming use of the concepts of "force" and "locomotion" for the explanation of a person's transformation of the life space. For Lewin, it was possible to be satisfied with a look at only those boundaries in a person's life space that could be described as strict and well-delineated—and that could be represented by topological diagrams, which he and his disciples were always fond of drawing. In contrast, the present theoretical framework does not use the concept of force in its explanatory terminology but concentrates on the canalizing role of different sets of zone boundaries instead. Therefore, in the present context, it is essential to analyze the concepts of boundary and zone in greater depth.

Lewin's suggestion for solving the problem of gradual boundaries in the life space was to describe them through the concept of a "boundary zone"—not a one-dimensional, but at least a two-dimensional region. According to the width of the boundary zones, it is then possible to talk about more or less "sharp" boundaries (Lewin, 1936a, p. 120). Through equating the width of the boundary zone with its "unsharpness," Lewin created a convenient way for his descriptive topology to reduce fuzzy-looking boundary zones into their strict descriptions by Jordan curves (see Lewin, 1936a, p. 121, for the argument in favor of this transformation). However, his treatment of the issues of boundary zone and sharpness of the boundary remains confused because of his efforts to talk of the field structure and its dynamics at the same time, as can be seen in the following quote:

> Sharp psychological boundaries correspond best to mathematical boundaries. On the other hand not every boundary with pronounced depth implies an unsharp transition. An example from social psychology may serve as a demonstration. While the boundary between different economic classes is in general relatively unsharp and is characterized by a gradual transition, the boundary of some social groups such as an exclusive club is sharply defined. This means that for every person it is clearly determined whether or not he belongs to the group. Nevertheless the boundary of such a group can have the character of a boundary zone. In order to join the club for example it may be necessary to have one's name put on a waiting list in advance. Sometimes several such stages are prescribed. Therefore the existence of a boundary zone does not necessarily lessen the sharpness of the boundary, for the boundary zone itself may be a region which is clearly structured and sharply defined as to its boundaries. (Lewin, 1936a, pp. 121–122)

The first part of this quote describes the structure of field conditions (with their fluid and sharp boundaries) in their static form. Both fuzzy (as in the case of social class boundaries) and strict (e.g., the example of the exclusive club) boundaries coexist within the same field. However, the second part of the quote refers to the microgenetic transformation of the person's field over time (e.g., the route by which a person can gradually maneuver into becoming a member of the club). The would-be member of the club gradually crosses the boundary, and, viewed over time, the boundary for him indeed constitutes a boundary zone that can be crossed only gradually. However, all through the period of *the given* person's movement to club membership, the strictness of the static nature of the boundary between the members and nonmembers of the group *remains the same for other persons*—both current members or outsiders. The person who is in the process of joining the club changes the boundary of the club membership *for himself or herself* while moving to become a member, but not for those who are already members, nor for those who remain nonmembers.

The mixing of structural-static and microgenetic perspectives in Lewin's definition of the nature of boundary zones may have contributed to Lewin's conceptual difficulties in defining the boundary concept in lieu of the existence of both strict and fuzzy boundaries in the field at the given time, and the change in the nature of these boundaries (e.g., fuzzy ones becoming strict, or vice versa) over time. Lewin usually used his concept of boundary where he provided analysis of phenomena from the perspective of their mostly static state of existence (e.g., Lewin, 1933, 1935a, 1935b, 1936a, 1936b). However, even in these cases, he tended to fuse the structural description of the person–environment fields with the dynamic functioning of locomotion and forces in that field. For example, he described the individual as a *relatively* closed system, where "how strongly the environment operates upon the individual will . . . be determined (apart from the structure and forces of the situation) by the functional *firmness of the boundaries* between individual and environment" (Lewin, 1933, p. 619). Similar emphasis on his boundary concept is evident in his efforts to analyze the psychological issues of minority groups, especially when he tried to explain the tragic history of the situation of Jews in Germany during and before the 1930s (Lewin, 1935b). As a new immigrant to the United States, Lewin was obviously interested in understanding the organization of life in his new country, and again his use of the boundary concept served the purpose in his comparison of Germany and America. Lewin argued that, in the personality structure of Americans, the most private regions are made inaccessible to others through excessively "thick" boundaries, whereas the comparable boundary in the personality structure of Germans covers a zone consisting of different, less "thick" boundaries to be crossed by others in their becoming close to the person (see Lewin, 1936b, pp. 283, 284). Again, in these examples, Lewin fused the functional and structural aspects of the psychological explanation *without* explicitly introducing the time parameter into the analysis. (He tried to correct this omission later—see Lewin, 1939, 1942, 1943a—but the emphasis on the nature of the boundaries in the field was negligible.)

Lewin's major interest in the functional organization of the life space explains the prevalence of the concepts of locomotion, force, and valence *(Aufforderungscharakter)* over those of boundary and zone in his theoretical analyses of phenomena. In *his* theoretical life space, the concept of boundary was narrowed down to the concept of barrier, which was defined strictly in connection with the force concept:

> We shall call boundaries (boundary zones) which offer resistance to psychological locomotion "barriers." We shall speak of barriers of different strength according to their degree of resistance.
>
> We shall continue to use the concept of boundary in a purely topological sense. The term "psychologically real" boundary therefore does not imply defined dynamic properties. (Lewin, 1936a, p. 124)

Lewin's definitional separation of barrier and boundary illustrates the conceptual dilemma that the originator of the field theory in psychology was in. On the one hand, the topological use of the boundary concept could fit the description of the static structure of the psychological field sufficiently well, but it offered no direct connections with the dynamic concepts that Lewin put an emphasis on. On the other hand, some notion of structural organization of the field was necessary as the context within which the locomotion, the work of forces and valences, can be clearly demonstrated. The concept of barrier was a functional (= locomotion-related) boundary served well for Lewin's theoretical purposes. In his empirical studies (e.g., Barker, Dembo, & Lewin, 1941), it is exactly the barrier behavior that was studied, rather than the structure of boundaries in the field, or the transformation of that structure. In summary, *Lewin's theoretical analysis of the microgenesis of psychological phenomena made use of structural concepts as a context for the dynamic ones,* in his efforts to analyze the processes that determine persons' actions within the environment. In contrast, the present theoretical framework sets up a balance between the context (structured environment) and the acting individual. The latter participates in the construction (or reconstruction) of the former, and the structured environment in its terms canalizes the development of the individual toward culturally acceptable and required achievements.

5.9 DEFINITION OF "ZONE" AND ITS DIFFERENT REPRESENTATIONS

The environment of the developing child is structured by sets of boundaries that define different environmental zones. The environment is zoned, or—to use a rare but fitting term from Webster's *Third International Dictionary* (1981)—it is *zoniferous.*

A range of meanings are provided for the term *zone.* The Latin root—*zona*—means girdle or belt, but usage has been subsequently extended to different domains of knowledge, particularly those where metaphors relate to spatial areas (geography, military organization, economics, anatomy, and physiology). One of the dictionary's explanations—"a region or area set off or characterized as distinct from surrounding or adjoining parts"—fits the general notion of the term as it is used in the present theoretical context.

Lewin's theoretical thinking included the zone concept. The Zone of Free Movement, which constitutes a part of the present theory, follows from Lewin's introduction of the concepts of region of freedom of movement (Lewin, 1933) and space of free movement (Lewin, 1939). Lewin's own use of the zone concept was related to the question of how boundaries in life space occupy areas of different width. He also discussed "zones of undetermined quality"—the frequent cases in which the boundary zones contain "undetermined sectors" or "psychologically empty" areas (Lewin, 1936a, pp. 130–131). Compared to Lewin's use of the zone concept, the present application of the term has a wider meaning and includes his notions of region and space.

The zone concept as it is used here can be clarified by examining Figure 5.2. The zone can be an area that is distinct from its surroundings in different ways.

The simplest way of depicting such a zone is as a region that is surrounded by a continuous and evenly sharp boundary [zone X in Figure 5.2(a)]. However, the surroundings of such a zone constitute a zone in itself (zone Y), which is observably bounded on one side (by the boundary of zones X and Y), but has an undetermined boundary on the other side of Y. This diagram helps to express the point that a zone need not be bounded (closed) on all of its sides. In reality, regularly bounded zones like zone X in Figure 5.2(a) are rare. Instead, the majority of zones that enclose areas of space are *partially discontinuous* and *unevenly bounded,* like zone X in Figure 5.2(b), which has a semipermeable

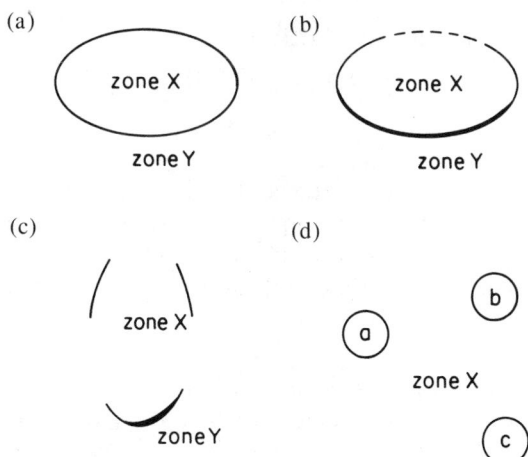

FIGURE 5.2.   Schematic illustrations of different explications of the zone concept: (a) separation of zones by homogeneous boundary with closed contour; (b) separation of zones by heterogeneous and semipermeable boundary with closed contour; (c) separation of zones by heterogeneous and discontinuous boundary; (d) determination of a zone in exclusive terms ("Zone X includes everything except a, b, and c").

boundary of zone X with zone Y in a particular locus. Furthermore, a zone may be specified by a *discontinuous boundary* [e.g., Figure 5.2(c)] that separates zone X from zone Y in some loci strictly, while allowing the two zones to be fused and inseparable in other areas. The example in Figure 5.2(d) moves one step further, specifying as zone Y all the field except for points a, b, and c, which have strict boundaries with Y and are the only areas in the field that are excluded from zone Y. It is easy to see that the excluded points are similar to zone X in Figure 5.2(d), since a point constitutes a zone with strict boundaries but of infinitely small area.

The four examples of different zones given in graphic form in Figure 5.2 do not constitute the full list of possible versions of all conceivable forms of zones. The function of these examples is to emphasize that the zone concept need not be limited to the intuitively most obvious case—a continuously bounded area. Instead, it can include fuzzy or semipermeable boundaries, or an undefined boundary in many areas of the zone. The epistemological usefulness of the zone and boundary concepts lies in their flexibility in capturing the often partially fuzzy or indeterminate nature of the phenomena, rather than in adding stricter preciseness to a description of inherently imprecise reality.

The present theoretical framework uses three basic zone concepts that are viewed as organizers of development, both interpsychologically (between persons) and intrapsychologically (in the semiotic regulation of one's own thinking, feeling, and acting). These three concepts are abstractions that can have particular real-life illustrations, yet remain theoretical terms. They are:

1. Zone of Free Movement (ZFM).
2. Zone of Promoted Action (ZPA).
3. Zone of Proximal Development (ZPD).

The relationship among these three zone concepts is meant to explain the process mechanism of development in its dynamic microgenetic flow. All zones are viewed as abstract organizational devices of a transient nature. Their explanatory value is in how they (and their relationship) become restructured "online," that is, where they actually regulate the ongoing developmental process. Later semistatic depictions of them as existing with relative stability are shorthand presentations.

5.9.1 The Zone of Free Movement (ZFM)

The concept of a Zone of Free Movement originated in the field theory of Kurt Lewin (Lewin, 1933, 1939). The ZFM structures (a) the child's access to different areas in the environment, (b) the availability of different objects within an accessible area, and (c) the child's ways of acting with the available objects in the accessible area. As a result of development, the child learns to set up a ZFM in his or her personal thinking and feeling—the ZFM becomes internalized.

When it is internalized, the Zone of Free Movement provides a structural framework for the child's cognitive activity and emotions; the latter are to be controlled in culturally expected ways in different social situations (see Cole, 1985; Lutz, 1983). Even when internalized, ZFMs regulate the relationships of the person with the environment. The Zone of Free Movement is therefore a *socially constructed cognitive structure of child–environment relationships* (Valsiner, 1984d, p. 68). It is socially constructed because it is based on adults' (and older siblings') cultural meaning systems, and is formed in inter-action with them. It is a cognitive structure because it organizes child–environment relationships on the basis of the cultural meanings of the society. These meanings become internalized by the developing children in the process of their acting within the environments. The ZFM is simultaneously a structure of the child's actions within the environment at the given time, and the future structure of the child's thinking. The development of internal cognitive processes starts with external acting of the child within its environment (Piaget, 1977; Vygotsky, 1956, 1960, 1978), and proceeds toward internalization of the external experience.

The Zone of Free Movement has a number of properties, as follows.

1. The ZFM is always based on the child's relationships with the structure of the given environmental setting. At any time in life, the child's (adult's) access to some areas in the environment is seemingly unlimited, whereas access to some other areas is blocked. In addition, for some areas in a person's environment, their status of being within limits or off limits is not exactly specified at the given time. An effort to clarify their status may lead to access or to their being blocked off. The notion of *area* can also be applied beyond the geographically organized space, and can include different objects in places and different actions with the same object. Last but not least, area can be extended to thoughts and feelings.

2. The ZFM is based on the meanings of different aspects of the environment for the social other (parent, sibling, schoolteacher, etc.), who is the leading organizer (but not the sole determiner) of the Zone of Free Movement for the child. Either the social other or the child may make the first move in structuring the ZFM. However, the child's caregiver is the gatekeeper of the ZFM as it is constructed—and reconstructed from time to time. For example, when a 2-year-old boy and his mother enter a new environment (e.g., during a visit to a friend's home), the child (who goes to a precious vase in the living room and tries to push it onto the floor) or the mother (who told the child immediately, when they entered the room, not to touch the vase) may start the construction of a particular ZFM. The construction of the ZFM may involve both proactive and reactive (see Holden, 1985) child-control techniques. Whether the adult or the child starts the construction, the resulting ZFM can be constructed by different routes. At one extreme, the caregiver may play an

overwhelmingly dominant role in its construction, leaving the child with the option of conforming to the ZFM as it has been unilaterally set up. At the other extreme are occasions where the social other of the child participates minimally in the construction of a ZFM, and the major role ends up being played by the child. In the majority of cases in contemporary European and North American societies, ZFMs are constructed in child–adult joint action. Through a series of alternate "moves" by both sides (the mother's efforts to set up limits on the child's action, and the child's actual actions, which may either cross the limits or stay within them), the ZFM is set up, maintained, and changed.

3. The ZFM is often set up on the basis of the parent's understanding of what the child *can* do in the given setting, in conjunction with what the child is doing or has done in the past. Orientation toward future possible actions is thus a part of the construction of ZFM.

4. The ZFM is reconstructed when the adult and the child enter a novel environment. The adult analyzes the new setting on the basis of his or her knowledge of the former action of the child, and the potential future action afforded to the child by the new environment. That analysis—based on cognitive simulation of scenarios of possible events—leads to the basic understanding of how the ZFM could be constructed. Beyond that, the actual behavior of the child may lead to further refinement, or change, of the simulated ZFM.

The ZFM is a means to an end, rather than an end in itself. It is set up to organize child–environment relationships, and through that organization, to canalize the development of the child in directions that are accepted in the given culture at large. As a means, a particular ZFM can become obsolete, once the child is past a certain age and his or her relationships with the environment are changed. It is particularly easy to bear this in mind, when one thinks of the physical constraining devices (playpens, baby-gates, cribs, car seats) that occupy the role of important organizers of infants' and toddlers' relationships with their Western middle-class environments. Once the functions carried out by them are no longer important in the child's development, these devices (and the ZFMs they helped to set up) are discarded and replaced by others.

In a set-theoretic denotation, a ZFM at a given time (t1) can be given as:

$$ZFM(t1) = \{a^*,b^*,c,d,e,f,?,??,g^*,h^*\} \tag{1}$$

In this set, members a . . . h constitute specified areas of the zone, ? and ?? denote existing but nondifferentiated areas, and the addition of * to some members of the set denotes boundaries with which those members are in immediate contact. Thus, a^*, b^*, g^*, and h^* indicate that these subparts of ZFM are *in direct contact with the boundary* of the ZFM, while c, d, e, and f belong to the "interior" (not-boundary-contacting) areas of the ZFM.

Bounded indeterminacy is encoded in two ways in this depiction: (a) the *-marked set members indicate the subareas of negotiations where uncertainty is present, and (b) the undifferentiated areas (? and ??) denote the part of the ZFM that is, at the given time, not yet specified, and its field structure is uncertain. The ZFM is *simultaneously* well defined (in boundary areas where specific parts of the ZFM are involved in boundary renegotiation, and in specified internal areas) and ill defined (through inclusion of ?- and ??-denoted undifferentiated areas). This formal depiction is meant to indicate the internally heterogeneous nature of ZFM (and other zone concepts; see below), and to elaborate, in structural terms, the situation in developmental phenomena that was depicted in Figure 3.4.

5.9.1.1   Primary Focus on ZFM Modulation.   The dynamic side of the zone concepts is viewed in this system as the regulator of development. Hence, the modulation of the ZFM system is expected to take place first at the areas of the zone that interact with a particular boundary or constraint (i.e., all the *-marked members of the set of areas within the ZFM).

Let us add to the formal description an "out-of-ZFM" phenomenon and denote it as j. We then assume that j is adjacent to h* but located outside the ZFM boundary. The contrast h*← BOUNDARY → j then gives us the location of the ZFM field where a particular change of the ZFM boundary is being negotiated. What may happen from time t1 to t2 can be variable: maintenance of the present status quo, or extension of ZFM to include j, or constriction of ZFM to exclude both h* and j, and so on. Here, the bounded indeterminacy is visible within the move from t1 to t2. Let us assume in this example that extension of ZFM takes place:

$$ZFM(t2) = \{a^*,b^*,c,d,e,f,?,??,g^*,h,j^*\} \tag{2}$$

In this case, the boundaries of the ZFM now include j, which becomes (instead of h) one of the boundary-marked members.

5.9.1.2   Known and Unknown Areas of ZFM.   ZFM entails both knowledge and ignorance. In parallel to boundary-contact action (i.e., h* ← BOUNDARY → j), most of the present ZFM content is not known even to the actors (e.g., as depicted by ? and ??). This is an inevitable implication that follows from the coconstructionist axiom of the theory. Human beings encounter their ZFMs (set up in joint construction) *not by exhaustive sampling of all of their content, but by detecting and creating boundary areas in an unsystematic way.* The process is akin to that of *bricolagé*—assembling of a building from occasional materials at hand, making up the plan along the way (Lévi-Strauss, 1966, pp. 16–19).

The experiencing of the ZFM is episodic: only one (or a few) subarea(s) of it can be experienced at a given time. Hence, persons are *necessarily* ignorant of numerous subareas—those not experienced contemporaneously—of their ZFM. This ignorance constitutes a "reserve" area for possible experiences, if the ZFM remains in a steady state for a while. Aside from the constructive exploration of the ZFM by the person, there can be pointed efforts by the social other (or, in the internalized case, from other levels of semiotic regulation) to orient the "explorer" of ZFM toward some, rather than other, subareas of that zone. This fits with the expectations of the individual-socioecological reference frame, and is captured by the second zone introduced here.

5.9.2   The Zone of Promoted Action (ZPA)

The ZFM, conceptualized here as an inhibitory psychological mechanism, has a counterpart oriented toward the promotion of new skills. That zone is called the Zone of Promoted Action (ZPA; Valsiner, 1984d, p. 68; 1985b, p. 136). The ZPA is a set of activities, objects, or areas in the environment, in respect of which the person's actions are promoted. Parents may get involved in special efforts to promote their child's actions with an object that they consider important for the child's development. The child may, but need not, be interested in acting with that object. The parents, however, may try to do whatever they consider feasible to promote the child's action with that particular object. The ways in which ZPA functions in everyday lives of families are easily observable at any age of children. For example, during a session of "free play" of the parents and their toddler in the living room at home, the parents may try to get (and keep) the child interested in reading a children's book, so that understanding of words and pictures, and knowledge of the alphabet, can promoted. The child, however, may be captivated by the book reading for only a short while, and will soon move on to other activities. The parents may try to get the child to continue with book reading, but if many other activities are available within the ZFM for the child, parents' efforts may be to no avail.

The important characteristic of ZPA is its *nonbinding nature.* When a ZPA is set up but the child does not follow the lead of the parents' promotional effort but acts with other objects (in other ways) within the ZFM, there is no way in which the child can be made to act within the ZPA (unless the ZPA is turned into a ZFM).

5.9.2.1   Set-Theoretic Depiction Continued: Mapping ZPA upon ZFM. In the original presentation of these zone concepts, it was claimed that the ZFM and ZPA are mutually intermapped and constitute a functioning system. The ZFM keeps the person's acting or thinking-feeling within the field of acceptable possibilities, and the ZPA provides further suggestions for the differentiation of the field. To continue the set depiction of the zones,

$$\text{ZFM/ZPA}(t\underline{X}) = \{a^*,\underline{b^*},c,d,\underline{e},f,?,??,g^*,h,\underline{j^*}\} \tag{3}$$

where denoted items are the same as in equations (1) and (2), with the addition of specification (by underlining) of the ZPAs within the set. The ZFM/ZPA complex here is specified to negotiate potential change in two boundary areas (b* and j*) as well as one nonboundary area (e). Again, the principle of bounded indeterminacy is shown here: The process under question is canalized by the set of ZFM-included options *and* by the ZPA highlights. For the latter, it is still not determined which of the highlighted areas (if any) actually leads to the change into the next nearest state of the ZFM/ZPA system. Change can come into being in other areas of the ZFM/ZPA complex as well, without the ZPA functions (or despite them)—for instance, via specification of the ? or ?? areas.

5.9.2.2 ZPA That Entails Areas Outside of ZFM. Although the example above was elaborated in ways that caused ZPA to highlight some subareas of ZFM, there is no reason to limit it to that case. ZPA can include areas that are currently outside of ZFM. The example (above) of integration of an out-of-ZFM element (j) into ZFM may be a result of the ZPA's promotion of such integration. Thus, onto a pattern of ZFM/non-ZFM distinction:

$$ZFM(t1) = \{a^*, b^*, c, d, e, f, ?, ??, g^*, h^*\} \wedge \text{non-ZFM}(t1) = \{j,?\} \qquad (4)$$

a ZPA can be mapped that includes both intra-ZFM and extra-ZFM highlights:

$$ZFM/ZPA(t1) = \{a^*, \underline{b^*}, c, d, \underline{e}, f, ?, ??, g^*, h^*\} \wedge \text{non-ZFM}(t1) = \{\underline{j},?\} \quad (5)$$

The ZPA here includes {b*, e, j}, uniting both intra-ZFM and extra-ZFM items. If the promotion effort is successful in the sense of guiding the developmental process toward integration of j into the ZFM in the next time moment, the ZPA *can* focus the developing process onto the boundary-crossing dialogue (of h* with j). Similarly, such dialogue can occur without ZPA-based highlighting (an example of the principle of equifinality in practice).

The reality of positing for ZPA a scenario that includes areas outside of ZFM, gets its substantiation in any setting in which "forbidden"—yet possible—actions are being suggested to the person. Such suggestions can entail actions that are indeed possible (i.e., belong to the ZPD; see below), as well as those for which possibility is a present illusionary construction (i.e., actions that are outside of ZPD). The principal uncertainty about the boundaries of the ZPD (see below, and 4.5) makes the construction of such illusionary highlighted actions or reflections possible. Similar suggestions of possible-but-ruled-out thought scenarios can occur in a person's intrasubjective world. Such suggestions may lead to reorganization of the zone system at the level of actions, by semiotic mediation at the level of reflection.

5.9.2.3 Emergence of Semiotic Level in ZFM/ZPA Complexes. The form of ZPA (relative to the ZFM) may provide canalization of the process. Thus, the ZFM boundaries are narrowed down to the absolute minimum (of *two* possibilities—to act/think *or not* to act/think, using the ZFM that includes only X). Equating the ZPA with that narrowly defined ZPA (e.g., it is best to act or think or feel X) is likely to lead to the expected outcome. Still, it is merely *likely* to reach that outcome; the coconstructing "target person" can always counteract the narrowly prescribed ZFM/ZPA complex by extending the set of meanings in the semiotic sphere and constructing a new personal relationship with the action–ZFM/ZPA domain (see Brockmeier, 1996a, 1996b, for examples). Even when the ZFM/ZPA system is overconstrained in one field, the coconstructive process can be transposed to another related field and become open-ended again. This usually happens between the domains of action and reflection. Our set-descriptive example may be modified as follows:

$$\text{ZFM/ZPA}(tX+1) = \{a^*, B\underline{b}^*, c, d, \underline{e}, f, ?, ??, Gg^*, h, \underline{Jj}^*\} \tag{6}$$

Here, we add denotations (by capital letters B, G, J) of emerging sign-mediated reflections on parts of the ZFM/ZPA complex adjacent to the particular areas of the ZFM action subzones. This description shows that *not all parts* of the ZFM/ZPA complex at the action level need to be semiotically mediated (i.e., they could be reflected by use of signs). Furthermore, not all of the mediational devices themselves become highlighted by ZPA (e.g., highlighting is the case for $\underline{Jj}^*$ but not for B$\underline{b}^*$ or Gg*). A particular sign-mediator may become attached to different parts of the ZFM/ZPA complex, as in:

$$\text{ZFM/ZPA}(tX+2) = \{a^*, B\underline{b}^*, c, d, B\underline{e}, f, ?, B??, Bg^*, h, \underline{Bj}^*\} \tag{7}$$

For instance, the general designation "This is good to do" can be applied to different parts of the ZFM/ZPA set, in some cases fortifying the ZPA function (B$\underline{b}^*$, B$\underline{e}$, $\underline{Bj}^*$), and, in others, just marking the action area in terms (Bg*).

5.9.3 Some Everyday Examples of ZFM/ZPA Relations

Perhaps an analogy from adults' world can clarify the difference between the ZFM and ZPA. Different producers of various products are interested in selling these products to customers. However, in a free-market economy, a producer cannot force any buyer to buy a particular brand. Instead, the producer can only persuade a potential buyer to act in ways that favor the producer. Hence, commercial advertising acquires prominence under the conditions of a free-market economy. All sellers advertise their products in a hyperactive way, but the buyer decides which of the competing products (if any) to buy. There is a direct analogy between that state of affairs in producer–consumer relations and the establishment of ZPA in adult–child relationships. In both cases, the side that establishes the ZPA cannot bind the other to accept it, but has to try persuasion to that end. In contrast, the nonbinding nature of ZPAs set in adults' consumer world disappears as soon as a monopoly on the production or distribution of some product is established. The producer (or distributor) then has full control over the market and need not try to persuade the potential buyer to buy the product—everything that can be bought is produced by one producer, and the buyer has no alternatives. State-controlled production and distribution systems in some non-Western countries provide many examples of how economic life is organized under these conditions. The ZFMs in child socialization, which are set up by parents, resemble such monopolies. The only options available to children are those they can choose among, and as long as it does not matter to the parents which option is chosen, no ZPA needs to be present.

More usually, both ZFMs and ZPAs are used by child caregivers in their socialization of children, at least in contemporary Western industrialized countries. Rather then separate the two zone concepts from each other, it is more accurate to consider them as parts of the same whole: the ZFM/ZPA complex. Zones of Free Movement and Zones of Promoted Action work jointly as the mechanisms by which canalization of children's development is organized. This applies equally to the development of children's actions and thinking. In the first years of life, the joint work of the ZFM/ZPA system is easily observable in naturalistic settings. During later childhood, however, some of the functioning of that complex becomes rarely observable as a result of children's internalization of control over their own actions and thinking.

In some environmental settings, the ZFM/ZPA complex remains observable for a time longer than childhood. One setting in which the relationships between ZFMs and ZPAs can be traced both historically and cross-culturally is education. This is not surprising; education involves a purposeful effort by adults to educate children in domains of knowledge that require more skillful and mature persons to acquire it. Every form of education, informal or formal (see Greenfield & Lave, 1982), contains some limits set up to constrain the developing children's exposure to, and participation in, some aspects of adults' lives. Certain efforts by children to observe and/or participate in some activities of adults are strictly prohibited. For example, contemporary American children do not learn about sexual activity by observing their parents engaging in it. In many traditional societies, youngsters may get their sexual education vicariously by observing others. However, these same youngsters may be kept away from some other kind of knowledge (e.g., their cultures' secret rituals), until they get their knowledge in those domains during their initiation rites.

The situation is not much different in the case of Western formal schooling. Parallels between different aspects of Western educational settings and traditional initiation ceremonies are noteworthy (see Lancy, 1975). In different settings where children get their formal education, the ZPA and ZFM relationships can be very variable.

The history of Western education provides an interesting account of how the schooling of children gradually progressed from the prevalence of strictly limited ZFMs to include more emphasis on the student's individual goal-directed actions in the process of learning. That change was part of the large-scale social changes that surrounded the process of the Reformation (Ozment, 1983). In Puritan England, an increasing emphasis on the active role of the student within a

ZFM (set by the teacher) can be observed in the child-oriented catechisms that appeared in the 17th century. Previous methods of educating children had emphasized rote memorization of texts (i.e., ZFM was set to equal ZPA—the rote-learning child was requested to repeat exactly the material that the teacher provided and was not allowed to do anything else). The Puritan catechisms widened the ZFM in this learning situation. For example, Herbert Palmer's catechism *An Endeavour of Making the Principles of Christian Religion . . . plaine and easie,* which appeared in 1640, approached the teaching task through a reflective method that would get the "truth" out of the child through the child's *own* (independently dependent) answers, instead of letting the child merely repeat the teacher's words. The method included presentation of the main question and then suggested to the child possibilities that could be answered in yes/no format. The main question was then followed by the right answer, provided by the teacher. Hearing the questions and answers from the teacher would suggest the right answer to the child, rather than give it to him or her directly (Sommerville, 1983). An example of teacher–child interaction taken from that early catechism illustrates this issue:

QUESTION: What is a man's greatest business in this world? Is it to follow the world, and live as hee list?
ANSWER: No.
QUESTION: Or is it to glorifie God, and save his own soule?
ANSWER: Yes.
QUESTION: So, what is a man's greatest business in this world?
ANSWER: A man's greatest business in this world is to glorifie God, and save his own soule.
QUESTION: How shall a man come to glorifie God and save his own soule? Can they do so that are ignorant?
ANSWER: No.
QUESTION: Or, they that do not believe in God?
ANSWER: No.
QUESTION: Or, do not serve him?
ANSWER: No.
QUESTION: Or, must they not needs learn to know God and believe in him and serve him?
ANSWER: Yes.
QUESTION: So how shall a man come to glorifie God and save his own soule?
ANSWER: They that will glorifie God, and save their own soules, must needs learn to know God, and believe in him and serve him. (Quoted with minor textual modifications via Sommerville, 1983, pp. 391–392)

This example illustrates how the ZFM/ZPA complex became gradually restructured in the history of Western education and in conjunction with the reformation of the Christian religion. In this example, the teacher narrowly defines the student's ZFM to the role of the listener to the message, the organization of which involves examples of answers that are considered "correct." The reflective organization of the teacher's text (in the question/answer format) prepares the students to become independent in answering the given set of questions on their own but in the "correct" ways.

This educational approach can be considered to be the historical forerunner of the widespread use of multiple-choice tests in contemporary psychology and education. The structural similarity of the two is astounding. In both the early catechisms and contemporary multiple-choice tests, the responder is given the question and possible answers, together with the task of reaching the single "right" answer. This task requires selection, rather than construction or reinvention, of the right answer. The respondent is guided by a narrow ZFM that includes the choice of "wrong" answers as possible answers but excludes the option of coming up with one's own answer to the question (the ZFM structure excludes respondent-initiated change). The availability of choice between different answers creates the illusion of independent decision making by the student (thus promoting the idea that the individual's choice is independent). In reality, the individual's independent choice is dependent on the ZFM as it is set.

An illustration of how contemporary school systems in different countries organize the ZFM/ZPA system comes from a comparison of two examples. The first example is taken from a description of a Qur'anic school in rural Morocco, where the ZFM and ZPA are set up in such a way that the students' freedom of choice is limited to the actions that the teacher is currently promoting. The limitation of the students' ZFM to the prescribed ZPA is evident from the following description of a lesson in a Moroccan grade school:

> The French writing lesson. The teacher calls for the chalkboards. . . . Teacher says, "Ready." Everyone is sitting up at his desk with chalkboard in left hand and a piece of chalk in the right. Right hands are poised. The teacher reads aloud a sentence from her notebook. Unexpectedly no one moves, right hands still remain poised. The teacher slaps the desk with a ruler. The children at once bend over their slates, working slowly and painstakingly with their chalk. Several minutes later the teacher slams the ruler again. All slates go straight up in the air at arm's length, facing forward in the fashion of a placard parade. The teacher marches up and down the aisles, saying "Wrong, correct, correct. . . ." She slams her ruler for the third time and the boards are lowered, erased, and chalk poised for the next sentence. (Miller, 1977, p. 146)

This description illustrates a classroom situation where, during the dictation, literally every movement of the children was exactly constrained. In everyday language, we may be tempted to talk about such instances as extreme examples of "discipline." In such a situation, the children's ZFMs equal their ZPAs—they can act only in ways that are allowed by the teacher, and have no choice of acting in any other way (what the children are required to do—ZPA—is the only option that they can possibly select as their ZFM). This situation represents the widespread form of the structural organization of human actions that bears the label "military discipline" in Western discourse. Military institutions have developed canalization of human actions to the maximum, where the boundaries of ZFM are narrowed down to match the boundaries of ZPA (the latter occurring in an extreme form of not promoted, but *required* action—on orders, of course).

A different way of organization of the ZFM/ZPA complex is evident in the context of a school in a middle-class neighborhood in Canada, described by Smollett (1975). The students are provided with strict frameworks of ZFM by the teacher, who at the same time promotes the idea of personal choice (between strictly given alternatives) within the ZFM:

> A bright, well-equipped third-grade classroom. Miss Simms explains that today they will begin work on their Christmas pictures. They will draw with crayons again today, as they did such a good job on their last set of crayon drawings.
>
> She explains the task. They will do, altogether, two Christmas pictures each, one today in crayon, one next week in paint. One picture will be on the religious side of Christmas, such as a manger scene, the wise men, or the like (henceforward referred to in class as "the manger picture"), the other on Santa Claus (St. Nicholas) or something on the non-religious side (henceforward referred to as "the Santa Claus picture").
>
> "Now, you have two choices," she declares. "You can do either the manger picture or the Santa Claus picture this week—as you like. Then you will do the other one next week. . . ."
>
> The children begin to draw. Miss Simms walks about, making suggestions, answering questions. "Do the figures first, Janet, then the background."
>
> Several children begin to put questions to Miss Simms, exploring the boundaries of their choices. "Can we do it in pencil?" asks Tom. "No, do it in crayon," says Miss Simms, "it must be in crayon." Little Brenda whispers to another child: ". . . hard to do manger in paint; . . . try it in crayon first." "Miss Simms," asks Brenda, "can I make both pictures of the manger?" "No," says Miss Simms, "you have a choice—one subject for one picture, one for the other." "Can both pictures be in crayon?" asks a boy. "No." Brenda tries again: "Miss Simms, can I make both pictures about the manger if I put Santa Claus in both of them?" Miss Simms walks to another part of the room without responding. After several minutes, Brenda begins to draw. (Reproduced with permission from Smollett, 1975, pp. 221–222)

This example of a student–teacher interaction about the ZFM boundaries in the classroom task may look at first glance very different from the Moroccan description. The students in this example are encouraged to make their own decisions about what to draw in what order, *but they are not allowed, by the teacher, to alter the boundary set through the ZFM* for their drawing activity. On the one hand, the teacher is available to the students to answer their questions (promoting active queries about different aspects of the drawing task), but she refuses to reciprocate any efforts by the children to redefine the ZFM of the task. The children are *free to choose only within the limits set,* and their use of this limited freedom of choice is promoted (by setting up the possibility to ask questions) by the teacher. Some of the questions asked are reciprocated by the teacher in a manner that leads to promotion of one or another of the children's drawing skills, but the basic issue of the ZFM boundaries remains inflexible.

Finally, it is possible to add to these examples the "open classroom" type of organization of school lessons that became widespread in the United States in the 1960s. Here the ZFM boundaries are set quite wide indeed, and the students are provided with excessive opportunities to make (and, therefore, to learn to make) their personal choices within the ZFM. Through setting up a set of different ZPAs for the students' actions (e.g., "You can work on task A, or B, or C, or D, etc."), the teacher leaves the choice to the students, which constitutes a step in the lengthy process of socialization of the American schoolchildren into the ethos of personal choice and becoming a "self-made-person" who is active in life and tends to attribute causality for events that happen in his or her relationships with the environment to his or her own credit.

Thus, from the structural point of view of ZFM/ZPA relationships, the classroom settings in the Moroccan and Canadian schools, as well as in the "open classroom," contain the universal presence of the limits set on children's actions by setting up ZFMs. The examples differ greatly in the ways in which ZPAs are set up for the children—in the Moroccan case, ZPA covers the (narrow) area of ZFM for the children; in the Canadian case, the bifurcation between possible choices for children is strictly determined by the structure of the ZFM, but the ZPAs are set up so that the children can decide on their own what to draw in what order. The "open classroom" has perhaps less promotion of any particular task by the teacher, but ZPAs are set for the particular content domains to be covered in the lesson. In all three cases, the teacher uses ZFM *to keep the children within the given field of actions,* not letting them leave that domain for another one (not allowing the children to redefine the function of the whole setting). The function of ZFMs is to block the possibility of the child's leaving the present field of actions, while possibly (but not necessarily) promoting some actions within the ZFM by setting up ZPAs for the child. A child can learn a new skill, provided that it is within the range of accessibility (in ZFM), even without adults' efforts to promote its acquisition (by ZPAs). Or, if such promotion is present, the child also learns the same skill, possibly a little sooner or at the same time as without promotion.

5.9.4   From Synchrony to Diachrony: The Function of the Zone of Proximal Development (ZPD)

The notion of a Zone of Proximal Development (ZPD) was borrowed from the intellectual heritage of Lev Vygotsky but reconstructed in an attempt to fit it with the other two zone concepts (ZFM/ZPA). ZPD is a narrowed-down extension of Vygotsky's concept, made subservient to the ZFM/ZPA complex. Thus,

ZPD entails the *set of possible next states* of the developing system's relationship with the environment, *given the current state* of the ZFM/ZPA complex and the system. The ZPD helps us to capture those aspects of child development that have not yet moved from the sphere of the possible into that of the actual, but are currently in the process of becoming actualized.

5.9.4.1 Mapping ZPD on ZFM/ZPA.   The ZPD concept here extends the immediate present constraint structures out toward the immediate future. Therefore, it needs to be mapped on the ZFM/ZPA system.

In the context of the theoretical framework presented in this chapter, the ZPD has a decisive role to play in child development because it provides a link between the ZFM and ZPA. That link can be characterized as follows.

1. If the ZPA is set up in ways that have no overlap with the ZPD, then any effort to promote the child's development within the ZPA thus set, will necessarily fail. In real life, if parents try to teach the child a new skill which, given the child's present state of development, is beyond his or her immediate learning possibilities, then the effort will fail. However, the promotion of the same skill in the same way, sometime later in the development of that child, may succeed—if the child by that time has reached a state from which he or she can learn that new skill with the adults' assistance and instruction. The practical question that is asked by parents and educators over and over is familiar: When is the "right time" to begin teaching a child how to use a spoon, or to toilet-train the child? It illustrates the layperson's concern with the issue of setting up ZPAs that would not be outside ZPD.

2. Where the range of the ZPA exactly matches the range of the ZPD, the instruction provided for the children by others can have the maximum possible effect—in terms of everyday life, if parents are knowledgeable about the full extent of what their child *could* learn with their help at a given developmental state. If the parents want to provide the full range of such instruction, then the child may show the expected development of new skills, provided that the child actively participates in the tasks that are the subject of the parents' instruction.

3. The relationship among ZFM, ZPA, and ZPD is constantly "filled in" with new content that depends on what is important in the life of the particular child at a given time. For example, a toddler starts to climb different objects in the home. This constitutes a new motor skill, which is canalized through ZFM and ZPA. The parents deny the toddler the possibility of climbing certain objects in the home (e.g., window sills, kitchen table, etc., which belong outside ZFM at the time), and at the same time may promote the development of safe climbing habits up, and down, the stairs (ZPA; cf. Valsiner & Mackie, 1985). If the given toddler's previous motor development has created a basis onto which, with instruction from

adults, the new skill of climbing stairs can easily be integrated, then ZPA fits into ZPD, and the new skill is learned relatively quickly and without difficulty. If that particular toddler's motor basis for learning to climb stairs is not yet sufficient to fit the parents' preferred ways of teaching the child to climb, then the ZPA does not fit the ZPD at that time, and the efforts to teach the child to climb may fail, or remain unsuccessful for a longer period of time. Some parents do not bother to teach their child how to climb (no ZPA set), but let their toddler try to ascend and descend the staircase (ZFM). In accordance with the equifinality principle, the child whose climbing is not "pushed," but who is allowed to try it alone, will also develop the capability for climbing stairs. However, after the child has learned to climb stairs, the whole issue of climbing may be redefined to include only ZFM (e.g., certain objects remain unavailable for the child to climb), and no ZPA is set up for the child's further development of that particular skill, despite the possibility that the child might be capable of further advancement of that skill under instruction by an adult, or in his own play (ZPD). Instead, another content domain may become important for the adults to promote after climbing skills have developed sufficiently, so the whole system of ZFM/ZPA that should fit ZPD is filled with that new content domain.

5.9.4.2   ZPD and the Contrast of Actional and Mediational Fields.   When taken to the realm of semiotic mediation, ZPD would entail the set of possible new personal senses that could become constructed, given the present person–environment relationship and the ZFM/ZPAs involved in it. Thus, negotiations of ZFM boundaries in the realm of actions can lead not merely to the reorganization of that "actions field," but also to the reorganization of the domain of semiotic mediation (the "mediational field"). Once the latter is reorganized, it regulates further the field of actions. Thus, we have a multilevel system of fields:

1. Tertiary (etc.) fields—metalevel semiotic constructions emerging from personal sense and regulating it, as well as the field of action. These fields can "grow hierarchically" on one another, thus making the metalevel semiotic constraining systems "open" for advancement of hierarchical (i.e., abstract) complexity.

2. Secondary field—a ZFM/ZPA system of personal sense that regulates the field of action, yet at times can operate in a semiautonomous fashion, regulating itself and possibly giving rise to phenomena at the tertiary field level.

3. Connections between fields—*ascending* (reconstruction of the higher field on the basis of the lower) or *descending* (regulation of the lower field by the restructured higher field).

4. Primary field—the ZFM/ZPA system at the level of actions in the particular context (e.g., children's mealtimes, as will be analyzed in Chapters 6 and 7).

Some directions of construction of a new personal sense of the person–environment situation at a given time are open to change as the system moves into the future. This happens interdependently between the levels of semiotic mediation and those of action. At both, there exist novel possibilities of action or of feeling and thinking. Those belong to the ZPDs at these levels; hence, ZPD is conditional on the given state of the ZFM/ZPA complex.

To continue with the set-theoretic depiction from above, the ZPD can be defined as a family of possible novel forms of change, given particular areas of the ZFM/ZPA complex:

$$\text{ZFM/ZPA(t)} \qquad \text{ZPD (t+1)} \qquad\qquad (8)$$

ZFM/ZPA(t)		ZPD (t+1)
{a*}	→	{a, a*, Aa, Aa*, A, ?}
(B<u>b</u>*}	→	{b, b*, Bb*, Bb, B, ?}
{c}	→	{c, c*, Cc, C, ?}
{d}	→	{d, d*, Dd, D, ?}
{B<u>e</u>}	→	{e, e*, Be, Ee, E, ?}
{f}	→	{f, f*, Ff, F, ?}
{?}	→	{?, ?*, X?, X, ??}
{B??}	→	{??, ??*, B??, X??, ???}
{Bg*}	→	{g, g*, Bg*, Bg, B, ?}
{h}	→	{h, h*, Hh, H, ?}
{B<u>j</u>*}	→	{j*, j, Bj*, Jj, J, ?}

This formal example specifies that the set of ZPD options is dependent on ZFM/ZPA in a number of ways. The nearest future can include maintenance of the previous ZFM/ZPA area (the depiction in the left column is included in the right-column set). In the ZPD case, possible new ZPA forms are not included (there are no underlined members in the sets in the right column). The novelty can be constructed in the nearest future by altering the boundary status of the areas (leaving or adding *), by constructing signs [indicated by capital letters, as in (6)], or by further open-ended options (?, ??, or ???). In this tabular format, the level of actions is described in its entire structure, plus the *linkages with the level of semiotic mediation* (see the capital letters). Yet the focus remains on the given level of actions—a corresponding depiction of the mediational field, or of the metamediational fields, can be constructed.

5.9.4.3 Summary: Zones Mapped on Zones. The previous formalistic exercise reflects a very simple general principle: The developmental process is constrained "from the outside inwards," so to speak. At each level of organization, starting from the primary (i.e., actions) level, the ZFM delimits the "outer boundaries" of the field at the given time. This defines those boundary areas where negotiation about further development is going on. Further differentiating that ZFM structure is the set of highlighted (promoted) actions (ZPA). It can include subzones of ZFM, but it can also entail suggestions to renegotiate the existing boundary of a ZFM. The ZFM/ZPA structure is a contemporaneous one—both zones are assumed to function in a coordinated fashion, simultaneously. ZFM "keeps the process within the field" and ZPA works toward providing it with loci of concentration within the field itself, or suggesting changes of the field.

The ZPD represents a further mapping—now of a *time*-extended kind. The set of possibilities (as those look from a present vantage point) is posited to exist for each differentiated part of the ZFM/ZPA field. The crucial point is again the notion of bounded indeterminacy—the range of possibilities within ZPD, given the previous ZFM/ZPA complex, is defined, yet *which of those options* is going to become actualized remains to be negotiated in the actual development. The use of ZFM/ZPA/ZPD terminology provides a framework for talking of the canalization processes in development, and for specifying the narrowed-down (but not strictly determined) arenas for the active negotiation processes that create actual development out of the narrowed-down set of immediate possibilities.

5.10 PARALLEL TERMINOLOGIES FOR MICROGENETIC CHANGE: SCAFFOLDING, FORMATS, FRAMES, AND SCRIPTS

Since the time of Vygotsky's and Lewin's efforts to create field-theoretic—yet largely metaphorical (London, 1944; Sorokin, 1956)—depictions of complex psychological processes, a number of investigators have been attempting to construct elaborations of field-theoretic and zoniferous models.

5.10.1 Extensions of ZPD and Other Zone-Terminological Concepts

Although Vygotsky used the term ZPD as a convenient metaphor in his disputes with educators of his time (see 4.5), later efforts have been in the direction of treating it as a theoretical concept. Recent work by a number of investigators indicates the theoretical difficulties that this concept entails, when turned into a scientific term (Cazden, 1983; Greenfield, 1984; Rogoff & Gardner, 1984; Rogoff, Malkin, & Gilbride, 1984; Saxe, Gearhart, & Guberman, 1984; Wertsch, Minick, & Arns, 1984). Numerous efforts to provide concrete elaborations for the ZPD concept exist. A number of investigators have attempted to measure differences between different posited "zones" of action (e.g., Calil, 1994; Cole, 1985; Ignjatovic-Savic, Kovac-Cerovac, Plut, & Pesikan, 1988; Moll, 1990; Newman, Griffin, & Cole, 1989; Portes, Smith, & Cuentas, 1994). Others have tried to clarify the relationship of that concept with other close concepts [e.g., "scaffolding" (Rojas-Drummond & Rico, 1994); "situated cognitive representations" (Saada-Robert, 1994)]. Efforts to create zone concepts parallel to the system of zones also exist, as outlined in the present theory in the area of communication (Reed, 1995) and in contexts of teaching and learning (Maciel, 1996).

Extensions of the ZPD model into the domain of semiotic mediation by concepts and reconstruction of external environment lead to relating ZPD with the meaningfulness of everyday-life contexts (Alvarez, 1994; del Rio & Alvarez, 1992). A particularly important elaboration of the zone terminology is the effort to capture the unity of person and sociocultural field through conceptualizing the syncretic nature of ongoing action processes. This has led to the formulation of the Zone of Syncretic Representation (ZSR; del Rio, 1990). Built up along the analogy with Vygotsky's ZPD metaphor, the notion of ZSR is used by del Rio to conceptualize the dynamic nature of child–environment relations in everyday contexts:

> [T]he developing child . . . acts, thinks, wants, considers, remembers, and so forth, using two main sources mutually integrated: the classical mind of psychologists, her or his brain under the skin; and the distributed mind, the loans, resources, funds, or mediational tools that are offered to her or him or his cultural space—mainly social mediations (the teacher that reminds us of a formula or a moral attitude, the mother that wakes us up in the morning, the friend that suggests going for ice cream) and instrumental mediations (the alarm clock, the table and the written papers on it, the room and its "cultural affordances," the TV, the diary). There is *continuous help* from the external operators to the internal, or vice versa. One can start an internal plan (to go and fetch a book to look up a reference) and to pass to another plan externally activated in the cultural space (find another book that evokes its own task or possibilities . . .). Each of these actions is a personal and freely initiated action, but their organization is syncretic, in the common territory of distributed operations of our internal-and-external mind . . . . The *current syncretic sum or system of operators that we have in every situation* (moment plus space) would be the zone of syncretic representation. (del Rio & Alvarez, 1995, pp. 394–395, italics added)

The ZSR is thus a concept that entails the present field of person–environment relations. As a field of the present, it is close to Kurt Lewin's focus on the personal life space and its transformation (Lewin, 1943a). The ZSR has a qualitative advantage over Lewinian space: It is semiotic. In parallel, it also has a disadvantage: The structure of the ZSR is not charted out. (Note the uncertainty in the above quote, regarding use of the notions of "sum" and "system" of operators.) In fact, it hardly can be charted out, because the ZSR is designated to capture the dynamic syncretism of human streams of acting and consciousness. It seems that the ZSR, as described by its inventors, is similar to the transitional form between associatively determined and apperceptively determined structures of behavioral processes—to use Mikhail

Basov's (1991) terminology. The relation of the person with the activity contexts flows in a continuous syncretic stream of encounters with culturally meaningful and directive objects. In that stream, cultural mediating devices are viewed as "continuously helpful." This axiomatic focus is widespread in many post-Vygotskian theoretical advances: The social world, in its many versions, is viewed as helpful (rather than ambivalent, or intentionally malevolent). The ZSR may also include beliefs in "evil eye," or in positive social values that lead to glorified death (e.g., Sande, 1992).

The meaning of "help" can indeed be considered broadly—for instance, the meaning of "witch" was helpful for the medieval witch-hunters to solve problems of power relations in their society. Nevertheless, help remains unspecific unless the particular objectives for which that help works are made explicit. What is help for one can be an act of "being made to feel inferior" by another. The active interpreter at secondary and tertiary field levels provides the particular action with its meaning and its general context.

5.10.2   Tutoring and Scaffolding

The concept of tutoring has been widely used in educational discourse (see Maier & Valsiner, 1996, for further analysis). Various research efforts emerged in conjunction with the intellectual stimulation by Jerome Bruner (1975, 1976, 1978, 1981). The emphasis on understanding the psychological role of instruction (tutoring) in child development, which has been consistently present in Bruner's interest (Bruner, 1960, 1972), has been ultimately connected with Vygotsky's explanations of development through the ZPD concept (Bruner, 1983, 1984).

The empirical research efforts around Brunerian perspectives on development have led to the use of the metaphor of "scaffolding" to describe the process of adults' instruction of children in the solving of specific tasks (Wood, 1980; Wood, Bruner, & Ross, 1976; Wood & Middleton, 1975; Wood, Wood, & Middleton, 1978). The explanation of the meaning of scaffolding reveals its explicit similarity, in its empirical coverage, to the ZFM/ZPA/ZPD complex that constitutes the core of the present theory:

> Adult and child together were achieving success on a task, but the nature of their individual contributions varied with the child's level of ability. Once the child could be lured into some form of task-relevant activity, however low level, the *tutor could build around him a supporting structure which held in place whatever he could manage.* That supporting activity served to connect the child's activity into the overall construction and to provide a framework *within which the child's actions could lead to and mean something more general than he may have foreseen.* As the child mastered components of the task, he was freed to consider the wider context of what he could do, to take over more of the complementary activity. The adult could "de-scaffold" those parts which now stood firmly on their own. Thus tutor and child shared in doing the task, the tutor helping the child succeed with those aspects he could not manage,

thus supporting his gradual mastery of the task. (Wood, 1980, pp. 281–282; italics added)

This quote illustrates how scaffolding relates to the same aspects of empirical reality as those covered by the concepts of ZFM and ZPA in the present framework. The child is "lured" into task-relevant activity, which can be promoted through ZPA while excluding alternative action options by ZFM. Once the child is "on-task," the adult keeps him or her acting by setting up constraints that help the child (ZFM), and suggests ways of acting (ZPA) that would contribute toward the solution of the problem. Once a particular action is perceived by the adult to be mastered by the child to a sufficient extent, the "descaffolding" process rearranges the set of constraints on the action mastered by the child, progressing to erect a similar scaffold around some other actions. The decision by the adult of how to proceed from supporting the development of the child's previous action to promoting and constraining some new action depends on the perception of the child's developmental possibilities on the adult's side. In this respect, the ideas covered by Vygotsky's ZPD concept relate to scaffolding:

[S]uccessful instruction involves more than the child's recognition of goals and the adult's encouragement to achieve them. It also involves what we have called the scaffolding of means. The successful teacher regulates his or her instructions, demonstrations, descriptions, and evaluations to the child's current attentions and abilities. The adult provides *just that level of intervention which is necessary to get the child over his current difficulties;* when the child can successfully take responsibility for a particular constituent of a task, the adult abandons that particular form of intervention and reacts at a more general level. Thus, adult intervention is contingent upon the child's activity, and the contingency is based upon the adult's interpretation of the child's errors and the fate of earlier interventions. (Wood, 1980, p. 294; italics added)

The process of matching the instructor's actions to the child's particular ZPDs in Wood's conceptualization was originally related to the empirical domain of children solving construction problems in laboratory settings. In such settings, the whole environment (the fixed-feature space of the laboratory, the objects present in it, and the social expectation that the child will stay in the room and act on experimental tasks) reveals the connection between the instructor's actions within ZFM/ZPA and the particular organization of the ZPD. The more exclusive role of ZFM—keeping the child "on task"—may have been easier, thanks to the laboratory setting. In the sense of the role of the structures of general settings in organization of action, the concepts of "script," "frame," and "format" are close to the present perspective.

These three concepts capture the *structural* aspect of the phenomena that they describe. Bruner's concept of format parallels scaffolding in substantial ways. It is "a little microcosm, a task, in which the mother and child share an intention to get something done with words. At the start, what the child cannot manage in the format, his mother does for him. Once he can, she requires him to do it thereafter. The format 'stores' presuppositions that become shared by the two partners" (Bruner, 1983, p. 171).

Bruner's empirical analysis of different formats (e.g., "peek-a-boo," Bruner & Sherwood, 1976; "book reading," Ninio & Bruner, 1978) revealed how the development of children's speech is canalized in the context of these formats. The idea of formats is related to two other concepts that are in use in cognitive psychology and anthropology: scripts and frames. Both are rooted in the concept of "schema" that has been used in psychological thinking in the past (Bartlett, 1932; Piaget, 1970a) and that has become used in contemporary psychology in conjunction with talk about a "knowledge base" or "knowledge structures" (see Abelson, 1981; Schank & Abelson, 1977). Scripts are defined as "conceptual representations of stereotyped event sequences" (Abelson, 1981; p. 715) that become activated when necessary to help the person to organize actions. A similar concept, although approaching the issue of knowledge from a slightly different angle, is Minsky's "frame": "a collection of questions to be asked about a hypothetical situation: its specific issues to be raised and methods to be used in dealing with them" (Minsky, 1982, p. 379).

All these concepts—format, script, and frame—are slightly different reincarnations of the recognition of the structured nature of organisms' psychological phenomena and their environments. These structurally oriented concepts, however, are largely assumed to preexist in some static (normative) structural form, and such assumption of the *existence* of these structures may be sufficient for the majority of nondevelopmental tasks in psychology, anthropology, and artificial intelligence research. However, in the case of developmental psychology, it becomes important to explain the emergence of the knowledge structures and action schemes. The theoretical framework outlined in this book can explain the development of scripts in children's ontogenies (see Nelson, 1981) through the general canalization explanation, which is made empirical by the notions of the ZFM/ZPA/ZPD complex as it works in particular conditions of child–environment relationships under the supervision of other people.

5.11   SUMMARY: ZONES CREATE THE ARENA FOR NEGOTIATION OF ACTUAL DEVELOPMENT

This chapter elaborated the theoretical system that clarifies how the general idea of bounded indeterminacy is actualized in microgenetic contexts of development where a person is "pushed" and "pulled" in one or another direction by some social other—or by personal goal orientations. The system entails construction and constant reorganization of constraint structures at different levels of the person's functioning. The actions level and semiotic mediational level are mutually separated yet interdependent (i.e., they constitute a case of inclusive separation). Their relative autonomy allows for increased capacities to deal with new life situations. Both levels are organized by *constraint structures,* conceptualized in terms of three kinds of zones. These zones specify the immediate present-to-future possibilities of the action (and mediation) system, and provide the here-and-now *temporary structure* for actual development. Thus, the constraint system reflects the deterministic—yet dynamically constantly changing—side of the developmental processes.

However, together with this structural deterministic moment in development, the processes of actual development entail two moments of indeterminacy. First, the constraint systems themselves (at any given moment) are *quasi*-defined. They are neither strictly given (i.e., in the form of a "crisp" set or a clearly charted "field structure"), nor are they random. All zones at any moment exist in semistructured form, which makes them open for further transformation.

The constraint systems constitute sets (areas) within which undifferentiated regions (and unknown set members) are theoretically acceptable. The possibility of emergence of novel (surprising) items in that *quasi*-defined set (or an area that includes undifferentiated regions) is accepted by the formal description of the zone concepts. It has been a constant problem in psychology to make sense of seimistructured empirical phenomena, which are usually forced into category systems that do not tolerate any semistructured or fuzzy nature of the phenomena (as was described in Chapter 3). The elaboration of the present zone concepts gives an example of a theoretical language in which the coexistence of well-structured, ill-structured, and unstructured aspects of psychological processes can be theoretically accepted.

In Chapters 6 and 7, the present theoretical system will be illustrated by an empirical analysis of children's action development in their first three years, and in very ordinary real-life contexts. These chapters remain largely as they were in the first edition of this book (in 1987), but the theoretical system since that time has been advanced in the direction of conceptualizing intrapsychological processes aside from interpsychological ones. Although it is not clearly specifiable which aspects of the model's empirical setting—children's mealtimes—become internalized (and externalized) by the developing persons, it is assumed that the continuity of the microgenetic context (of mealtime activity structures) on a daily basis leads to the turning of specific action patterns into ontogenetically generalized and semiotically mediated self-regulatory systems. The process of formation of such systems is discussed in Chapter 8.

6

Actions in Culturally
Organized Contexts:
Settings of Mealtimes

The theoretical system that was elaborated in the previous chapter needs to be illustrated with a cultural-historical organized setting of human development where the systems of meanings constructed in a society set up the basis for ontogenesis. The latter consists of many concrete actions that are organized—in their microgenetic form—by culturally structured everyday activities. Most of these activities are so ordinary that we barely stop and think about their intricate organization. The latter is taken for granted; we just act in our everyday lives as it "seems to fit." Yet, in this ordinariness of human action is a great puzzle for developmental science: How can human development proceed in some specifiable form in the myriad of everyday action contexts?

The goal in this chapter is to analyze the cultural organization of one everyday setting—young children's mealtimes. After elaboration of the meaning of action in psychological discourse, the history and field organization of mealtimes are given.

6.1 THE MEANING OF "ACTION"

On the side of empirical reality, this book deals with the development of children's action. The concept of action has been defined differently in different schools of thought in psychology. In its different versions, though, it has centered around an invariant emphasis on the *goal-directedness* and *conscious planning* of acting (Chapman, 1982; Harré, 1980; Herzog, 1984; Leont'ev, 1975; Von Cranach, 1982; and others). The conceptual roots of action theories lie within the German cultural-philosophical traditions where the concepts of *Handlung* and *Tätigkeit* have served as the language basis for action theories.

The English-language terms *act* and *action* relate to the Latin verb *agere* (= to do). The closeness in the meanings of these terms in the English language has facilitated their use in scientific discourse in more electic ways than the German equivalents afford, which has certainly complicated the English-translation difficulties of German or Soviet contributions to action research in psychology or sociology.

6.1.1 Summary of Concepts of Action in Psychology

In different theoretical systems in contemporary psychologies, the meaning of *action* and *act* (and their relationships) is conceptualized in various ways. Within one tradition, Harré (1980; Harré & Secord, 1972) and Von Cranach (1982) view action as goal-directed behavior, while act is reserved to denote the meaning of some set of actions within a culture. For example, the act of greeting can be accomplished by different actions: kissing, handshaking, nodding, smiling, saying "Hi" or bowing, and so on. All these actions (which can occur in combination, and/or in a sequence: saying "Hi!" followed by shaking hands) accomplish the same social act of greeting. Thus, act may be in different relationships with action: the relation can be one-to-one (e.g., in cases where a specific action has a specific meaning), or one-to-many (a certain act is carried out by a sequence of partially parallel actions, like the example of greeting).

In research on children's motor development, the term *action* is used in connection with the more general term, *skill*. A skill (e.g., walking, singing, using a spoon while eating, and so on) can be denied as a sequentially organized program of actions toward the attainment of a goal (Connolly, 1973, 1975), which is composed of different subroutines (Connolly, 1970). In the domain of motor skill research, the issues of the cultural meaning of the skills are usually not considered important—thus the discrepancy between an act and a skill. This discrepancy may be remedied by assuming partial overlap between the two: All motor skills of human beings are, or become, acts (or parts of acts) as their goals are culturally meaningful. However, not all acts involve readily available skills; the meaningful frame of an act may direct the development of a motor skill (action program) for its fulfillment.

The traditions of thinking about actions that have emerged within the Soviet psychology have branched off from the German traditions of viewing action in an object-related manner (exemplified by *Tätigkeit*). Vygotsky's writing about the role of cultural tools in human development (e.g., Vygotsky & Luria, 1930) served as a beginning stage for increased interest in the concept of activity in contemporary Soviet psychology. The most well-known effort in the Soviet psychology to construct a theory of activity is found in A.M. Leont'ev's thinking. His (Leont'ev, 1975) "theory of activity" (*deyatel'-nost* in Russian) involves a different use of the terms. Different *activities* (forms of human relationships with the object-world, distinguished and guided by their motives) include *actions* (*deistvie* in Russian—processes that are guided by conscious goals). Leont'ev explicitly defines action as "the process that is subservient to the representation of the result that must be reached, i.e., the process that is subservient to a conscious goal" (Leont'ev, 1975, p. 103). Actions, in turn, consist of *operations* (behaviors that are immediately dependent on the context of attainment of concrete goals). Leont'ev explains his use of the term *operations* in the following way:

> Every goal—even . . . "reach point N"—exists objectively in some object-related [environmental] situation. Of course, for the subject's consciousness the goal may be in the form of an abstraction from that situation, but his *action* cannot be abstracted from it. That is the reason why, aside from the intentional aspect (*what* must be accomplished), action includes also its operational aspect (*how,* in what way it can be accomplished), which is determined not by the goal in itself, but by the objective object-related [environmental] conditions of its accomplishment. In other words, the *action that is being carried out* matches the task; the task—that is the goal which is given under certain circumstances. That is why action has a special character that in special ways "creates" it—the ways for which it is carried out. I call these ways of accomplishment of action *operations.* (Leont'ev, 1975, p. 107)

Whereas the Harré–VonCranach tradition of thinking emphasizes the relevance of behavior and its existing social function, Leont'ev's emphasis is rooted in his understanding of motives as results of person–environment transaction. Motives, for Leont'ev, constitute the object (either existing in reality or constructed in the ideal sphere of a person) that directs the activity of the person toward self. Leont'ev posits the absolute existence of motives—according to him, "nonmotivated" activity cannot exist (if it seems to exist, it represents a case with hidden motives—cf. Leont'ev, 1975, p. 102).

6.1.2 The Concept of Action in the Present Theory

Any developmental perspective on children's actions has to deal with the issue of validity of teleological understanding of the young infant or child. Under what conditions is it reasonable to assume that the child's activities are goal-directed? This question is flavored by its nondevelopmental ethos—it is asked to verify the *existence versus nonexistence* of the child's purposefulness and even its intentionality. It overlooks the developmental aspect: How do purposefulness and intentionality develop from a state of the young organism in which it is not *yet* present? The latter question helps us to overcome the theoretical duality of action-theoretic handling of infancy, which either has to (a) posit the existence of intentionality in the infant and then analyze its actions, or (b) deny the existence of intentionality and consequently refuse to analyze infants' behavior as related to actions. A developmental solution to the problem of actions among infants is suggested by Thelen and Fogel (1986) in their effort to explain infants' motor coordination and interaction with adults in terms of *coordinative structures*—synergistic forms of organization of the particular functional structure (e.g., muscle complexes of the infant's body, or mother–infant interactive behavior) that are capable of advancing into qualitatively new states of organization. In this sense, conscious goals are not necessarily part and parcel of action, but emerge in its process and continue to participate in actions once they have emerged. The present perspective on children's action development emphasizes the *teleogenetic* nature of actions—the human capacity for practice of generating goals and acting toward attainment of such self-constructed goals (Coulter, 1973). This perspective contrasts with the teleonomic (goal-seeking) view of action, as well as with the rich behavioristic traditions in psychology that have attempted to eliminate the notion of future-oriented purposeful behavior from the realm of scientifically studied phenomena. The theory presented in this book is aimed at explaining how children's actions (observable behavioral episodes) and acts (culturally meaningful events) are *constructed in the process of transaction of the developing child and his or her social others, as that transaction regulates the relationship of the child to the particular environmental context.* In the process of such transaction, the directedness of the social others of the young child can be assumed from the beginning, but the child's intentionality and goal-direction constitute emergent developmental phenomena. In other words, the development of a child's actions starts from a state of no intentionality or goal-directedness and is gradually canalized toward culturally acceptable and prescribed forms of goal setting and goal attainment, as well as toward the cognitive construction of intentionality as a psychological device that underlies human actions in their adult form.

The empirical study of psychological phenomena from a teleogenetic perspective confronts three conceptual difficulties. First, the possible construction (and/or presence) of multiple goals makes it complicated to explicate the whole goal network that is functioning at a given time. Furthermore, some goals in that network may be eliminated from the network, and new ones constructed, at the next time moment—the goal-network is a dynamic entity that changes in connection with the actions related to it.

Second, many of the goals in the goal-network may be *fuzzily defined* at a given time. This is a very likely state of affairs because of the constructed nature of the goals—their construction starts from a state in which the given goal does not exist, moves through a state where its existence is unclear and its nature fuzzy, and only finally may reach a state of high clarity and clear differentiation. At any given time, some of the goals in the goal network are in the intermediate state of emergence in which they cannot be exactly delineated in an analysis. The empirical study of goal-directed action therefore has to assume their existence without their clear delineation.

The third difficulty of empirical research relates to the temporal organization of the goal network. Some goals are set up to be attained sooner rather than later; some more immediate goals serve as means of reaching more far-off or more general goals, and so on. Analysis of any future goals involves explication of an organism's projection of expected outcomes in the future, so such analysis depends heavily on the conscious self-reports of the organism. The latter is accessible to the investigator if the organism involved is a human being capable of introspection. Infants and toddlers are not particularly suitable subjects for introspective accounts of their goals, although from their behavior goal-directedness is easily implied by the socialized *adult* observer who treats his or her projections of goal-directedness into the child's actions as if these were necessarily true.

6.2   STRATEGIES OF SEARCH FOR RELEVANT EMPIRICAL REALITY

The theoretical system outlined in this book is based on assumptions that determine where to look for empirical phenomenology that would be relevant for the theory. First, the structured nature of the organism and its environment leads to looking for empirical phenomena in those domains where one can expect constraining of the actions of developing children to take place. This direction of search is quite opposite to the strategy of many child psychologists who want to observe children's "free" behavior in their habitats. A good example of the latter is the overwhelming interest in contemporary studies of adult–infant interaction in the setting called "free play"—where the adult and the baby "act naturally" in a situation where they "play freely." From the perspective of the present theory, such a free-play situation is the *least* interesting domain of empirical phenomena—exactly because the potentially present constraints on action (and thinking) are least likely to become evident in observations of such situations. The free (= constraint-free) nature of free play makes it highly unsuitable for the purposes of the present theory, whereas exactly the same free (= natural) aspect may make it valuable to investigators whose theoretical background is not based on the central relevance of limits or constraints. Furthermore, from the perspective described in this book, *no play, or any behavior of any organism, can be free in principle, because all behavior is embedded in its context, which sets some limits on its freedom.* Even if it is difficult to point to the constraints operating in the mother–child free play situation, the constraints are actually there; but because they are unlikely to be reached (because of the wide range of possibilities they afford), it is possible to imagine that they do not exist.

The everyday life of developing children is full of highly constrained (e.g., diapering, eating, riding in a car seat, or on mother's back, and so on) as well as minimally constrained (e.g., unsupervised play, sleep) events or happenings. The domain of toddlers' lives that is represented in this chapter (mealtimes) was selected because, in that domain, adults purposefully limit some of children's actions and promote others, thus canalizing the toddlers' further development. It is also important to view the functioning of the present theory inside the adults' minds when they think about children in their role as parents, or consider child-related activities. In both cases, the thinking of adults is canalized by some cognitive constraints that allow the adults to solve old problems under new circumstances. Such sets of cognitive constraints of thinking can be viewed as results of the internalization process of external constraints on action—internal reconstruction of external reality (Vygotsky, 1956, 1960). The question of the correspondence between thinking and acting as both of these are organized by sets of constraints remains beyond the scope of this book.

6.3   THE CULTURAL ORGANIZATION OF CHILDREN'S MEALTIMES

It would be trivial to state the importance of feeding from the perspective of any living organism. The fundamental importance of the alimentary functions makes human actions in feeding settings prime targets for cultural regulation. As Lévi-Strauss (1966, p. 587) has emphasized, cooking shares with human language the status of being truly universal forms of human activity—there is no society without a language, and no society that does not cook in some manner at least some of its food. The discovery of controllable fire and its purposeful use was an important milestone in human history—one that set human beings apart from other species. Some nonhuman primates may, under special circumstances, acquire artificial semiotic systems that may be called language, but no nonhuman primate has been observed or taught to cook a meal, either in the wild or in a laboratory!

The cultural organization of cooking and eating includes many facets, all of which are relevant for the developing child. In fact, the ontogeny of feeding constitutes for the infant the microcosm within which cultural patterning of behavior begins and where the child is confronted with cultural knowledge about the world of foods, tools, and feeders. Gesell and Ilg (1937, p. 33) remark:

> One of the basic developmental problems of the human infant is to use his hand adaptively, to grasp food, and to manage implements for conveying food through the short but troublesome route from hand to mouth. The beginnings of self-feeding by hand in the very primitive child would make a fascinating evolutionary tale if it could be reconstructed. The introduction of cooking and the development of feeding utensils are important chapters in the history of civilization. Cup and spoon are sufficiently sophisticated implements of culture to come into conflict with the infant's capacities. There is a discrepancy between his immature equipment and the demands of adult culture.

Children's knowledge about the cultural meanings embedded in food-related activities is gradually acquired. They observe how others cook and then eat what has been cooked; they are given cooked food to eat under the supervision of others; and they become aware of (and participate in) the practices involving the leftovers. The following specific aspects of cultural organization of eating are important in the process of child socialization in any culture:

1. The distribution of meals and occasional snacks in the culture, within the day/night cycle.

2. The nature of raw foods, the length of time spent in food preparation, and the public-versus-private nature of cooking different kinds of foods.

3. The distinction between feasts and everyday meals, and the meaning of the former within the religious belief system of the culture.

4. The rules of social organization of a mealtime (the social closeness and positioning of the people present; inclusion/exclusion of women and children in the mealtime; rules of serving food—who serves what in which order; rules of eating—"table manners"—and social interaction during the meal; rituals marking the beginning or end of the mealtime and connecting it with the religious belief system of the culture).

5. Rules of dealing with the leftovers: disposal or preservation.

6. The meaning of "clean" versus "dirty" as that distinction is applied to food objects before, during, and after the meal.

7. Rules for children's behavior in the context of the mealtime of the household: changes in expectations for children's behavior, depending on age and capabilities.

All these cultural issues are intricately intertwined with the nutritional and psychological events that take place during mealtimes. On the other hand, these events also depend on the physical structure of the particular settings, which itself is culturally organized.

6.3.1 Accounts of Children's Mealtimes in Psychology

The process of acquisition of cultural knowledge by children in conjunction with eating has been very rarely of interest to psychologists, at least as far as times after weaning are concerned. Earlier studies devoted directly to children's eating included topics such as eating habits (Baldwin, 1944) or food preferences and appetite (Duncker, 1938; Katz, 1928). Psychoanalytically oriented researchers have tended to give attention to psychological events that take place in connection with eating. Anna Freud (1963) interpreted the development of children's relations with food in the context of transitions in their relations with the mother. She outlined six approximate steps in the progression to fully self-controlled eating:

(1) Being nursed at the breast or bottle, by the clock or on demand, with the common difficulties about intake caused partly by the infant's normal fluctuations of appetite and intestinal upsets, partly by the mother's attitudes and anxieties regarding feeding; interference with need-satisfaction caused by hunger periods, undue waiting for meals, rationing or forced feeding set up the first—and often lasting—disturbances in the positive relationships to food. Pleasure sucking appears as a forerunner, by-product of, substitute for, or interference with feeding;

(2) weaning from breast or bottle, initiated either by the infant himself or according to the mother's wishes. In the latter instance, and especially if

carried out abruptly, the infant's protest against oral deprivation has adverse results for the normal pleasure in food. Difficulties over the introduction of solids, new tastes, and consistencies, being either welcomed or rejected;

(3) the transition from being fed to self-feeding, with or without implements, "food" and "mother" still being identified with each other;

(4) self-feeding with the use of spoon, fork, etc., the disagreements with the mother about the quantity of intake being shifted often to the form of intake, i.e., table manners; meals as a general battleground on which the difficulties of the mother–child relationship can be fought out; craving for sweets as a phase-adequate substitute for oral sucking pleasures; food fads as a result of anal training, i.e., of the newly acquired reaction formation of disgust;

(5) gradual fading out of the equation food–mother in the oedipal period. Irrational attitudes toward eating out now determined by infantile sexual theories, i.e., fantasies of impregnation through the mouth (fear of poison), pregnancy (fear of getting fat), anal birth (fear of intake and output), as well as by reaction formations against cannibalism and sadism;

(6) gradual fading out of the sexualization of eating in the latency period, with pleasure in eating retained or even increased. Increase in the rational attitudes to food and self-determination in eating, the earlier experiences on this line being decisive in shaping the individual's food habits in the adult life, his tastes, preferences, as well as eventual addictions or aversions with regard to food and drink. (Reproduced with permission from Freud, 1963, pp. 251–252)

Anna Freud's interpretation of the sequence of development of children's relations with food is strongly (and unsurprisingly) influenced by the explanatory system of Freudian thinking, which is cast within the intraindividual frame of reference (see 3.1.1). Similar intraindividual emphasis is often present in clinical-psychological literature on children's eating *disorders,* mostly concentrating on later childhood years and adolescence (Diepold, 1983; Garfinkel, Moldofsky, & Garner, 1980; Minuchin, Rosman, & Baker, 1978; Schwartz, Thompson, & Johnson, 1982; Slade & Russell, 1973). Some research involving children's mealtime in its social-interactional aspect has been conducted within studies of mother–infant interaction (Benigni, 1974; Golinkoff, 1983; Kindermann, 1985, 1986; Leenders, 1983). These studies, however, have made use of the mealtime setting without explicitly analyzing its constraint structure, because they have theoretically been based on context-free conceptual systems.

The most explicit and structured description of children's mealtime social interaction with adults that is currently available in psychological research literature is part of the extensive longitudinal study of child development that has been conducted in Nottingham, England (Newson & Newson, 1963, 1968, 1976; Shotter & Newson, 1982). The theoretical perspective of the "Nottingham school" of psychology (see also Gauld & Shotter, 1977; Shotter, 1975, 1983, 1984; Wood, 1980) emphasizes the relatedness of the emerging "selfhood" in children with the organization of their social environments. Mealtimes, among other settings, turned out to be situations around which much of the social interaction was found to center in the Nottingham longitudinal study, especially among children 4 years of age (Newson & Newson, 1968, Chapter 8). The mothers' accounts of their problems with their children's eating revealed three basic themes: (a) concern with children's nutrition, (b) instruction in table manners, and (c) parental strategies for coping with children's eating at mealtimes. The Newsons' interviews (Newson & Newson, 1968) with mothers of 4-year-olds revealed very interesting qualitative aspects of mothers' worries and action strategies at mealtimes. Literally, any aspect of a 4-year-old's behavior at mealtimes *may* become a problem for the mother, depending on *her* (and the whole family's) ways of structuring the mealtime settings. The problem status of the child's actions is determined by the adults' thinking regarding these actions, within the context of social norms that the adults accept and impose on children.

Some aspects of the Newsons' empirical findings about mealtimes of 4-year-olds in Nottingham are of direct relevance for the empirical data on American toddlers' mealtimes (reported in Chapter 7). By the time the children reached age 4, the sample of mothers in the Nottingham study showed overwhelming (although not absolute) institution of special rules for mealtime actions. Thus, 73 percent of mothers did not allow the child to bring toys or books to the table, 25 percent did not allow the child to get up from the table during the meal, and 65 percent minded the order in which the child ate the food items during the meal. The rules of using utensils for getting food into the mouth revealed some surviving flexibility among the mothers side toward children of that age. Only 10 percent of the mothers admitted that they would not let the child use a spoon instead of a knife and fork. The times when the use of fingers by the child was allowed were almost an event of the past for most of the sample. In situations where utensils are culturally prescribed to be used, 79 percent of the mothers admitted that they would not let the child use fingers while eating (Newson & Newson, 1968, p. 233).

Although utensils were used overwhelmingly within the sample, in individual instances the issue of the child's reverting to the use of fingers while feeding was reported to acquire greater specificity as a problem. Thus, the wife of a metal polisher described her son's actions:

> He does tend to use his fingers, but we try to break him of that habit, you know. It is a delicate situation at the moment as regards that, because he would *like* to use his fingers; but we keep pushing the fork in this hand. He knows about it—once I've spoken about it, he won't actually use his fingers for the rest of the meal. But every meal he *starts* to use them. (Newson & Newson, 1968, p. 236)

This example illustrates the possible reality of many 4-year-olds' mealtimes—the child's actions are aimed at keeping the Zone of Free Movement at its wider state (i.e., to include hand use to transport food for which adults' culture prescribes a utensil). On the other hand, parents' canalization of the child's actions involves gradual (and future-oriented) promotion of utensil use. What emerges as a basic finding from the Newsons' data on 4-year-olds' mealtime behavior is the long ontogenetic period (essentially covering all the preschool years). The lengthy time it takes children to begin to accept the cultural regulation of mealtimes may be due to the intricately structured nature of these settings. A view into our own cultural history may help us to understand better the complexity of the setting.

6.3.2   Cultural Organization of Children's Mealtimes in European History

In written records about European cultures and their history, information on children's behavior at mealtimes is scarce (Braudel, 1973; Elias, 1978). This is not surprising, given children's status in our cultural history: (a) there has been long-term breast-feeding of children on demand, and no great motivation to force them to succumb to adults' mealtime rules at an early age; (b) once the children are expected to learn new social rules, they do so without raising many problems; and (c) child-related aspects of everyday life have been largely left outside the sphere of interests of chronicle writers or social scientists, because these aspects have been considered too natural to be of relevance for the understanding of history or society. However, from the perspective of understanding how child socialization works, the history of the everyday life of children within their families is highly informative.

The cultural history of mealtime settings is determined by two interdependent lines of historical inventions. First, the history of cooking and eating technology (tools for food preparation, utensils for eating) provides a sequence of external objects that makes it possible to restructure the mealtime setting in different novel ways. Each of these inventions—from the discovery of the usefulness of fire for roasting meat, to the invention of the microwave oven—caters to some cultural and alimentary needs of the users of these inventions at a particular historical period. Second, the history of cooking/eating technology is closely intertwined with the history of social rules that have been constructed to regulate the processes of food preparation and eating, and that make prepared food into an object of social exchanges with particular meanings in the culture (e.g., gifts of food as regulators of kinship ties; see Fortes & Fortes, 1936). The feeding utensils lead to new rules of using them at mealtimes, which, in turn, may lead to the invention of new utensils.

The developing child has inevitably been a participant in, as well as an observer of, mealtimes, as those were organized in his or her culture at the particular time. The following is an excerpt from a text by C. Calviac, influenced by Erasmus Rotterdamus, from the year 1560:

> When the child is seated, if there is a serviette on the plate in front of him, he shall take it and place it on his left arm or shoulder; then he shall place his bread on the left and the knife on the right, like the glass, if he wishes to leave it on the table, and if it can be conveniently left there without annoying anyone.

For it might happen that the glass could not be left on the table or on his right without being in someone's way.

The child must have the discretion to understand the needs of the situation he is in.

When eating . . . he should take the first piece that comes to his hand on his cutting board.

If there are sauces, the child may dip into them decently, without turning his food over after having dipped one side. . . .

It is very necessary for a child to learn at an early age how to carve a leg of mutton, a partridge, a rabbit, and such things.

It is a far dirty thing for a child to offer others something he has gnawed, or something he disdains to eat himself, unless it be to his servant.

Nor is it decent to take from the mouth something he has already chewed, and put it on the cutting board, unless it be a small bone from which he has sucked the marrow to pass time while awaiting the dessert; for after sucking it he should put it on his plate, where he should also place the stones of cherries, plums, and suchlike, as it is not good either to swallow them or to drop them on the floor.

The child should not gnaw bones indecently, as dogs do.

When the child would like salt, he shall *take it with the point of his knife and not with three fingers.*

The child must cut his meat into very small pieces on his cutting board . . . and he must not lift the meat to his mouth now with one hand and now with another, *like little children who are learning to eat:* he should always do so with his right hand, taking the bread or meat decently with three fingers only. (Elias, 1978, pp. 90–92; italics added)

This description of "good" eating habits for 16th-century children (of indeterminate ago range—most likely in mid-childhood) illustrates a number of concerns for child socialization in conjunction with the increasing complexity of the social rules that regulate mealtime behavior. It is interesting to note the socially transformed meaning of a food object once it has been in the person's mouth (not offering others—except servants—food that had been in the child's mouth, and not putting food remains from the mouth back onto the cutting board).

Another text that dates back to the 16th century originated in the German town of Gotha, where it was written by a local shoemaker, Hans Sachs, in 1534:

Listen you children who are going to table,
Wash your hands and cut your nails.
Do not sit at the head of the table; this is reserved for the father of the house.
Do not commence eating until a blessing is said.
Dine in God's name, and permit the eldest to begin first.
Proceed in a disciplined manner.
Do not snort or smack like a pig.
Do not reach violently for bread, lest you may knock over a glass.

Do not cut bread on your chest, or conceal pieces of bread or pastry under your hands.
Do not tear pieces for your plate with your teeth.
Do not stir food around in your plate or linger over it.
Do not fill your spoon too full.
Rushing through your meals is bad manners.
Do not reach for more food while your mouth is still full, nor talk with your mouth full.
Be moderate; do not fall upon your plate like an animal.
Be the last to cut your meat and break your fish.
Chew your food with your mouth closed.
Do not lick the corners of your mouth like a dog.
Do not hover greedily over your food.
Wipe your mouth before you drink, so that you do not grease up your wine.
Drink politely and avoid coughing into your cup.
Do not belch or cry out.
With drink be most prudent.
Sit smartly, undisturbed, humble.
Do not toast a person a second time.
Fill no glass with another.
Do not stare at a person as if you were watching him eat.
Do not elbow the person sitting next to you.
Sit up straight; be a model of gracefulness.
Do not rock back and forth on the bench, lest you let loose a stink.
Do not kick your feet under the table.
Guard yourself against all shameful words, gossip, ridicule, and laughter, and be honorable in all matters.
If sexual play occurs at table, pretend you do not see it.
Never start a quarrel, quarreling at table is most despicable.
Say nothing that might offend another.
Do not blow your nose or do other shocking things.
Do not pick your nose.
If you must pick your teeth, be discreet about it.
Never scratch your head (this goes for girls and women too), or fish out lice.
Let no one wipe his mouth on the table cloth, or lay his head in his hands.
Do not lean back against the wall until the meal is finished.
Silently praise and thank God for the food he has graciously provided, and you have received from his fatherly hand. Now you rise from the table, wash your hands, and return diligently to your business or work. (Reproduced with permission from Ozment, 1983, p. 143)

The general inhibitive nature of the particular "Do not . . ." rules in this text may perhaps illustrate the relevance that had been given to proper structure of actions at mealtimes in our cultural history. It may also reflect the difficulty of forcing children to succumb to the rigorous cultural rules of adults, which were related to the general life conditions of all people at different times in history (e.g., the rule concerning not fishing out lice in the 1534 Gotha text).

In general, the history of mealtimes in the European cultures is character-ized by increasing differentiation of the individual participant's food and food-use utensils from communal usage, and by increased external mediation of food handling by specific tools used during mealtimes. The European cul-tural traditions of eating have developed from the sharing of a communal dish in which food was presented and from which it was extracted by hand, toward highly differentiated social organization of the meal setting, where each par-ticipant has a varied set of food-handling tools (plates, bowls, glasses, forks, spoons, knives, etc.) for his or her use only, and where these private tools are kept strictly separate from similar but jointly used utensils (e.g., forks or spoons for the delivery of food from a common plate to the person's plate) in the process of eating. This cultural-historical development leads to the follow-ing situation:

> On many occasions, not only the plates are changed after each course but the eat-ing utensils, too. It does not suffice to eat simply with knife, fork, and spoon in-stead of with one's hands. More and more in the upper class a special implement is used for each kind of food. Soup-spoons, fish-knives, and meat-knives are on the one side of the plate. Forks for hors d'oeuvre, fish, and meat on the other. Above the plate are fork, spoon, or knife—according to the custom of the coun-try—for sweet foods. And for the dessert and fruit yet another implement is brought in. All these utensils are differently shaped and equipped. They are now larger, now smaller, now more round, now more pointed. But on closer consider-ation they do not represent anything actually new. They, too, are variations on the same theme, differentiations within the same standard. And only on a few points—above all, in the use of the knife—do slow movements begin to show themselves that lead beyond the standard already attained. (Elias, 1978, p. 105)

Undoubtedly, such cultural-historical development of the mealtime setting makes the task of learning to act in such a setting increasingly more compli-cated for the developing child. In this respect, *mealtimes are one of the very few recurrent settings in the lives of developing children where they experience the cultural organization of the social life of their culture in its full complexity.* The contemporary state of cultural organization of children's mealtimes in Europe-rooted societies on both sides of the Atlantic is an outcome of the cul-tural histories of these societies. However, when we view children's mealtimes in a synchronic comparative-cultural perspective, the variability in the ways in which mealtimes are organized becomes very evident. As will be seen in 6.3.3, the ways in which contemporary Euro-American parents structure their chil-dren's mealtimes constitute very particular setting structures of little cross-cultural generality.

6.3.3   Cross-Cultural Diversity in Organization of Mealtimes
Among the variety of descriptions of mealtime customs in different cultures, only a few have included information about children's actions in these settings

(Fortes & Fortes, 1936; Goody, 1982; Lévi-Strauss, 1963, 1966; Richards, 1939; Richards & Widdowson, 1936). This oversight stems from the logic of interest in the stable cultural organization of the adults' society, which has traditionally been characteristic of anthropologists. Children, from that perspective, are not yet fully competent informants about their culture, because they are still in the process of being socialized. This view is, on the one hand, a reflection of the dominance of nondevelopmental thinking in cultural anthropology; on the other, it may characterize the difficulty of observing and recording children's actions during fieldwork.

It is not surprising to find very high diversity across cultures in the ways children's food intake is organized. First (and foremost), that organization depends on the *availability* of food. It would be ridiculous to present the situation of a child from some middle-class European or North American family as in any way a "typical" example of children's eating and mealtime organization. Such a child may have a surplus of food at every mealtime. Contrary to the expectations of the parents, the child may choose not to eat what is offered and end up being considered a problem eater by the parents. Newson and Newson (1968) reported a number of cases where British parents expressed serious concerns about their 4-year-olds' eating habits, and described in very vivid terms how they try to deal with the problem. Furthermore, the two clinical disorders of adolescence and young adulthood that have eating problems at their core—anorexia nervosa and bulimia—are mostly problems of the affluent members of the world's population. In contrast, a child in a Third World country who is malnourished because of the simple lack of food, would provide a very different perspective on the role of food-related actions in child socialization.

However, the cultural diversity of organizing children's food-related actions does not depend unidimensionally on the availability of food. The whole organization of life in a culture sets the stage for structural organization of children's food-related actions. For example, accounts of child care in different African cultures have regularly stressed the difference created by a mother's constant tactile contact with the infant attached to her back (e.g., see Curran, 1984; Konner, 1976). Such an "infant niche" prepares the child for a different way of relating to the mother, as the following description of a recently weaned Wolof boy (age, 2 years 2 months) having a snack illustrates:

> Lying against his mother's back Abdou is whimpering slightly and then clearly asks for something to eat. An elder brother brings him some rice. The mother tries to lift the child on to her lap. But he grumbles, pushes her away and spontaneously presses himself against her back, becoming immediately quiet. She hands him the bowl of rice over her shoulder; the child takes it and begins to eat all by himself, still leaning against her back. The mother lifts her arm and passes the child a small tin of water; he leans over, grabs the tin which the mother still holds and drinks in the same position. (Zempleni-Rabain, 1973, p. 224)

This description illustrates quite clearly how culture-specific the contemporary Western toddler in his high chair is. The same nutritional actions can be performed in front of the mother (as in the case of a child in a high chair) or behind the mother's back (as in the case of the Wolof boy), but they are performed anyway. It is also obvious from the Wolof example that it is not necessarily the mother in other cultures who is the primary helper of the younger child's eating, but an older sibling (in this case, an elder brother). The primary role of older siblings in taking care of young children (following the latter's weaning) is a dominant feature in the organization of home life in the majority of the world's cultures (see Weisner & Gallimore, 1977). The traces of effectiveness of such a caregiving arrangement even in European-type cultures becomes evident if we return to Karl Duncker's research on the role of social suggestion in children's food preferences (Duncker, 1938). He discovered the fact (which may be intuitively obvious to parents with two or more children) that an older child's example in the area of food preferences coincided with a younger child's similar preferences (in 26 out of 28 cases, the children were not siblings). The mothers in the cultures where sibling caregiving is used retain the leading (albeit indirect) role in the child care. The mother's role is changed from that of immediate caregiver (breast feeder) to that of supervisor of the older siblings' work at caring for the younger siblings (e.g., Ochs, 1982).

The child's elders—parents, relatives, older siblings—play the key roles in the organization of the child's mealtimes. They set up the mealtime setting in everyday life, provide the utensils and foods that are considered acceptable or necessary for the child, conduct or supervise the feeding process, and try to direct the child toward the acquisition of appropriate action patterns and culture knowledge in respect to foods and mealtime settings. The social role of meal organizers includes multiple facets—from planning the menu to actual food preparation, and to the plan for feeding the child. Knowledge about what sources of nutrients are, in principle, edible is culturally determined (see Fortes & Fortes, 1936; Tambiah, 1969) and guides the decisions about what the menu of a meal would include. The knowledge about the distinction between edible and inedible objects need not be simple or strict, and in many cases it can be age-bound. For example, Tambiah's ethnographic materials from Thailand revealed that certain animals (house rat and, to some extent, field rat) were eaten only by children, but not by adults (Tambiah, 1969, p. 448). Likewise, Tallensi children in the 1930s were found to eat field or domestic mice, a species of toad, and harmless snakes—all of which were despised by adolescents and adults (Fortes & Fortes, 1936, p. 251). These examples pertain to kinds of animals that children kill and use sporadically in their eating, rather than to the menus of the regular meals taken in the context of their families. In that context, the issue of how and when a child begins to participate in the regular adults' diet is important. In traditional cultures where food preparation for adults as a rule is a time-consuming process, and where the basic set of nutrients used is limited, the foods for participating children are unlikely to be foods that are different from those prepared for adults. In this sense, children's participation in adult meals involves their sharing of the adults' food. Only in Western industrialized cultures could the practice of cooking separate foods for children that would be eaten by children at the general mealtimes become possible—under the conditions of relative affluence and food preservation.

The social organization of mealtime settings is the next aspect that is under control of the adult participants of the meal. It is obviously dependent on the occasion (e.g., the difference between a feast and a regular meal), which itself includes a different set of participants (i.e., the presence of many visitors or kinspeople is likely during feasts but not necessarily at everyday meals). The participants of the meal are located spatially in the meal setting, which may take place in one of several places, public or private. The particular marriage form and the rules of relationship between sexes have an input to the spatial location of meal participants. Among the Tallensi, the practice was to separate the sexes during mealtimes: within the family compound, the husband usually ate with his senior wife (in the case of polygyny), and received food from the kitchens of his other wives as a prescribed donation. The man ate with his youngest weaned child (offspring who were still suckling stayed with their mothers)—a practice that was explained by the need of the recently weaned child to "eat properly in order to grow, and must be taught to do so" (Fortes & Fortes, 1936, p. 271). The role of the teacher of the child at mealtime was thus played by the father—who, in other settings in traditional Tale life, had little contact with the child. Older boys ate nearby, forming a separate group. Women and older girls formed still another separate eating group. This organization reflected the two basic principles of separation of social roles in the society: male/female and child/adult distinctions. In societies where such distinctions have been weak (or lessened), the spatial arrangements at mealtimes reflect it (see Dreyer & Dreyer, 1973, about the ethnography of contemporary middle-class American family dinners). Or, the subsistence needs of the given society may be cognitively related to the expected behavior at mealtimes, as the following description of Yurok Indians by Erik Erikson implies:

> The concentration on the sources of food is not accomplished without a second phase of oral training at the age when the child "has sense"—i.e., when he can repeat what he has been told. It is claimed that once upon a time, a Yurok meal was a veritable ceremony of self-restraint. The child was admonished never to grab food in haste, never to take it without asking for it, always to eat slowly, and never ask for a second helping—an oral puritanism hardly equaled among other primitives. During meals, a strict order of placement was maintained and the child was taught to eat in prescribed ways; for example, to put only a little food on the spoon, to take the spoon up to his mouth slowly, to put the spoon down while chewing the food—and above all, to think of becoming rich during the whole process. There was supposed to be silence during meals so that everybody could keep his thoughts concentrated on money and salmon. (Erikson, 1963, p. 177)

The spatial arrangement of participants of a meal and the cognitive activity prescribed for the occasion set the stage on which the whole spectacle of the meal is played out. First, cultural rules govern the sequential organization of the meal (see Douglas, 1975; Douglas & Gross, 1981). The meal may consist of any number of courses, and each course may involve the use of a different set of utensils. A transition from one course to the next is connected with actions that emphasize the sequential nature of the meal. For example, after the main course, the foods and dishes/utensils with which that course was served are taken away from the table, and a new course (dessert) is introduced by the use of new food and tools for its manipulation (e.g., a cake is brought to the table, on a special plate, and every participant in the meal receives a new—often visibly different—plate and utensil for eating the dessert). A young child who observes or participates in such a meal is socialized toward accepting the sequential organization of the meal, as well as understanding it cognitively. Furthermore, *parents' direct efforts to provide an infant or toddler with some foods first, followed by others, constitute the beginning of multicourse meals in the life of the young child.* For example, a toddler's meal may start with some crackers, followed by the "main dish" of lasagna, and end with fruit as dessert. The dessert (fruit) may be served by the mother only after the remains of the lasagna are removed from the high-chair tray and the child's hands are wiped of traces of the "mess" that this second course involved. Such sequential organization of the toddler's meal is a step in the long process of socialization of the child toward accepting the society's eating traditions.

Second, some psychologically relevant issues that occur during the meal are of important socialization value. The major relevant issue is the adults' regulation of the child's relationships with food and with other people, which are played out around the handling of food. As far as the child's eating is concerned, the adults decide which social rules are applied to the child's actions. This involves social regulation of the child's initiative in getting food (e.g., whether the child is given things to eat, is expected to demand them, or must choose between different foods); accepting (or trying to modify) the child's noisiness or diversion from eating; rules about dealing with food that the child has left over (e.g., demanding that the child finish eating it, or accepting it as leftovers and disposing of it by throwing it away or giving it to other children, to domestic animals, or to the parent to eat); and the regulation of child–child relationships where several children participate in the meal. An example from the organization of child socialization during mealtimes among the matrilocal Bemba in Zambia (in the 1930s) provides a suitable contrast with the European cultural traditions:

> [F]ood is also something that has to be shared, and in this attitude the Bemba baby is definitely trained even in the first year. Children share from one dish and the mother or elder sister tears off for each a lump of porridge with a little drop of relish rolled inside. An unexpected present or find must be divided

with any other babies sitting near. . . . I have seen a women seize a lump of pumpkin out of a baby's hand and say in most vehement protest: "You give some to your friend you child, you! You sit and eat alone! That is bad what you do. . . ."

In a society in which individual initiative is on the whole encouraged, and age has no particular prerogatives, we tend to see that the youngest child gets his fair share at the dinner table or in the nursery school and often teach the elder children to "Give it to Baby first." The Bemba mother on the contrary always says: "Let your elder brother have it! Give it to him first," and on this recognition of precedence the whole organization of daily life as well as the political system finally depends. (Richards, 1939, pp. 197–198)

It is evident that the social rules of relating to other people in the given society are particularly obvious in the context of meals, and thus mealtimes are the naturally occurring settings in which much of the cultural knowledge is acquired by the children. The examples provided here thus far have been of how children's actions at mealtime are *directly* constrained by the caregivers with some cultural goals in mind. However, the opportunities for cultural learning at mealtimes are not limited to such direct socializing actions and constraints. *Within* the structured occasion of meals, children are *indirectly exposed* to different ways of acting and thinking by others. Cultural transmission takes place at mealtimes, both in a goal-directed and an occasional manner. Consider the following example of an American family talking during a meal:

FATHER: Well, I'm sorry, but I forgot to bring home some whiskey for cocktails tomorrow night.

MOTHER: It's all right. I don't think we better serve cocktails.

FATHER: How come?

MOTHER: Well, the Pearsons are coming, and you know him.

SON: Is Dr. Pearson coming, mother, is he? Is he, mother?

MOTHER: Yes he is, and Mrs. Pearson is coming too.

DAUGHTER: Why don't we serve cocktails when Dr. Pearson comes?

MOTHER: Well, Dr. Pearson is a doctor, and he thinks cocktails aren't good for people. He says too many people have the cocktail habit.

SON: I like Dr. Pearson.

FATHER: Well, I like him, too. But this means a stupid party. [This to wife]

MOTHER: I think I'll serve tomato juice. Do you think that will be all right? The red glasses will look nice on that black tray.

FATHER: If Pearson doesn't want to drink that's O.K. with me, but I don't see why that should spoil the party for the rest of us.

MOTHER: Well, I do think that out of deference to his views we should have a dry dinner.

SON: I like Dr. Pearson. Is he a good doctor, mother?

This conversation carries these implications for the children: (a) A doctor whom I like does not approve of the social use of alcohol; (b) Father thinks a dry party is dull; (c) Mother sees her obligation as a hostess; (d) a difference of opinion is resolved with deference to a guest, regardless of the wishes of the host and hostess. There is no preaching, no moralizing. All the ideas are transmitted in a matter-of-fact way, incidental to a table conversation, chiefly between the parents, concerning a small dinner party. (Reproduced with permission from Bossard, 1948, pp. 174–175)

An important aspect of the indirect cultural transmission at mealtimes (or other settings) is its *coconstructive* nature on behalf of the recipients (children). The children who listen and observe what happens between adults at the dinner table have to integrate this information into their already existing knowledge structures *by their own active efforts.* The active role of the recipients of cultural messages leads to the possibility of novel ways of information integration. Rather than taking the parents' messages in their original form, the children adjust the information they receive to their own needs. In this sense, all cultural transmission involves parents' and children's joint construction of new culture, rather than children's passive acceptance of the teaching provided by the parents.

Apart from the social organization of participants' actions at mealtime in direct and indirect ways, cultural implements that are used during mealtimes tell the story of how child socialization in a particular culture takes place. Therefore, an analysis of these tools—furniture, covers, plates and bowls, eating utensils—constitutes a valuable source of information that has usually been little noticed by psychologists in their feverish quest for a limited access to reality, otherwise called "behavioral observations" or highly "controlled" experiments.

6.4 CULTURAL TOOLS FOR FOOD-RELATED ACTIONS

The whole meal setting, and the utensils used, create a culturally structured environment where the use of the cultural tools and the meaningful aspect of these tools coexist. The invention of implements to be used in feeding is not limited to *Homo sapiens.* In fact, the cases where higher primates have been observed to prepare and use an implement that supplements the capacities of the body largely occur in conjunction with feeding. Thus, wild chimpanzees' habit of making and using implements for catching termites (McGrew, 1977; McGrew, Tutin, & Baldwin, 1979) or making and using sponges to get water out of tree-holes (Kitahara-Frisch & Norikoshi, 1982), as well as the Japanese macaques' invention of a washing technology to separate food from sand, occur in connection with fulfilling alimentary needs. The same connection with food is widely exploited by animal psychologists who follow time-honored traditions of rewarding prehungered animals with food, after their successful solution of a problem.

The history of human cultures is closely tied in with the history of technology, of which food-processing and food-handling technologies constitute an important part. Within the history of food-related technologies, special inventions have enriched the scope of possibilities for the feeding of young children and are of particular interest in the present context.

The physical character of foods determines the nature of the utensils used to contain and transport them. In the case of *liquid* foods, the problems of feeding children might not have required extensive development of tools, because the norm of feeding young children these foods has, all through human history, been breast feeding. The breast has largely made it unnecessary to develop many additional utensils for normal feeding of milk to babies, at least up to the times in history when early weaning became emphasized in a culture. When the mother could not nurse, a lactating woman (wet nurse) was often hired to feed the child. Quite naturally, the need for utensils to be used to give milk to infants relates to the acceptance of milk produced by organisms other than humans (e.g., cows, goats) as an appropriate nutrient for babies. In the Middle Ages, special tools made of animal horns (with an aperture made in their end) were used to feed cows' milk to infants. The invention of a "bubby pot" in 18th-century England—the forerunner of the modern nursing bottle that was even named after the old word for the female breast—made the practice of feeding cows' milk to infants more convenient (Gesell & Ilg, 1937, pp. 37–39). The bubby pot lacked the softness of the natural breast but guaranteed that no milk got spilled in the process of its intake—a quality that no cup-feeding or even horn-type tool applied to very young infants could grant. The invention of the rubber nipple followed suit (in 1861), from which time onward, different kinds of milk containers furnished with nipples have developed into the contemporary baby-bottles as a substitute tool for the female breast.

The problem of cultural child-feeding utensils emerges more basically in the handling of *semiliquid* foods that, having been produced outside the maternal organism, could not be handled by the feeder's or child's hands only. Such semisolid foods may have been necessary supplements for mostly breast-fed infants whose masticulatory capacities were underdeveloped. These foods require containers for keeping them—either for a longer time, or for the period from their preparation to consumption. Furthermore, these foods require implements for their transport from the container to the mouth (unless the containing implement is also usable as a transport implement). Ontogenitcally, it means that, at first, the semisolid foods were to be transported from the container into the child's mouth by the person feeding the child; later, the child gradually learned the handling of the utensils and acquired the eating rules. Under the demand characteristics of making and eating semiliquid foods, we can view the cultural history of food containers (bowls, plates, saucers, bottles, pots) and transport utensils (spoons and forks; chopsticks in the Orient). Some feeding utensils emerged that are containers and transport utensils at the same time. For example, cups and glasses are used in both of these functions—they may contain liquid or semiliquid foods for the necessary period of storage, but are also used to transport the foods into the mouth repeatedly. The spoon is an interesting combination of the cup/bowl and a lever—its bowl part is essentially a

container capable of handling a *sufficient amount of food for one-time intake.*
Its handle functions as a lever that can be used to extract food from another container without inserting into the food the hand that holds the spoon.

Feeding utensils for semiliquid supplementary feeding of infants and young
children have been documented over a long period of cultural history. Special
urns, cups, saucers, and flasks that were made to fit children's needs were used
for centuries by the ancient Greeks, Romans, Egyptians, Assyrians, and others
(Gesell & Ilg, 1937, p. 37). Spoonlike tools date back to Paleolithic times.

Personally used forks are a relatively recent cultural invention. They
emerged in the European eating settings only in the 15th and 16th centuries
(Braudel, 1973). One can trace the history of the fork back to the dagger—a
sharpened metal stick that can be used to transport pieces of objects of solid
consistency. The history of personal forks was influenced by the spoon. Prior to
the 15th century, the forks lacked the bowl-like curve of the end that comes into
contact with food, which is so characteristic of contemporary forks and was developed under the conditions of similarity with spoons. That curvature, together with widening of the contact region of the fork (due to the addition of
tines—from two in the first forks in history, to four in the majority of contemporary ones), made the fork closer to the spoon, so that it could be used as an
imperfect substitute for the spoon if necessary (e.g., try eating semiliquid
puréelike food with a fork!), although that substitutability may work poorly in
practice. Some contemporary forks made for children are exaggerated in their
form to resemble spoons functionally, and the ends of the tines are not sharp
(the danger of hurting oneself leads to the elimination of the major role of the
fork as the instrument for picking up hard pieces of food).

However, forks are useful for food objects that are of proper size for handling and eating. To get food into that size usually requires additional tools,
which in cultural history has led to the invention of knives. Knives are the
proper tools for cutting different objects, including food objects of hard consis-
tency that cannot be reduced to smaller pieces otherwise. The use of knives to
cut food may be the most ancient human tool-using activity, and has been important for nutritional purposes. Isaac's (1978) findings of the use of stone
tools for cutting meat by protohominids in Africa at least 1.6 million years ago
illustrate the ancient nature of these implements that are useful for solid food
objects that are either too hard or too big to be handled by teeth. In contrast to
this long history of cutting instruments in general, the use of a knife as a personal eating utensil has had quite different fates in different cultures. Even in
the present day, one can observe differences among some Western industrialized cultures in the use of knives during meals. The majority of present-day
Americans find the European habit of continuous handling of knife by the right
hand and fork by the left, too complicated. Instead, they proceed to cut out a
number of pieces of food of appropriate size, using the fork in the left and knife
in the right hand, and then abandon the knife and continue eating the just cut
pieces, handling the fork by the right hand. That difference between Europe

and the United States illustrates the subtle differences, in the sequential organization of the meal (i.e., divided into cutting-then-eating episodes versus continuous cutting and eating), in cultures that share much historically.

The contemporary utensils meant for feeding infants and toddlers reflect in their form the cultural expectations for the children to become socialized eaters within their society. An analysis of the affordances for different actions that are purposefully coded into the structure of these cultural tools is enlightening. First, the objects of furniture that are used as the basic frame for infants' or toddlers' mealtimes—the high chair, infant seat, infant walker, and special toddlers' seats that are either attached to the table or put on a regular chair to bring the child to the level of the table—all share certain structural characteristics that represent cultural ideas (apart from serving as pragmatically useful in the meal process).

By far the most standard furniture for toddlers' mealtimes in our empirical observations is the *high chair* (see Figure 6.1). The high chair is a cultural tool into which the emphasis on toddlers' constrained freedom of action is coded in full accordance with the culture. On the one hand, it is a device that limits children's freedom of behavior during mealtime. This is accomplished by the tray, which does not allow the child to leave the meal situation, as it blocks exit from the chair. That limitation is further assisted by strapping the child to the high

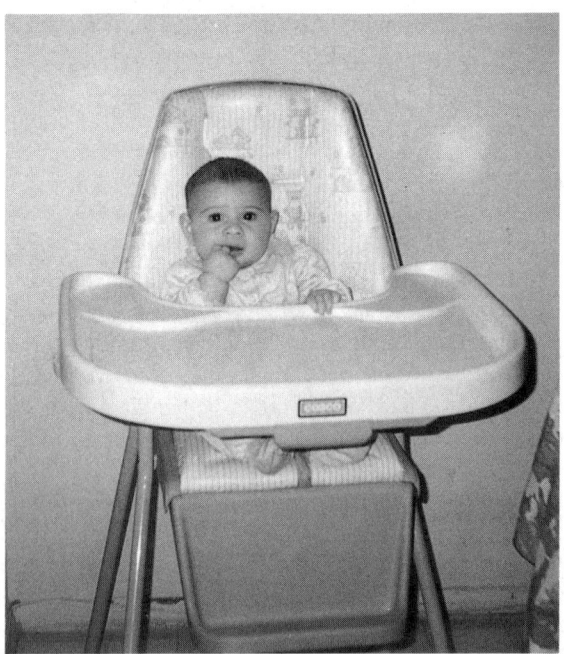

FIGURE 6.1.   Child within a constraining device: the high chair.

chair so that the remaining alternative routes for leaving the situation of meal-time (e.g., by sliding down under the tray, or standing up on the seat and climb-ing out of the chair over the tray) are excluded from the realm of possible actions. The high chair *affords the child a limited field of freedom of behavior*—including the set of actions that are possible to perform on the high chair tray (e.g, banging on it with hands or objects, manipulating objects on it, throwing objects across the board from it, etc.). Compared to the child's Zone of Free Movement before confinement in the high chair for a meal, the stay in the high chair brings greater restrictions on the child's behavior. However, if the high chair is compared to the arrangement where an adult keeps the child on his or her lap while feeding (e.g., using the left arm to limit the child's ZFM while feeding with the right hand), the high chair provides the child with greater *local* freedom of action *outside immediate tactile contact with the feeder.* On the feeder's side, the high chair makes it possible to move around in the environ-ment during the meal (e.g., for the purpose of fetching a new food, or perform-ing other tasks). The high chair also brings the child to the level at which adults eat their meals, thus promoting participation (through the possibilities for ob-servation and imitation, as well as direct intervention) in the adults' activities during the meals.

A number of cultural tools are used in the infant/toddler meal setting in the contemporary American middle-class subculture. These can be divided into *direct-action utensils* (e.g., spoons, forks, cups, bottles, bowls, plates) and *indirect-action utensils.* The latter category includes tools that set the stage for direct feeding actions—bibs that prevent the child's clothing from becoming dirty, special toys set up on the high chair tray that serve the function of keep-ing the child occupied, and so on. Some objects in the direct-action utensils cat-egory can be used for keeping the child occupied—for instance, the widespread practice of providing an extra spoon for the child, to keep the child from grab-bing the spoon used to spoon-feed the infant.

The specialized indirect-action utensils are themselves products of a cer-tain cultural patterning of infants' mealtimes. For example, if the infant were not provided with a certain local freedom of action during the meal, there would be no need for using objects to capture its attention and keep it away from intervening in the feeding process. That need for redirection of the in-fant's attention *emerges only in conjunction with the situation where the infant can possibly intervene in the feeder-controlled actions.* First, the adults provide the child with a ZFM, but the child begins to use its resources in ways that counteract the adults' goals, and consequently the adults have to deal with the situation. They may constrain the child's ZFM further so that the particular disturbing action possibility is eliminated. This happens, for example, when a parent holds down an infant's hands while continuing to spoon-feed the child. Another way out of the situation involves the creation of a ZPA with the help of an indirect-action utensil that is expected to occupy the child, retaining the present structure of ZFM.

The Wiggl-Egg (see Figure 6.2), one of the ingenious inventions of modern infant-feeding technology, constitutes an example of an indirect-action utensil *par excellence.* The function of the Wiggl-Egg is explained to the potential buyers (parents) thus:

> *A plaything that always remains within reach is an excellent way to keep a baby entertained while in his high chair or any other seat*—especially when a parent's attention must be temporarily elsewhere, such as during meal preparation. Wiggl-Egg's sure-grip suction base holds it securely no matter how hard a baby bats it to and fro. The colorful duck design will attract an infant's attention while the pleasant rattle encourages further interaction.

Certain cultural practices, based on the cultural meaning system (as well as practical considerations of parents' activity), are evident in this description of

FIGURE 6.2.   The Wiggl-Egg. (Photograph by Albrecht and Elzbieta Lempp.)

the tool. First, the idea that *the baby should be entertained* is explicitly taken for granted—in direct conjunction with the accepted necessity that the child's freedom of behavior has to be limited (but not fully eliminated) on some occasions (as when a hungry child intervenes in the parent's meal preparation activity in the kitchen). The tool invented for the purpose of providing the infant with an alternative action opportunity, thus redirecting his or her attention from what the adults are doing, has additional characteristics that promote the culturally valued positivity in expression of emotions. The duck figure on the Wiggl-Egg is depicted as smiling, and it is assumed that the egg will be set on the high chair tray *facing the child.* For the sake of an exercise in the strength of our culturally given expectations of what kind of environments we create for children, consider the two versions of the Wiggl-Egg in Figure 6.3, and ask yourself which of the two eggs you would prefer to give to a fussy

FIGURE 6.3.   Cultural coding of promotion of happiness: Which of the two Wiggl-Eggs would you choose for a child? (Photograph by Albrecht and Elzbieta Lempp.)

and hungry infant who is strapped into a high chair, while you as the caregiver are preparing a meal for the child.

The redirection of the child's interest thus involves canalization of the child toward the expression of positive emotions. The socialization of children's cultural "display rules" (Cole, 1985; Ekman, Friesen, & Ellsworth, 1972) of emotional expression may start from everyday life situations where parents surround the child with objects (indirect-action tools) that mark the environment of the child, thus gradually leading the developing child toward internalizing these rules.

The use of indirect-action utensils in different child-inclusive situations obviously goes beyond the limits of children's mealtimes. A highly interesting example—from a set of toy cooking utensils—is presented in Figure 6.4. The set constitutes an effort by adults to redirect the young child's play from adults' objects (real pots, pans, and food) to their toy replicas. Again, as in the case of the Wiggl-Egg in Figure 6.2, the pot is furnished with a schematic smiling face on one side. The goal of directing children toward play with toy replicas of cooking utensils is related to a potential danger, though. The text on the label of the toy set reveals it most directly:

> Important: Never allow your child to place the pieces of this set on the kitchen stove, in the oven or over any open flame.

Turning to the category of direct-action utensils, it becomes evident from the ways these are constructed how, in the given culture, the use of such

FIGURE 6.4.   The Smiling Pot. (Photograph by Albrecht and Elzbieta Lempp.)

utensils is guided. A promotional statement on the back of an infant spoon-and-fork training set package illustrates:

Allowing your baby to help spoon-feed himself as early as 9 to 12 months of age can help develop his independence and self-esteem. Early attempts at using a spoon are bound to be messy, but with practice your baby will learn to manipulate it with minimal spills. Use of a fork should follow at about two years of age.

This promotional message, printed on the reverse side of the spoon-and-fork set packaging, makes use of a number of cultural ideas that are prominent in the minds of contemporary American parents and that guide their actions in canalizing their children's development. First, the cultural core concepts of *independence* and *self-esteem* are explicitly emphasized in conjunction with the parents' allowing a 9–12-month-old infant to manipulate the spoon without help. Second, the spoon manipulation by the infant is referred to as "help" to the parent in the process of feeding the infant. That help, of course, is necessarily connected with nonfeeding actions with food by the child, which are culturally described as "being messy"—a price that parents, realistically, will have to pay if they give a spoon to their infant early. Note that the promotional text above explicitly acknowledges the messy aspect of early spoon manipulation by the infant, *and compensates for that with the use of another core idea of American culture—"practice."* That idea is based on the emphases on independent (= individual against environment) work and learning to work, which have guided the process of child socialization in the cultures where the Protestant work ethic has been dominant over some time in history. Finally, the *expectation of positive outcome* as a result of the child's individual learning of spoon use is emphasized. Parents are told essentially that practice makes perfect and that it is their responsibility to introduce the particular utensils *at the specified age period* (spoon at 2–12 months, fork "should" follow at about 2 years).

Important information about the psychology of child socialization is available from an analysis of the form of utensils that are meant for children at different ages. Infants' spoons are highly instructive in this respect. Infants' and toddlers' spoons are sometimes constructed to promote the use of one hand over the other. Figure 6.5 shows a spoon and a fork, with handles designed to make the left-hand use of these utensils in an appropriate manner increasingly difficult. The twisted handle of these utensils make it easier to use the right hand while self-feeding.

Furthermore, the first forks given to toddlers are often designed so as to eliminate sharp-ended tines, which makes the use of the forks increasingly difficult, and reduces their function practically to that of spoons (see Figure 6.6).

Cups, glasses, bottles, and other devices used for drinking at children's mealtimes occupy a unique position between the categories of *containers* and *transport utensils*—being simultaneously both. Bottles and cups are containers in which the drinkable liquid is held, and in which it is transported to the

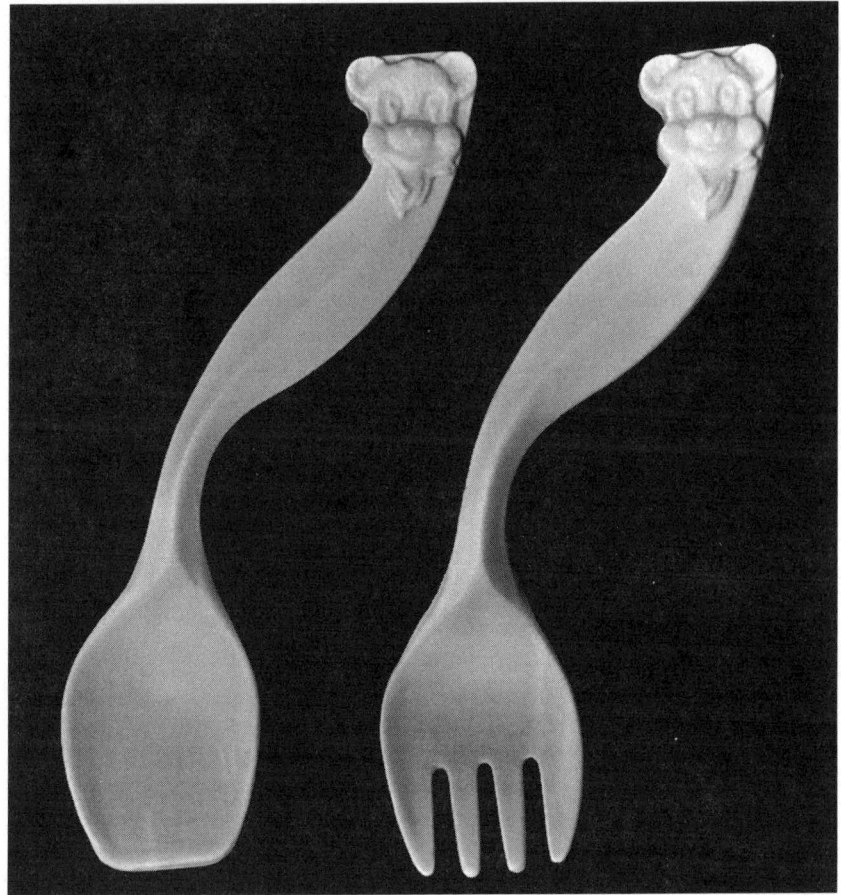

FIGURE 6.5. Cultural coding of the promotion of right-handedness: children's fork and spoon with twisted handles. (Photograph by Albrecht and Elzbieta Lempp.)

child's mouth—by either the adult or the child. Bottles appear on the scene of infant feeding earlier than cups (although in some families bottle feeding may be fully bypassed). The form of contemporary baby cups (see Figure 6.7) reflects a complex relationship between the goal of promotion of infants' self-feeding skills early in life, and the goal of preservation of the liquid in the container. Thus, the cups are provided either with a spout in the lid or with a trainer lid with apertures. The spout serves as an intermediate device between the infant's handling of the nipple (of the breast or a bottle) and "true" cup handling. The trainer lid with apertures (see Figure 6.7) is the device meant to bring the child's cup handling even closer to the adult skills of drinking. The

FIGURE 6.6.   Child's fork and adult's fork: compromises between functionality and potential stabbing danger. (Photograph by Albrecht and Elzbieta Lempp.)

FIGURE 6.7.   Toddlers' drinking cup and its accessories (lid with spout, trainer lid). (Photograph by Albrecht and Elzbieta Lempp.)

weighted base of the cup helps to bring it to the normal position if put down on its side—thus reducing spilling of milk when the child handles the trainer cup without help.

The present excursion into the analysis of cultural ideas and expectations that are coded into the cultural tools and structural units of the environment in which a child lives leads to the important conclusion that *cultural canalization of children's actions starts from the coding of some suggestive cultural messages into the form and function of objects that surround human beings.* This analysis illustrates the principle of the structured nature of the environment (cf. 4.1.2) in the particular setting of infants' or toddlers' mealtime environments—high chairs, trays, eating utensils, and attention-redirection devices—all of which are man-made objects that carry cultural expectancies for some goals-directed function from the makers to the children via their caregivers. Usually, behaviorally interested psychologists have bypassed the presence of these silent messages that are available to the acting child, as long as they constitute the environment. It should become evident that an approach in psychological research that claims to be cultural-historical in its scope cannot leave these objects outside the sphere of empirical analysis.

The cultural structure of children's mealtimes is only one domain of factors that act as bases for constraints that emerge in parent–child transactions in the process of canalization of actions. The ontogeny of motor capabilities provides the complementary set of structurally organized possibilities for the development of children's self-feeding skills. An analysis of psychological knowledge about the precursors of toddlers' self-feeding development in the motor development in infancy is therefore in order.

6.5 DEVELOPMENT OF MOTOR SKILLS NECESSARY FOR SELF-FEEDING

The infant's self-feeding behavior is dependent on both the nature of the food and the coordination of head-mouth-arm-hand-finger movements that can be used to transport the food from an external location to the mouth. Once an infant gains access to foods of different characteristics (beyond the first liquids—milk or otherwise—that are fed to the infant by the caregiver via breast or bottle), the food-transport problem emerges. The principal possibility of infants' self-feeding requires the development of certain motor coordinations. The requirement of such coordination differs for infants' "finger feeding" (the *natural line* in the development of feeding behavior) as compared to their use of a tool (utensil) for feeding purposes (the *cultural* developmental line). The latter case is, of course, the domain where the cultural organization of eating becomes most intimately intertwined with the children's developing motor behavior, because all self-feeding tools carry cultural information that is coded into their form and the social rules of their use.

6.5.1   Development of Motor Coordination

The natural line in the ontogeny of human feeding emerges earlier; it is based on the "natural facilities" that the anatomy and physiology of the developing organism provide. It is built on the general inclination of infants to transport different objects from their vicinity and try to insert them in their mouth. This behavior requires visually guided coordination of the fingers, hand, arm, and head and mouth. Coordination of the two motor systems—*reaching* and *grasping*—develops gradually. These two systems involve different neuromuscular mechanisms that develop heterochronically in ontogeny. The *grasping,* or manipulation, involves distal joints and muscle groups that are adapted to information about the affordances present in a particular object; the *reaching* part is based on the work of proximal joints in body-centered space (Jeannerod, 1984). Physiologically, the reaching component is realized through the work of the extrapyramidal tract, whereas the grasping part is under the control of the pyramidal pathway (Kuypers, 1962). The former begins to function earlier in ontogeny than the latter; thus, in the development of infant behavior, it is possible to observe discrepancies in the development of reaching and grasping (see Lockman & Ashmead, 1983). McDonnell's (1979) analysis of research findings on the development of reaching reveals that reaching in infants in the first 5 months of life is triggered (but not guided) visually. The arm movements used in such reaching are basically ballistic in nature. The development of visually guided reaching becomes evident at around 5 months of age and peaks at around 7 months. By that time, the reaching and grasping systems have become coordinated, so that at the approach to the target object, the grasping movements can be proactively prepared for making contact with the object. That coordination, at least in the adult case, is organized by the wrist rotation together with the movement of the reacher's index finger (Wing & Fraser, 1983). The development of grasping of objects of different sizes in infancy has been meticulously recorded by Halverson (1931) and Castner (1932). Halverson found that infants' grasping of a 26-mm cube progressed through a sequence of 10 distinctive grasping patterns between the ages of 16 and 52 weeks. These patterns first involved contacting the cube and squeezing it with the whole hand, followed by patterns in which the thumb and the index finger played a more active and precise role in the grasping process. Any particular observed series of stages in infants' development of grasping patterns is dependent on the object being grasped. Thus, Castner (1932), who studied infants' grasping of a 7-mm pellet, found that this grasping progressed through four stages: (a) whole-hand closure, (b) palmar prehension, (c) scissors closure, and (d) pincer prehension. In *whole-hand closure,* the prone hand is brought to a closed fist by simultaneous flexion of the fingers, with the thumb lying alongside the flexed forefinger. This type of closure upon the pellet was the only one observed among 20-week-old infants. This pattern was followed by *palmar prehension,* in which the fingers flex in such a way as to drag the pellet against the heel of the palm where it can be held. The third stage—*scissors closure*—involves the thumb being drawn in *against the side* of the flexing forefinger so that the pellet is secured between the thumb and the radial side of the forefinger. This movement is conducted in a manner similar to the action of these digits in operating a pair of scissors. This type of closure was observed predominantly at around 36 to 44 weeks. Finally, Castner observed the emergence of *pincer prehension*—the tips of the thumb and forefinger meet to secure the pellet between them. This latter type of prehension was observed in the majority of 52-week-olds, and develops further into the optional opposition of the thumb with digits other than the index finger (see Castner, 1932, pp. 178–179).

Research on infants' reaching and grasping has, in concordance with the meaning of reaching, concentrated on the analysis of how the infant's arm–hand system arrives at a target object (e.g., Bower, Broughton, & Moore, 1970; DiFranco, Muir, & Dodwell, 1978; VonHofsten, 1979), rather than on what the infant does *after* the target has been reached. The development of visually guided reaching is a neuromotor prerequisite for the infant's development of self-feeding behavior. Reaching out for an object, grasping it, and bringing it to the mouth is the complete sequence of behavior that makes self-feeding possible. Exploration of objects by mouth (rather than by hand) is ontogenetically the primary mode by which the infant seeks information about the nature of surrounding objects. Halverson described the development of infants' mouthing of the cube that he used in his study:

> [A]t 20 weeks, the few infants who secure the cube either push it away or hold it quietly without any further action. At 24 weeks the infants simply hold the cube, bring it to mouth, inspect it, and drop it. At 28 weeks, holding the cube occurs frequently, carrying it to the mouth and inspecting it also occur to a considerable extent. At 32 weeks, holding the cube and carrying it to the mouth are activities of frequent occurrence. These infants often put the cube down, pick it up again, and hold it in both hands. For the three oldest groups the activities are so diversified that none of them are particularly outstanding. However, at 36 weeks, perhaps the most common activities are carrying the cube to mouth, simply holding the cube, dropping and picking it up again, inspecting it, and exchanging hands on it. At 40 weeks the cube is not brought to the mouth as often as at 26 weeks; holding the cube, inspecting it, exchanging hands on it, and banging the table with it are the outstanding activities. At 52 weeks, manipulation of the cube by the fingers is the outstanding activity. (Halverson, 1931, p. 230)

The objects that are taken by the infant and handled one way or another (including mouthing them) are, at first, individual objects or their parts (e.g., where the child has happened to break an object and brings its pieces into the mouth). The mouthing of such objects is the prerequisite for the natural line in the development of self-feeding in infants: all "finger feeding" is possible on the basis of reaching for, grasping, and bringing to the mouth pieces of food that are of sufficiently small size. The cultural line of self-feeding, however, *requires the infant's capability of synthesizing two objects into a whole (united) object at least for the period of food transport from its original location to the mouth*. The example most obvious in this context is spoon or fork use. In order to self-feed with a spoon, the infant must put together the food-object and the tool-object in a certain way (i.e., taking food into the bowl part of the spoon), and must maintain the unity of the food + spoon whole at least for the time it takes to reach the mouth. After arrival at the destination, the synthesized object is disassembled (the spoon is taken out of the mouth, leaving the food in the mouth).

The context of infants' eating in contemporary home environments also provides examples where the utensil + food complex object is presynthesized by the feeders in order to facilitate the child's self-feeding while at the same time avoiding some side effects of that act. The example of giving an infant a baby-bottle, or, later, a cup covered with a special lid, so that he or she can drink from it, is a solution where such presynthesis has been provided. The lid (or bottle) decreases the possibility of unwanted side effects (spilling the liquid) while making it possible for the child to drink independently, once the motor action of lifting the bottle or cup up and holding it is mastered.

The development of the synthesis in infants' handling of objects has been documented in the existing research literature. The logic of the development of the synthesis of different behaviors was made explicit by Gesell and Thompson (1934) who, in accordance with their theoretical interests, attributed causality for that development to maturation:

> Developmentally, combining activity is closely articulated with patterns of individual or discrete activity. Two objects, A and B, lie adjacent. A elicits a discrete attentional-manipulatory response in its own right; so does B; so does A again. At a low stage of maturity these responses are independent events but at higher stages of maturity response B is influenced by stimulus A and tends to have a reference to B. It is not necessary to invoke a law of association or even learning to explain this fact of reference. The phenomenon seems to depend more upon the scope of regard and the range of manipulation and these factors are determined by maturation. (Gesell & Thompson, 1934, pp. 164–165)

The meticulous description of the development of infants' hand movement by Arnold Gesell and his colleagues in the 1920s and 1930s, which has remained unsurpassed in scientific value up to the present day, provides ample evidence about the gradual development of synthesizing objects in the process of their manipulation. One of the pairs of objects that was used by Gesell to study the development of coordination of behaving with multiple objects consisted of a cup and a spoon (Gesell & Thompson, 1934, pp. 154–165), which were presented together (in Gesell's standard testing situation) within the subjects' age range of 32 to 56 weeks. Gesell and Thompson described the development of combining the cup and spoon by the infants, first in their visual regard and then in their manipulation of these objects. Their description provides an overview of the richness of behavioral forms that can be observed in the process of establishing synthetic manipulatory behavior (although Gesell and Thompson themselves preferred to abstract away that richness in their summary descriptions of the generic child's development).

The sequence of observable combining of the cup and the spoon involves the following: (a) the child brings the spoon *over* the cup, without dipping it in or letting it fall (observed in some infants at 32 weeks, and in all infants of the sample at 56 weeks); (b) the child places the spoon in the cup, but does not release it (observed at 36 weeks in the earliest, and present in all infants by 56 weeks); and (c) releases the spoon in the cup after placing it there (observed first at 44 weeks, with 38% of the infants displaying it at the end of the administration of the task at 56 weeks). These three synthetic forms of behavior with cup and spoon were preceded by *combining* them (without putting the spoon either on top of or in the cup), as 59% of infants at 32 weeks were observed doing that, with all of them combining the two at 56 weeks (Gesell & Thompson, 1934, p. 157).

6.5.2 Social Heterochrony

The precursors of motor behavior with a spoon and a cup in a play (laboratory task) situation serve as the basis on which the caregivers of the infants build their efforts to socialize the child's developing use of cups and spoons in ways appropriate in the culture. It is possible to view the organization of socialization of children's actions from a perspective of the *principle of social heterochrony*. This principle is introduced here as an extension of the general heterochrony principle of developmental biology. That latter principle describes the emergence of subcomponents of a biological structure at diverse time periods during the organism's development (Anokhin, 1964). The heterochronical nature of biological ontogeny makes the developing organism open to different developmental paths that are decided on, depending on the organism–environment relations at the given time. Heterochrony provides for the plasticity of the organismic structure to become organized in novel complex forms that are built on the basis of the existing subcomponents at the given time. In the case of social heterochrony, these novel complex motor actions in children's development are wrought by caregivers' purposeful canalization of children's actions at a given age, toward learning new skills *on the basis of motor coordinations available to the child at the given time.*

The social extension of heterochrony introduced here is aimed at describing the *variety of possible ways in which the motor functions of a developing child can be socialized through social canalization within the culture.* The beginning of the efforts by social others of the developing child may be located at different places on the age scale. That information is determined by the cultural folk models about "when is the right time to start" with promoting a new skill to the child or expecting it to emerge in the child's individual development. This cultural knowledge may be only remotely connected with a realistic understanding of the actual developmental courses of motor (or cognitive) capabilities. The content of such cultural models is culture-specific and may fluctuate over time (e.g., Stendler, 1950; Wolfenstein, 1951, 1955; Zahorsky, 1934). The potential lower-age extreme application of the folk models of child socialization is corrected by the availability of new developments in children at different ages. In everyday terms, if a current ethos of infant education in the given culture prescribes a very early effort by adults for the beginning of socialization of a certain function, then all of those efforts would fail. However, under certain conditions—when appropriate teaching methods are used—the results may be attained (for example, see DeVries & DeVries, 1977, on Digo toilet training). The upper-end extremes in the application of folk models of child socialization are compensated for by the children's own learning of acting in culturally acceptable ways in respect to carrying out a given function, using the knowledge acquired by observation in the course of living in their social environments. If children are not instructed in certain motor actions, and these actions are relevant in their lives, then they learn those actions by themselves. Such asymmetry in the process of mapping the cultural planning of children's action socialization on the development of the neuromuscular body functions provides, in the case of social heterochrony, for redundancy in the socialization process, which is necessary for guaranteed success in it. If a child misses being explicitly taught a specially relevant skill, the child may acquire it on the basis of observations and trying. If a child is taught it, the skill will be acquired as well. If that teaching starts too early, it will not succeed until the time when it becomes available for the child in the context of ZPD in the teaching–learning situation. In any case, albeit by different routes, the particular important function is acquired by the children in the culture. This view of the role of social heterochrony in child socialization relates to the highly abstract notion of equifinality that is characteristic of all open systems (see 2.1).

6.5.3 Motor Skills in the Feeding Contexts

Despite the long tradition in child psychology of the study of infants' motor behavior, research on children's motor actions within contexts similar to meal settings has been almost nonexistent. The single coherent research group in contemporary developmental psychology that has studied the development of motor skills relevant for feeding has done it in conjunction with the issues of the development of children's motor program (Connolly, 1970, 1973, 1974, 1975, 1980, 1981; Connolly & Elliott, 1972; Elliott & Connolly, 1974, 1984). This interest involves the conceptual understanding of future-oriented control mechanisms in the organization of motor skills—an idea expressed and elaborated in movement physiology by Nikolai Bernstein (1966). Bernstein's theoretical emphasis is on the active, purposeful functioning of the moving individual who uses a future ideal outcome state as a criterion for adapting the ongoing action to the goal. This perspective fits well with the assumption that the motor skills that emerge in ontogeny become used by the child for some purposes, which, in turn, requires integration of knowledge about the environment of the actor, the action means, and the place of action goals in a wider scheme of the child's life-world. The concrete example provided by Connolly (1980) illustrates that issue more realistically:

> Consider the following circumstances, a child aged about 3 (and hence already quite skilled and experienced) is given a boiled egg to eat. The egg sits in an eggcup on a table in front of the child who is provided with a small spoon. The detail of the description of the ensuing encounter of the child and the egg could vary over a wide range, from simply, "eats with the spoon," to a minute analysis of the postures and movements employed. My purpose, however, is simply to indicate the great complexity of such commonplace actions which we take for granted. In order to solve the problem of eating the egg with the spoon the child must already have a richly developed cognitive system. He must have some idea of what he is aiming at—intention is implied on his part. Further, he must know something of the use and properties of a spoon, in itself a formidable achievement when one is called upon to explain it, which we shall assume. The child must pick up the spoon and hold it both appropriately (correct configuration of the hand on the spoon) and securely. Once this is done the child must take the spoon, correctly orientated, to a specific target location—the egg. The spoon must then be inserted into the egg, which requires postural adjustment of the spoon in the hand itself by the whole upper limb. Inside the egg controlled force must be applied through the spoon, here quite fine tolerance limits apply, too little force and the spoon is not loaded, too much and the egg is destroyed. Once this is done further postural adjustments must be made to extract the loaded spoon from the egg. The final part of the action consists in transporting the loaded spoon (which on the return journey must be managed under a different set of constraints if the egg is to remain on the spoon) to another target, the mouth, and there unloading it. Eating a boiled egg is such a commonplace activity that it causes little amazement and holds no puzzlement for most of us, but try and build a machine to do this, or gain some insight into the difficulty by watching the young child gain a mastery of the task. To master a skill such as this it is necessary first to master certain essential components such as holding a spoon in an adequate stable configuration. Once this is done the spoon can be grasped and used effectively for purposes other than eating boiled eggs. (Reproduced with permission from Connolly, 1980, p. 146)

The essential characteristic of motor skills, according to Connolly (1970), is flexibility in integrating different subroutines of action into a wide range of possible whole-action structures. That flexibility resembles the generative nature of human speech—with the help of its subroutines, ideas ranging from shallow TV commercials to communication of sophisticated feelings and thoughts of poets and writers can all be expressed. Likewise, motor skills, once developed, can be used for acting in very many different environments and in conjunction with an almost infinite variety of objects. On the one hand, the use of a particular motor skill (e.g., a child's eating a boiled egg) is highly context-specific. However, a skill that has been acquired in a specific context may lead to the development of action generation plans that adapt the subroutines of a learned skill to new conditions, modify them, and unite them into new complex wholes. In all human motor action, the actor–environment relationships provide the context in which any action skill gets developed and transformed.

Connolly's research on the development of spoon use in children is the part of existing research on motor skill development that is most directly connected with the empirical research described in this chapter. First, Connolly described the form of different grip types that 10–12-month-old infants were observed to use on a spoon when it was given to them (Connolly, 1974, p. 540). Different types of grips are differentially suitable for the use of the spoon in the adult ways. As the infants learn to use the spoon in meal settings, the range of different grip types is narrowed down gradually, and only those that make the adequate use of the spoon possible are retained. Second, the research by Connolly and his colleagues revealed how the structure of the complex motor skill of using a spoon to transport food to the mouth developed (Connolly, 1979). The task of spoon use can be divided into different phases (e.g., filling the spoon, lifting and transporting it, emptying it in the mouth, removing it from the mouth). Connolly found that the different parts of the motor skill—its "subroutines"—were first acquired separately (e.g., the spoon–food manipulation, and mouthing of the spoon), and only later integrated into the full action scheme. Finally, the child develops capabilities to recheck the state of affairs of the spoon and food at different times in the temporal structure of the action. For example, when the child has lifted a semifilled spoon from the plate, he or she may return it to the plate to get the spoon full of food before proceeding to the mouth with it (see Connolly, 1979, p. 248). The particular nicety of the motor skill of spoon use is its relevance in everyday life settings, which usually have been left unanalyzed in the research on motor skill development.

6.6   AN ANALYSIS OF THE STRUCTURE OF CHILDREN'S MEAL SETTINGS

Children's mealtime in the everyday life of contemporary European or North American middle-class families is a structurally organized setting with a usually clear-cut beginning and ending, and with a sequential organization, the rules of which are introduced by parents and accommodated to the child's behavior. No currently available formal-symbolic methodology is suitable for the description of the structural-dynamic organization of mealtimes (see Chapter 5).

Some theoretical analyses in the history of psychology have included passing efforts to explain the psychological side of children's mealtimes. Lewin (1936a) used the example of children's mealtime occasionally as an example of the application of his field theory. Lewin's first example involved the following setting and its interpretation:

> A mother has taken a year-old child away from play and wants to feed him on her lap. He does not want to eat. He is at the moment dominated by the tendency "away from eating" or "toward play." The mother holds the child on her lap and prevents the intended movement "away from eating." She puts her arm around him so that he cannot break away. The mother's interference has in this case the character of a barrier [b, in Figure 6.8] between the region of eating (e) and that of play (pl). This barrier at the same time keeps the child (C) from pulling away from the spoon (sp) as it is brought near his mouth. The child now begins to play on the mother's lap. The mother tries to put an end even to this possibility of action and limits the child's space of free movement still further. Thereupon the child tries to widen his region of free movement and begins to struggle with the mother. (Lewin, 1936a, p. 47)

The analysis of this episode in terms of the theory presented in this book would reject Lewin's attribution of "tendencies" ("forces") into the situation, but follows the description of the dynamic nature of the barrier setting (reorganization of the boundary of Zone of Free Movement). The mother's way of accomplishing the task of feeding the child by spoon is to narrow the child's ZFM sufficiently so that the feeding can take place. The child may (as in this example), but also need not, attempt to counteract the mother's actions. This example illustrates the process of negotiation that goes on between the mother and child about the boundaries of the ZFM in the meal situation.

The other example of mealtime actions of children that Lewin has provided involves the inclusion of objects in the framework of the whole situation.

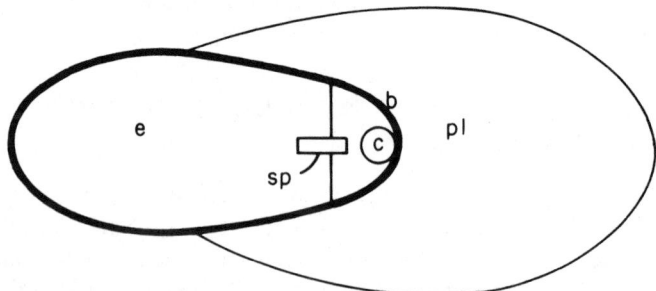

FIGURE 6.8. Topology of an eating situation—a child is prohibited from leaving for play (from Lewin, 1936, p. 47). Abbreviations: C = child; b = barrier, i.e., mother's interference; e = region of eating; sp = spoon; pl = region of play.

Lewin's example involves analysis of a case where a mother tries to get her child to eat some disliked food:

> . . . one of the most important means by which the adult induces the child to eat an undesired food is to bring him into the "eating situation." If a particular kind of food is not desired, the otherwise unified action of eating usually breaks up into a series of separate steps such as: putting the hand on the table (h); taking the spoon (sp); putting the food on the spoon (f); bringing the spoon halfway to the mouth (hw); bringing it to the mouth (m); taking the food into the mouth (i); chewing (ch); swallowing (sw). These steps correspond topologically to a series of regions [see (a) in Figure 6.9]. The procedure of the adult is sometimes to bring the child (C) step by step through these regions closer to the region of "real eating" (chewing and swallowing). In doing so he usually meets with increasing resistance in accordance with the fact that with approach to the undesired action the repulsive forces [represented

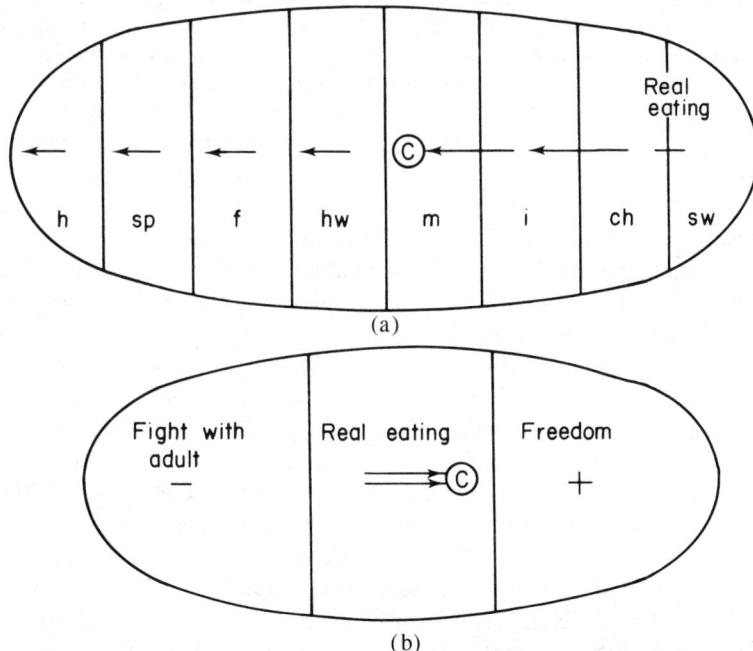

(a)

(b)

FIGURE 6.9.   Topology of a situation where a child faces disliked food: (a) before entering the region of real eating; (b) after entering the region of real eating (from Lewin, 1936, p. 97). Abbreviations: force (the direction of the arrow represents the direction of force, its length = the strength of the force, and its point = the point of application); locomotion (the point of the arrow designates the place of termination of locomotion; the other end, its departure point); + positive valence; – negative valence. Other abbreviations are similar to those in Figure 6.8.

as arrows in Figure 6.9] increase. However, as soon as the food is once in the mouth it is often not spit out, even when the adult has fed the child against its will. Instead the child goes on to chewing and swallowing the food. (Lewin, 1936a, pp. 96–97)

Lewin's example illustrates his observational sensitivity to changes that occur in the situation—the child, after rejecting the parent's pressure toward accepting food, may transform into the state of acceptance of that food, *once* it has reached the mouth. Likewise, the "breakdown" of a well-established (speedy) action pattern when the child does not like the task is a real enough event in everyday life. Lewin's analysis of the event is dynamic:

One can show that this change of behavior is brought about essentially by the fact that as the child enters the region of "real eating" his position and the direction of the field forces are entirely changed. When the child is in one of the preceding regions, for instance, when he holds the spoon halfway to his mouth, then a region of great unplasantness into which the adult tries to push him, still lies ahead. The adult therefore may have to exert great pressure to induce the child to make a locomotion into the disagreeable region. When the child is once within this region of real eating then the region which lies ahead of him is a more pleasant one of relative freedom [Figure 6.9b]. The child therefore often prefers a locomotion in this direction to spitting out, which is a locomotion in the direction of the disagreeable fight with the adult. (Lewin, 1936a, p. 98)

Again, the empirical analysis offered in this book relates closely to Lewin, with the exception of the implicit evaluative rationality that is projected into the child in the given example (e.g., a region assumed to be "more pleasant" by the child than another region). Lewin's use of the term *region* in this example seems to be synonymous with *setting* (rule-structured action situation). It is argued by Lewin that once the adult organizes the child's "movement" from one well-organized setting to another (e.g., from "play" to "real eating"), then the child may accept expectations of the new setting without difficulty, although these same expectations in the previous setting were rejected by the child vehemently. An additional aspect of such movement from one setting to another is the extent to which knowledge about the roles of action within these settings is present in the child's mind. That knowledge emerges in the process of socialization as a result of the child's life history of actions being canalized by the social others in the particular social settings. The knowledge of the rules of the setting is maintained redundantly, both by external and internalized means. Conflict situations tend to occur at the transitions from one setting to another, where it is uncertain which rules apply to action regulation (those of the previous, or of the new, setting). This state of uncertainty in the nature of the settings makes it possible for the interactants to *construct new settings* where new sets of rules (which may partially overlap with existing settings) apply. Put another way, the existence of well-structured settings with stable action rules is a means whereby persons try to escape the uncertainty inherent in social situations. When a situation is poorly structured, the actors who are present in that situation construct rules that provide them with a structure (Sherif, 1936). Settings as structured social situations with elaborate scripts for action are socially constructed cultural means for people to lead their lives, rather than rules given to them by some external agent.

What, then, are the implications of this social-constructive view of the ontogeny of mealtime settings? First, *from the perspective of a particular individual child,* the mealtime setting is constructed initially in the context of an infant–caregiver–environment transaction *and does not exist outside of the child's experience.* Second, *from the perspective of the caregivers,* the rules of the infant's mealtime exists as *the caregivers' decision about organizing the child's meal setting in accordance with knowledge about the setting in the culture.* The mother knows how to feed the infant, or if she does not know, or is unsure about some aspects of it, she turns to the available cultural sources (her mother, friends, books, and so on) to get information that will enable her to accomplish the task adequately. In that need, mothers are helped by their social networks. The ways in which babies are fed (e.g., the basic decision between breast and bottle feeding) are determined not by the mother (and father) of the child by themselves, but under the influence of the whole kinship network within which cultural traditions of child feeding are transferred from generation to generation (Bryant, 1982). In this way, the mother translates information present in the culture into the organized setting of *her* child's mealtime. However, the cultural knowledge that she starts from is not abstract but includes the very personal advice being given to her by others who are related to her (her mother, mother-in-law, aunts, sisters) and whom she may trust. The individuals who provide the mother with cultural information usually add their personal modifications. As a result, no two families within a culture can be expected to organize the child's mealtime in an exactly similar way, because the individual mothers interpret the cultural knowledge differently and construct the mealtime setting for their children in their own ways. However, some basic cultural patterns that are coded in the organization of mealtimes for children in the given (sub)culture are invariably present within the idiosyncratic organizational forms of mealtimes in different households (Lévi-Strauss, 1966; Tambiah, 1969).

6.7   SUMMARY

The physical and cultural structure of children's mealtime contexts was described in this chapter, together with an overview of psychology's knowhow of infants' and toddlers' motor development. Children's self-feeding actions develop in the mealtime contexts along two lines. The natural developmental line depends on the child's developing sufficient motor coordination to allow self-intake of food, without using cultural utensils. The cultural line—involving the use of food-transport utensils and food containers in culturally prescribed ways—develops under direct canalization by the child's caregivers, and with the help of observational learning by the child.

In Chapter 7, observational data on children's development of action in mealtime settings are presented. The children who were observed acted within culturally structured settings that involved high chairs, Wiggl-Eggs, children's spoons, forks, training cups, and many other highly specialized tools that are used at the present time in child care in American middle-class homes. The ways in which cultural information is coded in the form of such objects were analyzed here as a preview to the presentation of the empirical observations and their analysis.

7

Cultural Regulation and the Development of Children's Action at Mealtimes

With all the necessary theoretical ground and description of the cultural structure of children's mealtimes completed (Chapters 1–6), I now present observational data. The data in this chapter are derived from videotaped observations of a small number of children from a larger sample. The way the data are presented in this chapter follows from the metatheoretical assumptions that were analyzed in Chapter 2, and illustrates the application of the theoretical framework (outlined in Chapter 4) to the real-life setting of meals. No attempt will be made to introduce formal-structural analysis techniques to the present data, because the epistemological status of the few available techniques of that kind was found to be limited (Chapter 5).

7.1 THE SAMPLES AND PROCEDURES

The empirical material analyzed here is based on two naturalistic studies of toddlers' mealtimes in contemporary American middle-class families. It started with a study of a cross-section of 34 families when their child was 11–14 months of age. That study was followed by a longitudinal observation of 30 other families in the course of 1.5 years; the children's ages ranged from 6–7 months at the start to 24–26 months at completion. In both samples, all the families were of high educational background (both mothers' and fathers' education ranged from 12 years to PhD level). The parents of the children were within an age range of 24 to 40 years (mothers: 24 to 40; fathers: 27 to 38). The majority of the families were selected on the basis of the local birth records. They were contacted first via a letter explaining the aims of the study. If the family was interested in participation, they returned a prestamped postcard to the investigator via mail. This contacting procedure served as an effective filtering device that ensured the inclusion of only those families who were actively interested in research participation, and/or in contacting a child psychologist, and who had or were able to develop their own understanding of the relevance of the research. The investigator subsequently visited the family for a brief (30-minute) meeting where he explained the goals of the study and got to know the parents and the children.

The procedure used for at-home observations of mealtimes was built up around continuous videotaping of the events into which a free-format interview with the caregiver was inserted. At a time previously agreed on with the parent(s), the investigator arrived in the home with the video equipment and started videotaping the child's behavior, including any behavioral events that the child was involved in that were accessible to the investigator and permitted by the parent. (Some parents were reluctant to let the investigator videotape their changing the infant's diapers. That reluctance was traced in the parent's actions and the camera was stopped for the time of that event.) Otherwise, the unfolding of behavioral events was recorded continuously. The videotaped segment included some of the child's behavior before the meal started, the sequence of the whole meal, and some time after the meal had ended. The exact timing of these parts in that sequence of settings depended on particular circumstances, but, in general, each home visited produced about an hour's length of videotaped observational material, including semistructured interviews with parents on their child's recent development, which were recorded on the audio channel of the videotape. If the target child had older siblings who were at home during a particular videotaping session, care was taken not to exclude them from the research process. Some activities of theirs were videotaped, and occasionally the camera moved from the target child to the sibling(s).

The interview with parents about the child took place at variable times during the videotaping session. In the beginning of the session, the parents were asked to describe their child's development since the previous home visit. In the middle of the videotaping, in time periods immediately following some action by the child, the parents were asked questions about their previous experience with that (or a similar) action by the child. The opportunity to question parents immediately after a behavioral event took place in the child's actions made it possible to get information from the parents based on their sharing of the behavioral observation with the investigator, without the need for verbally describing the given behavior pattern from memory. In the closing part of the session, immediately after the meal had ended, the parents were queried about how the just-observed mealtime was different from other meals, and how the observer's presence had influenced the child.

In addition to the videotaped mealtime observations, the parents were asked to fill out a questionnaire at the beginning of the study. The questionnaire asked for information about the demographic–sociological background of the parents, and an account of their child's development from birth to the time when the study started. Two other questionnaires were administered to parents in the longitudinal sample. These additional questionnaires were administered when the target children were 14–16 months of age, and at the end of the study, at age 24–26 months. These questionnaires included information about the child's recent development that complemented the interview information recorded on videotape.

The research materials collected in this longitudinal study were analyzed as *case histories of individual children's mealtimes in the context of their families*, rather than by aggregating the material into group data. Aggregated data obscure the investigator's picture of psychological phenomena that are structured within, or around, the individual in reality (Valsiner, 1986). Therefore, the structure of mealtime settings and the development of children's self-feeding actions over time in these settings are analyzed here in selected cases of particular families studied. Only a limited number of cases could be included in this book because of space limitations and a redundancy in the knowledge that emerged from the study. Therefore, the major source of empirical data reported in this chapter comes from a longitudinal follow-up of individual cases during the 6–26-month study. During that period of time, the whole structure of the children's meal settings underwent substantial change.

7.2 STRUCTURAL ORGANIZATION OF MEALTIMES AND ITS CHANGE

The structural organization of children's mealtimes, as observed in the empirical material referred to here, provides a good basis for an analysis in terms of the present theoretical concepts. First, the Zone of Free Movement (ZFM—see 4.3.1) of all infants and toddlers is *narrowed down for the purpose of organizing the mealtime*—from the very beginning of the infants' lives until at least the time when no externally restrictive furniture is used (e.g., an infant seat or high chair). After the external devices of narrowing of the ZFM boundaries are discarded, the child is expected to have internalized certain social rules of acting in the meal setting that carry out the same function. *In general, internalized social norms replace the use of external devices as constraints upon the person's ZFMs in particular situations in ontogeny.* Even with infants and toddlers, for whom external constraining devices are actively used, additional *behavioral constraints* on actions while in the high chair are applied to narrow the ZFM further. For instance, many parents in our sample did not allow the child to throw objects (food and/or utensils) down on the floor from the high chair tray. Those who did allow that action usually took some measures to prevent that freedom of the child from spoiling the floor or carpet, by putting plastic covers on the area in which the high chair was located during the mealtime. Furthermore, a child sitting in the high chair may be additionally strapped to it (which eliminates the freedom of either standing up in it, or sliding down). During the feeding, the parent is in control of what objects appear within the child's reach (i.e., on the high chair tray), the combinations in which these objects appear, and the time when they are withdrawn from the tray. *The feeding of infants and toddlers in high chairs of contemporary middle-class American homes demonstrates all the ambivalence about the child's independence–dependence relationships dialectic of the given society at large,* where almost unlimited freedom of action is provided for individuals in some domains of life, whereas the boundaries of that freedom are strictly controlled by some agent—individual or collective. In the meal situations in the high chair, the toddlers may have remarkable possibilities of manipulating food objects and utensils in many ways. At the same time, the feeder has full control over the child's freedom of action in the high chair—when necessary, the ZFM can be further narrowed, leaving the child with very little freedom of action in order to attain a goal of the parent. Likewise, once the particular feeding goals are attained, the boundaries of the ZFM can be restructured to become wider again. The following episode from an observed mealtime provides an example of such purposeful narrowing and subsequent widening of the ZFM. It involves a mother and her toddler son (age: 14 months, 9 days) during the final minutes of a lunchtime. The child is sitting in a high chair, manipulating a plastic spoon that the mother had given him to distract him from grabbing her spoon. The mother is facing him and spoon-feeding him cottage cheese, episodically explaining her strategies to the videotaping investigator or interacting with older children. The following episode is an example of the restructuring of the ZFM:

CHILD: Drops his plastic spoon on floor.

MOTHER: "Oh-oh! Did it fall on the floor? Did it fall on the floor?" Picks up some spilled cottage cheese from the child's bib with her spoon, saying: "We are not supposed to leave that, are we?" She approaches the child's mouth with the spoonful of food.

CHILD: Turns his head away, hits the tray with his right arm.

MOTHER: Withdraws the spoon, tries to approach the child's mouth with it again, asking: "Can you have one more bite?"

CHILD: Turns his head away, starts leaning over the side of the high chair.

MOTHER: Grabs the child's head with her left hand and turns the child back to face her, saying: "Come on, pumpkin!" Then grabs the child's chin with her left hand, forcing the child to open his mouth, saying: "One more little bite!"

CHILD: Struggles himself free by kicking, with his arms in the air, and withdraws his head.

MOTHER: Withdraws spoon, then attempts to approach the child's mouth with the spoon again.

CHILD: Struggles himself free by kicking, with his arms in the air, and withdraws his head.

MOTHER: Withdraws spoon, asks: "Are you finishing eating?"

CHILD: Hits high chair tray with his hand.

MOTHER: "You mean, after all that—you have finally finished eating?" Approaches the child's mouth with the spoon again.

CHILD: Turns his head away to avoid the food, then turns it back to the central position.

MOTHER: Tries to approach the mouth again with the spoon, *captures the child's right hand with her left,* says to investigator: "He reaches for me, too."

CHILD: Frees his hand, kicks, with arms in the air.

MOTHER: Withdraws the spoon, then approaches again with it.

CHILD: *Accepts the spoonful, then spits it out immediately.*

MOTHER: Captures with the spoon the food that the child spit out.

CHILD: Hits the mother's left hand with his right.

MOTHER: *Grasps the child's chin with her left hand, forces the mouth open, puts the food in,* saying: "Come on, one more little bite, one more little bite!"

CHILD: Kicks, with arms in the air, tries to withdraw his head, finally gets free, but *accepts the food.*

This episode illustrates how the mother, having the goal of getting "one more little bite" of food into the child, first tries to get that bite into the child by recurrent back-and-forth action with the spoon, waiting for the time when the child would be receptive to it. When this fails, and the mother's immediate goal of getting the bite in remains, she proceeds to narrow the child's ZFM within the existing mealtime situation. First, she takes the child's hand into hers, so that the child's kicking himself free is restricted. When that is not sufficient, she grasps the child's face and forces the child to open his mouth and accept the food. In this situation, the child's ZFM is reduced to two options (spit the food back out again, or swallow it), the latter of which ends this episode of a mother–child "fight."

Situations like the one described here were rare in the generally *laissez-faire* organization of feeding in the families in our sample, and perhaps are rare in the population as a whole. However, certain situations of life (e.g., the necessity of getting a child to accept a certain food, or medicine) may lead parents to occasional extremes of narrowing the ZFM in order to attain their goals. A ZFM-narrowing strategy is effective in general; it has been tested all through the history of child rearing in many cultures.

Beyond the organization of ZFMs and the regulation of their boundaries dynamically in the context of mealtimes, the Zone of Promoted Action (ZPA; see 4.3.2) is at times used to promote the learning of some new skills. Parents who are feeding their toddler may pursue both immediate (e.g., getting the child fed) and distant goals. The latter may be the reason why ZPAs are introduced, either in the parent-child joint action, or (later) through distal communication between the parents and the self-feeding child. Within ZPAs, certain particular actions that *the child is capable of performing individually but might decide not to use in the given situation,* can be promoted by parents. If the child, however, does not succumb to the promotion effort, the parents need not force the exercise of the new skill on him or her. For instance, if a child has learned to use the spoon independently but reverts to finger feeding, the parent may organize the ZPA in different behavioral (pointing to the spoon, putting the spoon into the child's hand) or communicative (telling the child to use the spoon) ways. Here, an important aspect of the ZPA is evident: *The ZPA's function is to promote the further development of some actions that the child has already basically acquired, through the child's own decision to exercise these actions.* For example, a mother may point to a spoon on the tray as part of the ZPA-establishing action because *she knows that the child is already capable of handling it,* and is currently refraining from demonstrating and exercising that skill for some (unspecifiable!) motivational reasons. ZPA is a structure that canalizes the child's own motivation to act, whereas ZFM canalizes the actions themselves without an emphasis on the child's wishes or will. Not surprisingly, ZPAs emerge in the history of child rearing in conjunction with the ideology of thinking about children as independent human beings whose self-worth (or self-esteem) is developed by their own action preferences and (seeming) independence of thinking (see Sunley, 1955, for an account of different ideologies in American child rearing in the 19th century).

The actual beginnings of the child's development of new actions are embedded *within adult–child action in the Zone of Proximal Development* (ZPD). Structuring of the learning of the new action is assisted by setting up a ZFM to organize the new action, starting from its narrowest state, and gradually releasing different parts of the action to be controlled by the child (widening of the given ZFM). The ontogeny of learning the use of spoons provides an example. The adult at first helps the child to use the spoon by accomplishing the whole action (TAKE FOOD FROM CONTAINER ONTO SPOON → PREPARE FOR TRANSPORT (judge the readiness of the child for accepting food) → TRANSPORT → FOOD RELEASE), which provides the child with perceivable information about the whole action. When the baby starts to grab for the spoon (or when the adult considers it appropriate to involve the child in the action), the organization of action within ZPD begins. The adult gradually relinquishes control over some parts of the action, while retaining control over the others as well as over the action in its totality. For example, usually HOLDING OF SPOON is the first part of the whole action into which the child's behavior becomes integrated—the adult puts the spoon into the child's hand, *and controls the movements of the hand + spoon in the process of carrying out the whole action.* The child is kept in the subordinate role with no control over any part of the action, but is being prepared for further learning of it by the adult's guiding the whole motion of the hand + spoon. Next, some parts of the action may become "liberated" from the adult's control and delegated to the control of the child. For example, the adult may give the spoon to the child *and let him or her dip it into the container with food,* after which the adult may help the child to: get food onto the spoon, withdraw the spoonful of food from the container, take the hand + spoon + food to the mouth, and release the food. Likewise, the penultimate part of the action (hand + spoon + food reaching the child's mouth) may be delegated to the child—the spoon is filled under the adult's control, and is set into a starting position for the journey toward the mouth by the adult. The adult then guides the child's hand + spoon + food halfway toward the child's mouth, releases it, and lets the child complete the transport part of the action. The adult may then regain control over the spoon and help the child to release the food in the mouth and return the spoon. Further development of the action leads to even less control by the adult, where the child is allotted control over different parts of the action, at last reaching full control over all components of the action. To be successful in teaching the child the new skill, the process of guiding the learning of the skill by structuring (and restructuring) its emergence through ZFMs has to be coordinated with the ZPD of the particular child (previous life experience, up to the given time). If the ZFM is set so that it allows the child to control a part of the action that still cannot be mastered, the ZFM has to be reset in a way that takes care of that part, until the child is ready to learn it. *The dynamic restructuring of ZFM in the context of learning a particular type of action canalizes the emergence of that action so that it provides the child with selective learning experience for some of the parts of the action earlier than others, in correspondence with what is empirically (by trying, not succeeding, and trying again) found to be available to the child within the ZPD.*

7.3 ANALYSIS OF INDIVIDUAL CASE HISTORIES OF THE CANALIZATION OF MEALTIME ACTIONS IN INFANTS AND TODDLERS

From all the theoretical considerations outlined at length in the present book, it follows that the most appropriate strategy for developmental research is the analysis of the process of development by looking at individual developing systems longitudinally over a period of time, and interdependently with the contexts of their existence at every available step. Sections 7.4 through 7.6 present research materials on three children from the longitudinal (6–7 to 24–26 months of age) sample. All these cases are analyzed along similar lines. First, some background information about the child and her family is given. That is followed by a quantitative analysis of the amounts of time spent by the child and parent(s), during each of the mealtimes studied, on one or another kind of self- or other-feeding activity or merely in contact with food. This information provides the background for the most central topic of the empirical analyses—the structural description of the canalization process, which is represented by narrative descriptions of the sequence of events within the mealtimes that were observed, and by more specific analyses of sequences of particular child–parent–environment transaction episodes that occurred in one or another "crucial" moment during a particular meal. These crucial episodes are usually not the most frequent ones when viewed within the quantitative domain. They are usually single, rare, episodic events that are more informative than the dominant, recurrent, well-mastered actions.

All three cases presented here happen to be those of female toddlers. This clear dominance of one sex in the data is of no importance here, because the study is cast in the individual–socioecological reference frame, rather than the usual (interindividual) one. In the latter case, the issue of sex differences would be of interest, but, given the emphasis on the former frame, it is of no relevance for the empirical analysis that is outlined in this chapter.

7.4 THE CASE OF LAURA

7.4.1 Family Background

Laura is the first child of a college-graduate mother (26 years of age at the time of the child's birth) who works as a technical secretary, and a dental technician father (also 26 years of age). Laura was born healthy ($\frac{1}{5}$ minute Apgar rating 8 and 9 at birth), after a pregnancy without medical complications or psychological difficulties. The parents were involved in Lamaze preparations for childbirth. The mother reported some "postpartum blues," which disappeared after a few weeks. Laura was given her own room (next to her parents' bedroom) for sleeping from the first day at home. Her health between birth and the beginning of participation in the study was reported to have been very good (parents reported one virus infection and two colds during that period).

Laura's mealtimes were observed seven times, at the following ages (months: days): (1) 6:27, (2) 9:01, (3) 13:19, (4) 15:08, (5) 18:03, (6) 21:03, and (7) 25:17. The feeding was usually organized by her mother, with the father being present on some occasions and helping the mother in her work. Due to an equipment failure, the fifth videotaping session did not cover the whole meal, but only the end part of it.

7.4.2 The Time Distribution of Food-Contact Activities

The data on time distribution of Laura's food-contact actions (feeding or otherwise, by herself, her mother, or by both herself and her mother) are presented in Table 7.1. Laura's general (summary, percentagewise) time spent in contact with food changed dramatically over the 19-month period.

As expected, the dominant (100% time) way of getting fed at 6:27—the mother spoon-feeding Laura—was gradually substituted by, first, the dominance of the child's self-feeding with the use of her hands (e.g., at 13:19 that method occupied 91.6% of the time). Later on, Laura was seen to use the spoon—first, predominantly for handling the foods on the high chair tray (dipping the spoon into food, trying to get food onto spoon, banging with spoon on tray and food—anything except transporting food to the mouth region). At the end of the observations, she spent most of the time spoon-feeding herself adequately, with occasional (21.5% of all the mealtime spent in contact with food) use of finger-feeding herself. This wide general picture of the basic change toward utensil-mediated self-feeding proves that the child's eating habits became culturally organized during the period of the observations. More interestingly, certain events that were observed only rarely and proved to be transitory in the bigger quantitative picture of the mealtime events provide more direct and structured information about the process of mother–child interaction. These include the mother–child joint action with the spoon in the process of feeding (observed at 15:08 and 18:03) and their joint action in the process of drinking from a regular glass (observed at 21:03).

TABLE 7.1. Developmental Changes in Mealtime Food-Contact Time Allocations between Different Child-Centered Actions (Case: Laura)

	Observed Mealtimes at Child's Age												
	6:27		9:01		13:19		15:08		18:03		21:03		25:17	
Action Category	f	%	f	%	f	%	f	%	f	%	f	%	f	%
M spoon feeds CH	574	100.0	367	55.9	70	6.0	128	12.8	—	—	—	—	—	—
M finger-feeds CH	—	—	7	1.1	—	—	—	—	—	—	—	—	—	—
CH finger-feeds	—	—	282	43.0	1074	91.6	729	73.0	34	7.9	168	22.5	117	21.5
CH drinks from cup with lid	—	—	—	—	29	2.4	136	13.6	—	—	80	10.7	—	—
M–CH joint action with spoon	—	—	—	—	—	—	6	0.6	15	3.5	—	—	—	—
CH plays with food or utensil	—	—	—	—	—	—	—	—	373	86.1	69	9.2	—	—
CH spoon-feeds herself	—	—	—	—	—	—	—	—	11	2.5	407	54.6	428	78.5
M–CH joint action with regular glass	—	—	—	—	—	—	—	—	—	—	22	3.0	—	—
Total	574		656		1173		999		433		746		545	

M = mother; CH = child; f = frequency of 1-second time units.

259

7.4.3   Changes in the Mealtime Setting and the Development of Utensil Use

The sequence of events during the observed mealtimes provides better information about the process of child-feeding and its socialization than the summary time budgets. At age 6:27, Laura's mealtime had a very simple sequential structure. After the child was made ready for the meal (by being put into an infant seat located on a table, and attaching a bib to the child), the mother proceeded to spoon-feed her without interruption for 6 minutes, 19 seconds (6.19). The first time Laura was observed to turn her head away from the approaching spoon-with-food was at 4.50 (4 minutes, 50 seconds) into the meal. Then followed her mother's recurrent attempts to get the spoonful of food into her mouth (L turns head away → M withdraws spoon → L turns head back → M approaches with spoon again → L either accepts the food now, or turns head away again, with repetition of the subsequent maternal effort). There was an 8-second pause (from 6.30 to 6.38) in the meal, followed by continuous spoon-feeding in the course of which the child continued to display head turned away at times. This led the mother to ask (at 7.50): "Are you through?" She adjusted the child's position in the seat (8.18–8.25), and continued spoon-feeding until 9.00. That was followed by a period of waiting to see whether the child might accept some more food, tickling her, wiping her mouth and face, and cleaning off the dipped food from the bib. After that (at 10.40 into feeding), Laura was removed from the infant seat. This marked the end of the mealtime. At no time was Laura attempting to touch the spoon. The movement of her limbs was characterized by nonspecific activation (kicking feet and extending arms back and forth, being practically in a semireclining position in the seat). On no occasion did the mother attempt to get her to touch the food, its container, or the spoon.

The sequential picture of Laura's mealtime at 9:01 is already different. The child is put into the high chair. Maternal spoon-feeding is still prevailing (the mother feeds her uninterruptedly from 0.03 to 6.10 of the mealtime). At 6.00, the mother asks, referring to Laura's refusal to accept food, "Is that all?" The child's mouth and hands are subsequently wiped, after which the mother offers Laura a cracker *which the latter accepts by hand*. The acceptance of the cracker is followed by a long (from 7.05 to 11.47) period of Laura's bimanual and unimanual manipulating of the cracker, and mouthing it (together with eating it). The mother observes Laura finger-feeding herself, once helping her daughter by putting a piece of cracker into her mouth with her (mother's) fingers (11.47–11.50). After that, Laura drops the cracker on the floor (where the dog gets it). Laura continues to sit in the high chair without food until 13.18, after which the mother wipes the child's mouth, face, and hands, and cleans up the tray. Laura gets into fussing, and by 14.19 the meal is over as she is taken down from the high chair.

This second observed mealtime involved a mother–daughter exchange of food (cracker) *from hand to hand* and the subsequent finger-feeding by the child. Laura's finger-feeding during this mealtime could not be characterized as an efficient action, because it involved excessive manipulation of the food together with mouthing/eating it. The mother essentially provided Laura with a two-course meal—feeding her semiliquid food with the spoon herself, then cleaning up the child, followed by the second course of finger-food. Again, no opportunity was given to the child to manipulate any of the feeding utensils, and neither was Laura observed to try to grab the spoon during the first course of the meal.

Laura's third observed mealtime (at 13:19) included the appearance of new forms of meal organization. Although spoon-feeding by the mother was still present, it was not organized into long time periods, but present intermittently with the provision of finger-foods for the child, for self-feeding (putting pieces of ham *on the tray, rather than into the child's hands*). The presence of a drinking cup (with a lid with spout) was evident episodically. Laura indicated her wish to drink by a gesture (arms raised at the level of shoulders, pointing toward mother, sometimes accompanied by a vocalization). *After the child displayed that gesture, the mother immediately gave Laura the cup into her hands,* and she raised the cup bimanually to drink. After drinking was accomplished, *the mother immediately removed the cup from the child's reach (i.e., the tray),* until the child displayed the gesture again. The child was not given access to the cup other than when drinking, which was communicated by the child and immediately understood by the mother, who provided the cup. No use of spoon, nor grabbing of it, was observed among the child's actions during this observed meal.

The novel action type of *the mother and child cooperating in handling the spoon* was first observed in Laura's case during the fourth session (at 15:08). After the usual preparations for the feeding (until 0.38 into the mealtime) the mother proceeded to provide food for the child's finger-feeding, intermittently with spoon-feeding by the mother, until 5.14 of the mealtime. The first episode of mother–child joint action with the spoon was observed between 5.14 and 5.20: the mother gave the spoon (with food on it) to the child, who accepted it with her left hand. The mother did not release the spoon, but guided the child's hand (with the spoon) to the mouth. After that episode, the mealtime proceeded by the child's finger-feeding or drinking (the cup, as previously, was given to the child on demand and removed after the child had drunk and released the cup). The mother also tried to continue to spoon-feed Laura, with greater refusal efforts on behalf of the child toward the end of the meal (at 24.46).

A qualitatively new picture of the child's actions at mealtime, mediated by the use of utensils, was observed at 18:03 (unfortunately, this was when equipment failure made it impossible to record the whole meal, so only the final 7.20 of that meal constitute the observational basis here). The qualitative novelty of action during that observation session is evident even from Table 7.1—most of Laura's food-contacting time was spent *using the spoon while manipulating food.* The child acted with the spoon in different ways, mostly dipping it into the plate (with some solid food—like cheesecake—in it), hit the food with the spoon, took some food from the plate and put it on the tray. Actual self-feeding with the spoon (i.e., food transport from plate or tray to mouth) was observed only occasionally, and mother–child joint feeding with the spoon, only twice. The child's finger-feeding was likewise rare, although the nature of the food (solid cake) and the location of its pieces (both on the plate and on the tray) made it possible to finger-feed.

Laura's next meal was observed at 21:03. At that observation, the structure of the mealtime had reached a state where Laura fed herself most of the time with the spoon, and mother–child joint action while spoon-feeding was not observed. However, when Laura abandoned the spoon for some time, the mother reminded her of it. The following summary of events from the end of the sixth minute to nearly the tenth minute of the meal provides the action sequence:

6.58–7.54—Laura uses spoon to feed herself.

7.54–8.00—Quits feeding, bangs with spoon on the lid of the cup on the tray.

8.00–9.01—The child continues with finger-feeding. AT 8.39 MOTHER INTERVENES VERBALLY, SAYING: "You are supposed to be using your spoon." Laura continues to finger-feed, mother does not repeat her reminder.

9.01–9.12—Mother cleans the tray and wipes Laura's face and hands.

9.12–9.26—Laura grabs the spoon from tray, manipulates it. MOTHER COMMENTS: "That's right, use your spoon." Laura proceeds to spoon-feed herself, and drops the spoon on the floor at the end of the time period.

9.26–9.42—Mother wipes the tray, Laura talks to mother.

This action sequence illustrates the reality of the ZPA as it is ontogenetically transformed from the sphere of joint action to communication—the use of the spoon is promoted (verbally) when the child temporarily abandons the use of the spoon and reverts to finger-feeding.

Another important novelty in the way the child drank from the cup (with lid) was observed: after the child had asked for the cup, the cup was given *and not taken away after Laura had drunk,* but was left on the tray. Laura was observed to handle the cup for the first time unimanually (as well as continuing the bimanual hold of the cup sometimes). The mother did not help the child to act with the cup, but *on the one occasion when she offered Laura a drink from a regular glass she held the glass herself, letting Laura hold it bimanually, and helped the child to lift the glass for drinking,* not releasing the glass.

Laura's coordination of the actions of the left and right hands in the self-feeding context was observed particularly in the final half of the meal, when the mother gave her a spoon and a jar with some semiliquid prune purée (10.43–14.28). The jar and the spoon were put *on the tray* (rather than either of these into the child's hands). Previously, the child had been given a cookie which she continued to handle when the jar and spoon were given to her. At first, Laura used the cookie as a dipping tool to get the food from the jar and carry the food + cookie to the mouth, intermittently with manipulation of the spoon, jam, and the cookie on the tray. Between 12.40 and 12.50 of the mealtime, an interesting novel form of interlimb coordination in this action context was observed: Laura *took the jar into her left hand* and raised the jar approximately 4–5 cm from the tray, and then *took the spoon into her right hand* and spoon-fed herself from the jar. The importance of this observation lies in the child's reconstruction of the eating setting by her nonuse of the available support (the tray) for the jar, and in the coordination of manual handling of both tools involved—the container and the food-transport instrument.

The final observation of Laura's mealtime (at 25:17) revealed general consolidation of the self-feeding with spoon. This took the form of *exchange of hands* while spoon-feeding herself. During the first 6.11 of the mealtime, Laura was observed to feed herself with the spoon in her left hand (intermittently with finger-feeding, for which the right hand was used). Then the spoon was changed from the left to the right hand, and used by that hand until 10.42, when it was changed back to the left (until 10.51, after which the meal moved into its end phase). In terms of frequencies, the spoon was used approximately equally by the left (20 self-feeds) and the right (19 self-feeds) hands during the meal. However, the use of the two hands was not "random," but involved longer sequences of the use first of one, and then the other, hand.

Another important observation during this mealtime was the child's action (at 4.48–4.58) where, *holding the spoon in her left hand, Laura used her right hand to take some food in her fingers, put it on the spoon, and then transport the spoon + food to her mouth.* This structure of action was observed twice in a row. It illustrates the integration of the natural and cultural lines in the ontogeny of self-feeding.

7.5   THE CASE OF SOPHIE

7.5.1   Family Background

Sophie was born as the second child into a family where the mother (age 29 at the child's birth, secondary education) is from Africa and the father is American (38 years of age, PhD-level education). The family's first child (daughter) was 8 years old when Sophie was born.

Sophie's mealtimes were videotaped five times, at the following ages: (1) 8:05, (2) 12:10, (3) 15:13, (4) 17:10, and (5) 25:00 months. All mealtimes were recorded at lunchtimes, around noon.

7.5.2   The Time Distribution of Food-Contact Activities

The data on the distribution of time that Sophie spent in contact with food at each of the longitudinally observed mealtimes are presented in Table 7.2.

These summary data are instructive in two respects. First, they replicate the finding of the role of child's play with food and utensils (see Table 7.1) as an immediate concomitant of the development of both Laura's and Sophie's

TABLE 7.2. Developmental Changes in Mealtime Food-Contact Time Allocations between Different Actions of the Child (Case: Sophie)

Action Category	Observed Mealtimes at Child's Age									
	8:05		12:10		15:13		17:10		25:00	
	f	%	f	%	f	%	f	%	f	%
M spoon-feeds CH	270	39.1	—	—	—	—	—	—	—	—
M fork-feeds CH	—	—	—	—	—	—	38	6.2	—	—
M gives drink	25	3.6	—	—	—	—	—	—	—	—
CH plays with food and utensils	395	57.3	398	31.4	133	38.7	77	12.7	—	—
CH finger-feeds (= hand-feeds)	—	—	604	47.7	112	32.5	112	18.4	420	67.8
CH spoon-feeds	—	—	—	—	—	—	—	—	—	—
CH fork-feeds	—	—	—	—	47	13.7	209	34.4	110	17.8
CH drinks by herself	—	—	84	6.7	52	15.1	48	7.9	65	10.5
M–CH joint action: with fork	—	—	—	—	—	—	43	7.1	—	—
with cup/glass	—	—	—	—	—	—	20	3.3	—	—
CH feeds other actor (mother, father, doll)	—	—	180	14.2	—	—	61	10.0	24	3.9
Total	690		1266		344		608		619	

M = mother; CH = child; f = frequency of 1-second time units.

264

self-feeding actions in mealtime contexts. By the end of the first year of life, Sophie's mother had reversed her strategy of *not* giving the child the opportunity to manipulate utensils and food. Because that manipulation thus occurred in the ZFM of Sophie's actions in the immediate environment (high chair tray), both the manipulation of food and utensils and finger-feeding herself became possible. The food and utensil play that was first observed at 12 months subsequently declined in its quantitative share of the mealtime, as the child's self-feeding actions (both with fingers/hands and utensils) became more skillful.

The second useful piece of information that data in this table denote is the *dependence of the particular actions on the structural conditions set for the meal setting by the mother.* The mother has full control over the way she structures the mealtime setting. The child may (and indeed—was observed to) demand one or another alteration in the ZPA/ZFM structure that the mother had set up, and the mother may (and did) "give in" on the issues that the child tried to change, but the ultimate control over the whole situation remained in the mother's hands. She made the decision to provide the child with a fork and not with a spoon—thus resulting in nonoccurrence of the child's spoon-feeding herself during the observed mealtimes. She made it possible for the child to play the game of feeding another person—initiating the period at 12:10, when Sophie was observed finger-feeding the mother. She provided a soft animal-toy (which Sophie subsequently "fed") for the child in the high chair at 17:10. The mother's decision to give the child a sandwich at 25:00 resulted in extensive hand-feeding by the child during the meal observed at that age.

7.5.3   Changes in the Mealtime Setting and the Development of Utensil Use

As is evident from the summary data in Table 7.2, the longitudinal course of Sophie's mealtime organization progressed toward greater differentiation of the action repertoires that could be observed. At 8:06, the child is confined in the high chair and no food is made constantly available to her. This is evidenced in the mother's keeping the food container (a child's three-partition feeding plate) not on the high chair tray but on the table next to it, out of the reach of the child. The mother explicitly acknowledges that she does not give to the child any utensil (except the cup) to handle during the meal. The course of the meal at that age verifies that strategy—the mother spends the first 2.05 of the meal spoon-feeding the child. At some spoon-feeding attempts, the mother opens her mouth widely at the time that she expects the child to do likewise (1.29), and withdraws the spoon-with-food when the child occasionally refuses to open her mouth. The cup emerges in the situation at 2.05 to 2.30 feeding time. The mother gives the child a cup (with a lid and spout), putting it onto the tray in front of the child. The child looks at it and examines it with her right hand, pushing it off onto its side. The mother lifts it back up. The child pushes the cup around on the tray, the mother intervenes (at 2.26) and puts it back up in front of the child. This episode of negotiation of ZFM boundary (child playing with cup, mother taking it and setting it upright) is followed by *the mother giving a drink from the cup without releasing control over it.* Once the child has finished drinking, the mother retrieves the cup and puts it on the table out of the child's reach, but in her visual field. The next longer period of time (2.38–4.53) during that meal is again spent in the mother's spoon-feeding the child (at 3.54 an example of mother's mouth opening occurs; at 4.17–4.31, the mother tries to spoon-feed twice with no effect but gets the food to the child on the third try). After a brief side-oriented activity (interaction with father), the mother's spoon-feeding of the child continues until 6.08.

The events of the meal continue: the mother tries to give the child an apple (putting it onto the tray) but the child shows no interest, after which the apple is retrieved to the starting position (a plate). After wiping the child's mouth, the mother offers her a drink from the cup (by putting the cup on the tray), but the child does not take it. The mother proceeds to give the child a drink from the cup herself; the child drinks with arms stretched out in air at shoulder level, making no attempt to grab the cup. After drinking is finished, the mother leaves the cup on the tray. The child at first watches it, then proceeds to grab the cup by its handles bimanually, then releases her right hand and keeps it only in her left, mouths the spout, seems to drink. The mother takes the cup away from the child and gives her a piece of apple. The rest of the meal is spent by Sophie's mouthing of the piece of apple.

The second mealtime that was observed in the study took place at Sophie's age 12:10. The mother's strategy of organizing the mealtime is quite different from the previous session—instead of keeping utensils and food (except for the cup with lid) away from the high chair tray, now the mother *gives different utensils to the child and puts food onto the tray,* thus creating the possibility (ZFM) for the child to manipulate the food and utensils, and promoting the child's acting with food in particular ways (ZPA). The latter is evident in the mother's triggering of the child-feeds-mother game (see below).

The actual structure of the second mealtime starts from a relatively lengthy preparatory phase—the mother prepares food and brings it to Sophie while the child is ready in the high chair, with bib attached, ready to eat. At 1.31, the mother puts the child's three-section feeding plate *onto the high chair tray* (a qualitative change from the previous observation session), while continuing to mix the food in the different sections of the plate, explaining to the child a number of times: "That's hot." The child proceeds to manipulate the food with her hands, and then starts finger-feeding herself with her right hand.

At 2.46, the mother gives the child a plastic spoon (with a twisted handle, similar to the one in Figure 6.5) *in a way that forces the child to accept it in her right hand* (i.e., keeping the handle of the spoon to the right, from the child's point of view). The child accepts the spoon by the handle, using her right hand, brings it to contact with the food, but proceeds to put it down on the tray. The mother takes it away and puts it back on the tray (on the child's right side) immediately. The child uses her right hand to manipulate it on the tray. At 3.28, another similar plastic spoon is given into the child's left hand. It is accepted by the child, who then puts both spoons down onto the plate. The mother acts to adjust one of the two for right-hand use and withdraws the other (3.38). The child uses the spoon to touch food, manipulates the spoon, at 4.10 points toward the other spoon (on the table, outside the child's reach but in her visual field) which the mother gives to her, after which the child continues to manipulate the two spoons on the tray and plate, making no effort to bring either of them close to her mouth or into it, with or without food. This is followed by a relatively long period (4.23–7.39) of finger-feeding (using the right hand). The mother takes away both spoons.

A drinking episode follows at 7.39. The child vocalizes and points in the direction of the cup (which has a lid and spout, but no handles) that is on the adjacent table, out of reach. Mother gives the cup—*by putting it on the tray in front of the child,* from where the child lifts it bimanually and drinks. After the child has finished drinking and puts the cup down on the tray, the mother leaves the cup there (rather than removing it to the adjacent table) while the child proceeds to finger-feed herself. At 8.58, the mother gives the child a plastic fork, which she accepts with her left hand. After some manipulation, the child puts it into her right hand, contacts food with it, and abandons it on the tray, resuming finger-feeding.

An episode concerning attempts to cross ZFM boundaries in respect to actions with utensils followed at 9.48–12.53 of the meal:

CHILD: Takes fork into right hand, touches food, manipulates it with fork, vocalizes and points with left hand toward other utensils on the table.
MOTHER: Gives a plastic spoon into her left hand.
CHILD: Manipulates both fork and spoon on the plate, in contact with food, but no self-feeding effort with these utensils is observed. At 11.25 gets a piece of food onto spoon, transports it to the edge of the tray, and releases the food overboard.
MOTHER: Catches the piece of food in her hand.
CHILD: Fusses, gives the spoon to mother, continues to manipulate with the fork.
MOTHER: Accepts the spoon.
CHILD: Continues manipulation of fork, at 12.28 for the first time puts the fork in mouth in adequate way (handling it with left hand) but with no food on it, keeps mouthing it (until 12.51).

This episode illustrates the boundary condition of the ZFM being located at the subset of actions involving the throwing of objects (here, food) over the edge of the tray onto the floor. The child is allowed to play with food and utensils on the tray, and is not pushed to use the utensils in a particular way (although the utensil use is promoted by the mother's returning of utensils to the child from time to time).

This episode is followed by another drinking episode that was observed to include an important novel aspect (at 12.53–13.14). The child takes the cup from the tray bimanually and drinks, then puts it back onto the plate, where it loses balance and falls onto its side. *The child proceeds to adjust it*—first by trying to set it upright on the food in the plate, with no success. She then puts it down upright in the place from where she had taken it when she started to drink (left of plate, on far end of tray). She then proceeds to manipulate the fork. At 13.14–14.10, an effort toward getting the fork into a piece of food is observed: the child holds the fork in her right hand and adjusts a piece of food on the plate with her left hand. That action fails, since she uses the whole right arm, which is unsteady, to aim the fork at the food.

At the fifteenth minute, the mother introduces new food on a different plate. In the process of that introduction, the boundary of ZFM is again observable. When the mother puts a new (round, regular) plate with food on the tray, the child makes an effort to lift the plate from the tray, which is counteracted by the mother who pushes the plate back onto the tray surface. The child proceeds to manipulate the food with her fingers, and to finger-feed herself.

At 19.05, the investigator triggers a demonstration of the child's feeding the mother. The mother asks the child to feed her, makes herself available for that, and the child proceeds to finger-feed the mother (during the period 19.20–21.28). A couple of minutes later (at 23.55–24.47), and after finger-feeding herself, the child initiates feeding the mother—starting from high-pitch vocalization and holding up right arm/hand with food. When the mother comes, the child puts food in her mouth. The second time, the child begins to play an approach/withdrawal game with mother—when the mother approaches, the child withdraws her hand with food, leading to the mother's withdrawal, after which the child then approaches the mother's mouth with her hand again. The most interesting observation occurred when the child's hand was arriving at the mother's mouth—while putting the food into the mother's mouth, the child opened *her own* mouth wide.

The *actual use of a utensil for transport of food to mouth* was observed, starting from the third videotaping session (at 15:13). That session began with the child sitting in the high chair, having the (three-sectional) plate and cup (with lid and spout) on the tray, and a fork in her right hand. The child mouths the fork, and at 1.19 uses the operation of her left hand to *dip the fork in food and bring the fork with some food to the mouth,* after which she continues mouthing the fork. This event is repeated at 2.12.

Between 2.52 and 3.18, another action version with the fork takes place: the child, while holding the fork in her left hand, gets some food onto the fork (some of it is between the fork's tines). Then, using her right (free) hand, she takes the food from the fork and puts it into her mouth in the regular fashion of finger-feeding. The importance of this little episode lies in the demonstration of flexibility in the child's actions—once the utensil use has emerged ontogenetically in the social context, the child continues to have the freedom to decide when *not* to use the utensil and reverts to using the hand pure and simple. The cultural organization of mealtimes generates *redundancy in action possibilities,* which affords an increased number of different possible ways to solve the food transport problem. However, such shifting back and forth between utensil and hand use may be seen in actual mealtime practices only in early ontogeny. Later, when the structure of mealtime settings becomes internalized, it takes an adult quite a bit of courage to grasp food in a hand during some formal dinner party when the luxurious situation has furnished each person with a set of forks or spoons.

Sophie's third mealtime session proceeds with mouthing the fork and playing with the food on the tray. At 4.05, the child starts to push the plate away from the tray, the mother takes it away, and new food (banana) is given to the child (4.54). For the rest of the mealtime (until it ends at 9.09), the child finger-feeds herself banana pieces, drinks from the cup, and occasionally interacts with the mother in a manner not related to eating.

The fourth observed mealtime (at age 17:10) includes some further novelties in its structure. First, a regular (metal instead of plastic) fork is given to the child. Second, for the first time in the course of observations, the cup used for drinking lacks the lid (with spout), and is thus equivalent to a regular cup (with a handle).

The session begins with the mother putting the child in the high chair and lowering the tray. The mother then puts the three-section plate on the tray, uses a steel fork to stir some food, leaves it all for the child, who is engaged in finger-feeding herself. At 0.40–1.07, the child takes the fork with her right hand and *adequately transports food to her mouth*. She does not release the whole forkload but only part of it, withdraws the fork with the rest of the load to the plate, and then advances to the mouth again with the same load and releases all of it in the mouth. This is the first episode where the child was observed to use the fork independently in ways that guaranteed adequate food transport, which in this case was related to withdrawal of some of the food on the fork and eating it at the next action.

The session proceeds with the child finger-feeding, then playing with the fork and food (holding the fork by all five fingers at the very end of the handle, dipping it into the food), drinking from the cup, finger-feeding again, mouthing the fork. At 4.56, an episode of mother–child joint action starts. The mother says, "Let me help you," to which the child answers with a "No!" Nevertheless, the mother takes some food onto the fork, gives it to the child to be accepted by the right hand, and the child finishes the action by accepting the fork + food from the mother, taking it to the mouth, and releasing it in the mouth (5.38). After a period of the child feeding herself with the fork, a similar episode of joint action occurs, after the child begins to play (pointing with the fork to a drawing on the side of the cup on the tray). That episode again is connected with the issue of ZFM boundary regulation:

MOTHER: Takes the fork, prepares its foodload, and puts the fork + food on the tray so that the handle is on the child's right side.
CHILD: Picks up the fork with the right hand, manipulates it, tries to take the load off the fork with her left hand.
MOTHER: Says: "No, that's OK."

CHILD: Finally transports the fork + food to the mouth, helps with her left hand to keep the food in the mouth when withdrawing the fork with the right hand. Goes on to hit the plate with the fork, then tries to dip the fork into the cup.

MOTHER: Interrupts the dipping action and redirects child's hand with fork.

CHILD: Tries again to dip the fork in the cup.

MOTHER: Takes away cup.

CHILD: Throws fork down onto the floor, bangs on tray with the right hand.

MOTHER: Picks up the fork, wipes it clean, and gives it back to the child.

CHILD: Uses the regained fork to hit the tray.

MOTHER: "No!"

CHILD: Throws the fork down on the tray.

MOTHER: Takes the fork away.

CHILD: Bangs on the tray with hand, reaches out toward mother.

MOTHER: Remains inactive, asks "Eat more!"

CHILD: "No."

This episode ends as the child switches into finger-feeding herself. The negotiation involved in the episode illustrates the ways in which the ZFM for acting with the fork during the meal is negotiated. The mother excludes the banging on the tray with the fork, and throwing it (or other objects) overboard onto the floor, from ZFM. The child, however, begins to display these actions and persists in doing so (e.g., after the mother returns the fork). The boundary is reinstated by eliminating the fork from the situation and suggesting (ZPA) that the child continue eating more without the fork (i.e., the child's reaching out toward the mother at the end of the episode may have been a gesture to get the fork back).

After some time of the child's finger-feeding, the mother returns the fork into the situation (at 7.43)—again by getting a load of food onto it herself first. Then she puts the fork on the plate so that it is ready for right-hand use. The child, who has been episodically interested in the camera, then takes fork + food and transports it to the mouth, after which the child continues using the fork to feed herself. Suddenly she gives the fork to the mother, who collects a forkload and tries to feed the child while holding the fork herself. The child refuses (by withdrawing head); the mother abandons the feeding effort and puts the fork on the plate, ready for right-hand use. The child pays no attention to the food—sits, looks at mother, points at camera, no food-related action. Only 20 seconds later does the child take the fork, manipulate it, and proceed to use it to feed herself. After putting the food in the mouth with it, she puts the fork back on the plate. The mother takes the fork, again collects food onto it, gives fork + food to the child, who takes it, first *offers to feed the mother,* then transports it to her own mouth.

The next minute of the mealtime (9.40–10.36) is spent in occasional joint action of the mother and child around drinking from the cup, and using the fork again. An interesting episode starts at the end of this period, when the child requests a soft toy (Kitty-cat) which is located on the table next to the high chair. The mother puts the Kitty-cat to sit next to the child in the high chair, on the left side of the child. The presence of the toy animal in the structure of the meal creates new possibilities for the child's actions and for the mother's regulation of these actions. At 10.36–10.47, the child grasps the cup with her right hand only (as her left arm is around the Kitty-cat). The mother immediately says: "Two hands! Two hands only!" The child releases Kitty-cat, and the mother adjusts it in the sitting position, saying "Kitty-cat, she sits there." The child proceeds to take the cup with both hands and drinks. This little episode illustrates how the addition of a new object into the situation triggers the canalization effort of otherwise well-established action—the child had been seen previously many times to lift the cup bimanually, but tried to do it unimanually when her left hand was not available. Immediately, the mother intervenes to reinstate the ZFM boundary condition.

The following period (10.47–11.50) is spent in the mother's fork-feeding the child while the latter is playing with the toy—e.g., lowering the Kitty-cat to "eat" from the plate. As a result, the toy gets dirty with ketchup, the mother retrieves and cleans it, then returns it to the position in the high chair. At 11.50, the next interesting episode begins. The mother prepares a forkload and gives it to the child, who accepts it in her right hand. She starts to "feed" the Kitty-cat with the fork and then transports the forkload into her own mouth. This action sequence is repeated, until, at 12.35, the mother prepares a forkload and attempts to fork-feed the child, who refuses and plays with Kitty-cat, adjusting it in the high chair. The action then proceeds to eating broccoli—the mother takes a piece of broccoli in her hand and gives it into the child's right hand. The child tries to feed it to the Kitty-cat by her hand, then transports broccoli into her own mouth. The child is observed finger-feeding the Kitty-cat repeatedly, with no maternal intervention. This, however, ceases to be the case when the child takes the cup and tries to give the Kitty-cat a drink (14.19–14.35)—the mother intercepts the child's hands holding the cup when she predicts that the next thing the child is going to do is to raise it in front of Kitty-cat's nose. She also verbally reminds the child: "Not kitty! No!" The child gives in, and the mother proceeds to clean the tray while the child remains inactive. After some efforts by the mother to fork-feed the child and to offer more food (refused by the child), the mother proceeds to end the mealtime (16.05).

The fifth observed mealtime took place at the child's age of 25:00 and was characterized by a number of previously unobserved novelties. First, the child is no longer *put* into the mealtime position—sitting in the high chair—by the mother but is urged by her to climb into the high chair (and down from it at the end of the meal) "all by herself," which she does. Second, the high chair is used as an equivalent of an ordinary chair—instead of lowering the tray to confine the child after she has climbed into the sitting position, the mother pushes the whole chair with the child to a position at the regular table. Third, the mother uses a regular plate as the food container, putting it together with a regular fork in front of the child. The fork, not coincidentally, is placed at the right side of the child's plate. A napkin is also provided within the child's reach.

The child, at first, hand-feeds (a sandwich) with her right hand, then (at 0.33) fork-feeds, holding the fork by the very end of the handle in her right hand. This is followed by the child's wiping her own mouth/nose with the napkin (taken from the table). The meal proceeds with the child hand-feeding, drinking from the open (no lid) cup, using the fork to manipulate food; at 7.25, the child says "OK" and stands up on the chair, calling "Mommy!" The mother takes away the plate, the child sits down, and the mother brings another plate with new food.

The child proceeds to hand-feed herself. In the period 9.58–10.22, the father appears episodically in the situation, insisting that the child feed him. The child feeds the father by hand, and then comments, "He took a bite," pointing toward him with her finger. The rest of the meal is uneventful (from the perspective of the present investigator, of course): the child hand-feeds herself with her left hand (10.22–12.20), talks, says her name at her mother's insistence, and talks about a recent visit to the zoo, while holding food in the left hand but not acting with it (12.20–14.00). She then proceeds to hand-feed and talk intermittently (14.00–15.48), after which she demands "Down!" which leads to the mother's cleaning of her mouth and moving away the chair from the table, so that the child can get down—by herself.

7.6   THE CASE OF SARAH

7.6.1   Family Background

Sarah was the second child of educated parents (mother's age 31 at the time of Sarah's birth, nurse by professional training; father's age 30, occupation: pediatrician). The mother's pregnancy was medically uneventful, and Sarah's condition immediately after delivery was very good ($\frac{1}{5}$ minute Apgar ratings 9 and 9). Her health from birth until the beginning of participation in this study had been generally good. The mother reported only occasions of jaundice on the fourth and fifth days of life, and otitis media at the sixth month. Sarah's older sister Emily was 2 years old when Sarah was born. The older sister was psychologically prepared for the birth of the sibling during the mother's pregnancy, and, according to the mother's report, she was "excited initially and then began sharing in caring routine" after Sarah was born. In the first 6 weeks of life, Sarah was sleeping in her parents' bedroom, after which she began to share the older sister's bedroom. At the beginning of the study, Sarah was still nursing, although the mother reported that she had just started her on solid foods.

Sarah's actions in the home environment were videotaped seven times. The first videotaping session (at child's age 6:07) did not include any episodes of feeding. The data reported in this section are derived from the remaining six sessions, which occurred at the following ages: (2) 8:01, (3) 12:11, (4) 14:26,

(5) 17:02, (6) 19:02, and (7) 21:28. After the seventh videotaping session, coverage of Sarah's development ended because of the family's relocation from the area.

7.6.2   The Time Distribution of Food-Contact Activities

The quantitative information relating to the child's time spent in different versions of contact with food is summarized in Table 7.3.

Longitudinal observations at Sarah's mealtime reveal a pattern of change from mother-controlled feeding, and child-controlled feeding without the use of utensils, to the child's feeding herself independently with a utensil, sometimes reverting back to the use of fingers and hands. As in the cases presented earlier, the time spent in mother–child joint action on feeding with a utensil (fork, spoon, or cup) occurred infrequently in general and was seen to decline after the control over utensils was delegated to the child. Unlike the other mothers presented, Sarah's mother was observed to nurse her at the earliest age (8:01). On the child's side, the fluctuations in the percentages of time spent in different food-contact actions reveal the relevance of situational specificity of the time allocation. When a spoon was made available (at 14:26 and 21:28), it was used in conjunction with finger-feeding. Likewise, when a fork was provided (12:11, 17:02, and 19:02), that utensil was used in conjunction with finger-feeding. Remembering that the form of forks given to toddlers makes them functionally similar to spoons, the motor skills used by the child while using either of those utensils can be observed to demonstrate similarity. However, what remains to be stressed in respect to the quantitative overview of the time allocation at mealtimes is the copresence of utensil-mediated and utensil-nonmediated feeding actions, together with a substantial amount of time spent on manipulation of the food, the utensil, or both.

7.6.3   Changes in the Mealtime Setting and the Development of Utensil Use

The longitudinal observation of Sarah's mealtimes revealed a general developmental pattern similar to those observed in the other two cases. However, the practical arrangements of Sarah's mealtimes excluded the usual framing device used in other families—during the videotaped sessions, Sarah was not observed to be put into a high chair (although the interview with the mother revealed that they sometimes do use a high chair—on those occasions when the family is having dinner together and they want to include Sarah). The rare use of a high chair, however, was supplemented by active use of other furniture or human child-restraining devices. Thus, the setting at session 2 (at age 8:01) was organized by the mother's holding the child on her lap while spoon-feeding was performed. During sessions 3 (12:11) and 4 (14:26), the child was observed sitting in a small wooden chair (with arm restraints) that was drawn close to a low table. This organization of the setting was functionally very similar to that of the high chair. During the remaining three sessions, the child

TABLE 7.3. Developmental Changes in Mealtime Food-Contact Time Allocations between Different Child-Centered Actions (Case: Sarah)

	Observed Mealtimes at Child's Age											
	8:01		12:11		14:26		17:02		19:02		21:28	
Action Category	f	%	f	%	f	%	f	%	f	%	f	%
M spoon-feeds CH	150	27.3	—	—	—	—	—	—	—	—	—	—
M nurses CH	163	29.6	—	—	—	—	—	—	—	—	—	—
CH finger-feeds	—	—	48	23.4	43	12.4	53	19.9	255	36.4	39	9.3
CH drinks (open cup)	—	—	—	—	97	28.0	94	35.2	69	9.8	49	11.7
CH fork-feeds	—	—	3	1.5	—	—	85	31.8	191	27.3	—	—
CH spoon-feeds	—	—	—	—	57	16.4	—	—	—	—	185	44.0
CH plays with food or utensils	237	43.1	121	59.0	138	39.8	28	10.5	160	22.9	131	31.2
M–CH joint action on food and utensil	—	—	33	16.1	12	3.4	7	2.6	25	3.6	16	3.8
Total	550		205		347		267		700		420	

M = mother; CH = child; f = frequency of 1-second time units.
Note: The observed mealtimes represent sessions 2 through 7. No videotaping of mealtime was done at session 1.

was observed to sit on a plastic chair (with no arm supports) at a plastic, round, children's table. This arrangement made it possible for the child to move out of, and back into, the chair without the help of the others. As will be evident from the description of the child's actions, Sarah made use of that freedom of action repeatedly during the mealtimes.

7.6.4   The Description of Actions at Mealtime

When Sarah was 8:01, session 2 took place in the morning, beginning at 9 o'clock. The mother is feeding yogurt to the child, who is sitting on the left side of the mother's lap, being constrained by the mother's left arm. The first two minutes of the mealtime (from 0.00 to 2.09) are filled by the mother's spoon-feeding the child, and adjusting the child. The mother is talking with the investigator about Sarah's behavior. The child is not observed to try to catch the spoon.

At 2.09, the first observed episode of the transfer of the spoon from the mother to the child is observed. The mother puts a plastic spoon (which she had been using for the feeding) into the child's left hand. The child transports the spoon's handle to her mouth, sucks the handle, then takes the handle out of her mouth, and manipulates the spoon bimanually. She then puts the spoon into her right hand, mouths the bowl part of the spoon, takes the spoon out of her mouth, manipulates it, and mouths the bowl part again. She then arches her back while the mother is adjusting her shoes; she fusses; the mother wipes the child's mouth with a cloth.

This episode is followed by the mother's carrying the child (on her arm) to the kitchen, washing an apple, and returning to the table. When the child is again sitting on the mother's lap at the table, the apple is given to her. At 4.39–4.49, the mother attempts to resume spoon-feeding, but the child holds the apple in such a way that it blocks the approach of the spoon. The mother abandons spoon-feeding attempts, and the child's mouthing of the apple continues; at 5.15, the apple gets loose from the child's hands and falls onto the floor. Between 5.15 and 5.31, the mother responds to the situation—she holds the child under her left arm, stands up, takes the fallen apple from the floor, carries it to the kitchen, washes it, returns to the table, and gives the apple back to the child. The child continues to mouth the apple. However, now the mother's right hand supports the apple, preventing it from falling.

At 6.20, the mother takes the apple away from the child and puts it on the table. The child fusses. The mother resumes spoon-feeding. By the end of the period (at 6.54), the child refuses to accept another spoonful. The mother responds by returning the apple to the child. The child holds and mouths it, while the mother assists with her right hand. Finally, the child releases the apple. The mother holds it and tries to get the child to take more of it, but the child does not.

The session then proceeds into nonmeal activity (at 7.42, the mother puts the child down onto the floor). After the child fusses and does not take interest in objects promoted by the mother, she is picked up again (at 8.12) and set to nurse (at 8.33). The nursing (at the table) lasts until 11.16. It is followed by another episode involving the apple. The mother removes the child from the breast, holds her on her arm, prepares food with the other hand. At 11.41, she sits down at the table, still holding the child on her arm. The child reaches out for the apple that is on the table and at 12.23 gets hold of it, but it drops onto the floor. The mother retrieves it from the floor and offers it to the child, who continues to handle the apple and mouth it, while the mother's right hand supports the apple. The meal ends at 12.29.

The data reported here are particularly interesting from the perspective of the beginning of the socialization of the child for accepting the adults' cultural meaning of "dirty." The two episodes in which the apple is dropped to the floor—at 5.15 to 5.31, and at 12.23 to 12.29—with the subsequent varied action by the mother, are relevant. In the first instance, the mother changes the whole situation (i.e., carrying the child to the kitchen sink while she is washing the fallen apple) in order to resume the previous activity state of the child (mouthing the apple). Note that after the fall of the apple the mother's hand is used to protect the apple from falling again. In the second episode, the mother is inconsistent in her action—no washing ritual is organized when the apple falls again. Nevertheless, the mother proceeds to use her right hand to prevent further drop of the apple.

The third videotaped meal session took place when Sarah was 12:11. The mealtime lasted for 4 minutes, 40 seconds, and was videotaped during the midday. The child is sitting at a low table in a chair (which is moved to the table so that she can't fall—practically a substitute for a high chair). Food is located in front of the child on a special "warming" plate that has three sections. The child holds a fork in her right hand while she finger-feeds herself banana pieces with her left hand. Her older sister is sitting in a similar chair at the same low table, facing Sarah.

At 0.35, the mother adds some banana pieces onto Sarah's plate. The child uses the fork in her right hand to mash them in the plate. At 0.51, the fork is transferred from the right to the left hand, and the child continues to manipulate food with her right hand. Thus far, the child's feeding process has been that of self-feeding. However, the situation changes into an episode of mother–child joint action. During the period 1.12–1.39, the mother intervenes, puts the fork into the child's right hand, and helps the child's hand to get food onto the fork. The mother then leaves it up to the child to finish the transport of food to the mouth. However, the child continues to manipulate food with the fork. The mother intervenes again, guiding the child's hand to get some food onto the fork, and to move the hand + fork to the child's mouth. Following the success, the child is left to her own resources again and continues to manipulate food on the plate with the fork. The mother intervenes again, helping the child to get food onto the fork, and leaving it to her to finish food transport. Sarah, however, does not use the fork. She switches to finger-feeding with her left hand while holding food on the fork in her right hand, up in the air above the level of her right ear.

This episode of mother–child joint action about the use of the fork in feeding is interesting as a example of the mother's promotion of the fork use (by setting up a ZPA) that persists over the period of the episode. The joint action occurs three times in a row. When the first "help" by the mother (reducing the child's freedom of movement to use of the fork) is not followed by the child's independent completion of the food-transport task, the mother intervenes again *and guides the child's hand (with the fork) to the mouth.* In the present terminology, the mother decreased the ZFM in the context of the child's action of food transport by eliminating alternative actions other than straight food-to-mouth transfer. However, immediately after that, the ZFM boundaries are rearranged again toward leaving greater degrees of freedom to the child's action. In the third joint action, the mother again only helped the child to get food onto the fork, leaving it up to the child to finish the action. Despite the fact that the child did not proceed along the expected way (and reverted to finger-feeding with the left hand while holding the fork up in the air with the right), the mother did not intervene another time.

The meal continues with the child's individual actions—she finger-feeds, manipulates food with the fork, finger-feeds again. Following an episode of the child's banging on the table with the fork, a brief (from 2.24 to 2.27) effort by the mother to guide the child to use the fork is then recorded: She takes the child's right hand (which already is holding the fork) and guides it back to the plate toward the food, releasing it there. The child continues to manipulate food on the plate, using both the right hand (with the fork) and the left hand. Finger-feeding is resumed by the child, and then she manipulates food on the plate with the fork.

At 3.15, the child tries to slide her body down under the table. The mother comes and adjusts her back into a sitting position on the chair. The mother talks to the older child, while the child slides herself again under the table. The mother takes her from the chair, sets her to stand on the floor, asks: "Are you all done? All done?" (moves the plate further away from the edge of the table). The child moves toward the table, looking at the plate, and grabs the edge of the plate with her left hand. The mother sets the child back onto the chair in a sitting position, brings the plate closer, and assists the child's right hand to get some food with the fork. The child's hand is then released. She goes on to manipulate food on the plate with the fork held in her right hand. In the brief period from 3.53 to 3.56, the child is observed to transport the fork, with some food, to her mouth on her own, with her right hand.

The end of the meal period is initiated by the child. At 3.56, she starts to slide down under the table. The mother comes and sets her to stand on the floor, removing the chair farther from the table. The child goes back to the chair and climbs up on it; the older sister comes over to the chair and assists her. The child stands up briefly on the chair, looking at the plate on the table. The table is moved away from the chair (at 4.40)—which serves as the actual event that marks the end of the meal. The child turns around and starts climbing down from the chair, with the mother's assistance.

Theoretically, the most interesting aspect of the observed actions at session 3 was the episodic organization of the mother–child joint action. Only occasionally did the mother intervene to promote the use of the fork and to assist the child in fork use by jointly performing a subpart of the action. It is clear that the child *can* accomplish the food transport with a fork at this age (as is evidenced by the single self-feeding instance with the fork at 3.53–3.56). It is equally clear that the mother is trying to promote the use of the fork more often than the child actually ends up using it. However, the mother's fork-promotion efforts were triggered under some specific conditions that occurred in the feeding situation: the child's manipulation of food with the fork (before the first joint-action episode that started at 1.12), beating on the table with the fork (before the second episode), and general body-position readjustment in the chair. Following these diversions from the feeding activity, which were wrought by the child's actions, the mother tried to guide the child toward the use of the fork in the context of her self-feeding action. However, the mother's guidance was not consistent in two of the three episodes, and in the third she quit her instruction efforts after three repetitions of the joint-action sequences with the fork.

The episodic nature of parent–child joint action that serves the promotion of new cultural motor (or cognitive) skills may be a general characteristic of child socialization processes in any culture. No time-urgency is involved in parents' efforts to get their children to master new skills. Instead, the parents may only episodically, on some (but not many) occasions, direct their children's actions toward the desired end results. Time and the cultural organization of the children's environments make such episodic guidance efforts functional, because the development of utensil use while eating is redundantly organized. If the parents do not guide their child to the use of the spoon or fork, but provide an example of the utensil use in their own everyday actions at mealtimes, the child will eventually be canalized into the use of these implements anyway.

The next videotaped meal (session 4) took place at a lunchtime when Sarah as 14:26. As in the previous session, the child is sitting at a small table on a small chair, holding a spoon in her left hand. The same warming-plate that was seen in the previous visit is in front of the child, on the table. From the very beginning of the meal, the child is observed to spoon-feed herself. The mother occasionally adjusts the plate (to bring it closer to the child) and says "M-mm" when the child's food transport to her mouth succeeds. After the initial 39 seconds of the mealtime, the child manipulates the food on the plate with the spoon in her left hand. She then drops the spoon onto the plate and proceeds to finger-feed with her left hand. During 0.47 to 1.01, the mother takes the spoon and rearranges the food on the plate. This is followed by a promotion effort. The mother takes the child's left hand, saying, "Here . . . ," puts the spoon in her left hand, and then releases the hand. The child manipulates food on the plate with the spoon for 7 seconds, after which she resumes spoon-feeding herself for 6 seconds. This is followed by unhurried eating efforts—the child sits with the spoon in her left hand, looking around. She then tries to get food from the corner of the plate with the spoon (no success), switches to getting it with fingers of her right hand (succeeds), and then transports the piece of food to her mouth with her right hand. The mother reenters the situation and adjusts the plate. The child drops the spoon into the plate.

At 1.56, a drinking episode starts (which lasts until 3.18). The child reaches out for the cup (no lid; standing on the left side—from the child's perspective—of the plate). The mother puts out her hand to safeguard the cup on its way to the child's mouth, then withdraws her hand. The child handles the cup with her left hand, holding it by the rim, then utilizes a bimanual grip to drink. Drinks.

Following the drinking episode, the mother adjusts the plate, then puts the spoon in the child's right hand. After than, the child spoon-feeds herself, and the mother vocalizes "M-mm!" after each successful food-transport action. The child tries to get food on the spoon, then loses some that falls onto the table. The child picks it up with left-hand fingers and takes it to her mouth. The meal proceeds with food manipulation by the child with the spoon, the mother's adjusting of the cup and plate, and the child's independent drinking and playing with the cup.

At 5.09, an interesting encounter between the mother and the child begins. The child takes a piece of food from the plate with her left hand and puts it into her mouth. She then takes another piece from the plate and drops it into the cup. The mother immediately interferes, saying: "No!" and moving the cup farther away from the child, after rescuing the piece of food from the cup. The child draws the cup closer by hand, and looks for the piece of food in it. She then takes the spoon from the plate with her left hand, looks at it, holds it up in air, drops it—it falls onto the floor—and looks after it. The mother picks it up and puts it back onto the plate, turning the plate so that the spoon's handle is close to the child.

During the time from 5.39 to 6.10, the child grabs the spoon and bangs with it on the plate, then takes a piece of food from the plate with her left hand and puts it into her mouth, continues banging on the plate with the spoon in her right hand, moves on to bang on the table. The mother intervenes when banging is extended to the table; she redirects the child's hand-with-spoon back to the plate. The child continues to bang the spoon on the plate, then again on the table. Finally, she abandons the spoon onto the plate and finger-feeds. At 6.20, she turns to her left side and looks down over the side of the chair, sliding (climbing) down from the chair. The mother moves in to safeguard, then picks her up and sets her down to stand on the floor. The child walks away to the living room, and the meal is over.

The description of session 4 reveals that, by this time, the child is in the habit of using the implement (this time, a spoon) on her own. The mother's efforts to promote the child's actions have also been transformed. Whereas some episodes are similar in structure to those in session 3 (e.g., putting the utensil into the child's hand), no longer is there any recurrence of these efforts, nor active help to the child in getting food onto the utensil. It is quite reasonable to expect that this feature of no-help in action depends strongly on conditions (e.g., nature of food, child's activity level, utensil used), so generalizations about absolute change of maternal guidance strategies may be unwarranted here.

Session 5 took place at morning breakfast when Sarah was 17:02. She is sitting at a little children's table made of plastic. This is a new table that has not been seen before (was purchased only recently). More importantly, she is sitting on a new plastic children's chair. The chair has no armrests and therefore does not constrain the child to stay at the table, but allows getting down/up easily. The food is on the table, in the warming-plate in front of the child. She manipulates food on the plate with a fork (in the right hand), and with her left hand.

The observation of session 5 is interesting for its actions relating to the event of dropping food onto the floor. The first episode of that kind takes place at 0.22–0.44. Apparently, some food has fallen onto the floor, so the child looks down and slides off the chair to stand up. The mother comes to her, picks up the food, *and puts it back onto the plate.*

The second episode is similar. Between 0.44 and 1.10, the child picks food onto the fork (in her right hand) and starts to transport it toward her mouth. The mouth opens in expectation of getting the food. The food, however, falls from the fork onto the floor. The child slides herself down onto the floor, picks up the food from the floor with her left hand, and puts it into her mouth. (The older sister comments: "Yucky.") The child returns to sit in the chair. The mother did not intervene in this episode.

The child continues to sit, manipulate food with the fork, fork-feed, and look around. The third episode involving the food dropped onto the floor begins at 1.43. The child slides herself down from the chair to stand on the floor. Picks up some food from the floor with her left hand, puts it into her mouth. (At the same time, the mother passes by to bring a cup to the older sister; puts it on the table.) The child looks at the mother, runs away from the table, and ends up sitting on the floor at the refrigerator (about 6 feet from the table). Gets up, runs back to the table. The mother helps her to sit down on the chair, sets a plastic cup (no handle, no lid) on the left of the plate (from the child's perspective), saying: "Here we go." The child drinks from the cup, using a bimanual hold, puts the cup back on the table where it was, and then plays with the cup.

The period from 2.51 to 4.16 includes the child's feeding herself with a fork, finger-feeding, manipulating food, and banging on the plate with her right hand. The fourth episode of handling the food dropped onto the floor emerges from the child's self-feeding efforts. The course of events was noted by the observer as follows:

4.16–4.36—The child takes food by fingers of right hand, manipulates food in hand, transports part of it to the mouth. Some food remains in hand when it is withdrawn from the mouth, gets loose and falls onto floor.

4.36–5.38—The child looks down at the fallen food. Slides down from chair, and while standing starts to push the fallen food with her foot, looking in the direction of the mother. Mother: "What are you doing there?" The child keeps pushing food on floor. The mother intervenes, saying: "Aeh-aeh! Pick it up and put in the garbage, O.K.!" Child picks the food up. Mother: "Put in the garbage." The child turns to the table and tries to put the picked-up food onto the plate. Mother intervenes: "No, aah-aah! Nn-nh!"; picks the pieces that the child had put back onto plate up again and puts them into child's right hand, directing child toward the garbage can. Child toddles over to the garbage can, opens it, throws the food into the can, and lets the garbage can cover fall down to close the can. Then opens the cover again, and begins to take something out from it (5.20). The mother intervenes, saying "Yakky," taking the objects/substance from child's hands and throwing it back into the can. At 5.27 picks up the child and takes her to the kitchen sink, where she washes the child's hands. Then puts the child back onto the floor.

This episode is followed by the child's returning to the table, resuming self-feeding and drinking, looking around. Another episode involving the garbage can follows, beginning at 7.28 (which is the actual endpoint of the meal). The child sits idle, then slides herself onto the floor and toddles to the garbage can (at 7.39). Opens the cover, looks inside, grasps something (which turns out to be a big piece of cardboard inside), takes it out. Mother shouts: "Sarah!" and rushes to the child; takes the object from her hands and throws it back into the can, saying: "No!" The mother closes the lid, picks up the child, goes to the kitchen sink and washes her hands there, then puts the child down.

In this session, the four episodes that involved the child's handling of food that had fallen onto the floor constitute an interesting sequence that allows us to trace the process of canalization of the child's actions with food in conjunction with the cultural meaning of "dirty." A certain variability in the mother's actions in the four episodes is evident. In the first episode, the mother herself returned the fallen piece of food onto the child's plate. In the second episode, the child picked up the food and put it into her mouth. This recurs during the third episode, during which the mother also does not intervene. Only during the fourth episode is the handling of the food from the floor moved beyond the ZFM boundary. The child—imitating how the mother acted in the first episode—tried to return the piece of food that she had picked up to the plate. However, the mother had already cognitively restructured the ZFM in the situation (evident in the verbal direction given to the child, to take the piece to the garbage). Thus, an action that previously had been within ZFM (returning food onto the plate, and/or eating it) was now outside the ZFM, while the mother set up the ZPA for getting the child to throw the food into the garbage. The child indeed acts as the mother wants her to—by going over to the garbage can and putting the piece of food in it. However, this action is followed by a separate action *concerning garbage*—the child opens the can again and starts to manipulate its content. The mother intervenes, and, at the end of *both* of the episodes involving garbage, the child is taken to the kitchen sink for washing her hands.

It is interesting to note the episodic nature of the mother's structuring of the situations where food is picked up from the floor. At times, the child can experience no change (the food is still edible after being on the floor), but at other times she is subjected to active and extensive coding of the cultural meaning of "dirty" in a similar context. Paradoxically, the *child* in episode 4 behaves in a consistent manner (by trying to put the food back onto the plate—which she observed the mother doing during episode 1!). In the given observational context, this is not surprising—the mother's task of taking care of two children, doing things in the kitchen, and interacting with the investigator make it only very natural that her observations of the child do not include all the occasions when some food falls onto the floor and the child picks it up. In contrast, the child in the meal setting is in a position to have a fuller observational experience of these situations. From the child's perspective, the mother's noninterference in some cases, and active interference in others, creates the demand of decision making under conditions of uncertainty.

Videotaping of Sarah's mealtime at session 6 took place at the child's age of 19:02 and included a midday meal. Sarah was observed sitting at the same plastic children's table as during session 5. An ordinary (adult) plate with food is in front of the child, on the table. The mother says: "Here's your fork" and puts it into the child's right hand. The child proceeds by sucking her fingers, holding the fork up in the air with the right hand, and looking at the camera. At 0.36, she tries to manipulate food on the plate with the fingers of the left hand, holding the fork up in the air with her right. Mother: "Can you use your fork? Use your fork, please!" The child looks in the direction of the mother and continues to manipulate food on the plate with her left hand. She then proceeds to finger-feed with the left hand, while holding the fork in her right hand in the air. When she reaches back with the left hand for more food, the mother comes close, points to the fork in the child's right hand, and says: "Use the fork, please!" The mother guides the child's right hand + fork to get some food onto the fork, then releases the child's hand. The child proceeds to use the fork in the right hand to transport food to the mouth. Then sits, idle. Continues intermittent finger-feeding of pieces of cheese and meatballs for the next 2 minutes (1.20–3.21).

The next joint-action episode takes place at 3.21–3.31. The child picks up a meatball in her left hand, looks in the direction of the mother. The mother comes and takes hold of the child's right hand (which holds the fork). She guides the child's left and right hands so that the fork in the right hand enters the meatball in the child's left hand. The mother then guides the child's right hand with fork + meatball to the child's mouth. The meatball is swallowed by the child. The mother guides the child's right hand-with-fork back to the plate. This is followed (during 3.31–4.30) by the child's independent actions. She picks up food with the fork (in her right hand), transports it halfway to her mouth, keeps the fork up in the air, then proceeds to mouth + swallow the food. Finger-feeding is repeated, accompanied by looking in the direction of the mother. At 4.30, a brief episode of food-drop and retrieval is observed. A piece of food falls from the child's fork onto the floor. The mother comes, picks it up, and returns it to the child's plate. The child uses the fork to feed herself.

An episode of drinking follows (at 4.42–5.15). The child moves the fork from right hand to left hand, reaches out in the direction of the mother with her right hand (toward her right), vocalizes. Mother: "Juice, please?" and places a plastic open cup into the child's right hand. The child takes the cup and proceeds to drink from it unimanually (right hand). After drinking, she stretches the right hand with cup toward the mother, who takes the cup.

An episode of complex motor action involving food and utensil follows immediately after the drinking episode (during 5.15 to 5.51). The child takes a meatball from the plate with her right hand and manipulates it. Then she exchanges hands: the fork from the left hand is put into the right, and the meatball into the left. Holding the meatball steady in the left hand, she tries to push the fork with the right to get it into the meatball (all this happens in the air, above the plate). She does not succeed and ends up transporting the meatball to her mouth with her left hand, while holding the fork in her right hand (up in the air). She mouths the meatball but cannot be seen to bite it, takes it out of her mouth with the left hand, and resumes the effort with the right hand to get the fork into the meatball (again held up in the air by the left; then the left hand is lowered to the table and gets support from it). In this way, she succeeds in getting the fork into the meatball, and then transports it to the mouth with the fork + right hand. She mouths the meatball-on-fork, bites, takes it into her mouth, and removes the fork from her mouth.

The meal proceeds with the child manipulating the fork and food, looking around, feeding herself by hand and by fork. At 8.55, she takes a big piece of food onto the fork with her right hand, transports it to her mouth, and mouths it. Mother: "You can use your fingers with that." The child puts the food from her mouth back onto the plate, uses her left hand to get the piece off the fork and onto the plate. Mother: "Here you go." Child looks at mother. Mother: "You can pick that up with your fingers." Looks at the mother. Mother: "Use your hand." The child takes the piece again onto the fork. Mother: "You don't have to use a fork for that." The child transports the piece to her mouth with the fork and puts it *all* in her mouth. The mother intervenes immediately, calling out: "Oh, oh! Here!" and takes the piece out of the child's mouth. She cuts it up on the child's plate, then sets one small piece onto the fork, puts it into the child's hand, and releases hand + fork + food. The child takes an additional piece onto the fork and transports it toward her mouth, but part of it falls down on its way. The child looks down while mouthing the fork. The mother comes, picks up the fallen piece, and puts it back onto the plate. Sarah continues to mouth the fork, then goes on to feed herself with the fork, manipulate food, look around, and hit the plate with the fork. This continues intermittently until 11.46, when the child gets down from the chair. The mother comes and wipes her hands and mouth. The child then gets the cup from the mother, who says: "Use both hands!" while giving the cup to her. The child drinks while standing on the floor. The meal is over at 13.10.

The observations during session 6 are noteworthy in two respects. First, developmentally, the transition of the mother's action-promotion efforts from direct joint action with the child to distal communication and then to verbal means is nicely demonstrated. The mother was observed giving verbal suggestions from a distance, and intervening only when the child happened to act in a potentially dangerous way (putting an excessively big piece of food into her mouth). Second, the child (at 5.15–5.51) displayed a sequence of complex motor action of a synthetic kind, relating the utensil to the food under difficult problem-solving conditions that required precise dosage of force applied bimanually on the fork and the food.

The last session (7) when Sarah was videotaped during a mealtime took place at her age of 21:28 and involved a morning meal. The child is again at the small plastic table (as in sessions 5 and 6); in front of her is a big soup plate (with cereal). A spoon is in the plate (ready for right-hand grasp). The child holds a blanket by both hands, and pulls it up to cover her lap.

At 0.08, the child takes the spoon in her right hand; the mother assists by drawing the plate closer to the child on the table. The child spoon-feeds, then holds the spoon in her right hand, up in the air at shoulder level. She looks at the camera and in the direction of her mother; no action. She then proceeds with intermittent spoon-feeding, finger-feeding, looking around, mouthing her hand, and manipulating food on the plate.

At 4.00, an episode of food-drop begins. The child spoon-feeds with her right hand. Some cereal falls onto her shirt. The child abandons the spoon on the plate, raises her shirt with both hands (exposing the breast region), vocalizes, looks around, mouths her left hand. The mother brings a napkin, gives it into the child's right hand, adjusts the food on plate with a spoon, and sets the spoon onto the plate. The child wipes the table on both sides of the plate with the napkin (which is in her right hand), while holding her left hand in her mouth, then looks at camera. She stretches out her right hand with the napkin in the direction of the mother. The mother comes, takes the napkin, wipes the child's face; the child coughs, looks at her left hand, gives it to the mother (who wipes it), examines it after wiping. The mother proceeds to wipe the child's lap while the child watches. The episode is over by 6.00, when the child grabs the spoon with her right hand, spoon-feeds; the older sister sings and the child looks around, holding the spoon in midair. This is followed by sitting (holding the spoon in midair with the right hand), looking around, spoon-feeding, mouthing the spoon, and stirring the food in the plate with the spoon.

At 8.26, she has difficulty getting more food onto the spoon. She abandons the spoon on the table (on the right side) and uses both hands to lift the plate to the mouth and drink. She puts the plate back on the table, then mouths both hands, and at 9.00 resumes spoon-feeding.

Another episode relating to cleaning starts at 9.24. The mother comes and wipes the child's mouth with a napkin. The child looks in the mother's direction, stretches out the right hand-with-spoon, and vocalizes. The mother takes the spoon, puts it into the plate, and hands a napkin into the child's right hand. The child wipes her mouth herself, then abandons the napkin on the table, and proceeds to drink (getting the cup from the mother at 9.58).

The child's actions at the table come to a close at 10.25. She gets down, holding the cup in her right hand, and, dragging the blanket along with her left hand, walks over to the kitchen oven. She stands in front of the mother, who wipes her mouth and face. The meal is over at 10.52.

7.7   CONCLUSIONS: LONGITUDINAL ANALYSIS OF INDIVIDUAL CHILDREN'S ACTIONS AT MEALTIMES

The three longitudinal cases analyzed in this chapter revealed quite clearly (a) the general direction in the development of independent self-feeding (shared in all of the cases), and (b) the idiosyncratic particular joint-action forms that were observed at different mealtimes and that changed over time. The quantitative analyses of the time that each of the three children spent in contact with food revealed a fact that, at the first instance, may seem paradoxical: The adult–child joint action in meal settings that is related to the children's learning of the use of culture-given utensils *is a remarkably rare phenomenon during everyday meals,* at least in the cases described. Nevertheless, the same impression also emerges from other cases (not reported here) of contemporary American children of middle-class backgrounds. However, the quantitative time distribution data are illusionary in a very informative way, demonstrating again the notion that was well understood by Lewin (1931): *The rare (rather than frequent) structured psychological phenomena may be of decisive relevance for children's development.* During mealtimes at any age (e.g., see Newson & Newson, 1968) the children's ZFM may include the use of hands and fingers, which are perfectly sufficient for transporting food to the mouth. The extension of the hand by attaching to it a utensil provided by the culture is part of the socialization of children that is redundantly guaranteed by the universal use of these utensils in the society. As a result, the task of canalizing children toward utensil use takes the form of *episodic direction* of the child's action by an adult (or older sibling), rather than that of an intensive instruction session. The conditions for triggering the adults' episodic acting in the ZPA of utensil use can be highly variable, relating both to the child's action at the time (e.g., a child banging on a tray with a spoon, followed by the mother's redirection of hand + spoon to food on a plate) and to the adult's goals and time resources (e.g., a mother in a hurry in the morning has simply no time to promote spoon use to her toddler and knows well indeed that the child can learn to use the spoon if given time). This episodic nature of canalization of child development in real-life settings may seem to lead to inconsistency in parental child-oriented actions and is definitely different from the picture of children's learning process that is presented by the majority of learning theorists. These theorists, however, may have been looking at the phenomena as those are reduced to their elements. They have tried to find explanations for children's development in particular, and frequently occurring behavior-reinforcement adjacencies in which the structured and culturally meaningful nature of the contexts in which behavior occurs have been overlooked. In contrast, cultural canalization of child development may be adequately described by a sequence of variable and largely nonrepetitive events that take place in the child's life and provide impetus for further individual action of the child within the culturally set constraints that make up the structure of the settings. In that way, rare but subjectively important events in humans' lives may have longer-term impact on their future, whereas the majority of high-frequency recurrent behaviors or life events become automatic and lose their canalizing relevance for a person's development.

7.8 SUMMARY

This chapter linked the theoretical system outlined in previous chapters with one particular example of empirical investigation—a longitudinal study of infants' and toddlers' action development in their everyday meal situations. Meal situations are a good example of settings that are socially organized so as to attain both immediate (e.g., getting the child fed) and longer-term goals (e.g., canalizing the child toward culturally appropriate ways of acting with food and with the utensils used to keep or transport the food).

The empirical longitudinal case observations of the mealtime situation give evidence for the gradual transition from fully parent-controlled feeding (the most extreme example of that would be the parent's spoon-feeding of the infant through the whole meal) to fully child-controlled actions with the relevant utensils for feeding. The general control of the mealtime organization remains with the parent—she decides what food is given, when, in conjunction with what utensils, and how the child's demands are to be reacted to. The children's actions—which sometimes leave the impression of being unconstrained—remain independently dependent on the setting that the parent has constructed in accordance with parental goals and cultural knowledge. Parental active participation in canalization of children's actions in a structured setting like mealtime is often a rare occasion that emerges when necessary—that is, at times when the child may cross a ZFM boundary or try to renegotiate it, or when the parent sets herself the goal of promoting a particular new action to the child (ZPA). As was evident from the longitudinal description of the mealtimes in individual cases, the particular parent–child–environment relationships can be highly variable, depending on the circumstances, whereas the general process by which the parents regulate child–environment relationships and canalize their future development in some (again, variable in their particulars) directions is built along similar lines. The empirical analyses presented in this chapter provide one (but not the only) possible way in which the relatively abstract ideas of cultural-historical thinking in psychology can be transposed from the level of theory to the domain of direct empirical work at deriving meaningful data from the richness and fluidity of phenomenology of child development.

8

Cultural Autoregulation of the Self: Semiotic Mediation of the Intrapsychological Realm

As is obvious from the previous chapters, the core of this book is dedicated to the constraining of human actions in early childhood. Yet the theoretical system of constraining needs to be extended to the intrapsychological realm of human development as well (Valsiner, 1997a). Like the externally visible cases of action-constraining (described in detail in Chapters 6 and 7), the intrapsychological constraining entails semiotic organizers—signs. However, the functioning of such signs is not immediately observable in action itself. Still, it is clear from introspective evidence that it guides the whole of human activity through setting it up in meaningful ways.

Two issues are relevant for making sense of cultural regulation of the human intrapsychological domain. First, there is the question of *sociogenetic origins* of human intrapsychological functions. This takes the form of focus on internalization and externalization processes in a person's encounters with the world. Second, there is the issue of the *relative autonomy* of the person's intrapsychological processes from their immediate interpersonal (social) contexts. This is the issue of the "dependent independence" (see 5.4) that persons display in any social setting. Relative autonomy of the person—or of "the self"—is made possible by semiotic mechanisms of psychological distancing of the self relative to the given context. That distancing takes many forms and allows for emergence of goal-oriented planning of actions that transcend the demands of the given setting. For the latter, semiotic means make it possible for humans to act on the basis of *future desired* (i.e., meaningful) *objectives,* transcending the given context in ways constrained by the meanings imbued in fantasy, assumed social roles, and pretend play.

8.1   INTERNALIZATION AND EXTERNALIZATION

In contemporary cultural psychology, we often hear about the "mutual constitution" of persons and social worlds. For instance:

> [One can describe] social reality . . . as participating in the creation of [a] subject's functioning, and not as an outside factor. The subject is part of (or participates in) social reality. Self-regulation is assumed to be created *on the basis of* inter-regulations. (Góes, 1994, p. 126, italics added)

Much of contemporary cultural psychology is caught in the web of the "outside–inside" distinction. That distinction has two facets: (a) whether it is made in terms of inclusive or exclusive separation of the two (see 2.1), and (b) whether it is conceptualized with or without considering time. Where there is exclusive separation of the person and the social world without viewing that relation as time-based, a dualistic picture surely emerges. The picture is very different if the inside is viewed as systemically interdependent with the outside in time—microgenetic or ontogenetic. This latter inclusive form of separation allows one to theoretically maintain the intrapsychological processes as distinct from their interpsychological counterparts. Thus, it becomes possible to consider the emergence of the "inner" on the basis of the "outer." We need to conceptualize the process by which this emergence takes place.

The process by which this self-regulation emerges is internalization/externalization. The use of these parallel-process terms is similar to the unity of Piaget's assimilation/accommodation terminology (see 4.2.3)—both processes work as parts of the same whole. Thus, internalization can be observed only via some form of externalization, and externalization results feed into a further internalization process. The use of internalization/externalization terminology entails a clear decision to separate the person and the social world in inclusive ways that allow us to look at the process of their relation. That process has clear *directionality* in that some cultural "materials" are "brought inward" from the outside, and others are taken outward from the intrapsychological sphere. The use of internalization/externalization concepts would be axiomatically rendered impossible if the inner/outer distinction is denied. Given the axiomatic nature of such denial (e.g., by theorists who prefer an "appropriation" concept), there is no need to dispute the use of one or another set of axioms. Here, the axiom of person–environment as an inclusively separated duality is accepted, and hence the question of internalization/externalization processes is legitimized. Furthermore, it is claimed that both of these processes are active and constructive.

8.1.1   Selective and Constructive Ways of Being Active

Human beings can be active in two ways. First, they can actively *select* from the myriad of fixed (pregiven) cultural messages. Any view of internalization that defines the active role of a person as an agent who *takes choices* assumes that view. Likewise, a person who is assumed to "have preferences" is basically selecting from among different pregiven options. Preferences are subjective choices that already exist, whereas the issue of being active in a developmental sense requires a corollary question: How have these preferences emerged in the first place?

The selection process may be active, but *it is not necessarily constructive.* The person as an active choice-taker is not developing beyond the set of choices that the social world has laid out in front of him or her. That set of choices can be very large, in which case it is possible to build one's development entirely on the choice-taking within a hyperlarge set, without ever creating a new one. The distinction that constructivity introduces is that between a finite and an open set of choices: If the person can create new choices (= the set is open), then we can talk of the constructive nature of choice-*making.*

The picture is further complicated if we look at the person's active role from the standpoint of personal life course. *Relative to one's personal past,* taking choices from a socially given set is a version of creating novelty. If I buy a new computer program (which I cannot modify myself), it is a novel event, relative to my personal past experiences with other computer programs. This would be the case if the ZPD (as elaborated in Chapter 5) were to constitute (at any time) a set in which all members (for time $t + 1$) were well known to the developing person at time t. In this case, the person can select one of the "ready" versions from the ZPD, and this would amount to novel development, relative to the ZFM/ZPA system at t.

There are, of course, serious theoretical difficulties with that assumption, as could be seen from the argument in Chapters 3 (3.7.8) and 5 (5.9). Only part of the ZPD may be knowable in advance as a crisp set of next-moment possibilities, and much of it is not clearly set up. It includes subzones of an ill-defined nature, as well as unknown (surprising) parts. The same is true for the contemporaneous ZFM and ZPA concepts. Hence, only in a special case can one describe the active notion of *person* as a selection of given options; the general case should be described differently. Here, the assumptions of hyper-game theory are helpful. When dealing with the unknown strategies of the other player (in this case, the social world), the person's best option is to construct his or her own new strategies.

Thus, the second way of being active is by *constructing new choices*—for oneself and for others. This can be a general view that subordinates the selection notion; in any new setting, the person can select some suggested way of acting, feeling, or thinking, or can also create a new one. The new one is thus a result of personal psychological synthesis (along the lines of Vygotsky, 1971), which may entail a selection as a subcase (or a "short cut," when such selection opportunity fits). There may be some psychological "economy" in using a readily suggested choice (yet in a necessarily new context), rather than creating a new one. Yet the core of the process is construction rather than selection, because the now-available choices were created by somebody at some time.

8.1.2 Internalization and Externalization as Constructive Processes

Internalization and externalization involve a reciprocal cyclical process within which "personal sense" (in Vygotsky's sense—a complex of personally signified unique experiences; see 4.5) leads the construction of the meanings that are made available in the interpersonal domain. Internalization is the process by which meanings that relate to phenomena and that are suggested for the individual by "social others" who pursue their personal goals while assuming social roles, are "brought over" into the individual's intrapsychological system. That bringing-over process entails constructive modification of the brought-over material by the person. The meanings change into the complex of personal senses (in Vygotsky's terms), and acquire their unique personal organization. The reciprocal process of externalization connotes activities by which the once-social—but now personal—set of meanings is constructively moved into novel contexts within the social environment (Valsiner & Lawrence, 1996). The semiotic code used in interpsychological communication is translated into a different code for the intrapersonal communication. As a result, the person constantly "imports" meanings, changes them (through his or her personal sense construction), and "exports" these newly reorganized meanings to the domain of social action. This process is similar to the different forms of interdependence of "voices of the mind" that are elaborated by Wertsch (1990, 1991, 1995) and Bandlamudi (1994) along the lines previously indicated by Mikhail Bakhtin.

8.1.3 Phenomenology of Internalization, and Its Social Guidance

It is obvious that any information about internalization can be available via two possible channels: (a) the person's introspective experience, and (b) some product of externalization. In fact, any reporting of introspective experience is also a form of externalization. Introspective methods can be used at levels of development at which reflection on one's intrapsychological processes is possible (e.g., Crawford, Kippax, Onyx, Gault, & Benton, 1992). In the case of young children, we are limited to viewing externalization of internalized phenomena in action contexts.

In adulthood, any phenomenon of self-reflexive thought—feeling about oneself, about one's action—is an example of the phenomenological reality of internalization. Intrapsychological dialogues, or songs that "sing in one's head," are likewise of such a nature. In ontogeny, the internalization and externalization of musical materials precedes the same processes operating on verbal materials (Baldwin, 1893). The power of rhythmic input of a social kind into persons' psychological systems is utilized in settings of purposeful socialization, such as in Quaranic pedagogy:

> A Muslim should be able to read the Quaran [Koran] even without being able to understand the words, because the ability to read the Quaran itself has been known to evoke in people a response to the teachings of Islam which sociologically has been very valuable. Beyond this most of those people will hardly go,

but *provided they learn in their childhood to respond to the music of Arabic consonants and vowels, and to the rhythms of the Quaran,* they will continue throughout their lives to have an emotional attachment to it. (Husain & Ashraf, quoted in Wagner, 1983, pp. 185–186; italics added)

Similar reliance on guiding efforts by social institutions to penetrate the internalization sphere of persons can be found in abundance in modern TV commercials and in many forms of political symbolic actions. Through the construction of combined (musical–verbal–visual) messages, the socioinstitutional communicator attempts to "break through" the relative autonomy of the target person, and succeed in inserting a suggested message into the internalization/externalization system. The person is dependently independent in relation to the social world—he or she can ignore most of the social suggestions arriving from outside, yet at the same time these messages exist, and are related in some ways.

Aside from the obvious goal orientation of social guidance of internalization for *accepting* suggested messages, there exists a parallel effort to limit the person's acceptance of alternative ones, and a promotion of making the accepted message separated from specific parts of the personal sense system. For instance, political, religious, or advertising messages entail promotion of the absolute truthfulness of the message, thus downgrading the possibility of doubt. An example of the remarkable success of such efforts can be found in the demonstrations (in cross-cultural studies) that subjects' experience with formal schooling is the major factor that leads to their acceptance of syllogistic reasoning tasks *as those are given* by the investigator (Luria, 1976). Thus, consider the following syllogism:

All X are Y.

This is X.

———————

This is Y.

The uncritical acceptance of the major premise ("All X are Y"), which the formal schooling system has succeeded in promoting for persons' internalization/externalization system, makes "correct solutions" of this syllogism possible, and, usually, the efforts of solution proceed without doubt. The absence of doubt in the adequacy of the major premise can vary on the basis of specific meanings inserted into the syllogism (compare two extremes: "All metals sink in water" versus "All Estonians belong to an inferior race"). Yet, for those meaning domains that do not encounter personal-senseful rejection of the content of the major premise, the formal schooling institution has largely succeeded in establishing a form of direct "pipeline" into the schooled persons' intrapsychological system.

Social guidance of a person's self toward some state is always simultaneously an effort to guide it away from the opposite state. One can claim that an important control strategy (by social institutions) over individual persons is the attempt to reduce the dialogicality of self-construction processes to some monological form, eliminating the opposite "voice." These efforts exist in social constructions of national identity (Wertsch, 1997). Hence, all canalization of a developmental process—by oneself or a social other—leads simultaneously toward knowledge *and* ignorance. The latter has an important role to play in society and in personal worlds (Moore & Tumin, 1949), being an important counterpart of the former. Thus, it is possible to guide developing children toward hyperactive participation in different "activity settings," and thus lead to possible underdevelopment of the intrapsychological domain. At the other extreme, it is possible to orient the developing persons toward intrapsychological meditation, in the context of a school built around the philosophy of Krishnamurti:

> Every evening, all the pupils and house-parents are expected to watch the sunset for above twenty minutes from an appointed place, located at a slight elevation with a clear view of the sun setting behind three hills. . . . Pupils and teachers sit on the ground, or the rocks surrounding the area, facing the hills. A bell is rung to announce the commencement of the event. Some pupils sit with closed eyes while most of them rivet their gaze on the three hills in the distance in complete silence. (Thapan, 1986, p. 208)

Similar promotion of moments for internal mediation can be found in other societies and institutional contexts. Here, the target of promotion is intrapsychological meditation, and children are guided away from external action. No social institution can guarantee that, by its actual nature, the intrapsychological meditation is of a kind that is ideologically desired. The actual content remains in the decision sphere of the persons who mediate. Yet the external activity setting is organized for a focus on meditation, and the ritual meditation is carried out daily.

Ontogenetically, the socialization efforts by social institutions can be observed to lead to persons' construction of different versions of control beliefs in person–environment relations (Rothbaum, Weisz, & Snyder, 1982). These control beliefs—whether "primary" (an individual personal agent acting upon a context) or "secondary" (an individual personal agent aligning self with a powerful other)—can belong to the repertoire of personal worldviews constructed by internalization/externalization processes and turned into relatively permanent dispositions. These control beliefs can be viewed as internal semiotic mediators of a person's participation in situated activity contexts.

8.1.4   Activity Theories as Partial Solutions to the Question of Human Development

From the examples on social guidance of internalization, it is possible to see how activity-theoretic perspectives on human development (see 6.1) cover only the external part of psychological development, leaving the psychological processes of the acting person without a central role. These theoretical accounts elaborate the contexts in which the person is embedded (e.g., Bronfenbrenner, 1979, 1989; Bronfenbrenner & Crouter, 1983; Ratner, 1991, 1996; Rogoff, 1990). It is true that all human development is organized by "activity settings" in accordance with cultural meanings, but these are only a part of the whole system of human development. The internalization/externalization concept complements the focus of activity theories by providing an emphasis on the constructive processes within the interchange between the intrapsychological and interpsychological spheres of phenomena. This is in line with the open-system nature of development (3.7.1). Activity theories, in and by themselves, cannot represent an adequate solution to the problems of human development because they fuse the notion of person ↔ environment relations with the undifferentiated notion of "activity" and overlook the intrapsychological coconstruction of the activity by the meaning-making agent (see Josephs, 1996b).

The developing person is viewed by activity theories as "participating in" different activity settings, yet the variety of personal forms in which that participation takes place depends on the personal construction by the participants. The latter are always in some version of distanced relations with the activity settings. Hence, analysis of external activity settings is only a *precursor* for understanding actual activity settings, rather than a full-fledged solution.

8.2   INTERNALIZATION/EXTERNALIZATION AND PSYCHOLOGICAL DISTANCING

Constructive internalization and externalization necessarily leads to some form of psychological distancing. This takes numerous forms. First, it entails the intrapsychological counterpositioning of personal and socially lived-through experiences in the "here-and-now" setting. While being an active participant in such a setting, the person may reflect on the ongoing events in ways that are not immersed in the actions by which the participation takes place. Any reflections on one's action (e.g., any intrapsychological question: "What am I doing here and now?") constitute a form of psychological distancing that allows the person to transcend the present setting *while remaining* a participating actor.

Distancing also takes different, more permanent forms. In ontogeny, one can observe the differentiation of the child's intrapsychological world, which is kept hidden from adults' efforts to peep into it. All persons (as well as social institutions) develop different forms of knowledge that are kept "confidential" or "secret" in various forms, and hence are not immediately available to others in activity contexts. The development of phenomena of secrecy has relevance for human development (Simmel, 1906) because it serves as the basis from which social participation can be contemplated. In general, any personal decision not to disclose one's private thoughts or feelings in an activity setting indicates the functioning of distancing mechanisms. Such a person is mostly a *peripheral* participant in the myriad of activity settings in which he or she participates, and is buffered against purposeful social invasions into personal privacy by various distancing mechanisms.

The person can regulate his or her own immediate perception and cognition through semiotic mechanisms of psychological distancing. The notion of psychological distancing is not new in psychology (Bullough, 1912), and its uses continues in our present time (Sigel, 1993). In Bullough's description of "psychical distance," a contrast emerges between immediate relating with a context and a person's subjective separation of self from the context. Both immediacy and distancing are affect-laden; it could be said that, thanks to the affective personal-sense construction, it becomes possible for the person to achieve *both* immediacy and distancing:

> Distance does not imply an impersonal, purely intellectually interested relation. . . . On the contrary, it describes a *personal* relation, often highly emotionally coloured, but *of a peculiar character*. Its peculiarity lies in that the personal character of the relation has been, so to speak, filtered. It has been cleared of the practical, concrete nature of its appeal, without, however, thereby losing its original constitution. (Bullough, 1912, p. 91)

Different persons in the same context necessarily construct their personal— and discrepant (from one another)—meaningfulness of the context, using semiotic means of different levels of generalization. For instance, using Bullough's example, consider the experiencing of fog at sea:

> . . . for most people . . . is an experience of acute unpleasantness. Apart from the physical annoyance and remoter forms of discomfort such as delays, it is apt to produce feelings of peculiar anxiety, fears of invisible dangers, strains of watching and listening for distance and unlocalised signals. The listless movements of the ship and her warning calls soon tell upon the nerves of the passengers; and that special, expectant, tacit anxiety, and nervousness, always associated with this experience, make a fog the dreaded terror of the sea (all the more terrifying because of its very silence and gentleness) for the expert seafarer no less than for the ignorant landsman.
>
> Nevertheless, a fog at sea can be a source of intense relish and enjoyment. Abstract from the experience of the sea fog, for the moment, its danger and practical unpleasantness, just as everyone in the enjoyment of a mountain-climb disregards its physical labour and its danger (though, it is not denied, these may incidentally enter into the enjoyment and enhance it); direct the attention to the features "objectively" constituting the phenomenon—the veil surrounding you with an opaqueness as of transparent milk, blurring the outline of things and distorting their shapes into weird grotesqueness . . . ; note the

curious creamy smoothness of the water, hypocritically denying as it were any suggestion of danger; and, above all, the strange solitude and remoteness from the world, as it can be found only on the highest mountain tops: and the experience may acquire, in its uncanny mingling of repose and terror, a flavour of such concentrated poignancy and delight as to contrast sharply with the blind and distempered anxiety of its other aspects. This contrast, often emerging with startling suddenness, is like a momentary switching on of some new current, or of the passing ray of a brighter light, illuminating the outlook upon perhaps the most ordinary and familiar objects . . . . (Bullough, 1912, pp. 88–89)

Bullough's introspective example—the transformation of the immediate (i.e., the dangers involved in the immediate action context) personal sense of a person on a ship deck in a fog (or climbing a mountain) into an overwhelming feeling of aesthetic pleasure—reflects the role of affective-semiotic processes in their constructive action. The mechanism of distancing is seen as tension between what is and what is not. It is here that the "as-if" psychological construction mechanisms (*à la* Vaihinger) can be seen to be at work in human psychological worlds. Distancing entails comparison of the here-and-now with a desired ideal (future) state, or with a hypothetical alternative (opposite) state.

8.2.1   Modulation of Distancing

The dynamic side of psychological distancing as a semiotic self-regulation device entails constant modulation of the person's relation with the given context—moving between various forms of immediacy and intermediacy. The internalization and externalization processes make it possible to set up intrapsychological constraints (via semiotic means) that change the whole personal sense of some ongoing action. Thus, when a mother feeds her child during a mealtime, her construction of how much food "is enough" for her child guides and constrains her actions. Yet, at any moment, she can distance herself from the immediate feeding process by constructing the notion that "The child actively resists me," and then proceeding in the direction of either intensifying action ("I must get him to stop resisting") or de-intensifying it ("I don't want to fight with my child; let him eat as much as he wants"). The intrapsychological self-regulation by the mother thus can move her—in the same setting as for a mealtime—to be even more actively involved in her actions, or distanced from the given setting. Furthermore, any train of thought or feeling that proceeds in the mother's intrapsychological field while performing the routine actions of feeding, and is totally unconnected from the action task, indicates the power of semiotic means in distancing.

8.3   CREATING *AS-IF* STRUCTURES BY INTERNALIZATION/EXTERNALIZATION

From very minimal externally given signs, human beings can construct elaborate intrapsychological scenarios via the internalization process. These scenarios may stand as possible desired contexts for future action. They entail abstraction of the specific meanings from the given context.

Continuing with the example of a mother feeding her child (and arriving at the notion of "The child actively resists me"), the abstraction process can bring out a generalization about the child's character (e.g., "My child knows how to stand out for himself" or "My child has difficult character"). Such leaps in inference then become semiotic organizers of future actions relative to the child, well outside of the given context (mealtimes). Furthermore, in the given context, these generalizations constitute cases of *as-if* structures of meaningful organization of the given setting. Thus, via abstraction, the mother creates her own meaning structure as if her child has that difficult character, and may then act in ways different from her primary (immediate) goal orientation (i.e., get the child fed). The latter changes in the sphere of actions are products of externalization of the constructed as-if meaning structure. All abstract concepts that cannot be defined but are applied constantly to concrete settings—such as "love," "friendship," "fairness," "justice," and so on—are semiotic vehicles for flavoring the given concrete situation by including the overriding generic meaning. The recontextualization of these abstracted meanings constitutes creation of an as-if structure of the situation. The same phenomenon—for example, an effort by the mother, at the end of a mealtime, to get "one more spoonful" of food into the child's digestive system—can be viewed extremely differently by outside observers who recontextualize their abstracted meanings to the given specific context. Thus, some of these observers would view that episode as if it reflects the "great love" of the mother for her child; others, as a case of a mother's "dominance"; and still others, as "good feeding tactics." The as-if nature of any interpretation of a setting is made possible by the role of the observers, who constantly modify their position relative to the observed phenomenon (the process of *attunement;* see Rommetveit, 1992). All meaning structures therefore are related to the objects they attempt to make sense of, on the one hand, and to the meaning-makers' goal orientations and positions, on the other. Communication becomes a process of coordinating these different positions through the semiotic messages. Hence, the crucial feature of communication is the discrepancy between different positions of the intercommunicating persons, rather than the "shared" basis for mutual sense making.

8.3.1   Karl Bühler's Theory of Communication

Bühler's Organon Model is the central concept of all of his language philosophy (Bühler, 1990, pp. 34–39). It is based on the idea that three functions are involved in the process of communication. First, there exists an external state of affairs—some reality—that the two partners, Sender and Receiver, want to communicate about. That reality can have *representation* through the use of language, yet never in the exact form of that reality because language does not map reality in an isomorphic way. Second, the Sender's subjective understanding, together with the desired goals, guides the Sender to create some form of message. This creation of the message is an *externalization*. Third, after the message has been created and becomes available to the Receiver, it undergoes active *reconstruction* in accordance with the Receiver's own position toward the reality, the Sender, and the relation of the message to his or her goals. Thus, the Receiver and Sender necessarily hold different positions relative to the same object, and they construct (create) and reconstruct the message differently.

This discrepancy leads to the functions of abstraction in the process of communication. This problem was explicitly treated by Bühler in the Organon Model (Bühler, 1990, pp. 52–54). The *principle of abstractive relevance* was his answer to the question of what happens to the communicative message when it has been externalized by one partner and becomes internalized by another. According to Bühler, the externalized message is not the same one that becomes internalized (because of the constructive nature of the internalization and externalization processes). The discrepancy between them creates the tension necessary for internalization, which leads to the construction of abstraction from the message in the process.

This tension entails immediate "fielding" (= placing into a field context) of any new receivable message at (and across) three levels, or representational fields, that are mutually interdependent. The *primary* representational field is the field (place) that the speech sign "brings with itself" when it is actualized. The sign, given its form, evokes a particular field of relations within which its meaningfulness can be further constructed by the interpreter. Bühler's example is that of a geographical map—a reference to some city or route evokes (as its necessary context) *the whole reference system of the map* (with all of its representational parts). Any answer to a specific geographic question can be given only within this reference system. The primary field is the cognitive semantic field, within which the representational nature of the signs is contextualized within a system of appropriate opposites and neighboring concepts.

The *secondary* representational field entails the field of personal memories and productive fantasies that the speech act evokes in the coconstructive hearer. This representational field frees the construction of the hearer's understanding from the immediate here-and-now, and leads to the development of internalized control functions of the speech signs in the personal world of the hearer. The person brings past experiences to the personal senses that are fielded within the secondary field. It can be said that the secondary field relates the personal past with the present, via fielding a particular sign in the realm of subjective lived-through experiences. The contrast between the primary and secondary fields can be considered in parallel with the distinction between *semantic* (= Bühler's primary field) and *episodic* (= Bühler's secondary field) kinds of memory (Tulving, 1972).

The *tertiary* representational field entails the syntactic schemata that are generated in the direction of the nearest possible future. The Receiver must be made to understand the specific intentions of the Sender. Thus, the tertiary field is a starting point for the "speech act theory," which operates with pragmatics of language use—that is, the usual example of "Can you pass the salt?"

This sentence, when viewed at the different field levels, can lead to three different answers by the Receiver:

1. "Yes, I can"—a statement about the Receiver's ability, without corresponding action (PRIMARY field).
2. "Why are you doubting my abilities again?"—here, the Receiver links the here-and-now event with some past event, flavored by a sense of personal offense (SECONDARY field).
3. "Yes, here it is"—(the Receiver has understood the goal and acted accordingly) (TERTIARY field).

The crucial feature of the system is the coordination of three representational fields. A particular message becomes internalized by the Receiver by *some version* of coordination of the three fields. The simplest forms of coordination are those that exclude at least one field from the structure. Thus, it is possible to overlook the elocutionary function of the message (TERTIARY field) and respond to the message only by coordinating the other two fields. Or, if the Receiver does not know the language used by the Sender, the PRIMARY field may be missing in the interpretation, but the message can still be fielded in undifferentiated secondary ("He seems to be friendly as always") and tertiary ("He seems to want something") fields. And, of course, the secondary field can be absent (e.g., when meeting a person with whom one does not have a common history of personal encounters).

Rommetveit's pet example of "Mr. Smith" may be used here as an elaboration of how the three-field structure (à la Bühler) functions when it entails a person's perception of the perspectives of different social others, referring to the same ongoing event. In this scene, Mr. Smith is mowing the lawn in his yard/garden, on a Saturday morning, and his wife, Mrs. Smith, is communicating with different persons over the telephone:

> What is going on in Mr. Smith's garden . . . may under different dialogically established background conditions be made sense of in a variety of different ways and brought into language by expressions such as MOW THE LAWN, BEAUTIFY THE GARDEN, ENGAGE IN PHYSICAL EXERCISE, WORK, ENGAGE IN LEISURE-TIME ACTIVITY, and NOT WORK. A neighbour prying into the miserable relations of the Smiths may even tell us that he "sees" Mr. Smith AVOID THE COMPANY OF HIS WIFE. And this may indeed also be the way in which Mr. Smith, left alone in the kitchen with the morning coffee in front of her, makes sense of what is going on. . . . We hear her say, "He is once more avoiding a confronta . . . ." At that moment her bitter voice is drowned by the sound of telephone, and she picks up the receiver. It is her friend Betty who is calling, and Betty initiates their chat by asking: "That lazy husband of yours, is he still in bed?" To which Mrs. Smith answers: "No,

"Mr. Smith is WORKING this morning, he is mowing the lawn."
A short time afterwards Mrs. Smith receives another call, this time from Mr. Jones, who, she tacitly takes for granted . . . wants to find out whether Mr. Smith is free to go fishing with him. He asks: "Is your husband working this morning?" And Mrs. Smith answers: "No,

"Mr. Smith is NOT WORKING this morning, he is mowing the lawn."

(Rommetveit, 1992, pp. 25–26)

The changes of position in Mrs. Smith's three reflections upon Mr. Smith's activity result from coordination of the secondary and tertiary fields with the specific fielding on the primary field (AVOIDING—WORKING—NOT WORKING). Depending on her assumptions about the positions of the others—Betty; Mr. Jones—relative to the given activity of Mr. Smith, Mrs. Smith changes her representation of the event in a cardinal way. The intersubjectivity created in these telephone conversations was organized by subjective projection of the intentions of the others (tertiary field) upon the response message.

8.3.2   From Intersubjectivity to Subjectivities

What follows from Bühler's Organon Model is that the communicator necessarily fails in his or her attempts to communicate a particular message exactly as it is constructed. The Receiver will field it in some hierarchical/representational field structure, and will abstract new nuances of personal sense from the message. Communication is thus an effort to overcome misunderstanding (Robinson, 1988), rather than a "sharing" of joint semiotic reference system.

Surely there exists *some* common understanding between the communicating persons—a field of mutually constructed intersubjectivity (Rommetveit, 1979a, 1979b, 1992). Yet that intersubjectivity is of different kinds (Markova, 1994), entailing *as-if* and *striven-for* forms. The former is set up by interaction partners to attempt to construct the latter.

The relation between as-if and striven-for forms of intersubjectivity yields a mismatch between the communicator's and the recipient's versions of the present state of intersubjectivity. If the as-if form is set up with a notion of commonality assumed on both sides, then the striven-for forms would differ for both partners. Both of these forms can be semiotically organized by abstracted ill-defined meanings (e.g., a mother: "My child and I *are so close* and *I want us* to stay this way"—the as-if form of the intersubjectivity claim is related to its maintenance in the striven-for case as stated by the mother; nothing is stated for the child).

The canalizing function of all semiotic mediation guarantees the eternally fuzzy nature of meanings used in setting up both the as-if and striven-for intersubjectivity. Language entails *approximate* suggestions—constraints on feeling and thinking—which, when used, lead to personal abstractions and their recontextualizations. Language is not a static set of forms; it is a constantly changing semiotic mediating reservoir for human life:

> Language does not flow along tranquilly in a ready-made bed; at every turn it must dig out its channel anew—and it is this living flow which at every step produces new and more highly developed forms. Herein lies its true and fundamental strength, but from the standpoint of the concept and of conceptual thought also its weakness. For the concept in the strict sense tends to set a goal for this surge and flow; it demands stability and unambiguousness. In its *being* it seeks to transcend and negate everything that language must tolerate in its becoming. (Cassirer, 1957, p. 336)

The function of meanings as both disambiguating and ambiguating the given context of here-and-now is important for a constraining-based theory of human development. By abstracting a general meaning from a specific context, human beings create powerful means for transfer of meanings to novel contexts. These meanings act as preconstrainers of novel settings, whatever those may be like.

8.4   CONCEPTUAL UNIVERSALS AS ABSTRACTED ILL-DEFINED SEMIOTIC MEANS

Construction of universals necessarily starts from an axiomatic basis. Here I would like to posit the universality (for humans) of a semiotic–psychological process—that of *constant construction and reconstruction of collective-cultural meanings and personal-cultural senses* of the experienced world. I assume that this process constitutes the universal psychological basis for all cultural phenomena in society and personal worlds.

The main problem of human meaning-making is that of immateriality and incorporeality of the signs used in the mental processes, through which real interpersonal actions are mediated. Again, the focus is on the vagueness of the semiotic tools. Boesch (1991, p. 124) has used the notion of fantasm to refer to personally meaningful overarching ego-world relationships (e.g., general terms such as *happiness, order,* and *self-realization,* when filled in with personal cultural sense, become what Boesch called *fantasms*). Because the construction of such fantasms is an individual–experiential process, the exact complex field of connotations of those fantasms cannot be verified. Yet they are of crucial relevance in the regulation of a person's actions, anticipations of the future, and understanding of the world. The persons who construct fantasms make use of common general terms. Thus, through personal-cultural fantasms, people reach out to assume intersubjectivity, and construct myths as a result. Myths are externalized and socially shared fantasms that feed into further construction of fantasms.

Discourse about universal concepts is based on the assumption that behind the observable heterogeneity of phenomena there exists some "kernel" of a universal kind, which could be revealed in scientific study. This hope for finding such an ontological kernel has been around for a long time (see Jahoda, 1993, for an intellectual history of cultural psychology), and was well expressed over a century ago by Adolf Bastian:

> What a tremendous and exciting advance could be made if we could assemble an index, or statistic, of ideas which showed that the same number of psychological elements (like cells of a plant) is circulating in regular and uniform rotation in the heads of all people, and that this is so for all times and places! . . . There are surprising analogies in mythological thoughts and world views amid both the fetishism of the savage and the aesthetics of the civilized, and in metaphysical ideas, in abstract philosophies and the mystical raptures of believers: in all these, after removing the flesh of local and temporal variations in language and idiom, we encounter the same small number of psychological kernels. Thought is merely psychological arithmetic, and arithmetic's laws are immutable; each ethnic group will arrive at the same answer for its life, although of course the results will appear different according to the varying perfection of the mode of operation. (Bastian, 1860, quoted in Koepping, 1983, p. 180)

As can be seen here, cultural psychology as such as been ontological in its scope—it has been looking for the immutable psychological universals. From the perspective of a developmentalist, theoretical difficulties (as well as practical lack of success) in the 19th century in revealing such immutable kernels are no surprise. If human psychological functions are assumed to develop, both ontogenetically and through cultural history, and to lead to constant innovation of meaning systems by abstraction processes, then no immutable kernels can be found. Instead, the investigators are confronted with constantly novel forms of general meanings.

8.4.1   Universal Concepts in Action: A Reanalysis of Twin Infanticide

The notion of "action of spirits" is a widespread generalization used, in a variety of forms, in religious systems all through human history. Thus, the differential constraining of thinking, feeling, and acting by this universal concept could provide an example of the ways in which human life (and death) is culturally regulated by *omniscopous* concepts (Aphek & Tobin, 1990).

Different kinds of assumed "spirits" (or deities; see Horton, 1967) can be separately marked as benevolent or malevolent. If a specific action (event) is an unusual happening in everyday life (e.g., the birth of twins, or of otherwise unusual children), and some immediate action concerning the event is needed (the specific sense prescribes action rather than nonaction), then the same universal systemic mechanism leads to a number of possible scenarios of action and their interpretations:

1. Possible scenario: Because a twin birth indicates the effects of malevolent spirits, the twins must be killed. (Possible alternative action:

Instead of killing the twins, devise special rituals that will neutralize the effects of malevolent spirits.)

2. Possible scenario: Because a twin birth indicates the effects of benevolent spirits, the twins must be kept alive at all costs, and protected (by way of appropriate amulets, body markings, or rituals) against possible attacks by malevolent spirits.

3. Possible scenario: Although it was believed long ago that a twin birth was related to the action of spirits, we now do not believe that "old stuff." Hence, we treat and care for the twins as we would any other children.

4. Possible scenario: Anyone who believes in the role of spirits in leading to the birth of twins is stupid. Modern medicine has simple explanations for why twins are born, and requires that we keep all children alive and healthy. The twins, like any other children, should be well cared for, vaccinated against diseases, and played with.

The same general hierarchical structure is present in all four scenarios, regardless of the described outcomes of action: killing the twins (scenario 1), specially preserving them (scenario 2), or treating them as any other children in accordance with modern medical beliefs (scenario 3). In scenarios 3 and 4 (in contrast with 1 and 2), the belief in a spirit world becomes attenuated and is replaced by the acceptance of modern medical beliefs about infant care.

This example tells us that there exists a modulated process of recontextualization of universal terms into the reasoning processes about general life events. Real-life examples of such recontextualization exist in the empirical evidence about legal discourse during abortion trials in the United States (Danet, 1980), as well as contemporary discourse analysis of interpersonal negotiations (Edwards, 1995). Human internalization/externalization processes work when concrete and abstract levels of semiotic mediation are linked with concrete activity contexts. At times, the activity context is directly organized by the results of such linking; at other times, the semiotic mediation works in disjunction with the activity contexts.

8.5   ACCESS TO INTERNALIZATION/EXTERNALIZATION PROCESSES

One of the technical reasons for the notion of internalization/externalization is the need for methods that can access the relevant phenomena to derive data from them. The use of introspection as an adequate route to intrapsychological processes has been consensually blocked and stigmatized in the psychology of the 20th century. Even in versions of methods that *de facto* make use of introspective tendencies—such as "thinking-aloud" techniques in cognitive psychology, or rating scales (which work on the basis of subjects' minimal superficial introspection)—theoretical conceptualization of the relevance of introspection has been rare or absent.

Any access to processes of internalization is possible only through the revival and further development of introspective methods. Intramental processes are accessible only if their externalization is the target of investigation. The externalization can be based on subjects' verbal or nonverbal (e.g., graphic) efforts to report their intrapsychological phenomena. A similar kind of externalized reporting is involved in any effort to study intrapsychological issues via their externalization by action (e.g., children's pretend- or role-play). In any case, both the speech and the action-based information sources provide the investigator with the hurdle of interpretation: how one can adequately conceive the data that are constructed by the subject without ever gaining direct access to the phenomena → data-derivation process.

In William James's terms, the *stream of consciousness* of any person is immediately available only to the person who is constructing it in the course of one's experiencing. As researchers, our access to it is the same as that of our subjects—our own intrapsychological phenomenology appears to us in the flow of our experiencing, and is mediated by our intrapsychological semiotic system (that of "personal sense"). Any effort to bring it to the attention of another—or even to myself as I reflect and "feel through" whatever is happening in my own stream of experiences—constitutes an act of externalization. In this respect, my semiotically constructed image of my own intrapsychological events is already a result of externalization, even if I never communicate it to anyone else.

Thus, in general terms, all information about internalization/externalization processes depends on our interpretation of our own or others' already interpreted (i.e., externalized) accounts of the intrapsychological processes. As a semiotic construction, that second-level interpretation may be organized in terms of necessary processes that can be assumed to take place, that is, in a sequence that moves from the person's "periphery" toward the "center" of the subjective world. A model of concentric layers of the person, surrounding the "center" and the boundaries that have to be overcome, has been proposed by Kurt Lewin in his comparison of personal conduct styles in the United States and Germany (Lewin, 1936b).

8.6 A LAMINAL MODEL OF INTERNALIZATION/EXTERNALIZATION

If we follow Lewin's concentric boundaries depiction in setting the stage for viewing internalization/externalization processes, we are creating a *laminal* model of the intrapsychological world. The internalization process needs to pass through two layers (laminae)—layers I and II in Figure 8.1—before reaching the "inner" sphere (layer III). The externalization process needs to proceed correspondingly, in the reverse direction.

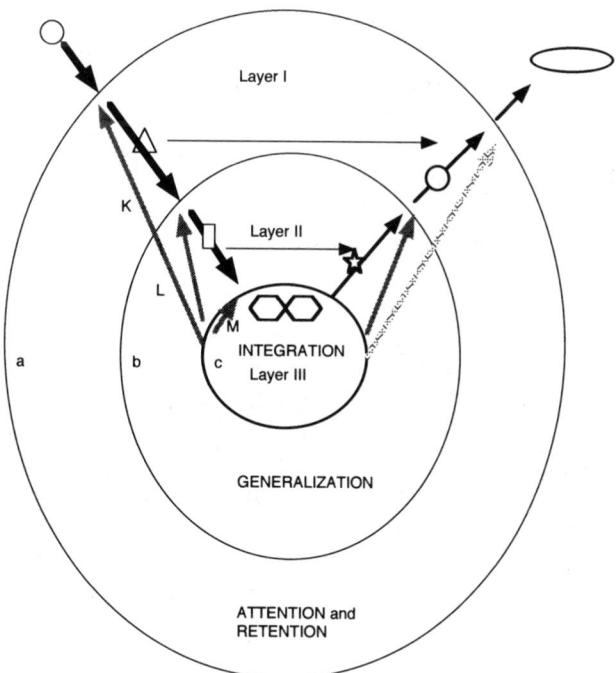

FIGURE 8.1.   A multilayer model of internalization and externalization.

In the process, three boundaries—a, b, and c—are to be penetrated by the internalization process. Because the process is constructive, the "inner core" of the person regulates each of the boundary crossings by a specific social (semiotic) regulating device. Boundary a can be selectively open for some communicative messages from the external social world, while remaining closed for others. The specific "boundary regulator"—K—recognizes those messages that the person is ready to internalize, and ignores or blocks others.

Once a message is brought into layer I, it becomes potentially internalizable. It is noticed as a message by the intrapsychological system, but not integrated into it. The latter requires opening of boundary b for the message—by way of the social regulator, L. Given the latter's action, the message takes on a new form; in Layer II, the message becomes generalized (see Bühler's focus, above). This generalization in and by itself is not yet part of the structured intrapsychological world (layer III), but it creates the basis for its potential integration. It must be let through boundary c under the action of social regulator M. If that happens, the generalized and reconstructed message becomes integrated into the structure of the intrapsychological phenomena (in layer III).

This hypothetical model of internalization/externalization is a sequentially structured parallel to Piaget's assimilation/accommodation model (see 4.2.3). The boundary between "inside" and "outside" is reconstructed here into a sequence of three boundaries—a, b, and c—that need to be passed before external communicative messages can become integrated into the internal structure. Layers I and II describe the realm of contact between the person and the external social world. Directionality in the processes is strictly assumed. The incoming message is acted on by the social regulators. Internalization then entails coconstructive passing of boundary a → layer I → boundary b → layer II → boundary c, in that order. Externalization entails the opposite order.

The final result of internalization is the process of hierarchical integration of the transformed incoming message into the structure of intrapsychological phenomena. This puts into its place Heinz Werner's focus on differentiation (see 4.4). However, we cannot be specific about the content of layer III, other than positing the existence of some form of hierarchy of the intrapsychological phenomena.

The model advanced here has been utilized in research on children's development of understanding of religious miracles (Josephs & Wolgast, 1996). Its value is in the structural elaboration of the domain of contact between a person and the "social voices" that the person encounters. Furthermore, the general talk of the person who is active in the internalization process is being replaced by positing concrete actions on the transformed incoming messages by specific social regulation devices that operate as boundary maintainers and "openers." However, in general, the scheme remains an abstract construction that needs specification.

8.6.1   Phenomena in Layer I: Retention of "Brought-In" Material

After a message has passed boundary a and has been transported into layer I, it is maintained in the attention sphere of the intrapsychological system, but its fate in layer I may be variable. It can be maintained and slowly attenuated. Alternatively, it can be maintained in its steady state or even escalated. Yet none of these developments would guarantee that the message is taken further (into layer II). That transformation depends on the action of the social regulation device (L).

Phenomena that can be viewed as located in layer I are most widespread in our introspective worlds. For example, a tune (or phrase) from a TV commercial may keep reverberating in the mind for a long time. Any effort to suppress the silly reverberation may be ineffective. That material is not brought to any form of generalization (which would indicate its layer II state), nor is it ever integrated into an intrapsychological personal-sense structure. After some time, the tune or phrase "dies out," yet the memory of suffering from the futile efforts to suppress it can be reactivated later. Thus, the message was clearly noticed, maintained, and limited to the outermost layer of the internalization/externalization system.

8.6.2 Phenomena in Layer II: Generalization without Personal Integration

If a message from layer I is brought to layer II, it is observable by the act of generalization in the introspective sphere. Yet the generalization remains just that—it is not integrated into the personal-sense system. It remains an abstract generalization, without being added to the person's feeling tone. It amounts to a rational concept formation (*à la* Vygotsky), which is not linked with the person's core of intersubjectivity. For instance, a concrete story (which was brought into layer I) of how my next-door neighbor was mugged by a gang of youngsters whom I have attended to has been present in my internal sphere since I heard the story, and I let it pass into layer II by my intrapersonal generalization: "Young people these days are very inconsiderate and aggressive." I can externalize this generalization in many different versions—as a generalization; as a summary or retelling of my neighbor's story; or as an ironic comment while watching some youngsters in the street (who may be actually hanging out there in a perfectly peaceful manner). Thus, I have constructed a generalization, but it is not integrated into my personal-sense system—it is not yet "populated" with my personal feelings, which would be the case if the generalization were to reach the integration layer (III). Nevertheless, I may become involved in many rational discussions—within myself or with others—about the downfall of the mores of the youngsters in our time.

Most of ordinary human interactions on issues of politics, business, and psychology may be of the layer II type. Discussion of abstract problems that are sufficiently far from one's own core self may be an activity that seems to create an image of the person's participation in social issues. Yet that participation remains at the level of abstract discourse. Thus, discussions of persons who are located very far from the dangers of some lethal virus (Ebola, or HIV) can, in abstract terms, look like efforts to participate in the solution of a "problem" (= another abstraction); yet, through that discourse, the issue involved is *not* allowed to become integrated with the personal-sense system (layer III). In contrast, if any of the eager talkers actually encounters the problem, it may be taken into the layer III realm, and the person may find it too difficult to externalize any (or some) of the personal-sense aspects of the newly integrated phenomenon.

Two important aspects follow from this elaboration of internalization layers. First, the glorification of the abstract thinking "in concepts" (à la Vygotsky) as the highest level of human reasoning processes looks very different from this point of view. It constitutes an *intermediate* level of internalization and can be followed by a highly subjective synthesis of ideas that takes place in the form of pseudo-concepts or complexes (in Vygotsky's terminology), rather than in terms of concepts. Second, the relativity of a person's participation in external activity contexts (i.e., moving between central and peripheral roles in a joint action setting) has its counterpart in the intrapsychological sphere. Here, it is organized by way of maintaining different kinds of internalized materials in different layers, and selectively (and episodically) letting them become integrated into the personal-sense system. The person is a *relative*—sometimes peripheral, sometimes central—*participant in one's own life,* thanks to the differentiated system of internalization/externalization.

8.6.3   Phenomena in Layer III: Another Look at Bakhtin's Ideas

In layer III, the personal-sense structure transforms the permeating message with the help of the person's subjectivity, and the integrated incoming message acquires a clearly affective flavor. From the perspective of the laminal model, the oft-quoted key idea of Mikhail Bakhtin may acquire a new role. The usual quote from Bakhtin (used to emphasize the unity of the social and the personal in the appropriation process) is:

> The word of language [*slovo iazyka,* in Russian] is [a] half-alien [*chuzoye*—not belonging to me and unknown, in Russian] word. It becomes "one's own" when the speaker inhabits [*naselit,* in Russian] it with his intention, with his accent, masters [*ovladeet,* in Russian] the word, brings it to bear upon his meaningful and expressive strivings. Until that moment of appropriation [*prisvoenie,* in Russian], the word is not existing in neutral and faceless language (as the speaker does not take the word from a dictionary!), but [it exists] on the lips of others, in alien contexts, in service of others' intentions: from here it has to be taken and made into one's own. (Bakhtin, 1934/1975, p. 106)

The word "exists on the lips of others"; it constitutes an externalized version of the words by these others. As for the given person, the word is always "half-alien"; it is simultaneously *also constructed to be one's own,* in that "other half." The speaker "inhabits" it with his or her "intention," and, through that inhabiting, masters or takes control over the word. The Russian *prisvoenie* (in contrast to appropriation) carries a two-directional connotation: some external agent can make the person accept something (e.g., an award—*prisvoenie nagrady*), and the person can attribute some quality to an external aspect of the world, making that aspect thus his or her own.

This double-directedness of *prisvoenie* works well within the present laminal model of internalization/externalization. The person is involved in *prisvoenie* exactly by way of internalization/externalization. The populating of the word can be seen as the subjective integration of the incoming message into the personal-sense system in layer III.

The externalization process proceeds in direct complementarity with the internalization process. Different layers can enter into a dialogue—some material that is by now "populated with intention" (à la Bakhtin) is taken from layer III outward to layer II. If, after talking much about the sad incident of my neighbor's being mugged, and blaming modern-day youngsters for being aggressive, I myself am mugged by some adolescents, I might integrate the generic talk of before (layer II) with my lived-through experience, and my talk about youngsters' aggressivity may become "populated by my personal sense" and highly affective in its tone. That may become translated into more vehement general talk about youngsters (layer II), but now a dialogue exists between layer II and layer III phenomena in my intrapsychological system.

8.7 CONCLUSION: SEMIOTIC REGULATION OF ONESELF

The aim of this chapter has been to demonstrate how the constraining processes described elsewhere in this book could be seen to operate in the intrapsychological sphere of a person. Furthermore, it is assumed that this intrapsychological constraining emerges in human ontogeny on the basis of interpersonal constraining. This elaborates the usual "sociogenetic law" of cultural-historical psychology—that is, the move from mostly interpsychological to mostly intrapsychological regulation of human action in ontogeny. Both levels of regulation remain functional and complementary as the intrapsychological level develops and takes over the control. They can be combined to create situations of *redundant* control over a person's conduct (i.e., both external and internal social regulators constrain the person's conduct in the same direction). When operating in a discordant fashion, one of the control levels makes it possible to counteract constraining at the other. Thus, the most general intrapsychological social regulator—"my own will"—can override an elaborate set of external constrains upon conduct, and lets the person resist the canalization efforts of others, and force the external constraint systems to change. Or, in another solution, the intrapsychological system allows the person to provide a personal interpretation of the external constraint system that neutralizes its canalization efforts, and to be psychologically distanced from the goal-directed efforts of the "social others." The emergence of an intrapsychological self-constraining system guarantees the person's dependent independence even in situations where the external actions of the person are maximally limited. The co-construction of one's development includes ways to reorganize any constraint system at both interpsychological and intrapsychological levels. In that, the principle of "bounded indeterminacy" gains its general theoretical value.

9

Conclusions: "Bounded Variability" in Human Psychological Development, and the Methodology for Its Study

This book is theoretical and methodological in its intention, and it has illustrated a selected phenomenon (child–adult joint actions at mealtimes). As was pointed out in Chapter 1 (see Figure 1.1), the research process in any science traverses the complex issues of phenomena, method, data, theory, and general assumptions, making up a dynamic process along the lines of a "wheel" of methodology. Methodology is the general systemic structure of researchers' efforts to construct new knowledge about phenomena, from their own constructed intellectual perspective. All knowledge exists relative to the particular ways in which that methodology cycle operates in the approach used by a particular researcher or a collective research tradition. However, the particular researcher's construction of the methodology cycle is further embedded in the "symbolic market" of ideas in a given society, which is in a particular state of historical development. Still, symbolic markets do not create new ideas; they can only facilitate the emergence (or nonemergence) of new ideas by way of setting up selective and promotional orientations for scientists' thinking. This book has outlined the general methodology of the study of human development, building on well-established theoretical directions within the social sciences and developmental biology.

9.1 DEVELOPMENTAL PSYCHOLOGY AND ITS CONSTRAINING BY SOCIETIES

Social sciences at large, and psychology in particular, have developed in ways that have made them highly vulnerable to the expectations of the society. On the one hand, psychology as a science strives to transcend the sociocultural context of any given society. By constructing general knowledge about psychological functions, it reaches the status of a basic science. However, on the other hand, psychology is—independently—dependent on the social institutional background of the society, because it takes over, from other social institutions, a number of functions in that society. Thus, fortune telling, soul healing, provision of communally meaningful explanations, legitimization for social actions, and many other functions that have been the realm of other institutions, may be taken over by psychology.

This establishment of psychology as a social institution within a society leads to a state of affairs where it cannot transcend its own sociocultural context, because success in that context amounts to a lessening of the immediate social value. The discipline is caught within a debilitating paradox: *In order to arrive at basic knowledge, it would have to diminish its immediate social usefulness* (i.e., potential for application). However, *as long as it tries to build up knowledge on the basis of applied concerns* (which are relevant for its success in any society), *it cannot advance its basic knowledge.* The ethos of psychology's image as a socially helpful science makes it helpless in its own epistemological advancement.

Developmental psychology is subject to this paradox, along with its nondevelopmental counterpart. Societal canalization of its focus can already be seen in what is included in its structure and what is not. Thus, developmental psychology has often been viewed as a synonym for *child psychology*—thus leaving out investigation of psychological processes in the early ontogenies of other species. Since the 1970s, the study of the elderly has been added to the area—not without a connection to the fact that European and North American societies have discovered the economic problems of care for the elderly. The study of old age has been labeled *life-span* developmental psychology, yet full coverage of the whole span (e.g., the middle-age years) has been absent. The invention of the label *life-course* developmental psychology adds some focus on the middle years, yet it leads researchers toward the formal trajectories of life, rather than toward study of the complexity of human beings' personal subjective experiences. Despite the "discursive turn" in contemporary social sciences, the focus on subjective construction (and reconstruction) of experience has been rarely under study. A phenomenological turn in psychology is still to reappear on the symbolic market of our knowledge-construction enterprise in developmental psychology.

Similar social selectivity is present when preferred topics are suggested for researchers' study. Thus, no reason other than the social market value of the topic of children's attachment to adults would make attachment research a core topic for developmental psychology. In fact, in its actual implementation (e.g., "predictions" of future outcomes from early childhood "attachment types"), this research tradition has nothing in common with the study of development (as outlined in this book).

All in all, developmental psychology as a discipline is constantly being re-constructed on the "symbolic market" of a given society at a given time. Its focus usually remains either culture-specific or centered on the social demands of a given (domineering) society at a given time. The general societal value given to children by adults sets up the easy constraining of the focus of developmental psychology on one (childhood) rather than another (adulthood) part of life-course development. Furthermore, the initial position from which the developmental psychologist is expected to look at child development is also pre-given by societal constraining of what is the "right" way to assume that children's development takes place. Thus, themes like "secure attachment" leading to harmonious life (in contrast to "insecure attachment" which is expected to lead to "problems"), or the whole psychology of adolescence, written from the point of view of adults, are examples of such canalization.

The potential danger inherent in such canalization is in the discipline's becoming a "colonial" (or "neo-colonial") version of a social science, serving the purposes of the powerful (at the given time) societies in working out their relationships with the less powerful ones. Thus, exportation of the knowhow of child psychology from one society to another may evolve into a social missionary effort to change the other society's ways of dealing with children, turning the recipient society toward the ways used and cherished in the "donor" society at the given time. As the relations of (economic) power between societies change, cultural inventions from the previous recipient society may become imported into the previous donor (e.g., in organizational management practices, the efforts to use "Japanese management styles" in U.S. enterprises). Uses of child psychology's culturally constructed knowledge may take more time to reach a phase of reverse importation. Yet, in one scenario, instead of trying to export from Occidental to Oriental societies the focus on "making children independent," we may see efforts to import Chinese "parental strategies" that promote the development of "filial piety" into the United States in the future.

The focus in this book has been on a basic science of development that takes the cultural-historical embeddedness of both developing children and developing developmental psychology into account. Hence, it is considered important to transcend most of the "practical" or "applied" issues of dealing with children, in favor of a generic account of human development within (and through) culture. The empirical phenomena selected here for illustration were from the most ordinary, everyday realms of human life. Yet it is in exactly the most inconspicuous settings that development is somehow taking place. This book has been an exercise of elaborating one possible way in which that "somehow" can be elaborated.

9.2 COMPLEXITY OF CHILDREN'S PSYCHOLOGICAL DEVELOPMENT

The elegance of child development is in its complex organization, which is so closely intertwined with the cultural environment that it easily remains unaffected by the occasional fads in education and child psychology. That robust reality of child–environment relationships guarantees sufficiently adequate socialization of children in the majority of cultures and at any historical period.

Furthermore, ideas *about* children's development have themselves emerged in cultural-historical contexts. Therefore, any theoretical explanation of children's development is a by-product of human cultural history. It is a constructed explanatory system—created by adults who have been curious about the children for one or another reason. Ideas that have enjoyed wide popularity among child psychologists and educators at different times have happened to match with the cultural background of adults in the first place. Only as a result of purposeful socialization of children under the guidance of adults do these ideas become transferred to those whom they are thought to represent—the children themselves. Children within a culture are socialized to become adults within that culture. If the science of psychology, including child psychology, is a differentiated part of the adults' culture, children are socialized to accept it as such. That socialization may involve both the conceptual (e.g., what kinds of ideas "make sense" when used as explanations in psychology) and applied aspects. In the latter case, former children are socialized toward asking child psychologists certain kinds of questions, and refraining from expecting answers to other questions from these specialists.

Undoubtedly, there exist vastly different ways in which child psychologists have become part of their cultures in different areas of the world. In some, child psychologists may enjoy the status of "experts" in the eyes of parents who may turn to them for advice—often to find out that their questions have no simple answers. In others, psychologists may be in the process of establishing their "expert" role in fierce competition with the knowhow of folk psychology of children that is available to parents through the mothers' social networks and the availability of folk remedies and curers. Whatever is the status of child psychology in a particular society at this time, child psychologists are involved in complicated societal discourse about their own role in the culture. Quite often, psychologists' thinking is carried away by that (undoubtedly important) participation in such discourse, and the more fundamental scientific foundations of their views of child development are not analyzed in sufficient depth by them.

It was the goal of this author, pursued all through this book, to make available to the interested reader an analysis of the process of child development that recognizes the inevitable dependence of that process on the one hand, and is general enough to transcend the limits of any particular culture on the other. This goal made it necessary to address issues at different levels of generality, ranging from the most abstract (philosophical) axioms (labeled "basic assumptions" in this book) to a detailed presentation of empirical observations from a very limited action context (children's mealtimes) and age range (toddlerhood) in a cultural context (that of the contemporary middle class in the United States of America) that is highly atypical as compared with the majority of cultures around the world.

9.3   THE ROLE OF HISTORY OF DEVELOPMENTAL IDEAS

A central tenet in the theory elaborated in this book is its historical connected-
ness of ideas. The reader may have noticed clear preference for connecting the
ideas used in this theory with their historical predecessors—rather than with
our "contemporary literature." Despite the frequent use of the label "developmental psychology" in the contemporary literature on child psychology, little
explicit interest in the theoretical analysis of development as a process seems to
be widespread in contemporary psychology. The earlier theoretical efforts to
analyze development as a process—by James Mark Baldwin, Jean Piaget, Lev
Vygotsky, Mikhail Basov, Heinz Werner, and others—have been either largely
forgotten, or transformed into an interest in the outcomes of development.

The reason for such pervasive loss of interest in the process of development
stems from the application of nondevelopmental data-derivation techniques
to developmental phenomena. This has become an established practice in child
psychology. As a result, it is in the domain of developmental psychology, first
and foremost, that Wittgenstein's observation of "the problems and methods
passing one another by" is especially true as a description of contemporary affairs. The habitual use of the term *the scientific method* in child psychology, in
the sense of the Baconian ideology (rather than the systems approach of natural
philosophies), has led psychologists either to avoid asking (and thus, answering)
developmental questions in child psychology; or, in case some developmental
questions are asked, to answer them in ways that do not represent the developmental phenomena in the area of empirical data derivation and analysis.

History of ideas in general informs us of previous efforts at construction of
knowledge, some of which have failed (but in ways from which we can learn),
others—left unfinished. The role of history of a science in its contemporary
development is crucial for new advancements. Hence the "reading span" of contemporary developmental psychologists needs to be the "literature" published
in the last 100, rather than 10, years. Undoubtedly such reading is highly selective, yet it constructs structured theoretical positions, rather than tries to make
sense of accumulated piles of empirical papers.

9.4   DEVELOPMENT THROUGH PERSON–ENVIRONMENT RELATIONS

The process of child development is embedded within a structurally organized
environment that is interconnected with the system of *cultural meanings* of the
society a child is born into, and whose member the child eventually becomes.
Furthermore, the culturally structured environment of a developing child is *dynamic*. It undergoes constant changes, only some of which are produced by the
child's own acting upon it. The environment can be changed by the actions of
the other people among whom the child develops. In this respect, purposeful
actions by parents, older siblings, or teachers organize many sides of a child's

environment in order to attain *their* goals in respect to the child's development. The environment may also change due to the actions of social groups in a given society, on whom the particular child and his or her immediate social network have minimal or no influence. For example, a war between rival political groupings in a country restructures the whole environment of families (and developing children within those families) in drastic ways. From those conditions, there is often no way out, other than adaptation to the circumstances with as little loss as possible. Finally, all the environment of human beings is vulnerable to changes that nobody can directly control once they happen—or can even prevent from happening (e.g., natural disasters).

All these four major kinds of environmental change create situations where the environmental dynamics are unpredictable in principle, even regarding their own nature. The process of child development that takes place under these conditions has to cope with such environmental uncertainty, in ways that guarantee a satisfactory result of the process. This can be possible under conditions of high flexibility in the ways in which the developing child interacts with his or her environment. Also, the developing psychological processes of the child are to be buffered against occasionally excessive fluctuations in the environmental conditions. Such buffering can be achieved by the child's active role in relations with the environment. The environment does not have a direct and long-lasting "molding" effect on the child. Instead, the child's own activity determines which particular aspects of the environmental input become influential. This perspective is the core of Piaget's "constructivist" perspective, which has been widely known in psychology. However, its actual implications in the form of the study of the assimilation–accommodation system as a process has largely evaded further development and concretization in developmental psychology.

9.5 DEVELOPMENT IS POSSIBLE ONLY IN OPEN SYSTEMS

Developmental phenomena represent an open-systems process in which the exact predictability of outcomes is impossible, because these outcomes are constructed over time in the process of organism–environment transaction. However, thinking about the processes of development is usually oriented to the task of trying to predict future outcomes. Possibly that is the case for the very reason that the uncertainty of future development needs to be reduced at a given time, at least in the thinker's mind—all the more on those occasions when it is the least realistic. At different times and across all cultural conditions in human history, fortune tellers, priests, and psychologists have been asked to reduce the uncertainties about the future by providing people with ways of thinking that help them to construct at least some (although often illusionary) certainty about the relative stability of things, organisms, and persons.

The Western culture-based common sense has largely guided theoretical endeavors in child psychology, canalizing it in ways that are congenial with laypersons' ideologies. Laypersons may be asking developmental psychologists questions about the relative stability of the development of particular children in order to reduce the excessive uncertainty that is hidden in the future. These questions are regularly answered as part of applied (and necessary) social-cognitive support to the laypersons in their practical efforts and concerns. However, these answers cannot adequately represent the reality of developmental processes since these, as open-systems phenomena, are, in principle, unpredictable in any exact way.

9.6 SUMMARY OF THE THEORY AND ITS HISTORICAL ANTECEDENTS

The present theoretical system relies on different aspects of earlier theoretical systems in psychology. It follows James Mark Baldwin, Jean Piaget, and Lev Vygotsky in their emphasis on the active nature of the developing child in the process of development. It uses Piaget's notion of "progressing equilibration" (3.2.2) in conjunction with the notion of *increasing disequilibration,* borrowed from the thinking currently used in contemporary thermodynamics (3.2.4). However, the present theoretical system goes beyond Piaget's traditions of empirical study of children's actions within environments, the structure of which is not explicitly studied in most of Piagetian research. This task is accomplished here by looking at the ways in which caregivers structure the child's environment in various concrete ways. In this respect, the present system relates to Kurt Lewin's thinking about the structure of the psychological field and its change (3.6). However, the present author stops short of accepting Lewin's major domain of interests—projection of the causality for happenings in the psychological field to different "field forces." Instead, the developing child and his caregivers are viewed as being engaged in constant negotiation and renegotiation processes involving different "boundaries" in their relationships with one another and the environment at large. These boundary conditions define (and redefine) the structured nature of the child–environment relationships, which (following Vygotsky's key idea of internalization of external experience—3.5.1) is gradually carried over from the realm of the child's (externally constrained) actions on the environment into internally constrained thinking, feeling, and programming of actions. The process of sociocultural constraining of child development is referred to as *canalization,* a term that has been used in theoretical biology (Waddington, 1942, 1966). However, Waddington's original notion of canalization is used here in an altered meaning. In this context, the term refers to the directive, but not determinative, role of structurally organized child–environment relationships, rather than to the presence of strictly determined developmental pathways among which the organism at times may choose but which the organism cannot participate in constructing by its own actions (4.1.4).

The theoretical system outlined in this book was built around three abstract concepts of *zones* that are applicable to real phenomenology in concrete ways:

(a) the Zone of Free Movement, (b) the Zone of Promoted Action, and (c) the Zone of Proximal Development. The Zone of Free Movement (ZFM) characterizes the set of what is available (in terms of areas of environment, objects in those areas, and ways of acting on these objects) to the child's acting in the particular environmental setting at a given time. The ZFM is a functional structure; it is constantly generated and regenerated as the child and the caregiver move from one environmental setting to another, and from seeking one set of goals to trying to attain other ends. Thus, the structure of ZFM is dynamic; given the change in goals or conditions, the boundaries of ZFM are constantly being reorganized. That reorganization may be initiated by the child, the caregivers, or all of them at the same time. The ZFM is also episodic. Any particular ZFM is constructed in accordance with the local conditions of the environment and the child and adult(s), and serves its purposes under these conditions. Once no longer functional, a particular ZFM can be abandoned, replaced by another, or gradually transformed into another. Finally, the ZFM is exclusive. It delineates the domains of children's actions that the caregivers do not let the children get involved in.

The second zone concept used in the theory is the Zone of Promoted Action (ZPA). This, in contrast to ZFM, is an *inclusive* concept. It illustrates the directed effort of the people around the child to guide his or her actions in one, rather than another, direction. ZPA, like ZFM, is also episodic (it is set up in particular situations, and can be abandoned later) and dynamic. It works in conjunction with the ZFM, and the way child development is culturally canalized can be characterized by the relationships the particular ZFM and ZPA have with each other. For example, a narrow ZFM (i.e., one that allows the child to act in only one way), when paired with a ZPA that matches the ZFM, leads to the most controllable situation one can think of in parent–child relationships: The child *can* act in only one way, the parent urges or commands the child to act in that way, and the child can either revolt (refuse to act in that way), or will act in the expected way. The latter is particularly the case if the only action in ZFM is not only promoted but strictly required—without an acceptance of the no-action solution (see 4.3.3). It is not surprising that the social institution of military discipline makes efficient and purposeful use of narrow ZFMs paired with strictly required ZPAs.

In the other extreme, the provision of a "wide" ZFM with a "narrow" ZPA in it creates situations where, seemingly, the children are given very great freedom for the development of their "selves." The child has a large number of possible actions available in a given setting, and very few of those are supported by active promotion on behalf of the caregivers. The latter may act in the belief, based on an ideology prominent in the culture, that children need a wide margin of freedom to develop in the best possible ways, and that constraining them may hamper their natural development. The actual development of children under such conditions may lead them to choose a pathway of development on their own. That pathway might not please their parents, though. Not all actual uses by

children, when a wide range of freedom is provided for them, will lead to outcomes that are to the liking of the freedom-providers. In this sense, the parents
may facilitate the potential future development of their children in *both* positive
and negative directions (as those are viewed by the parents). Such arrangements
logically lead to the socialization of children toward becoming "free-willed"
individuals, in concordance with the complex expectations that are accepted in
the culture. In interactions between free-willed individuals, however, clashing
of wills is a frequent and expected phenomenon.

The use of zone terminology makes it possible to conceptualize some aspects
of child rearing that, at first glance, seem to be irreconcilable opposites. For
example, the opposition between "strict" versus "permissive" parenting styles
disappears when viewed from the perspective of ZFM/ZPA complexes. The
strict version of parenting involves setting up the ZFM and ZPA so that the latter covers most (or all) of the former, and so that parental promotion of actions
in the ZPA approaches the conditions of requiring them. The permissive version
of parenting involves relatively loosely defined ZPAs in conjunction with wide
ZFMs. In that case, the child is left to his or her own devices to make decisions
about actions. Both these versions of parenting can be described by the same
system of concepts (ZFM/ZPA). Furthermore, this unitary explanation allows
one to understand how sometimes permissive parents become strict with their
children, or vice versa. Instead of describing the style of parenting that is
attributable to the parents' personalities, the zoniferous view of the process of
development affords description of conditions in parent–child–environment relationships that are interpreted in everyday language in the terminology of the
static qualities of permissiveness or restrictiveness.

The ZFM/ZPA system is not yet sufficient to explain the progression involved in development. Even if parents very much want to make a good piano-
player out of their infant child by limiting the child's freedom of action (e.g.,
imagine a ZFM that includes only the "manipulation" of piano keys while the
infant is held at the piano) and strictly demanding the desired action (e.g.,
ZPA = ZFM: parent pushing the infant's touching of the piano keys), the child
need not become a great pianist. Instead, the ZPA/ZFM system, which is set
up in ways that do not take into account what is possible for a child at a particular age, and on the basis of the child's particular developmental history, fails
in its function. The third core concept of the theoretical system is taken from
Vygotsky's contribution to psychology, and is redefined here to fit the basic
idea of selective limitation of variability as the mechanism of development. It
functions to determine when the ZPA/ZFM system can fulfill its expected
function. This is the Zone of Proximal Development (ZPD)—a set of actions
that are not yet available to the child in his or her individual acting. The ZPD
is the zone within which promotion efforts of the caregivers (ZPA) can lead to
the accomplishment of particular actions done by the child jointly with an
adult, whereas these actions are not yet observed among the child's actions
within the non-ZPA portion of the ZFM.

It needs to be emphasized that the use of the terminology of the three zones—ZFM, ZPA, and ZPD—is in this book put into practice in the microgenetic sense, and has no direct transferability to the issues of ontogeny. The zones are always temporary, constantly changing structures that organize the immediate construction of the future state out of a here-and-now setting. However, in that process of organization of microgenetic change, some feed-forward cultural organization devices are constructed, which may be reconstructed at a later time when necessary. The latter are mostly located in the intrapsychological sphere of the persons (adults, and—in ontogeny—children) and take the form of semiotic constraining devices. These devices operate in the intrapsychological sphere similarly to the action sphere—*constraining processes* are the core of both interpsychological and intrapsychological cultural regulation phenomena of human development.

9.7 AN EMPIRICAL APPLICATION: CHILDREN AND ADULTS AT MEALTIMES

The role of empirical research is crucial in the context of knowledge construction, yet it remains subdominant to the construction of theoretical knowledge as a whole. Empirical evidence corrects different inadequate assumptions inserted into the lower levels of the theoretical system, and is thus crucial. However, empirical evidence *in and by itself* (i.e., without theoretical and axiomatic argumentation) cannot disprove or falsify a theory. Theory becomes modified by way of its reconstruction within the whole methodology cycle, and not as a result of merely new data that happen to accumulate collectively. The final organizer of the data and the theory is the researcher's constructing mind.

The generic, constraining-based theoretical system elaborated in this book was brought to bear on empirical phenomena (and sought to derive data from them) in Chapters 6 and 7. These chapters illustrate a possible use of the theoretical system in the case of a very limited, although culturally highly important, setting of child socialization. In line with the context-sensitive nature of the theory, the culturally organized structure of the mealtime setting and the necessary development of infants' motor skills were analyzed in Chapter 6. That was followed by presentation of individual case histories of three toddlers and their parents at mealtimes from 6–7 to 24–26 months of age.

The mealtime context includes cultural expectations that are coded into fixed-feature objects that surround the child in this context. Some of these objects are directly usable by the child; others serve to make up the structural context for the development of new actions. The cultural canalization of children's actions thus starts from the structuring of the setting for those actions. For example, if a mother sits a toddler in a high chair, provides food and feeding utensils (by putting them on the tray), and subsequently leaves the child to its own resources for eating, the child's *behaviorally individual* process of self-feeding is still canalized socially because *the action context and action tools carry the cultural canalization function.* Furthermore, in the majority of cases observed, the mother remained neither an impartial observer of the self-feeding toddler, nor a domineering feeder. The mother provided the child with help *at points of acting where it was considered necessary,* but not all the time. Once a child had acquired the basic skills for handling feeding utensils, the mother would let the child act without assistance unless he or she started to act in ways that went beyond the ZFM established at the given time. The children were consistently helped when the actions they tried to perform were not yet fully established in their action repertoires. However, the caregivers gradually started to delegate control over parts of the developing action sequence to the children, retaining their helping role in other parts. The adult–child *joint action* in these situations created the system of zones (involving ZPA and ZFM) for the acquisition of particular motor skills (e.g., use of spoon, fork, or cup). Once the particular action sequence had been securely established in the child's motor repertoire, the caregivers allowed it to be exercised further in the course of the children's individual acting. They provided help only when it was perceived to be necessary or when the acquisition of a new skill began. The "informal education" of toddlers' actions at mealtimes was observed to take place in a low-key manner. Toddlers were observed to eat largely by themselves, alternating between hand and utensil use. They were often given ample time to feed themselves. However, the whole setting of mealtimes was fully under the organizational control of the caregiver, who could intervene by restricting some action by the child, or promoting utensil use, at times that she termed necessary. No highly "economical" picture of children's mealtimes emerged in the course of this author's empirical observations. The children were not trying to act in ways that would maximize some aspects of the eating process while minimizing some costs. For example, they could proceed to take time off eating to play with the food and the utensil, or they could revert to finger-feeding themselves long after their handling of spoons or forks had become well established. The mothers were not observed to try to make their children eat more quickly, or excessively, or with less mess, despite the fact that the method of collection of empirical materials (videotaping in homes) facilitated showing-off the children to the eyes (and videocamera) of the investigator. Instead, the mothers seemed to organize the children's mealtimes in accordance with the nutritional needs of the children at the time, and by pursuing culturally given socialization goals, the attainment of which was expected to be a future event. The mealtimes gave evidence for the use of the principle of satisficing, a basic principle that is the foundation of most human problem-solving in complex real-life situations (Simon, 1956).

9.8   EXTENSION OF THE THEORY TO OTHER PHENOMENA

Turning to other empirical phenomena in developmental psychology, it must be emphasized that the present theoretical system is not limited to the particular kind of phenomenology that was used as the example of the empirical elaboration of the theory. Besides mealtimes, many other domains of child socialization where goal-directed actions take place would fit as empirical grounds on which specific propositions stemming from the present theory can be tested. For instance, the way infants are dressed (see Benigni & Valsiner, 1984; Brackbill, 1971; Mead, 1954), in accordance with historical traditions, sets limits on their motor activity while they are not yet ready to locomote themselves. Furthermore, when they begin to creep or crawl (McSwain, 1981), and to walk in two- or three-dimensional space (i.e., climb; Valsiner & Mackie, 1985), their actions are selectively restricted by purposeful organization of child–environment relationships by the caregivers. All these phenomena have the same functional organization in common, although the particular details of the actions and the environments differ a great deal.

This invariant basic organization has been the topic of this book. The caregivers set limits on the general *range* of children's action opportunities, rather than determine the prototypic actions that the child can perform. Determination of the exact typical form of actions is practically impossible in reality. The contexts in which a given action can occur are highly variable, and, in each particular case, the action is adapted to the context, which is the only way in which the developing child will not only survive but develop further.

There exist, of course, psychological phenomena to which the theoretical system presented in this book is *not* applicable in any conceivably fruitful ways. These phenomena are characterized either by an absence of an environmental or person-based structural organization or by a highly complicated structural organization (e.g., a variety of partially conflicting goals of the persons involved in a situation). The theoretical system assumes that the reality is structurally organized, and is built on this assumption. Any phenomena for which the structural organization cannot be assumed (e.g., subjects' responses to a set of randomly presented stimuli) are not of interest for empirical research that is based on the theoretical framework outlined in this book.

Extension of the theory to the cultural regulation of intrapsychological domains is fruitful. Thus, the semiotic constraining of the personality processes (Valsiner, 1997a) has been conceptualized. The field-theoretic ethos of the theory makes it potentially applicable to domains that have been rarely studied in their complexity—such as feeling, desiring, hoping, believing, valuing—and to other intrapsychological processes in the realm of adults' or children's subjective worlds that guide their actual conduct.

9.9 ACTIVE CONSTRUCTION OF NOVELTY IN ASYMMETRIC SOCIAL POWER RELATIONS

The earlier version of the constraining theory offered insufficient emphasis on the active and constructive nature of all persons involved in the process of human development. Constraining was *not* meant to reflect external canalization of the child's development of specific forms of culturally overde-termined skills (such as spoon use), but rather a field where the whole struc-ture of the interactive setting—which involves persons in asymmetric power relations (e.g., the adult determining the setting for the child—a mealtime)—is maintained and reorganized by continuous, multisided setting of constraints. Thus, in the mealtime setting, the adult constrains the child's actions, *and* the child's actions constrain those of the adult. The adult's (mother's) feeling and thinking are further constrained by her abstraction of new generalized mean-ing from the given setting (as elaborated in Chapter 8). So, the adult and the child are equally active coconstructors of the mealtime event and of the gener-alized meanings that stem from it. These meanings can further constrain the conduct of both of them, in similar (or other) settings.

Human development entails a bidirectional culture-transmission process across generations. All human beings are in some form of asymmetric power relations most of the time (i.e., equality of power would be the exception, rather than the rule); yet, in settings organized through such asymmetric rela-tions, they jointly participate in the reconstruction of cultural messages. In a manner similar to Karl Bühler's Organon Model, the cultural messages gener-ated by some Senders are not received in the way they are presented, but, rather, in the ways the Receiver personally reconstructs them. A specific power role's differential may act as an additional constrainer of the width of the zone of possibilities for the Receiver, yet the latter always is assigned the active and constructive role of being subservient. This is particularly possible because of the development of intrapsychological semiotic reflection possibili-ties. Our ontogenetically emergent capacity for internal dialogue makes us rel-atively free from external action control efforts by powerful others. The maximally overcontrolled child (or adolescent), in some settings, can set his or her mind free in a fantasy world that substitutes imaginary there-and-then set-tings for the enforced action in a here-and-now setting. The two-level organi-zation of constraining processes—composed of an action level and a level of reflection—opens up the developmental contexts of human beings for unex-pected advancements. Or, in other terms, the system of action-constraining is made open (when overdetermined) by distancing from it through the reflection level, thereby dissociating the latter from the former. Development by con-straining is a coconstructive event.

9.10   THE FINAL POINT: *LIMITED* INDETERMINACY
         OF DEVELOPMENT

Perhaps the most important general effort that was embedded in the building of this theory was an attempt to solve a basic philosophical controversy that underlies any account of development. This is the controversy between *deter-ministic* and *indeterministic* general models of development. Usually, in psy-chology, either one or the other model is assumed. Development is either viewed as a predetermined process (which may seem to be not that because of the "noise" from the environment), or as a case of total *ad hoc* construction in which "anything goes" and nothing can be taken for granted. Both of these extremes are obviously inadequate. Development is neither "fully closed" nor "fully open," but partially (episodically) open and *at the same time* maintaining itself in rather conservative ways. Hence, the treatment of issues of determinism and indeterminism are not the either-or kind (see Fogel, Lyra, & Valsiner, 1997); they require some intermediate philosophical construction.

Hence, the perspective of this book can be viewed as one of *"bounded"* (or "limited") *indeterminacy.* This is close to the notion of *probabilistic epigenesis* (Gottlieb, 1976, 1992), which is oriented to resolving the same controversy in slightly different terminology. The main course of development is *deterministically indeterministic:* the specifiable constraint systems (which at the moment represent the deterministic state of the developmental process) are the basis for "surprises"—novelty constructions (which represent the indeterministic side of development). This deterministic (bounded) indeterminacy guarantees stability and instability, continuity and change, and rigidity and flexibility in development.

As was elaborated in Chapters 3 and 5, a deterministically indeterministic view on human development requires a basic change in the methodological habits of developmental psychology (or even developmental science in general; see Cairns, Elder, & Costello, 1996). The issues to be studied is the emerging and fluid structure of developmental phenomena, rather than any quantitative translation of these phenomena into static and nonsystemic "measures." Much of the rigor of contemporary qualitative mathematical systems remains to be elaborated for the purposes of such developmental science. The inevitable embeddedness of all developmental phenomena in the context of irreversible time sets up a special status for developmental science that has not been encountered by other sciences thus far (with the exception of nonequilibrium thermodynamics).

Thus, in an interesting way, the everyday phenomena we easily take for granted—such as mealtimes—turn out to be very complex intellectual puzzles for developmental theory and methodology. Human development entails multilevel dynamic complexity, and only those theoretical models that recognize this feature of development can be considered seriously in the realm of developmental science. The main difficulty for all of those has been lack of recognition of novelty construction on the basis of what already has come into existence. After all, human development entails novelties both in the realm of actions and in reflections that previously did not exist. Under these conditions, human progress can proceed in its curious ways, with advances and drawbacks, and can result in a myriad of the never-ending activities and imaginations of ordinary human beings within their constantly changing, culturally structured life environments. Developmental science can be science only if it constructs theoretical systems that explicitly account for that reality.

References

Abelson, R.P. (1981). Psychological status of the script concept. *American Psychologist, 36*(7), 715–729.

Albury, R. (1983). Science teaching or science preaching? Critical reflections on school science. In R.W. Home (Ed.), *Science under scrutiny* (pp. 159–172). Dordrecht, The Netherlands: D. Reidel.

Allen, P.M. (1981). The evolutionary paradigm of dissipative structures. In E. Jantsch (Ed.), *The evolutionary vision: Toward a unifying paradigm of physical, biological, and sociocultural evolution* (pp. 25–72). Boulder, CO: Westview Press.

Allen, P.M. (1982). Self-organization in the urban system. In W.C. Schieve & P.M. Allen (Eds.), *Self-organization and dissipative. structures: Applications in the physical and social sciences* (pp. 132–158). Austin: University of Texas Press.

Allen, P.M., & Sanglier, M. (1980). Order by fluctuation and the urban system. In M. Zeleny (Ed.), *Autopoiesis, dissipative structures, and spontaneous social orders* (pp. 109–132). Boulder, CO: Westview Press.

Allport, G.W. (1940). The psychologist's frame of reference. *Psychological Bulletin, 37*(1), 1–28.

Allport, G.W. (1942). The use of personal documents in psychological science. *Social Science Research Council Bulletin,* No. 49.

Alvarez, A. (1994). Child's everyday life. An ecological approach to the study of activity systems. In A. Alvarez & P. Del Rio (Eds.), *Explorations in socio-cultural studies. Vol. 4. Education as cultural construction* (pp. 23–38). Madrid: Fundación Infancia y Aprendizaje.

Anokhin, P.K. (1964). Systemogenesis as a general regulator of brain development. In W.A. Himwich & H.E. Himwich (Eds.), *Progress in brain research* (Vol. 9, pp. 54–86). Amsterdam: Elsevier.

Anzai, Y., & Simon, H. (1979). The theory of learning by doing. *Psychological Review, 86,* 124–140.

Apel, K.-O. (1989). Linguistic meaning and intentionality: The compatibility of the "linguistic turn" and the "pragmatic turn" of meaning-theory within the framework of transcendental semiotics. In G. Deledalle (Ed.), *Semiotics and pragmatics* (pp. 19–70). Amsterdam: John Benjamins.

Aphek, E., & Tobin, Y. (1990). *The semiotics of fortune-telling.* Amsterdam: John Benjamins.

Arievich, I., & Van der Veer, R. (1995). Furthering the internalization debate: Gal'perin's contribution. *Human Development, 38,* 113–126.

Asendorpf, J.B., & Valsiner, J. (1992). Editors' introduction: Three dimensions of developmental perspectives. In J.B. Asendorpf & J. Valsiner (Eds.), *Framing stability and change* (pp. ix–xxii). Newbury Park, CA: Sage.

Bakhtin, M.M. (1975). Slovo v romane [Discourse in the novel]. In M. Bakhtin, *Voprosy literatury i estetiki* (pp. 73–232). Moscow: Khudozhestvennaya Literatura. (Original work written in 1934)

Baldwin, A.L. (1940). The statistical analysis of the structure of a single personality. *Psychological Bulletin, 37,* 518–519.

Baldwin, A.L. (1942). Personal structure analysis: A statistical method for investigating single personality. *Journal of Abnormal and Social Psychology, 37,* 163–183.

Baldwin, A.L. (1944). An analysis of children's eating habits. *Journal of Pediatrics, 25,* 71–78.

Baldwin, A.L. (1946). The study of individual personality by means of the intraindividual correlation. *Journal of Personality, 14,* 151–168.

Baldwin, J.M. (1892a). Suggestion and will. *Proceedings of the International Congress of Experimental Psychology* (2nd session, pp. 49–54). London: Williams & Norgate.

Baldwin, J.M. (1892b). Origin of volition in childhood. *Science, 20,* 286–287.

Baldwin, J.M. (1893). Internal speech and song. *Philosophical Review, 2*(4), 385–407.

Baldwin, J.M. (1894). Personality-suggestion. *Psychological Review, 1,* 274–279.

Baldwin, J.M. (1895). *Mental development in the child and the race.* New York: Macmillan.

Baldwin, J.M. (1896). Consciousness and evolution. *Psychological Review, 3,* 300–309.

Baldwin, J.M. (1897). *Social and ethical interpretations in mental development.* New York: Macmillan.

Baldwin, J.M. (1902). *Fragments in philosophy and science.* New York: Charles Scribner's Sons.

Baldwin, J.M. (1906). *Thought and things: A study of the development and meaning of thought, or genetic logic: Vol. 1. Functional logic, or genetic theory of knowledge.* London: Swan Sonnenschein.

Baldwin, J.M. (1908). *Thought and things: A study of the development and meaning of thought, or genetic logic: Vol. 2. Experimental logic, or genetic theory of thought.* London: Swan Sonnenschein.

Baldwin, J.M. (1911a). *Thought and things: A study of the development and meaning of thought, or genetic logic: Vol. 3. Interest and art being real logic.* London: Swan Sonnenschein.

Baldwin, J.M. (1911b). *The individual and society.* Boston: Richard G. Badger.

Baldwin, J.M. (1915). *Genetic theory of reality.* New York: Putnam.

Baldwin, J.M. (1930). James Mark Baldwin. In C. Murchison (Ed.), *A history of psychology in autobiography* (Vol. 1, pp. 1–30). New York: Russell & Russell.

Bandlamudi, L. (1994). Dialogics of understanding self/culture. *Ethos, 22*(4), 460–493.

Bandura, A. (1983). Temporal dynamics and decomposition of reciprocal determinism: A reply to Phillips and Orton. *Psychological Review, 30,* 166–170.

Barker, R., Dembo, T., & Lewin, K. (1941). Frustration and regression: An experiment with young children. *University of Iowa Studies in Child Welfare, 18*(1), 1–312.

Bartlett, F.C. (1932). *Remembering.* Cambridge, England: Cambridge University Press.

Basar, T., & Oldser, G.J. (1982). *Dynamic noncooperative game theory.* London: Academic Press.

Basov, M. (1929). Structural analysis in psychology from the standpoint of behavior. *Journal of Genetic Psychology, 36,* 267–290.

Basov, M. (1931). *Obshchie osnovy pedologii* [General foundations of pedology]. Moscow and Leningrad: Gosizdat.

Basov, M. (1991). The organization of processes of behavior. In J. Valsiner & R. Van der Veer (Eds.), Structuring of conduct in activity settings: The forgotten contributions of Mikhail Basov. Part 1. *Soviet Psychology, 29*(5), 14–83.

Bateson, G. (1972). *Steps to an ecology of mind.* New York: Ballantine Books.

Bem, D., & Allen, A. (1974). On predicting some of the people some of the time: The search for cross-situational consistencies in behavior. *Psychological Review, 81,* 506–520.

Bem, D., & Funder, D.C. (1978). Predicting more of the people more of the time: Assessing the personality of situations. *Psychological Review, 85,* 485–501.

Benigni, L. (1974, October). *Dipendenza alimentare e sviluppo communicativo nel primo anno di vita.* Paper presented at the 8th Congress of the Societa Italiana di Neuropsichiatria Infantile, Taormina, Italy.

Benigni, L., & Valsiner, J. (1984). Il corpo del neonato i suoi confini sociali. In L. Gandini (Ed.). *Dimmi come lo vesti* (pp. 89–135). Milano: Emme Edizioni.

Benigni, L., & Valsiner, J. (1985). Developmental psychology without the study of developmental processes? *ISSBD Newsletter,* No. 1.

Bennett, P.G., & Dando, M.R. (1979). Complex strategic analysis: Hypergame study of the fall of France. *Journal of the Operations Research Society, 30*(1), 23–32.

Bensaude-Vincent, B. (1983). A founder myth in the history of sciences? The Lavoisier case. In L. Graham, W. Lepenies, & P. Weingart (Eds.), *Functions and uses of disciplinary histories* (Vol. 7, pp. 53–78). Dordrecht, The Netherlands: D. Reidel.

Bergson, H. (1911). *Creative evolution.* New York: Henry Holt.

Bergson, H. (1945). *L'Evolution créatrice.* Geneva: Éditions Albert Skira. (Original work published 1907)

Bernstein, N.A. (1966). *Ocherki po fiziologii dvizheniya i fiziologii aktivnosti* [Studies in the physiology of movement and physiology of activity]. Moscow: Meditsina.

Berresford, A., & Dando, M.R. (1978). Operational research for strategic decision making: The role of world-view. *Journal of the Operations Research Society, 29*(2), 137–146.

Berry, R.S., & Andresen, B. (1982). Thermodynamic constraints in economic analysis. In W.C. Schieve & P.M. Allen (Eds.), *Self-organization and dissipative structures: Applications in the physical and social sciences* (pp. 323–338). Austin: University of Texas Press.

Bertalanffy, L. von. (1950). The theory of open systems in physics and biology. *Science, 111*, 23–29.

Bertalanffy, L. von. (1960). Principles and theory of growth. In W.W. Nowinski (Ed.), *Fundamental aspects of normal and malignant growth* (pp. 137–259). Amsterdam: Elsevier.

Bertalanffy, L. von. (1981). *A systems view of man.* Boulder, CO: Westview Press.

Bickhard, M.H. (1992). Myths of science: Misconceptions of science in contemporary psychology. *Theory & Psychology, 2*(3), 321–337.

Bloom, L. (1982). Applying psychology in the Third World. *Bulletin of the British Psychological Society, 35,* 143–146.

Boesch, E.E. (1991). *Symbolic action theory and cultural psychology.* New York: Springer.

Bohm, D. (1980). *Wholeness and implicate order.* London: Routledge & Kegan Paul.

Boole, G. (1854). *An investigation of the laws of thought, on which are founded the mathematical theories of logic and probability.* London: Walton & Maberly.

Bossard, J.H.S. (1948). *The sociology of child development.* New York: Harper & Brothers.

Bourdieu, P. (1981). Men and machines. In K. Knorr-Cetina & A.W. Cicourel (Eds.), *Advances in social theory and methodology: Toward an integration of micro- and macro-sociologies* (pp. 304–317). London: Routledge & Kegan Paul.

Bourdieu, P. (1985). The social space and the genesis of groups. *Social Science Information, 24*(2), 195–220.

Bourdieu, P. (1988). *Homo academicus.* Stanford, CA: Stanford University Press.

Bourdieu, P. (1991). *Language and symbolic power.* Cambridge, MA: Harvard University Press.

Bourdieu, P., & Wacquant, L.J.D. (1992). *An invitation to reflexive sociology.* Chicago: University of Chicago Press.

Bower, T.G.R., Broughton, J.M., & Moore, M.K. (1970). Demonstration of intention in the reaching behavior of neonate humans. *Nature, 228,* 679–681.

Brackbill, Y. (1971). Cumulative effects of continuous stimulation on arousal level in infants. *Child Development, 42,* 17–26.

Branco, A.U., & Valsiner, J. (1997). Changing methodologies: A co-constructivist study of goal orientations in social interactions. In G. Misra (Ed.), *Psychology in developing countries.* New Delhi, India: Sage.

Brandt, L.W. (1973). The physics of the physicist and the physics of the psychologist. *International Journal of Psychology, 8*(1), 61–72.

Braudel, F. (1973). *Capitalism and material life 1400–1800.* New York: Harper & Row.

Brent, S. (1984). *Psychological and social structures.* Hillsdale, NJ: Erlbaum.

Bridgman, P. (1927). *The logic of modern physics.* New York: Macmillan.

Brockmeier, J. (1996a). Construction and interpretation: Exploring a joint perspective on Piaget and Vygotsky. In A. Tryphon & J. Vonèche (Eds.), *Piaget–Vygotsky: The social genesis of thought* (pp. 125–143). Hove, England: Psychology Press.

Brockmeier, J. (1996b, May 31–June 1). *Verstehen, Interpretieren, Verhandeln: Zur psychologischen Hermeneutik des Verhältnisses von Zeichen und Bedeutung.* Paper presented at the conference *Lernen und Entwicklung aus kulturhistorischer Sicht: Was sagt uns Wygotski heute?* at the University of Potsdam, Germany.

Bronfenbrenner, U. (1977, July). Toward an experimental ecology of human development. *American Psychologist,* 513–531.

Bronfenbrenner, U. (1979). *The ecology of human development.* Cambridge, MA: Harvard University Press.

Bronfenbrenner, U. (1989). Ecological systems theory. In R. Vasta (Ed.), *Annals of child development.* Greenwich, CT: JAI Press.

Bronfenbrenner, U. (1993). The ecology of cognitive development. In R. Wozniak & K. Fischer (Eds.), *Development in context* (pp. 3–46). Hillsdale, NJ: Erlbaum.

Bronfenbrenner, U., & Ceci, S. (1994). Nature–nurture reconceptualized in developmental perspective: A bioecological model. *Psychological Review, 101*(4), 568–586.

Bronfenbrenner, U., & Crouter, A.C. (1983). The evolution of environmental models in developmental research. In W. Kessen (Ed.), *Handbook of child psychology: Vol. 1. History, theory, and methods* (pp. 357–414). New York: Wiley.

Brown, R., & Fish, D. (1983). The psychological causality implicit in language. *Cognition, 14,* 237–273.

Bruner, J.S. (1960). *The process of education.* Cambridge, MA: Harvard University Press.

Bruner, J.S. (1972). The nature and uses of immaturity. *American Psychologist, 27,* 1–22.

Bruner, J.S. (1975). The ontogenesis of speech acts. *Journal of Child Language, 2,* 1–19.

Bruner, J.S. (1976). From communication to language—a psychological perspective. *Cognition, 3,* 155–187.

Bruner, J.S. (1978). Acquiring the uses of language. *Canadian Journal of Psychology, 32,* 202–218.

Bruner, J.S. (1981). The organization of action and the nature of adult–infant transaction. In G. D'Ydewalle & W. Lens (Eds.), *Cognition in human motivation and learning* (pp. 1–13). Hillsdale, NJ: Erlbaum.

Bruner, J.S. (1983). *In search of mind: Essays in autobiography.* New York: Harper & Row.

Bruner, J.S. (1984). Vygotsky's zone of proximal development: The hidden agenda. *New Directions for Child Development,* No. 23, 93–97.

Bruner, J.S. (1990). *Acts of meaning.* Cambridge, MA: Harvard University Press.

Bruner, J.S., & Sherwood, V. (1976). Early rule structure: The case of "peekaboo." In R. Harré (Ed.), *Life sentences* (pp. 57–62). Chichester, England: Wiley.

Bryant, C.A. (1982). The impact of kin, friend and neighbour networks on infant feeding practices. *Social Science and Medicine, 16,* 1757–1765.

Bühler, K. (1990). *Theory of language: The representational function of language.* Amsterdam: John Benjamins.

Bullogh, E. (1912). "Psychical distance" as a factor in art and an aesthetic principle. *Journal of Psychology, 5*(2), 87–118.

Bush, R.R., & Mosteller, F. (1955). *Stochastic models for learning.* New York: Wiley.

Buss, A. (1978). The structure of psychological revolutions. *Journal of the History of the Behavioral Sciences, 14,* 57–64.

Buss, A. (1979). The historical context of differential psychology and eugenics. In A. Buss, *A dialectical psychology* (pp. 27–42). New York: Irvington.

Cairns, R.B. (1983). The emergence of developmental psychology. In W. Kessen (Ed.), *Carmichael's handbook of child psychology: Vol. 1. History, theory, and methods* (4th ed., pp. 41–102). New York: Wiley.

Cairns, R.B., Elder, G., & Costello, E.J. (Eds.). (1996). *Developmental science.* New York: Cambridge University Press.

Cairns, R.B., & Ornstein, P.A. (1979). Developmental psychology. In E. Hearst (Ed.), *The first century of experimental psychology.* Hillsdale, NJ: Erlbaum.

Cairns, R.B., & Valsiner, J. (1982). *The cultural context of developmental psychology.* Paper presented at the 90th APA Convention, Washington, DC.

Cairns, R.B., & Valsiner, J. (1984). Child psychology. *Annual Review of Psychology, 35,* 553–577.

Calil, E. (1994). The construction of the zone of proximal development in a pedagogical context. In N. Mercer & C. Coll (Eds.), *Explorations in socio-cultural studies: Vol. 3. Teaching, learning, and interaction* (pp. 93–98). Madrid: Fundación Infancia y Aprendizaje.

Castner, B.M. (1932). The development of fine prehension in infancy. *Genetic Psychology Monographs, 12*(2), 105–193.

Catán, L. (1986). The dynamic display of process: Historical development and contemporary uses of the microgenetic method. *Human Development, 29,* 252–263.

Cattell, R.B. (1944). Psychological measurement: Normative, ipsative, interactive. *Psychological Review, 51,* 292–303.

Cazden, C. (1983). Peekaboo as an instructional model: Discourse development at home and at school. In B. Bain (Ed.), *The sociogenesis of language and human conduct* (pp. 33–58). New York: Plenum Press.

Chapman, M. (1982). Action and interactions: The study of social cognition in Germany and the United States. *Human Development, 25,* 295–302.

Chapman, M. (1988). *Constructive evolution.* Cambridge, England: Cambridge University Press.

Chomsky, N. (1959). A note on phrase structure grammars. *Information and Control, 2,* 393–395.

Chomsky, N. (1966). *Topics in the theory of generative grammar.* The Hague: Mouton.

Chomsky, N. (1976). On the biological basis of language capacities. In R.W. Rieber (Ed.), *The neuropsychology of language* (pp. 1–24). New York: Plenum Press.

Chomsky, N. (1980a). On cognitive structures and their development: A reply to Piaget. In M. Piatelli-Palmarini (Ed.), *Language and learning: The debate between Jean Piaget and Noam Chomsky* (pp. 35–52). Cambridge, MA: Harvard University Press.

Chomsky, N. (1980b). *Rules and representations*. New York: Columbia University Press.

Cole, M. (1985). The zone of proximal development: Where culture and cognition create each other. In J.V. Wertsch (Ed.), *Culture, communication, and cognition: Vygotskian perspectives* (pp. 146–161). Cambridge, England: Cambridge University Press.

Cole, M. (1995). Culture and cognitive development: From cross-cultural research to creating systems of cultural mediation. *Culture & Psychology, 1*(1), 25–54.

Cole, P.M. (1985). Display rules and the socialization of affective displays. In G. Zivin (Ed.), *The development of expressive behavior: Biology–environment interactions* (pp. 269–290). Orlando, FL: Academic Press.

Connolly, K.J. (1970). Skill development: Problems and plans. In K.J. Connolly (Ed.), *Mechanisms of motor skill development* (pp. 3–21). London: Academic Press.

Connolly, K.J. (1973). Factors influencing the learning of manual skills by young children. In R. Hinde & J. Stevenson-Hinde (Eds.), *Constraints on learning* (pp. 337–363). London: Academic Press.

Connolly, K.J. (1974). The development of skill. *New Scientist, 62*(900), 537–540.

Connolly, K.J. (1975). Movement, action and skill. In K.S. Holt (Ed.), *Movement and child development* (pp. 102–110). London: Heinemann.

Connolly, K.J. (1979). The development of competence in motor skills. In C.H. Nadeau, W.R. Halliwell, K.M. Newell, & G.C. Roberts (Eds.), *Psychology of motor behavior and sport* (pp. 229–252). Champaign, IL: Human Kinietics.

Connolly, K.J. (1980). Motor development and motor disability. In M. Rutter (Ed.), *Developmental psychiatry* (pp. 138–153). London: Heinemann.

Connolly, K.J. (1981). Maturation and the ontogeny of motor skills. In K.J. Connolly & H.F.R. Prechtl (Eds.), *Maturation and development: Biological and psychological perspectives* (pp. 216–230). London: Heinemann.

Connolly, K.J., & Elliott, J. (1972). The evolution and ontogeny of hand function. In N.G. Blurton Jones (Ed.), *Ethological studies of child behavior* (pp. 329–383). London: Cambridge University Press.

Coulter, N.A. (1973). Contributions to a mathematical theory of synergic systems. In A. Locker (Ed.), *Biogenesis, evolution, homeostasis* (pp. 57–61). New York: Springer.

Cox, B.D., Ornstein, P.A., & Valsiner, J. (1991). The role of internalization in the transfer of mnemonic strategies. In L. Oppenheimer & J. Valsiner (Eds.), *The origins of action: International perspectives* (pp. 101–131). New York: Springer.

Crawford, J., Kippax, S., Onyx, J., Gault, U., & Benton, P. (1992). *Emotion and gender: Constructing meaning from memory*. London: Sage.

Crick, F. (1988). *What mad pursuit: A personal view of scientific discovery*. London: Penguin Books.

Curran, V.H. (Ed.). (1984). *Nigerian children: Developmental perspectives*. London: Routledge & Kegan Paul.

Czikszentmihalyi, M., & Rochberg-Halton, E. (1981). *The meaning of things*. Cambridge, England: Cambridge University Press.

Dalton, T.C. (1993). *"Everything within the revolution": Cuban strategies for social development since 1960.* Boulder, CO: Westview Press.

Danet, B. (1980). Baby or fetus?: Language and the construction of reality in a manslaughter trial. *Semiotica, 32*(3/4), 187–219.

Danziger, K. (1985). The methodological imperative in psychology. *Philosophy of the Social Sciences, 15,* 1–13.

Danziger, K. (1990). *Constructing the subject.* Cambridge, England: Cambridge University Press.

Daston, L. (1992). Objectivity and the escape from perspective. *Social Studies of Science, 22,* 597–618.

Davis, K. (1938). Mental hygiene and the class structure. *Psychiatry, 1,* 55–65.

Davydov, V., & Radzikhovskii, L.A. (1980). Vygotsky's theory and the activity principle in psychology, I. *Voprosy Psikhologii,* No. 6, 48–59.

Davydov, V., & Radzikhovskii, L.A. (1981). Vygotsky's theory and the activity principle in psychology, II. *Voprosy Psikhologii,* No. 1, 67–80.

Del Rio, P. (1990). La Zona de Desarollo Proximo y la Zona Sincrética de Representación: El espacio instrumental de la acción social. *Infancia y Aprendizaje, 51–52,* 191–244.

Del Rio, P. (1994). Extra-cortical connections: The sociocultural systems for conscious living. In J. Wertsch & J.D. Ramirez (Eds.), *Explorations in socio-cultural studies: Vol. 2. Literacy and other forms of mediated action* (pp. 19–31). Madrid: Fundación Infancia y Aprendizaje.

Del Rio, P., & Alvarez, A. (1992). Tres pies al gato: Significado, sentido y cultura cotidiana en la educación. *Infancia y Aprendizaje,* 59–60.

Del Rio, P., & Alvarez, A. (1995). Directivity: The cultural and educational construction of morality and agency. Some questions arising from the legacy of Vygotsky. *Anthropology & Education Quarterly, 26*(4), 384–409.

DeVries, M.W., & DeVries, M.R. (1977). Cultural relativity of toilet-training readiness: A perspective from East Africa. *Pediatrics, 60*(2), 170–177.

Diepold, B. (1983). Essstörungen bei Kindern und Jugendlichen. *Praxis der Kinderpsychologie und Kinderpsychiatrie, 32*(8), 298–304.

DiFranco, D., Muir, D., & Dodwell, P. (1978). Reaching in very young infants. *Perception, 7,* 385–392.

Dolby, R.G.A. (1977). The transmission of two new scientific disciplines from Europe to North America in the late 19th century. *Annals of Science, 34,* 287–310.

Douglas, M. (1975). Deciphering a meal. In M. Douglas, *Purity and danger.* London: Routledge & Kegan Paul.

Douglas, M., & Gross, J. (1981). Food and culture: Measuring the intimacy of rule systems. *Social Science Information, 20*(1), 1–35.

Draguns, J.G. (1984). Microgenesis by any other name. . . . In W.D. Froehlich, G. Smith, J.G. Draguns, & U. Hentschel (Eds.), *Psychological processes in cognition and personality* (pp. 3–17). Washington, DC: Hemisphere.

Dreyer, C.A., & Dryer, A.S. (1973). Family dinner as a unique behavior habitat. *Family Process, 12,* 291–301.

Duncker, K. (1938). Experimental modification of children's food preferences through social suggestion. *Journal of Abnormal and Social Psychology, 33,* 489–507.

Duncker, K. (1945). On problem-solving. *Psychological Monographs, 58*(5), 1–112.

Edwards, D. (1995). Two to tango: Script formulations, dispositions, and rhetorical symmetry in relationship troubles talk. *Research on Language and Social Interaction, 28*(4), 319–350.

Edwards, D., & Potter, J. (1992). *Discursive psychology.* London: Sage.

Ekman, P., Friesen, W.V., & Ellsworth, P. (1972). *Emotion in the human face.* New York: Pergamon Press.

Elias, N. (1978). *The civilizing process: The development of manners.* New York: Urizen Books.

Elliott, J., & Connolly, K.J. (1974). Hierarchical structure in skill development. In K.J. Connolly & J. Bruner (Eds.), *The growth of competence* (pp. 135–168). London: Academic Press.

Elliott, J., & Connolly, K.J. (1984). A classification of manipulative hand movements. *Developmental Medicine and Child Neurology, 26,* 283–296.

Engeström, Y. (1990). *Learning, working, and imagining.* Helsinki, Finland: Orienta-Konsultit Oy.

Enriquez, V.G. (1992). *From colonial to liberation psychology: The Philippine experience.* Quezon City: University of the Philippines Press.

Ericsson, K.A., & Simon, H.A. (1993). *Protocol analysis: Verbal reports as data.* Cambridge, MA: MIT Press.

Erikson, E.H. (1963). *Childhood and society.* New York: Norton.

Espiritu, A.C. (1989). The limits of applicability of Western concepts, values and methods in the social sciences to the concrete realities of Asian societies. In R. Pe-Pua (Ed.), *Sikolohiyang Pilipino: Teorya, metodo at gamit* (pp. 111–119). Quezon City: University of the Philippines Press.

Eyferth, K. (1976). The contribution of William and Clara Stern to the onset of developmental psychology. In K.F. Riegel & J.A. Meacham (Eds.), *The developing individual in a changing world* (Vol. 1, pp. 9–15). The Hague: Mouton.

Eysenck, H.J. (1985). The place of theory in the world of facts. In K.B. Madsen & L.P. Mos (Eds.), *Annals of theoretical psychology* (Vol. 3, pp. 103–114). New York: Plenum Press.

Feliciano, G.D. (1989). The limits of Western social research methods in rural Philippines: The need for innovation. In R. Pe-Pua (Ed.), *Sikolohiyang Pilipino: Teorya, metodo at gamit* (pp. 99–110). Quezon City: University of the Philippines Press.

Festinger, L., Riecken, H.W., & Schachter, S. (1956). *When prophecy fails.* Minneapolis: University of Minnesota Press.

Flanagan, O. (1981). Psychology, progress and the problem of reflexivity: A study in the epistemological foundations of psychology. *Journal of the History of the Behavioral Sciences, 17,* 375–386.

Fogel, A., Lyra, M., & Valsiner, J. (Eds.). (1997). *The question of determinism and indeterminism in development.* Hillsdale, NJ: Erlbaum.

Ford, D.H., & Lerner, R.M. (1992). *Development systems theory.* Newbury Park, CA: Sage.

Fortes, M., & Fortes, S.L. (1936). Food in the domestic economy of the Tallensi. *Africa, 9,* 237–276.

Franck, I. (1982). Psychology as science: Resolving the idiographic–nomothetic controversy. *Journal for the Theory of Social Behavior, 12*(1) 1–20.

Fraser, N.M., & Hipel, K.W. (1979). Solving complex conflicts. *IEEE Transactions on Systems, Man, and Cybernetics, smc-9*(12), 805–810.

Freud, A. (1963). The concept of developmental lines. *The Psychoanalytic Study of the Child, 18,* 245–265.

Fu, K.S. (1970). Learning control systems—A review and outlook. *IEEE Transactions on Automatic Control, 15,* 210–221.

Fu, K.S. (1974). *Syntactic methods in pattern recognition.* New York: Academic Press.

Fuller, S. (1991). Is history and philosophy of science withering on the vine? *Philosophy of the Social Sciences, 21*(2), 149–174.

Galton, F. (1904). Eugenics: Its definition, scope and aim. *Nature, 70,* 1804, 82.

Gardner, H. (1985). *The mind's new science: A history of the cognitive revolution.* New York: Basic Books.

Garfinkel, P., Moldofsky, H., & Garner, D. (1980). The heterogeneity of anorexia nervosa. *Archives of General Psychiatry, 37,* 1036–1040.

Gärling, T., & Valsiner, J. (Eds.). (1985). *Children within environments: Towards a psychology of accident prevention.* New York: Plenum Press.

Gauld, A., & Shotter, J. (1977). *Human action and its psychological investigation.* London: Routledge & Kegan Paul.

Geison, G.L., & Secord, J.A. (1988). Pasteur and the process of discovery: The case of optical isomerism. *ISIS, 79,* 6–36.

Gergen, M.M., & Gergen, K.J. (1984). The social construction of narrative accounts. In K.J. Gergen & M.M. Gergen (Eds.), *Historical social psychology* (pp. 173–189). Hillsdale, NJ: Erlbaum.

Gesell, A., & Ilg, F.L. (1937). *Feeding behavior of infants.* Philadelphia: Lippincott.

Gesell, A., & Thompson, H. (1934). *Infant behavior: Its genesis and growth.* Westport, CT: Greenwood Press.

Geuter, U. (1984). *Die Professionalisierung der deutschen Psychologie im Nationalsozialismus.* Frankfurt/Main: Suhrkamp.

Gieryn, T.F. (1983). Boundary-work and the demarcation of science from nonscience: Strains and interests in professional ideologies of scientists. *American Sociological Review, 48,* 781–795.

Gigerenzer, G. (1987). Probabilistic thinking and the fight against subjectivity. In L. Krüger, G. Gigerenzer, & M.S. Morgan (Eds.), *The probabilistic revolution: Vol. 2. Ideas in the sciences* (pp. 11–32). Cambridge, MA: MIT Press.

Gigerenzer, G. (1991). From tools to theories: A heuristic of discovery in cognitive psychology. *Psychological Review, 98*(2), 254–267.

Gigerenzer, G. (1993). The superego, the ego, and the id in statistical reasoning. In G. Keren & C. Lewis (Eds.), *A handbook for data analysis in the behavioral sciences: Methodological issues* (pp. 311–339). Hillsdale, NJ: Erlbaum.

Gigerenzer, G., Swijtink, Z., Porter, T., Daston, L., Beatty, J., & Krüger, L. (1989). *The empire of chance.* Cambridge, England: Cambridge University Press.

Gilbert, S.F. (1991). Epigenetic landscaping: Waddington's use of cell fate bifurcation diagrams. *Biology and Philosophy, 6,* 135–154.

Gilmore, R. (1981). *Catastrophe theory for scientists and engineers.* New York: Wiley.

Góes, M.C.R. (1994). The modes of participation of others in the functioning of the subject. In N. Mercer & C. Coll (Eds.), *Explorations in socio-cultural studies: Vol. 3. Teaching, learning, and interaction* (pp. 123–128). Madrid: Fundación Infancia y Aprendizaje.

Goldstein, K. (1971). Concerning the concept of "primitivity." In A. Gurwitsch, E.M. Goldstein Haudek, & W. Haudek (Eds.), *Selected papers of Kurt Goldstein* (pp. 485–503). The Hague: Martinus Nijhoff.

Golinkoff, R.M. (1983). The preverbal negotiation of failed messages: Insights into the transition period. In R.M. Golinkoff (Ed.), *The transition from prelinguistic to linguistic communication* (pp. 57–78). Hillsdale, NJ: Erlbaum.

Goody, J. (1982). *Cooking, cuisine and class.* Cambridge, England: Cambridge University Press.

Gottlieb, G. (1976). The roles of experience in the development of behavior and the nervous system. In G. Gottlieb (Ed.), *Neural and behavioral specificity* (pp. 25–54). New York: Academic Press.

Gottlieb, G. (1992). *Individual development & evolution: The genesis of novel behavior.* New York: Oxford University Press.

Gould, S.J. (1984). Relationship between individual and group change: Ontogeny and phylogeny in biology. *Human Development, 27,* 233–239.

Graves, N.B., & Graves, T.D. (1978). The impact of modernization on the personality of a Polynesian people. *Human Organization, 37*(2), 115–135.

Greenfield, P. (1984). A theory of the teacher in the learning activities of everyday life. In B. Rogoff & J. Lave (Eds.), *Everyday cognition: Its development in social context* (pp. 117–138). Cambridge, MA: Harvard University Press.

Greenfield, P., & Lave, J. (1982). Cognitive aspects of informal education. In D. Wagner & H. Stevenson (Eds.), *Cultural perspectives on child development* (pp. 181–207). San Francisco: Freeman.

Grossmann, K. (1986). From idiographic approaches to nomothetic hypotheses: Stern, Allport, and biology of knowledge, exemplified by an exploration of sibling relationships. In J. Valsiner (Ed.), *The individual subject and scientific psychology* (pp. 37–69). New York: Plenum Press.

Guckenheimer, J. (1978). Comments on catastrophe and chaos. *Lectures on Mathematics in the Life Sciences, 10,* 1–47.

Hakfoort, C. (1992). Science deified: Wilhelm Ostwald's energeticist world-view and the history of scientism. *Annals of Science, 49,* 525–544.

Halverson, H.M. (1931). An experimental study of prehension in infants by means of systematic cinema records. *Genetic Psychology Monographs, 10*(2/3), 107–286.

Hardesty, F.P. (1976). Louis William Stern: A new view of the Hamburg years. *Annals of the New York Academy of Sciences, 270,* 31–44.

Hardie, R.P., & Gaye, R.K. (1930). *Aristotle's* Physica. Oxford, England: Clarendon Press.

Harkness, S., & Super, C. (1983). The cultural construction of child development. *Ethos, 11*(4), 221–231.

Harré, R. (1980). *Social being: A theory for social psychology.* Totowa, NJ: Rowman & Littlefield.

Harré, R. (1981). Rituals, rhetoric and social cognition. In J.P. Forgas (Ed.), *Social cognition* (pp. 211–224). London: Academic Press.

Harré, R., & Secord, P.F. (1972). *The explanation of social behavior.* Oxford, England: Blackwell.

Harsanyi, J.C. (1982). *Papers in game theory.* Dordrecht, The Netherlands: Reidel.

Haslerud, G.M. (1979). Which paradigm is both relevant to concerns of psychologists and also scientifically feasible? *Psychologia, 22,* 177–188.

Henle, M. (1977). The influence of gestalt psychology in America. *Annals of the New York Academy of Sciences, 291,* 3–12.

Henle, M. (1978). Kurt Lewin as a metatheorist. *Journal of the History of the Behavioral Sciences, 14,* 233–237.

Herbst, D. (1995). What happens when we make a distinction: An elementary introduction to co-genetic logic. In T. Kindermann & J. Valsiner (Eds.), *Development of person–context relations* (pp. 67–79). Hillsdale, NJ: Erlbaum.

Hermans, H.J.M. (1991). The person as co-investigator in self-research: Valuation theory. *European Journal of Personality, 5,* 217–234.

Hermans, H.J.M. (1996). Opposites in a dialogical self: Constructs as characters. *Journal of Constructivist Psychology, 9,* 1–26.

Hermans, H.J.M., & Bonarius, H. (1991a). The person as co-investigator in personality research. *European Journal of Personality, 5,* 199–216.

Hermans, H.J.M., & Bonarius, H. (1991b). Static laws in a dynamic psychology? *European Journal of Personality, 5,* 245–247.

Hermans, H.J.M., & Hermans-Jansen, E. (1995). *Self-narratives: The construction of meaning in psychotherapy.* New York: Guilford Press.

Hermans, H.J.M., & Kempen, H.J.G. (1993). *The dialogical self.* San Diego, CA: Academic Press.

Hermans, H.J.M., & Kempen, H.J.G. (1995). Body, mind, and culture: Dialogical nature of mediated action. *Culture and Psychology, 1*(1), 104–114.

Hermans, H.J.M., Kempen, H.J.G., & van Loon, R.J.P. (1992). The dialogical self: Beyond individualism and rationalism. *American Psychologist, 47*(1), 23–33.

Herzog, W. (1984). *Modell and Theorie in der Psychologie.* Göttingen, Germany: Hogrefe.

ʻproving educational outcomes for children with disabilities: ʻment, program planning, and evaluation.* Baltimore:

ʻlogy in utopia.* Cambridge, MA: MIT Press.

Ho, D.Y.F. (1995). Selfhood and identity in Confucianism, Taoism, Buddhism, and Hinduism: Contrasts with the West. *Journal for the Theory of Social Behaviour, 25*(2), 113–139.

Holden, G.H. (1985). How parents create a social environment via proactive behavior. In T. Gärling & J. Valsiner (Eds.), *Children within environments: Toward a Psychology of accident prevention* (pp. 193–215). New York: Plenum Press.

Holland, D.C., & Quinn, N. (Eds.). (1987). *Cultural models in language and thought.* Cambridge, England: Cambridge University Press.

Holy, L., & Stuchlik, M. (1981). *The structure of folk models.* New York: Academic Press.

Hoppe, F. (1930). Erfolg and Misserfolg. *Psychologische Forschrung, 14,* 1–62.

Horton, R. (1967). African traditional thought and Western science. *Africa, 37,* 50–71, 155–187.

Howard, N. (1971). *Paradoxes of rationality: Theory of metagames and political behavior.* Cambridge, MA: MIT Press.

Howard, N. (1974). "General" metagames: An extension of the metagame concept. In A. Rapoport (Ed.), *Game theory as a theory of conflict resolution* (pp. 261–283). Dordrecht, The Netherlands: Reidel.

Hume, D. (1854). *Philosophical works of David Hume* (Vol. 1). Boston: Little, Brown.

Hutchinson, G.E. (1948). Circular causal systems in ecology. *Annals of the New York Academy of Science, 50,* 221–246.

Ignjatovic-Savic, N., Kovac-Cerovac, T., Plut, D., & Pesikan, A. (1988). Social interaction in early childhood and its development. In J. Valsiner (Ed.), *Child development within culturally structured environments: Vol. 1. Parental cognition and adult–child interaction* (pp. 89–153). Norwood, NJ: ABLEX.

Inhelder, B., Garcia, R., & Voneche, J. (Eds.). (1976). *Épistémologie génétique et équilibration.* Neuchâtel, Switzerland: Delacjaux & Niestle.

Isaac, G. (1978). The food-sharing behavior of protohuman hominids. *Scientific American, 238*(4), 90–109.

Jahoda, G. (1993). *Crossroads between culture and mind.* Cambridge, MA: Harvard University Press.

Jantsch, E. (1980). *The self-organizing universe.* Oxford, England: Pergamon Press.

Jeannerod, M. (1984). The timing of natural prehension movements. *Journal of Motor Behavior, 16*(3), 235–254.

Jevons, W.S. (1958). *The principles of science.* New York: Dover. (Original work published 1873)

Joravsky, D. (1989). *Russian psychology: A critical history.* Oxford, England: Basil Blackwell.

Joseph, G.C., Reddy, V., & Searle-Chatterjee, M. (1990). Eurocentrism in the social sciences. *Race and Class, 31*(4), 1–26.

Josephs, I.E. (1996a). Challenging science's holy inquisition: Illegitimate psychological phenomena and their study. *Culture and Psychology, 2*(2), 211–221.

Josephs, I.E. (1996b). Does cultural psychology need the concept of activity? *Culture and Psychology, 2*(4), 435–456.

Josephs, I.E., & Valsiner, J. (1996, September 11). *How does dialogue work? Coordinating the mundane and the miraculous in religious understanding.* Paper presented at the 2nd Conference for Socio-Cultural Studies, Geneva.

Josephs, I.E., & Wolgast, M. (1996). Die Ko-Konstruktion religiöser Bedeutung aus kulturpsychologischer Perspektive: Eine Analyse von Eltern-Kind-Interaktionen. In F. Oser & K.H. Reich (Eds.), *Eingerbettet ins Menschsein: Beispiel Religion.* Lengerich, Germany: Pabst-Verlag.

Jürgensen, H. (1976). Probabilistic L-systems. In A. Lindenmayer & G. Rozenberg (Eds.), *Automata, languages, development* (pp. 211–225). Amsterdam: North Holland.

Kahneman, D., Slovic, P., & Tversky, A. (Eds.). (1982). *Judgment under uncertainty: Heuristics and biases.* Cambridge, England: Cambridge University Press.

Kasai, T. (1970). An hierarchy between context-free and context-sensitive languages. *Journal of Computer and System Science, 4,* 492–508.

Katz, D. (1928). La Psychologie de la faim et de l'appétit, en particular chez l'enfant. *Journal de Psychologie, 25,* 165–180.

Keats, D.M. (1982). *Cultural bases of concepts of intelligence: A Chinese versus Australian comparison.* Paper presented at the 2nd Asian Workshop on Child and Adolescent Development, Bangkok, Thailand.

Kelly, G.A. (1955). *The psychology of personal constructs: A theory of personality* (Vol. 1). New York: Norton.

Kelso, J.A.S., Holt, K.G., Rubin, P., & Kugler, P. (1981). Patterns of human interlimb coordination emerge from the properties of non-linear, limit cycle oscillatory processes. *Journal of Motor Behavior, 13*(4), 226–261.

Kessen, W. (1981). Early settlements in New Cognition. *Cognition, 10,* 167–171.

Kindermann, T. (1985, July 6–10). *A learning theoretical perspective on dependent and independent behaviors in children.* Paper presented at 8th biennial meetings of the International Society for the Study of Behavioural Development, Tours, France.

Kindermann, T. (1986). *Entwicklungsbedingungen selbständigen und unselbständigen Verhaltens in der fruehen Kindheit.* Unpublished doctoral dissertation, Free University of Berlin.

Kitahara-Frisch, J., & Norikoshi, K. (1982). Spontaneous sponge-making in captive chimpanzees. *Journal of Human Evolution, 11,* 41–47.

Koepping, K.-P. (1983). *Adolf Bastian and the psychic unity of mankind.* St. Lucia, Australia: University of Queensland Press.

Köhler, W. (1925). *The mentality of apes.* New York: Liverright.

Konner, M. (1976). Maternal care, infant behavior and development among the Kung. In R.B. Lee & I. DeVore (Eds.), *Kalahari hunters-gatherers* (pp. 218–245). Cambridge, MA: Harvard University Press.

Kozloff, M.A. (1994). *Improving educational outcomes for children with disabilities: Principles for assessment, program planning, and evaluation.* Baltimore: Brookes.

Kozulin, A. (1984). *Psychology in utopia.* Cambridge, MA: MIT Press.

Kozulin, A. (1990). *Vygotsky's psychology.* Cambridge, MA: Harvard University Press.

Kreppner, K. (1992). William L. Stern, 1871–1938: A neglected founder of developmental psychology. *Developmental Psychology, 28*(4), 539–547.

Kugler, P.N., Kelso, J.A.S., & Turvey, M.T. (1982). On the control and coordination of naturally developing systems. In J.A.S. Kelso & J.E. Clark (Eds.), *The development of movement control and co-ordination* (pp. 5–78). Chichester, England: Wiley.

Kugler, P.N., Turvey, M.T., & Shaw, R. (1982). Is the "cognitive penetrability" criterion invalidated by contemporary physics? *Behavioral and Brain Sciences, 5*(2), 303–306.

Kuhn, J.R.D., Hipel, K., & Fraser, N. (1983). A coalition analysis algorithm with application to the Zimbabwe conflict. *IEEE Transactions on Systems, Man, and Cybernetics, smc-13*(3), 338–352.

Kuhn, T.S. (1970). *The structure of scientific revolutions* (2nd ed.). Chicago: University of Chicago Press.

Kuhn, T.S. (1977). Objectivity, value judgment, and theory choice. In T.S. Kuhn, *The essential tension; selected studies in scientific tradition and change* (pp. 320–339). Chicago: University of Chicago Press.

Kuipers, B. (1984). Commonsense reasoning about causality: Deriving behavior from structure. *Artificial Intelligence, 24,* 169–203.

Kuipers, B., & Kassirer, J.P. (1984). Causal reasoning in medicine: Analysis of a protocol. *Cognitive Science, 8,* 363–385.

Kuklick, H. (1991). *The savage within: The social history of British anthropology, 1885–1945.* Cambridge, England: Cambridge University Press.

Kumarin, V. (1976). *Anton Makarenko: His life and his work in education.* Moscow: Progress.

Kurtz, S.N. (1992). *All the mothers are one: Hindu India and the cultural reshaping of psychoanalysis.* New York: Columbia University Press.

Kurzweil, E. (1980). *The age of structuralism: Lévi-Strauss to Foucault.* New York: Columbia University Press.

Kuypers, H.G. (1962). Corticospinal connections: Postnatal development in rhesus monkeys. *Science, 138,* 678–680.

Lakatos, I. (1978). *The methodology of scientific research programmes* (Vol. 1). Cambridge, England: Cambridge University Press.

Lakshmivarahan, S., & Thathachar, M.A.L. (1973). Absolutely expedient learning algorithms for stochastic automata. *IEEE Transactions on Systems, Man, and Cybernetics, smc-3*(3), 281–286.

Lamiell, J.T. (1991, August). *Great psychologists resurrected: William Stern.* Paper presented at the 99th annual convention of the American Psychological Association, San Francisco.

Lancy, D. (1975). The social organization of learning initiation rituals and public schools. *Human Organization, 34*(4), 371–380.

Lang, A. (1993, October). *Das Semion als Baustein und Bindekraft—eine einheitliche Semiosekonzepttion von Struktur und Prozess, welche Zeit konstituiren und analysieren kann.* Paper presented at the 7th International Congress of the German Society for Semiotics, Tübingen.

Langer, J. (1970). Werner's comparative organismic theory. In P.H. Mussen (Ed.), *Carmichael's handbook of child psychology* (3rd ed., pp. 733–771). New York: Wiley.

Lawrence, J.A., & Valsiner, J. (1993). Conceptual roots of internalization: From transmission to transformation. *Human Development, 36,* 150–167.

Leenders, F.H.R. (1983). *Responsivity during lunch of mothers and their 3- to 4-year old children as a function of child's behavioral style.* Paper presented at the 7th biennial meetings of the International Society for the Study of Behavioural Development, München, Germany.

Leont'ev, A.N. (1975). *Deyatel'nost', soznanie, lichnost'* [Activity, consciousness, personality]. Moscow: Izdatel'stvo Politicheskoi Literatury.

Lerner, R. (1979). A dynamic interactional concept of individual and social relationship development. In R.L. Burgess & T.L. Huston (Eds.), *Social exchange in developing relationships* (pp. 271–305). New York: Academic Press.

Lerner, R. (1986). *Concepts and theories of human development* (2nd ed.). New York: Random House.

Lerner, R., & Busch-Rossnagel, N. (Eds.). (1981). *Individuals as producers of their development.* New York: Academic Press.

Lévi-Strauss, C. (1963). *Structural anthropology.* New York: Basic Books.

Lévi-Strauss, C. (1966a). The culinary triangle. *Partisan Review, 33,* 586–595.

Lévi-Strauss, C. (1966b). *The savage mind.* Chicago: University of Chicago Press.

Lewin, K. (1917). Kriegeslandschaft. *Zeitschrift für angewandte Psychologie, 12,* 440–447.

Lewin, K. (1931). The conflict between Aristotelian and Galileian modes of thought in contemporary psychology. *Journal of General Psychology, 5,* 141–177.

Lewin, K. (1933). Environmental forces. In C. Murchison (Ed.), *A handbook of child psychology* (2nd ed., pp. 590–625). Worcester, MA: Clark University Press.

Lewin, K. (1935a). *A dynamic theory of personality.* New York: McGraw-Hill.

Lewin, K. (1935b). Psycho-sociological problems of a minority group. *Character and Personality, 3,* 175–187.

Lewin, K. (1936a). *Principles of topological psychology.* New York: McGraw-Hill.

Lewin, K. (1936b). Some social-psychological differences between the United States and Germany. *Character and Personality, 4,* 265–293.

Lewin, K. (1938). *The conceptual representation and the measurement of psychological forces.* Durham, NC: Duke University Press.

Lewin, K. (1939). Field theory and experiment in social psychology: Concepts and methods. *American Journal of Sociology, 44,* 868–896.

Lewin, K. (1942). Field theory and learning. In N.B. Henry (Ed.), *The forty-first yearbook of the National Society for the Study of Education: Part 2. The psychology of learning* (pp. 215–242). Bloomington, IL: Public School Publishing Co.

Lewin, K. (1943a). Defining the "field at a given time." *Psychological Review, 50,* 292–310.

Lewin, K. (1943b). Cultural reconstruction. *Journal of Abnormal and Social Psychology, 38,* 166–173.

Lewin, K. (1943c). The special case of Germany. *Public Opinion Quarterly, 7,* 555–566.

Lewin, K. (1948). *Resolving social conflicts.* New York: Harper and Brothers.

Lewin, K. (1951). *Field theory in social science.* New York: Harper and Brothers.

Lewin, K., Lippitt, R., & Escalona, S.K. (1940). Studies in topological and vector psychology 1. *University of Iowa Studies in Child Welfare, 16,* 3.

Lewin, K., Lippitt, R., & White, R. (1939). Patterns of aggressive behavior in experimentally created "social climates." *Journal of Social Psychology, 10,* 271–299.

Lewin, R. (1984). Why is development so illogical? *Science, 224,* 1327–1329.

Lewontin, R.C. (1978). Adaptation. *Scientific American, 239,* 157–168.

Lewontin, R.C. (1981). On constraints and adaptation. *Behavioral and Brain Sciences, 4,* 244–245.

Lightfoot, C., & Folds-Bennett, T. (1992). Description and explanation in developmental research: Separate agendas. In J. Asendorpf & J. Valsiner (Eds.), *Stability and change in development: A study of methodological reasoning* (pp. 207–228). Newbury Park, CA: Sage.

Lindenmayer, A. (1968). Mathematical models for cellular interactions in development. *Journal of Theoretical Biology, 18,* 280–299, 300–315.

Lindenmayer, A. (1975). Developmental algorithms for multicellular organisms: A survey of L-systems. *Journal of Theoretical Biology, 54,* 3–22.

Lindenmayer, A. (1978). Algorithms for plant morphogenesis. In R. Sattler (Ed.), *Theoretical plant morphology* (pp. 37–81). The Hague: Leiden University Press.

Lindenmayer, A., & Rozenberg, G. (Eds.). (1976). *Automata, languages, development.* Amsterdam: North Holland.

Lockman, J.J., & Ashmead, D. (1983). Asynchronies in the development of manual behavior. In L.P. Lipsitt & C. Rovee-Collier (Eds.), *Advances in infancy* (Vol. 2, pp. 113–136). Norwood, NJ: ABLEX.

London, I. (1944). Psychologists' misuse of the auxiliary concepts of physics and mathematics. *Psychological Review, 51,* 266–291.

London, I. (1949). The development of person as a joint function of convergence and divergence. *Journal of Social Psychology, 40,* 219–228.

London, I., & Thorngate, W. (1981). Divergent amplification and social behavior: Some methodological considerations. *Psychological Reports, 48,* 203–228.

Luria, A.R. (1976). *Cognitive development.* Cambridge, MA: Harvard University Press.

Luria, A.R. (1979). *Iazyk i soznanie.* Moscow: Moscow State University Press.

Luria, A.R., & Artemieva, E. (1970). On two ways of achieving the validity of psychological investigation. *Voprosy Psichologii,* No. 3, 106–112.

Lutz, C. (1983). Parental goals, ethnopsychology, and the development of emotional meaning. *Ethos, 11*(4), 246–362.

MacDonald, N. (1983). *Trees and networks in biological models.* Chichester, England: Wiley.

Maciel, D.A. (1996). *Análise das interações professor-criança em situação de ensino-aprendizagem da leitura escrita.* Unpublished doctoral dissertation, University of São Paulo, Department of Education.

Magnusson, D. (1988). *Individual development from an interactional perspective.* Hillsdale, NJ: Erlbaum.

Maier, R., & Valsiner, J. (1996). Presuppositions in tutoring: Rhetorics in the concept. *Archives de Psychologie, 64,* 27–39.

Mark, L.C., & Todd, J.T. (1983). The perception of growth in three dimensions. *Perception and Psychophysics, 33*(2), 193–196.

Mark, L.S., Todd, J.T., & Shaw, R.E. (1981). Perception of growth: A geometric analysis of how different styles of change are distinguished. *Journal of Experimental Psychology: Human Perception and Performance, 7,* 855–868.

Markova, I. (1990). The development of self-consciousness: Baldwin, Mead, and Vygotsky. In J.E. Faulconer & R.N. Williams (Eds.), *Reconsidering psychology: Perspectives from Continental philosophy* (pp. 151–174). Pittsburgh, PA: Duquesne University Press.

Markova, I. (1993). On the structure and dialogicity in Prague semiotics. In A.H. Wold (Ed.), *The dialogic alternative: Towards a theory of language and mind* (pp. 45–63). Oslo: Scandinavian University Press.

Maruyama, M. (1963). The second cybernetics: Deviation-amplifying mutual causal processes. *American Scientist, 51,* 164–179.

Maruyama, M. (1982). Four different causal metatypes in biological and social sciences. In W.C. Schieve & P.M. Allen (Eds.), *Self-organization and dissipative structures: Applications in the physical and social sciences* (pp. 354–361). Austin: University of Texas Press.

McCall, R. (1977). Challenges to a science of developmental psychology. *Child Development, 48,* 333–344.

McDonnell, P.M. (1979). Patterns of eye–hand coordination in the first year of life. *Canadian Journal of Psychology, 33*(4), 253–267.

McGrew, W.C. (1977). Socialization and object manipulation of wild chimpanzees. In S. Chevalier-Skolnikoff & F. Poirier (Eds.), *Primate bio-social development: Biological, social, and ecological determinants.* New York: Garland Press.

McGrew, W.C., Tutin, C., & Baldwin, P.J. (1979). Chimpanzees, tools, and termites: Cross-cultural comparisons of Senegal, Tanzania, and Rio Muni. *Man, 14,* 185–214.

McSwain, R. (1981). Care and conflict in infant development: An East-Timorese and Papua New Guinean comparison. *Infant Behavior and Development, 4,* 225–246.

Mead, M. (1954). The swaddling hypothesis: Its reception. *American Anthropologist, 56,* 395–409.

Merton, R.K. (1936). Puritanism, pietism, and science. *Sociological Review, 28,* 1–30.

Michell, J. (1986). Measurement scales and statistics: A clash of paradigms. *Psychological Bulletin, 100*(3), 398–407.

Miller, G.D. (1977). Classroom 19: A study of behavior in a classroom of a Moroccan primary school. In L.C. Brown & N. Itzkowitz (Eds.), *Psychological dimensions in Near-Eastern Studies*. Princeton, NJ: Darwin Press.

Minoura, Y. (1996). A plea for the hypothesis-generating approach to link the individual's world of meaning and society's cultural orientation. *Culture and Psychology, 2*(1), 53–61.

Minsky, M. (1982). A framework for representing knowledge. In Y.-H. Pao & G.W. Ernst (Eds.), *Tutorial: Context-directed pattern recognition and machine intelligence techniques for information processing* (pp. 339–419). Piscataway, NJ: IEEE Computer Society.

Minuchin, S., Rosman, B.L., & Baker, L. (1978). *Psychosomatic families: Anorexia nervosa in context*. Cambridge, MA: Harvard University Press.

Mitroff, I. (1974). Norms and counter-norms in a select group of Apollo moon scientists: A case study of the ambivalence of scientists. *American Sociological Review, 39*, 579–596.

Mitroff, I., & Featheringham, T.R. (1974). On systemic problem solving and the error of the third kind. *Behavioral Science, 19*, 383–393.

Moll, L.C. (Ed.). (1990). *Vygotsky and education*. Cambridge, England: Cambridge University Press.

Monberg, T. (1975). Fathers were not genitors. *Man, 10*(1), 34–40.

Montero, M. (1990). Ideology and psychosocial research in Third World contexts. *Journal of Social Issues. 46*(3), 43–55.

Moodie, E., Marková, I., & Plichtova, J. (1995). Lay representations of democracy: A study in two cultures. *Culture and Psychology, 1*(4), 423–453.

Moore, W.E., & Tumin, M.M. (1949). Some social functions of ignorance. *American Sociological Review, 14*, 787–795.

Morgan, C.L. (1894). *An introduction to comparative psychology*. London: Walter Scott.

Moscovici, S. (1961). *La Psychoanalyse: Son image et son public*. Paris: PUF.

Moscovici, S. (1984). The phenomenon of social representations. In R. Farr & S. Moscovici (Eds.), *Social representations* (pp. 3–69). Cambridge, England: Cambridge University Press.

Moscovici, S. (1988). Notes towards a description of social representations. *European Journal of Social Psychology, 18*, 211–250.

Moscovici, S. (1990). Social psychology and developmental psychology: Extending the conversation. In G. Duveen & B. Lloyd (Eds.), *Social representations and the development of knowledge* (pp. 164–185). Cambridge, England: Cambridge University Press.

Moscovici, S. (1994). Social representations and pragmatic communication. *Social Science Information, 33*(2), 163–177.

Moscovici, S. (1995). Geschichte und Aktualität sozialer Repräsentationen. In U. Flick (Ed.), *Psychologie des Sozialen* (pp. 266–314). Reinbek bei Hamburg: Rowohlts Enzyklopädie.

Mukerji, C. (1989). *A fragile power: Scientists and the state*. Princeton, NJ: Princeton University Press.

Mulkay, M. (1993). Rhetorics of hope and fear in the great embryo debate. *Social Studies of Science, 23,* 721–742.

Nandy, A. (1974). The non-paradigmatic crisis of Indian psychology: Reflections on a recipient culture of science. *Indian Journal of Psychology, 49*(1), 1–20.

Narendra, K.S., & Thathachar, M.A.L. (1974). Learning automata—A survey. *IEEE Transactions on Systems, Man, and Cybernetics, smc-4*(4), 323, 334.

Nelson, K. (1981). Social cognition in a script framework. In J.H. Flavell & L. Ross (Eds.), *Social cognitive development* (pp. 97–118). Cambridge, England: Cambridge University Press.

Némedi, D. (1995). Collective consciousness, morphology, and collective representations: Durkheim's sociology of knowledge, 1894–1900. *Sociological Perspectives, 38*(1), 41–56.

Newman, D., Griffin, P., & Cole, M. (1989). *The construction zone: Working for cognitive change in school.* Cambridge, England: Cambridge University Press.

Newson, J. (1974). Towards a theory of infant understanding. *Bulletin of the British Psychological Society, 27,* 251–257.

Newson, J., & Newson, E. (1963). *Infant care in an urban community.* London: Allen & Unwin.

Newson, J., & Newson, E. (1968). *Four years old in an urban community.* Chicago: Aldine.

Newson, J., & Newson, E. (1975). Intersubjectivity and the transmission of culture: On the social origins of symbolic functioning. *Bulletin of the British Psychological Society, 28,* 437–446.

Newson, J., & Newson, E. (1976). *Seven years old in the home environment.* New York: Wiley.

Nicolis, G., & Prigogine, I. (1977). *Self-organization in nonequilibrium systems.* New York: Wiley.

Nicolopoulou, A., & Weintraub, J. (1996). On liberty, cultural relativism, and development. *Culture and Psychology, 2*(3), 273–283.

Ninio, A., & Bruner, J. (1978). The achievement and antecedents of labeling. *Journal of Child Language, 5,* 1–15.

Nixon, J., & Pearn, J. (1977). Emotional sequelae of parents and sibs following the drowning or near-drowning of a child. *Australian and New Zealand Journal of Psychology, 11,* 265–268.

Nunnally, J.C. (1967). *Psychometric theory.* New York: McGraw-Hill.

Obeyesekere, G. (1990). *The work of culture: Symbolic transformation in psychoanalysis and anthropology.* Chicago: University of Chicago Press.

Ochs, E. (1982). Talking to children in Western Samoa. *Language and Society, 11,* 77–104.

Oerter, R. (1996). Are there universals, and why? *Culture and Psychology, 2*(2), 203–209.

Oerter, R., Oerter, R.M., Agostiani, H., Kim, H.-O., & Wibowo, S. (1996). The concept of human nature in East Asia: Etic and emic characteristics. *Culture and Psychology, 2*(1), 9–51.

Oliveira, Z.M.R., & Rossetti-Ferreira, M.C. (1996). Understanding the co-constructive nature of human development. In J. Valsiner & H.-G. Voss (Eds.), *The structure of learning processes* (pp. 177–204). Norwood, NJ: ABLEX.

Oommen, T.K. (1991). Internationalization of sociology: A view from developing countries. *Current Sociology, 39*(1), 67–84.

Oyama, S. (1992). Ontogeny and phylogeny: A case of metarecapitulation. In P. Griffiths (Ed.), *Trees of life* (pp. 211–239). Dordrecht, The Netherlands: Kluwer.

Ozment, S. (1983). *When fathers ruled: Family life in reformation Europe.* Cambridge, MA: Harvard University Press.

Pankow, W. (1976). Openness as self-transcendence. In E. Jantsch & C.H. Waddington (Eds.), *Evolution and consciousness: Human systems in transition* (pp. 16–36). Reading, MA: Addison-Wesley.

Pastore, N. (1949). *The nature–nurture controversy.* New York: King's Crown Press.

Pattee, H.H. (1971). Physical theories of biological co-ordination. *Quarterly Review of Biophysics, 4*(2/3), 255–276.

Pattee, H.H. (1972). Laws and constraints, symbols and languages. In C.H. Waddington (Ed.), *Towards a theoretical biology* (Vol. 4, pp. 248–258). Chicago: Aldine.

Pattee, H.H. (1973). Physical problems of the origin of natural controls. In A. Locker (Ed.), *Biogenesis, evolution, homeostasis* (pp. 41–49). New York: Springer.

Paulhan, F. (1928). Qu'est-ce que le sens des mots? *Journal de Psychologie, 25,* 289–329.

Pearn, J., & Nixon, J. (1977). Bathtub immersion accidents involving children. *Medical Journal of Australia, 1,* 211–213.

Peirano, M.G.S. (1991). For a sociology of India: Some comments from Brazil. *Contributions to Indian Sociology, 25*(2), 321–327.

Peirce, C.S. (1892). Man's glassy essence. *The Monist, 2,* 1–22.

Peirce, C.S. (1893). Evolutionary love. *The Monist, 3,* 176–200.

Peirce, C.S. (1935). *Collected papers of Charles Sanders Peirce.* Cambridge, MA: Harvard University Press.

Piaget, J. (1970a). Piaget's theory. In P.H. Mussen (Ed.), *Carmichael's manual of child psychology* (3rd ed.) (Vol. 1, pp. 703–732). New York: Wiley.

Piaget, J. (1970b). *Structuralism.* New York: Basic Books.

Piaget, J. (1971a). *Insights and illusions of philosophy.* London: Routledge & Kegan Paul.

Piaget, J. (1971b). *Biology and knowledge.* Chicago: University of Chicago Press.

Piaget, J. (1972). *The principles of genetic epistemology.* New York: Basic Books.

Piaget, J. (1977). *The development of thought: Equilibration of cognitive structures.* New York: Viking.

Piaget, J. (1980). Reply to Thom. In M. Piatelli-Palmarini (Ed.), *Language and learning: The debate between Jean Piaget and Noam Chomsky* (pp. 368–370). Cambridge, MA: Harvard University Press.

Polanyi, M. (1958). *Personal knowledge.* London: Routledge & Kegan Paul.

Portes, P.R., Smith, T., & Cuentas, T.E. (1994). Crosscultural parent–child interactions in relation to concept of development: Structure and processes in the ZPD. In A. Alvarez & P. Del Rio (Eds.), *Explorations in socio-cultural studies: Vol. 4. Education as cultural construction* (pp. 97–108). Madrid: Fundación Infancia y Aprendizaje.

Prigogine, I. (1973). Irreversibility as a symmetry-breaking process. *Nature, 246,* 67–71.

Prigogine, I. (1976a). Genèse des structures en physico-chime. In B. Inhelder, R. Garica, & J. Voneche (Eds.), *Épistémologie génétique et équilibration* (pp. 29–38). Neuchâtel, Switzerland: Delachaux & Niestle.

Prigogine, I. (1976b). Order through fluctuation: Self organization and social system. In E. Jantsch & C.H. Waddington (Eds.), *Evolution and consciousness: Human systems in transition.* Reading, MA: Addison-Wesley.

Prigogine, I. (1982). Dialogue avec Piaget sur l'irréversible. *Archives de Psychologie, 50,* 7–16.

Prigogine, I., & Nicolis, G. (1971). Biological order, structure, and instabilities. *Quarterly Journal of Biophysics, 4,* 107–148.

Raikov, B. (1961). *Karl Baer: His life and works.* Moscow: Izdatel'stvo Akademii Nauk SSSR.

Rapoport, A. (1974). Prisoner's dilemma—recollections and observations. In A. Rapoport (Ed.), *Game theory as a theory of conflict resolution* (pp. 17–34). Dordrecht, The Netherlands: Reidel.

Ratner, C. (1991). *Vygotsky's sociohistorical psychology and its contemporary applications.* New York: Plenum Press.

Ratner, C. (1996). Activity as a key concept for cultural psychology. *Culture and Psychology, 2*(4), 407–434.

Ravetz, J.R. (1971). *Scientific knowledge and its social problems.* Oxford, England: Clarendon Press.

Reed, E.S. (1995). The ecological approach to language development: A radical solution to Chomsky's and Quine's problems. *Language and Communication, 15*(1), 1–29.

Richards, A.I. (1939). *Land, labour and diet in Northern Rhodesia.* London: International Institute of African Languages and Cultures.

Richards, A.I., & Widdowson, E.M. (1936). A dietary study in North-Eastern Rhodesia. *Africa, 9,* 166–196.

Robinson, J.A. (1988). "What we've got here is a failure to communicate": The cultural context of meaning. In J. Valsiner (Ed.), *Child development within culturally structured environments: Vol. 2. Social co-construction and environmental guidance in development* (pp. 137–198). Norwood, NJ: ABLEX.

Rocke, A.J. (1985). Hypothesis and experiment in the early development of Kekulé's benzene theory. *Annals of Science, 42,* 355–381.

Rogoff, B. (1990). *Apprenticeship in thinking.* New York: Oxford University Press.

Rogoff, B. (1993). Children's guided participation and participatory appropriation in sociocultural activity. In R.H. Wozniak & K.W. Fischer (Eds.), *Development in context* (pp. 121–153). Hillsdale, NJ: Erlbaum.

Rogoff, B., & Gardner, W. (1984). Adult guidance of cognitive development. In B. Rogoff & J. Lave (Eds.), *Everyday cognition: Its development in social context* (pp. 95–116). Cambridge, MA: Harvard University Press.

Rogoff, B., Malkin, C., & Gilbride, K. (1984). Children's learning in the "zone of proximal development." *New Directions for Child Development, 23*, 31–44.

Rogoff, B., & Wertsch, J. (Eds.). (1984). Children's learning in the "zone of proximal development." *New Directions for Child Development, 23*.

Rojas-Drummond, S., & Rico, J.A. (1994). The development of independent problem solving in pre-school children. In N. Mercer & C. Coll (Eds.), *Explorations in socio-cultural studies: Vol. 3. Teaching, learning, and interaction* (pp. 161–175). Madrid: Fundación Infancia y Aprendizaje.

Rommetveit, R. (1979a). On negative rationalism in scholarly studies of verbal communication and dynamic residuals in the construction of human intersubjectivity. In R. Rommetveit & R. Blakar (Eds.), *Studies of language, thought and verbal communication* (pp. 147–161). London: Academic Press.

Rommetveit, R. (1979b). On common codes and dynamic residuals in human communication. In R. Rommetveit & R. Blakar (Eds.), *Studies of language, thought and verbal communication* (pp. 163–175). London: Academic Press.

Rommetveit, R. (1992). Outlines of a dialogically based social-cognitive approach to human cognition and communication. In A.H. Wold (Ed.), *The dialogical alternative: Towards a theory of language and mind* (pp. 19–44). Oslo: Scandinavian University Press.

Rosa, A. (1994). History of psychology: A ground for reflexivity. In A. Rosa & J. Valsiner (Eds.), *Historical and theoretical discourse in social-cultural studies* (pp. 149–167). Madrid: Fundación Infancia y Aprendizaje.

Rosa, A. (1996a). The psycho-anthropological project of Bartlett. *Culture and Psychology, 2*(4), 355–373.

Rosa, A. (1996b). The past, intellectual histories, and their uses for the future. *Culture and Psychology, 2*(4), 397–405.

Rosa, A., & Valsiner, J. (1994). Coda: Discourse, meanings and knowledge—A reflection on the socio-cultural approach within the crisis of modernity. In A. Rosa & J. Valsiner (Eds.), *Historical and theoretical discourse in social-cultural studies*. Madrid: Fundación Infancia y Aprendizaje.

Rosenkrantz, D.J. (1969). Programmed grammars and classes of formal languages. *Journal of the Association of Computing Machines, 16*, 107–131.

Rothbaum, F., Weisz, J.R., & Snyder, S.S. (1982). Changing the world and changing the self: A two-process model of perceived control. *Journal of Personality and Social Psychology, 42*(1), 5–37.

Saada-Robert, M. (1994). Microgenesis and situated cognitive representations. In N. Mercer & C. Coll (Eds.), *Explorations in socio-cultural studies: Vol. 3. Teaching, learning, and interaction* (pp. 55–64). Madrid: Fundación Infancia y Aprendizaje.

Saada-Robert, M. (1995). Microgenetic analysis of adult–child interactions in school writing. *Infancia y Aprendizaje, 72*, 95–115.

Samelson, F. (1979). Putting psychology on the map: Ideology and intelligence testing. In A.R. Buss (Ed.), *Psychology in social context* (pp. 103–168). New York: Irvington.

Samelson, F. (1981). Struggle for scientific authority: The reception of Watson's behaviorism, 1913–1920. *Journal of the History of the Behavioural Sciences, 17*, 399–425.

Samelson, F. (1985). Organizing the kingdom of behavior: Academic battles and organizational policies in the twenties. *Journal of the History of the Behavioral Sciences, 21*, 33–47.

Sande, H. (1992). Palestinian martyr widowhood—Emotional needs in conflict with role expectations. *Social Science and Medicine, 34*(6), 709–717.

Sarbin, T.R. (1990). Metaphors of unwanted conduct: A historical sketch. In D.E. Leary (Ed.), *Metaphors in the history of psychology* (pp. 300–330). Cambridge, England: Cambridge University Press.

Saxe, G., Gearhart, M., & Guberman, S.R. (1984). The social organization of early number development. *New Directions for Child Development, 23*, 19–30.

Schank, R., & Abelson, R. (1977). *Scripts, plans, goals, and understanding.* Hillsdale, NJ: Erlbaum.

Schwartz, D.M., Thompson, M.G., & Johnson, C.L. (1982). Anorexia nervosa and bulimia: The socio-cultural context. *International Journal of Eating Disorders, 1*(3), 20–36.

Sewertzoff, A. (1929). Direction of evolution. *Acta Zoologica, 10*, 59–141.

Shanahan, M., Valsiner, J., & Gottlieb, G. (1997). The conceptual structure of developmental theories. In J. Tudge, M. Shanahan, & J. Valsiner (Eds.), *Comparative approaches in developmental science.* New York: Cambridge University Press.

Shanker, S. (1992). In search of Bruner. *Language and Communication, 12*(1), 53–74.

Shaw, R.E., & Pittenger, J. (1977). Perceiving the face of change in changing faces: Implications for a theory of object perception. In R. Shaw & J. Bransford (Eds.), *Perceiving, acting, and knowing* (pp. 103–132). Hillsdale, NJ: Erlbaum.

Sherif, M. (1936). *The psychology of social norms.* New York: Harper and Brothers.

Shermer, M. (1990). Darwin, Freud, and the myth of the hero in science. *Knowledge: Creation, Diffusion, Utilization, 11*(3), 280–301.

Shi-Xu (1995). Cultural perceptions: Exploiting the unexpected of the Other. *Culture and Psychology, 1*(3), 315–342.

Shotter, J. (1975). *Images of man in psychological research.* London: Methuen.

Shotter, J. (1983). "Duality of structure" and "intentionality" in an ecological psychology. *Journal for the Theory of Social Behaviour, 13*, 19–43.

Shotter, J. (1984). *Social accountability and selfhood.* Oxford, England: Basil Blackwell.

Shotter, J., & Newson, J. (1982). An ecological approach to cognitive development: Implicate orders, joint action, and intentionality. In G. Butterworth & P. Light (Eds.), *Social cognition: Studies of the development of understanding* (pp. 32–52). Chicago: University of Chicago Press.

Shweder, R. (1990). Cultural psychology—What is it? In J.W. Stigler, R.A. Shweder, & G. Herdt (Eds.), *Cultural psychology* (pp. 1–43). Cambridge, England: Cambridge University Press.

Shweder, R. (1991). *Thinking through cultures.* Cambridge, MA: Harvard University Press.

Shweder, R. (1995). The confessions of a methodological individualist. *Culture and Psychology, 1*(1), 115–122.

Siegfried, J. (Ed.). (1994). *The status of common sense in psychology.* Norwood, NJ: ABLEX.

Siegler, R., & Crowley, K. (1991). The microgenetic method: A direct means for studying cognitive development. *American Psychologist, 46,* 606–620.

Sigel, I.E. (1993). The centrality of a distancing model for the development of representational competence. In R.R. Cocking & K.A. Renninger (Eds.), *The development and meaning of psychological distance* (pp. 141–158). Hillsdale, NJ: Erlbaum.

Simmel, G. (1906). The sociology of secrecy and of secret societies. *American Journal of Sociology, 11*(4), 441–498.

Simon, H.A. (1956). Rational choice and the structure of the environment. *Psychological Review, 63*(2), 129–138.

Simon, H.A. (1957). *Models of man.* New York: Wiley.

Simon, H.A., & Rescher, N. (1966). Cause and counterfactual. *Philosophy of Science, 33,* 323–340.

Slade, P.~., ~ Russell, G.F.M. (1973). Awareness of body dimensions in anorexia nervosa: Cross-sectional and longitudinal studies. *Psychological Medicine, 3,* 188–199.

Smedslund, J. (1978). Bandura's theory of self-efficacy: A set of common sense theorems. *Scandinavian Journal of Psychology, 19,* 1–14.

Smedslund, J. (1980). Analyzing the primary code: From empiricism to apriorism. In D. Olson (Ed.), *The social foundations of language and thought* (pp. 47–73). New York: Norton.

Smedslund, J. (1982). Revising explications of common sense through dialogue: Thirty-six psychological theorems. *Scandinavian Journal of Psychology, 23,* 299–305.

Smedslund, J. (1988). *Psycho-logic.* New York: Springer.

Smedslund, J. (1994). What kind of propositions are set forth in developmental research? Five case studies. *Human Development, 37,* 280–292.

Smedslund, J. (1995). Psychologic: Common sense and the pseudoempirical. In J.A. Smith, R. Harré, & L. van Langenhove (Eds.), *Rethinking psychology* (pp. 196–206). London: Sage.

Smith, J.A., & Ross, W.D. (1908). *The works of Aristotle: Metaphysical* (Vol. 8). Oxford, England: Clarendon Press.

Smolka, A.L.B. (1993). A dinamica discursive no ato de escrever: Relações oralidade escitura. In A.L.B. Smolka & M.C. Goés (Eds.), *A linguagem e o outro paco escolar: Vygotsky e a construcão do conhecimento.* Campinas, Brazil: Papyrus.

Smollett, E. (1975). Differential enculturation and social class in Canadian schools. In T.R. Williams (Ed.), *Socialization and communication in primary groups* (pp. 221–231). The Hague: Mouton.

Sommerville, C.J. (1983). The distinction between indoctrination and education in England, 1549–1719. *Journal of the History of Ideas, 44*(3), 387–406.

Sorokin, P. (1956). *Fads and foibles in modern sociology and related sciences.* Chicago: Regner.

Sorokin, P. (1985). *Social and cultural dynamics.* New Brunswick, NJ: Transaction Books.

Sovran, T. (1992). Between similarity and sameness. *Journal of Pragmatics, 18,* 329–344.

Stendler, C.B. (1950). Sixty years of child training practices. *Journal of Pediatrics, 36,* 122–134.

Stent, G. (1981). Strength and weakness of the genetic approach to the development of the nervous system. *Annual Review of Neuroscience, 4,* 163–194.

Stern, D. (1974). The goal and structure of mother–infant play. *Journal of the American Academy of Child Psychiatry, 13*(3), 402–422.

Stern, W. (1906). *Person und Sache: System der philosophischen Weltanschauung.* Leipzig: J. A. Barth.

Stern, W. (1911). *Differentielle Psychologie.* Leipzig: J. A. Barth.

Stern, W. (1918). *Grundgedanken der personalistische Philosophie.* Berlin: Reuther & Reichard.

Stern, W. (1919). *Die menschliche Persönlichkeit* (2nd ed.). Leipzig: J. A. Barth.

Stern, W. (1930). William Stern. In C. Merchison (Ed.), *A history of psychology in autobiography* (Vol. 1, pp. 335–388). Worcester, MA: Clark University Press.

Stern, W. (1935). *Allgemeine Psychologie auf personalistischer Grundlage.* The Hague: Martinus Nijhoff.

Stern, W. (1938). *General psychology from the personalist standpoint.* New York: Macmillan.

Stevens, S.S. (1946). On the theory of scales of measurement. *Science, 103,* 667–680.

Sunley, R. (1955). Early 19th-century American literature on child rearing. In M. Mead & M. Wolfenstein (Eds.), *Childhood in contemporary cultures.* Chicago: University of Chicago Press.

Super, C., & Harkness, S. (1981). Figure, ground, and gestalt: The cultural context of the active individual. In R. Lerner & N. Busch-Rossnagel (Eds.), *Individuals as producers of their development.* New York: Academic Press.

Tambiah, S.J. (1969). Animals are good to think and good to prohibit. *Ethnology, 8,* 423–459.

Tawney, R. (1926). *Religion and the rise of capitalism.* New York: Harcourt, Brace.

Taylor, C.A. (1991). Defining the scientific community: A rhetorical perspective on demarcation. *Communication Monographs, 58,* 401–420.

Teigen, K.-H. (1984). A note on the origin of the term "nature and nurture": Not Shakespeare and Galton but Mulcaster. *Journal of the History of the Behavioural Sciences, 20,* 363–364.

Thapan, M. (1986). Aspects of ritual in a school in South India. *Contributions to Indian Sociology, 20,* 199–219.

Thathachar, M.A.L., & Ramakrishnan, K.R. (1981a). An automation model of a hierarchical learning system. In H. Akashi (Ed.), *Control science and technology for the progress of society* (pp. 1065–1071). Oxford, England: Pergamon.

Thathachar, M.A.L., & Ramakrishnan, K.R. (1981b). A hierarchical system of learning automata. *IEEE Transaction on Systems, Man, and Cybernetics, 11*(3), 236–240.

Thelen, E. (1983). Learning to walk: Ecological demands and phylogenetic constraints. In L.P. Lipsitt & C. Rovee-Collier (Eds.), *Advances in infancy research* (pp. 213–249). Norwood, NJ: ABLEX.

Thelen, E., & Fogel, A. (1986). Toward an action-based theory of infant development. In J. Lockman & N. Hazen (Eds.), *Action in social context: Perspectives on early development.* New York: Plenum Press.

Thom, R. (1973). A global dynamical scheme for vertebrate embryology. *Lectures on Mathematics in the Life Sciences, 5,* 3–45.

Thom, R. (1975). *Structural stability and morphogenesis: An outline of a general theory of models.* Reading, MA: Benjamin/Cummings.

Thom, R. (1976). The two-fold way of catastrophe theory. In A. Dold & B. Eckmann (Eds.), *Lecture notes in mathematics: Structural stability, The theory of catastrophes, and applications in the sciences,* (Vol. 525, pp. 235–252). Berlin: Springer.

Thom, R. (1980). The genesis of representational space according to Piaget. In M. Piatelli-Palmarini (Ed.), *Language and learning: The debate between Jean Piaget and Noam Chomsky* (pp. 361–368). Cambridge, MA: Harvard University Press.

Thompson, D. (1942). *On growth and form* (2nd ed.). Cambridge, England: Cambridge University Press.

Thorndike, R.M. (1982). *Data collection and analysis.* New York: Gardner Press.

Thorngate, W. (1986). The production, detection, and explanation of behavioural patterns. In J. Valsiner (Ed.), *The individual subject and scientific psychology* (pp. 71–93). New York: Plenum Press.

Todd, J.T., & Mark, L.S. (1981). Issues related to the prediction of craniofacial growth. *American Journal of Orthodontics, 79*(1), 63–80.

Todd, J.T., Mark, L.S., Shaw, R.E., & Pittenger, J. (1980). The perception of human growth. *Scientific American, 242*(2), 132–144.

Toulmin, S. (1978). Mozart in psychology. *New York Review of Books, 25*(14), 51–57.

Toulmin, S., & Leary, D.E. (1985). The cult of empiricism in psychology, and beyond. In S. Koch & D.E. Leary (Eds.), *A century of psychology as science* (pp. 594–616). New York: McGraw-Hill.

Tourney, G. (1965). Freud and the Greeks: A study of the influence of classical Greek mythology and philosophy upon the development of Freudian thought. *Journal of the History of the Behavioral Sciences, 3,* 67–85.

Trettien, A. (1900). Creeping and walking. *American Journal of Psychology, 12,* 1–57.

Trevarthen, C. (1977). Descriptive analysis of infant communication behaviour. In H.R. Schaffer (Ed.), *Mother–infant interaction.* London: Academic Press.

Trevarthen, C. (1979a). Communication and cooperation in early infancy. In M. Bullowa (Ed.), *Before speech: The beginnings of human communication* (pp. 321–347). Cambridge, England: Cambridge University Press.

Trevarthen, C. (1979b). Instinct for human understanding and for cultural communication: Their development in infancy. In M. Von Cranach, K. Foppa, W. Lepenies, & D. Ploog (Eds.), *Human ethology.* Cambridge, England: Cambridge University Press.

Trevarthen, C. (1982). Basic patterns of psychogenic change. In T.G. Bever (Ed.), *Regressions in mental development: Basic phenomena and theories* (pp. 7–46). Hillsdale, NJ: Erlbaum.

Tulving, E. (1972). Episodic and semantic memory. In E. Tulving & W. Donaldson (Eds.), *Organization of memory* (pp. 382–404). New York: Academic Press.

Tulviste, P. (1991). *The cultural-historical development of verbal thinking.* Commack, NY: Nova Science.

Tversky, A., & Kahneman, D. (1974). Judgment under uncertainty: Heuristics and biases. *Science, 185,* 1124–1131.

Tweney, R.D., Doherty, M.E., & Mynatt, C.R. (Eds.). (1981). *On scientific thinking.* New York: Columbia University Press.

Valsiner, J. (1983a, December). *A developing child in a developing culture: A relativistic synthesis.* Paper presented at the 26th annual meeting of the African Studies Association, Boston.

Valsiner, J. (1983b, August). *Parents' strategies for the organization of child–environment relationships in home setting.* Paper presented at the 7th meeting of International Society for the Study of Behavioral Development, Munich.

Valsiner, J. (1984a). Conceptualizing intelligence: From an internal static attribution to the study of the process structure of organism–environment relationships. *International Journal of Psychology, 19,* 363–389.

Valsiner, J. (1984b). Two alternative epistemological frameworks in psychology: The typological and variational modes of thinking. *Journal of Mind and Behavior, 5*(4), 449–470.

Valsiner, J. (1984c). *The childhood of the Soviet citizen: Socialization for loyalty* [Lecture]. Ottawa: Carleton University Press.

Valsiner, J. (1984d). Construction of the zone of proximal development in adult–child joint action: The socialization of meals. *New Directions for Child Development, 23,* 65–76.

Valsiner, J. (1985a). Common sense and psychological theories: The historical nature of logical necessity. *Scandinavian Journal of Psychology, 26,* 97–109.

Valsiner, J. (1985b). Parental organization of children's cognitive development within home environment. *Psychologia, 28,* 131–143.

Valsiner, J. (1986). Between groups and individuals: Psychologists' and laypersons' interpretations of correlational findings. In J. Valsiner (Ed.), *The individual subject and scientific psychology* (pp. 113–152). New York: Plenum Press.

Valsiner, J. (1988). *Developmental psychology in the Soviet Union.* Brighton, England: Harvester Press.

Valsiner, J. (1989a). *Human development and culture.* Lexington, MA: Heath.

Valsiner, J. (Ed.). (1989b). From group comparisons to knowledge: A lesson from cross-cultural psychology. In J.P. Forgas & J.M. Innes (Eds.), *Recent advances in social psychology: An international perspective* (pp. 501–510). Amsterdam: North Holland.

Valsiner, J. (1994a). Reflexivity in context: Narratives, hero-myths, and the making of histories in psychology. In A. Rosa & J. Valsiner (Eds.), *Explorations in socio-cultural studies: Vol. 1. Historical and theoretical discourse* (pp. 169–186). Madrid: Fundación Infancia y Aprendizaje.

Valsiner, J. (1994b). Uses of common sense and ordinary language in psychology, and beyond: A co-constructionist perspective and its implications. In J. Siegfried (Ed.), *The status of common sense in psychology* (pp. 46–57). Norwood, NJ: ABLEX.

Valsiner, J. (1994c). James Mark Baldwin and his impact: Social development of cognitive functions. In A. Rosa & J. Valsiner (Eds.), *Explorations in socio-cultural studies: Vol. 1. Historical and theoretical discourse* (pp. 187–204). Madrid: Fundación Infancia y Aprendizaje.

Valsiner, J. (1994d). Bi-directional cultural transmission and constructive sociogenesis. In W. de Graaf & R. Maier (Eds.), *Sociogenesis reexamined* (pp. 47–70). New York: Springer.

Valsiner, J. (1995). Processes of development, and search for their logic: An introduction to Herbst's co-genetic logic. In T. Kindermann & J. Valsiner (Eds.), *Development of person–context relations* (pp. 55–65). Hillsdale, NJ: Erlbaum.

Valsiner, J. (1996). Social utopias and knowledge construction in psychology. In V.A. Koltsova, Y.N. Oleinik, A.R. Gilgen, & C.K. Gilgen (Eds.), *Post-Soviet perspectives on Russian psychology* (pp. 70–84). Westport, CT: Greenwood Press.

Valsiner, J. (1997a). *The guided mind.* Cambridge, MA: Harvard University Press.

Valsiner, J. (1997b). The development of the concept of development: Historical and epistemological perspectives. In R. Lerner (Ed.), *Handbook of child psychology: Vol. 1. Theoretical models of human development.* New York: Wiley.

Valsiner, J., & Benigni, L. (1986). Naturalistic research and ecological thinking in the study of child development. *Developmental Review, 6,* 203–223.

Valsiner, J., Branco, A.U., & Melo Dantas, C. (1997). Co-construction of human development: Heterogeneity within parental belief orientations. In J.E. Grusec & L. Kuczynski (Eds.), *Handbook of parenting and the transmission of values.* New York: Wiley.

Valsiner, J., & Cairns, R.B. (1992). Theoretical perspectives on conflict and development. In C.U. Shantz & W.W. Hartup (Eds.), *Conflict in child and adolescent development* (pp. 15–35). Cambridge, England: Cambridge University Press.

Valsiner, J., & Lawrence, J.A. (1996). Human development and culture across the life span. In J.W. Berry, P.R. Dasen, & T.S. Saraswathi (Eds.), *Handbook of cross-cultural psychology.* (Vol. 2, 2nd ed.). Boston: Allyn & Bacon.

Valsiner, J., & Mackie, C. (1985). Toddlers at home: Canalization of climbing skills through culturally organized physical environments. In T. Gärling & J. Valsiner

(Eds.), *Children within environments: Towards a psychology of accident prevention* (pp. 165–191). New York: Plenum Press.

Valsiner, J., & Van der Veer, R. (1993). The encoding of distance: The concept of the "zone of proximal development" and its interpretations. In R.R. Cocking & K.A. Renninger (Eds.), *The development and meaning of psychological distance* (pp. 35–62). Hillsdale, NJ: Erlbaum.

Valsiner, J., & Van der Veer, R. (1996). From gesture to self: George Mead's construction of a socio-psychology. In D. Paez Rovira & A. Blanco (Eds.), *Social psychology and sociocultural theory: Current perspectives* (pp. 63–73). Madrid: Fundación Infancia y Aprendizaje.

Valsiner, J., & Van der Veer, R. (1997). *The social mind.* Cambridge, England: Cambridge University Press.

Van der Daele, L.D. (1969). Qualitative models in developmental analysis. *Developmental Psychology, 1*(4), 303–310.

Van der Veer, R. (1984). *Cultuur en cognitie.* Groningen, The Netherlands. Wolters-Noordhoff.

Van der Veer, R. (1996a). The concept of culture in Vygotsky's thinking. *Culture and Psychology, 2*(3), 247–263.

Van der Veer, R. (1996b). On some historical roots and present-day doubts. *Culture and Psychology, 2*(4), 457–463.

Van der Veer, R., & Valsiner, J. (1991). *Understanding Vygotsky: A quest for synthesis.* Oxford, England: Blackwell.

Van der Veer, R., Van IJzendoorn, M.H., & Valsiner, J. (Eds.). (1994). *Reconstructing the mind: Replicability in research on human development.* Norwood, NJ: Ablex.

van Geert, P. (1983). *The development of perception, cognition and language.* London: Routledge & Kegan Paul.

van Geert, P. (1984, August). *The structure of developmental theories.* Paper presented at the Inaugural European Conference on Developmental Psychology, Groningen, The Netherlands.

Van Geert, P. (1991). A dynamic systems model of cognitive and language growth. *Psychological Review, 98,* 3–53.

Van Geert, P. (1993). A dynamic systems model of cognitive growth: Competition and support under limited resource conditions. In E. Thelen & L. Smith (Eds.), *Dynamic systems in development.* Cambridge, MA: MIT Press.

Van Geert, P. (1994a). Vygotskian dynamics of development. *Human Development, 37,* 346–365.

Van Geert, P. (1994b). *Dynamic systems of development.* Hemel Hempstead, England: Harvester Wheatsheaf.

Van Ijzendoorn, M.H., & Van der Veer, R. (1984). *Main currents of critical psychology.* New York: Irvington.

Von Baer, K. (1828). *Über Entwicklungsgeschichte der Thiere: Beobactung und reflexion.* Königsberg: Bornträger.

Von Cranach, M. (1982). The psychology of goal-directed action: Basic issues. In M. Von Cranach & R. Harré (Eds.), *The analysis of action* (pp. 35–73). Cambridge, England: Cambridge University Press.

von Glasersfeld, E. (1974). *Because* and the concepts of causation. *Semiotica, 12,* 129–144.

VonHofsten, C. (1979). Development of visually directed reaching: The approach phase. *Journal of Human Movement Studies, 5,* 160–178.

Von Neumann, J., & Morgenstern, O. (1944). *Theory of games and economic behavior.* Princeton, NJ: Princeton University Press.

Vuyk, R. (1981). *Overview and critique of Piaget's genetic epistemology 1965–1980* (Vol. 1). London: Academic Press.

Vygotsky, L.S. (1956). *Izbrannye psikhologicheskie issledovnia. Myshlenie i rech.* Moscow: Izd. APN.

Vygotsky, L.S. (1960). *Razvitie vyshhikh psikhicheskikh funktsii.* Moscow: Izd. APN.

Vygotsky, L.S. (1962). *Thought and language.* Cambridge, MA: MIT Press.

Vygotsky, L.S. (1963). Learning and mental development at school age. In B. Simon & J. Simon (Eds.), *Educational psychology in the U.S.S.R.* (pp. 21–34). London: Routledge & Kegan Paul.

Vygotsky, L.S. (1966). Play and its role in the psychological development of the child. *Voprosy psikhologii, 12*(6), 62–76.

Vygotsky, L.S. (1971). *Psychology of art.* Cambridge, MA: MIT Press. (Original work published 1925)

Vygotsky, L.S. (1978). *Mind in society.* Cambridge, MA: Harvard University Press.

Vygotsky, L.S. (1981). The genesis of higher mental functions. In J. Wertsch (Ed.), *The concept of activity in Soviet psychology* (pp. 144–188). Armonk, NY: M.E. Sharpe.

Vygotsky, L.S. (1994). The problem of the environment. In R. Van der Veer & J. Valsiner (Eds.), *The Vygotsky reader* (pp. 338–354). Oxford, England: Blackwell. (Original work published 1935)

Vygotsky, L.S., & Luria, A.R. (1930). *Etiudy pa istorii povedinia.* Moscow—Leningrad: Gosudarstvennoie Izdatel'stvo.

Waddington, C.H. (1942). Canalization of development and the inheritance of acquired characters. *Nature, 150*(3811), 563–565.

Waddington, C.H. (1966). Fields and gradients. In M. Locke (Ed.), *Major problems in developmental biology* (pp. 105–124). New York: Academic Press.

Waddington, C.H. (1968). The basic ideas of biology. In C.H. Waddington (Ed.), *Towards theoretical biology* (Vol. 1, pp. 1–41). Chicago: Aldine.

Waddington, C.H. (1970). Concepts and theories of growth, development, differentiation and morphogenesis. In C.H. Waddington (Ed.), *Towards theoretical biology* (Vol. 2, pp. 1–41). Chicago: Aldine.

Wagner, D. (1983). Rediscovering "rote": Some cognitive and pedagogical preliminaries. In S.H. Irvine & J.W. Berry (Eds.), *Human assessment and cultural factors* (pp. 179–190). New York: Plenum Press.

Wagner, W. (1994). Fields of research and socio-genesis of social representations: A discussion of criteria and diagnostics. *Social Science Information, 33*(2), 199–228.

Wapner, S., & Demick, J. (1997). In R. Lerner (Ed.), *Handbook of child psychology: Vol. 1. Theoretical models of human development.* New York: Wiley.

Weber, M. (1930). *The Protestant ethic and the spirit of capitalism.* London: Allen & Unwin.

Webster's *Third New International Dictionary* (1981).

Weisner, T.R., & Gallimore, R. (1977). My brother's keeper: Child and sibling caregiving. *Current Anthropology, 18*(2), 169–180.

Weiss, P. (1969). The living system: Determinism stratified. In A. Koestler & J.R. Smythies (Eds.), *Beyond reductionism: New perspectives in the life sciences* (pp. 3–55). London: Hutchinson.

Weiss, P. (1978). Causality: Linear of systemic. In G. Miller & E. Lenneberg (Eds.), *Psychology and biology of language and thought.* New York: Academic Press.

Werner, H. (1937). Process and achievement—A basic problem of education and developmental psychology. *Harvard Educational Review, 7,* 358–368.

Werner, H. (1940). *Comparative psychology of mental development.* Harper and Brothers.

Werner, H. (1957). The concept of development from a comparative and organismic point of view. In D.B. Harris (Ed.), *The concept of development: An issue in the study of human behavior* (pp. 125–148). Minneapolis: University of Minnesota Press.

Werner, H., & Kaplan, B. (1956). The developmental approach to cognition: Its relevance to the psychological interpretation of anthropological and ethnolinguistic data. *American Anthropologist, 58,* 866–880.

Werner, H., & Kaplan, B. (1963). *Symbol formation.* New York: Wiley.

Wertheimer, M. (1981). Einstein: The thinking that led to the theory of relativity. In R.D. Tweney, M.E. Doherty, & C.R. Mynatt (Eds.), *On scientific thinking* (pp. 193–211). New York: Columbia University Press.

Wertheimer, M. (1985). The evolution of the concept of development in the history of psychology. In G. Eckhardt, W.G. Bringman, & L. Sprung (Eds.), *Contributions to a history of developmental psychology* (pp. 13–25). Berlin: Mouton.

Wertsch, J. (1981). Trends in Soviet cognitive psychology. *Storia e critica della psicologia, 2*(2), 219–295.

Wertsch, J. (1983). The role of semiosis in L.S. Vygotsky's theory of human cognition. In B. Bain (Ed.), *The sociogenesis of language and human conduct* (pp. 17–31). New York: Plenum Press.

Wertsch, J. (1984). The zone of proximal development: Some conceptual issues. *New Directions for Child Development, 23,* 7–18.

Wertsch, J. (1985). *Vygotsky and the social formation of the mind.* Cambridge, MA: Harvard University Press.

Wertsch, J. (1990). The voice of rationality in a sociocultural approach to mind. In L.C. Moll (Ed.), *Vygotsky and education* (pp. 111–126). Cambridge, England: Cambridge University Press.

Wertsch, J. (1991). *Voices of the mind.* Cambridge, MA: Harvard University Press.

Wertsch, J. (1995). Sociocultural research in the copyright age. *Culture and Psychology, 1*(1), 81–102.

Wertsch, J. (Ed.). (1997). History in national identity [Special issue]. *Culture and Psychology, 3*(1).

Wertsch, J., Minick, N., & Arns, F.J. (1984). The creation of context in joint problem-solving. In B. Rogoff & J. Lave (Eds.), *Everyday cognition: Its development in social context* (pp. 151–171). Cambridge, MA: Harvard University Press.

Wertsch, J., & Stone, C.A. (1984). The concept of internalization in Vygotsky's account of the genesis of higher mental functions. In J. Wertsch (Ed.), *Culture, communication, and cognition: Vygotskian perspectives* (pp. 162–197). Cambridge, England: Cambridge University Press.

West, M.J., & King, A. (1985, April 25). *The inheriting of parents, peers, and places in the genesis of behavior.* Paper presented at the biennial Society for Research on Child Development meeting, Toronto.

Wildgen, W. (1981). Archetypal dynamics in word semantics: An application of catastrophe theory. In H.-J. Eikmeyer & H. Rieser (Eds.), *Words, worlds, and contexts* (pp. 234–296). Berlin: Walter de Gruyter.

Wildgen, W. (1983). Modelling vagueness in catastrophe-theoretic semantics. In T.T. Ballmer & M. Pinkal (Eds.), *Approaching vagueness* (pp. 317–360). Amsterdam: North Holland.

Wildgen, W. (1984). Gestalt semantics on the basis of catastrophe theory. In T. Barbe (Ed.), *Semiotics unfolding* (Vol. 1, pp. 421–427). The Hague: Mouton.

Williams, L.P. (1973). Kant, Naturphilosophie and scientific method. In R.N. Giere & R.S. Westfall (Eds.), *Foundation of scientific method: The nineteenth century* (pp. 3–22). Bloomington: Indiana University Press.

Winegar, L.T. (1988). Children's emerging understanding of social events: co-construction and social process. In J. Valsiner (Ed.), *Child development within culturally structured environments: Vol. 2. Social co-construction and environmental guidance of development* (pp. 3–27). Norwood, NJ: ABLEX.

Winegar, L.T., Renninger, K.A., & Valsiner, J. (1989). Dependence–independence in adult–child relationships. In D.A. Kramer & M.J. Bopp (Eds.), *Transformation in clinical and developmental psychology* (pp. 157–168). New York: Springer.

Winegar, L.T., & Valsiner, J. (1992). Re-contextualizing context: Analysis of metadata and some further elaborations. In L.T. Winegar & J. Valsiner (Eds.), *Children's development within social context: Vol. 2. Research and methodology* (pp. 249–266). Hillsdale, NJ: Erlbaum.

Wing. A.M., & Fraser, C. (1983). The contribution of the thumb to reaching movements. *Quarterly Journal of Experimental Psychology, 35A,* 297–309.

Wittgenstein, L. (1958). *Philosophical investigations.* Oxford, England: Basil Blackwell.

Wober, M. (1972). Culture and the concept of intelligence. *Journal of Cross-Cultural Psychology, 3,* 327–328.

Wolfenstein, M. (1951). Trends in infant care. *American Journal of Orthopsychiatry, 23,* 120–130.

Wolfenstein, M. (1955). Fun morality: An analysis of recent American child-training literature. In M. Mead & M. Wolfenstein (Ed.), *Childhood in contemporary cultures.* Chicago: University of Chicago Press.

Wood, D. (1980). Teaching the young child: Some relationships between social interaction, language, and thought. In D.R. Olson (Ed.), *The social foundation of language and thought* (pp. 280–296). New York: Norton.

Wood, D., Bruner, J., & Ross, G. (1976). The role of tutoring in problem solving. *Journal of Child Psychology and Psychiatry, 17*(2), 89–100.

Wood, D., & Middleton, D.J. (1975). A study of assisted problem solving. *British Journal of Psychology, 66*(2), 181–191.

Wood, D., Wood, H., & Middleton, D.J. (1978). An experimental evaluation of four face-to-face teaching strategies. *International Journal of Behavioural Development, 1*(2), 131–147.

Wozniak, R. (1982). Metaphysics and science, reason and reality: The intellectual origins of genetic epistemology. In J.M. Broughton & D.J. Freeman-Moire (Eds.), *The cognitive-developmental psychology of James Mark Baldwin* (pp. 13–45). Norwood, NJ: ABLEX.

Yeo, R.R. (1986). Scientific method and the rhetoric of science of Britain, 1830–1917. In J.A. Schuster & R.R. Yeo (Eds.), *The politics and rhetoric of scientific method* (pp. 259–297). Dordrecht, The Netherlands: D. Reidel.

Zahler, R.S., & Sussmann, H.J. (1977). Claims and accomplishments of applied catastrophe theory. *Nature, 269,* 759–763.

Zahorsky, J. (1934). The discard of the cradle. *Journal of Pediatrics, 4,* 660–667.

Zeeman, E.C. (1974). Primary and secondary waves in developmental biology. *Lectures on Mathematics in the Life Sciences, 7,* 69–161.

Zeeman, E.C. (1977). *Catastrophe theory: Selected papers 1972–1977.* Reading, MA: Addison-Wesley.

Zeigarnik, B. (1927). Das Behalten erledigter und unerledigter Handlungen. *Psychologische Forschung, 9,* 1–85.

Zeigarnik, B. (1981). *Teoria lichnosti Kurta Levina* [Kurt Lewin's theory of personality]. Moscow: Moscow University Press.

Zempleni-Rabain, J. (1973). Food and the strategy involved in learning fraternal exchange among Wolof children. In P. Alexandre (Ed.), *French perspectives in African studies* (pp. 221–233). London: Oxford University Press.

Index